# PARTY
# POLITICS
# IN
# AMERICA

**FRANK J. SORAUF**

University of Minnesota

# PARTY POLITICS IN AMERICA

**FOURTH EDITION**

**LITTLE, BROWN AND COMPANY**
Boston Toronto

For My Mother and Father

# PREFACE

The purposes and outlooks of this book — even its eccentricities — will be apparent to readers without my writing a lengthy preface to alert them. And what prefatory materials on the parties ought to be read I have included in the introductions to the six parts of the book where they will be read.

The sins of commission of which I am guilty are on the pages of the book for everyone to see. I hope readers will not hesitate to call them to my attention. My sins of omission may, however, require a brief comment. With the scholarly literature on parties expanding so rapidly, I have been forced to make difficult, even arbitrary, selections from it. In the interests both of brevity and of logic I have also resisted the temptation to dwell at length on interest groups and on American voting behavior. It is a self-imposed limitation, and I think it can be defended on intellectual as well as practical grounds.

Readers familiar with earlier editions of the book will find that the basic approach and structure of the book remain the same. But there are a number of changes. I have thoroughly updated the book to reflect both new aspects of American politics and the new scholarly literature of the last four years. I have also done some minor rewriting on many pages in the interests of clarity. Beyond these usual changes, there are two more substantial ones; I have included additional historical materials, and I have substantially rewritten the final chapter. My aim in all of these revisions has been to make the book clearer and more useful.

Finally, I should like to acknowledge some of the debts that I have incurred in putting this book into a fourth edition. This one bears enough similarity to the first three editions for the debts incurred there to continue here. To the thanks I gave in the prefaces to those editions I should like to add a few more. Many individual students, friends, and professional colleagues have made useful comments to me about the book. I hope they will forgive such a brief and collective acknowledgment. Among that group I am especially indebted to Milda Hedblom and Richard Watson for their reports "from the classroom." Herbert Alexander and Gerald Elliott went well out of their ways to help me locate materials. I am also grateful for the splendid work of my typist, Gloria Priem, and my assistants, Steven Clauser, Wallace Hilke, and Anita Neumann. Finally, the people at Little, Brown were, as usual, helpful and forbearing.

# CONTENTS

# PARTY
# POLITICS
# IN
# AMERICA

# I

# PARTIES
# AND PARTY
# SYSTEMS

The open and aggressive pursuit of personal advantage will probably never win the admiration of any society. It certainly has not won the admiration of ours. Yet the things men and women want for themselves and for others — status, security, justice, and wealth, for example — are in short supply. People compete for them by trying to influence government to recognize their claims rather than those of others. This striving to win the things one thinks desirable — a striving we call "politics" — is therefore as widespread as those desires are.

The pervasiveness of politics is a central fact of our times. We have seen in the twentieth century an enormous expansion of governmental activity. It seems most unlikely that the tides of governmental authority will soon, if ever, recede. The demands of a complex, increasingly urbanized, industrialized society, and the dictates of a world beset by international tensions, do not easily permit a return to limited government. For the foreseeable future a substantial proportion of the important conflicts over the desirable things in American society will be settled within the political system. The really meaningful issues of our time will surely be how influence and power are organized within the political system, who wins the rewards and successes of that political activity, and to whom the people who make the processes and decisions are responsible. It will increasingly be within the political system that we will decide, in the candid phrase of Harold Lasswell, "who gets what, when, how." [1]

In the United States these political contestings are directed largely at the regular institutions of government. Few political scientists believe that the real and important political decisions are made clandestinely by murky, semivisible elites and merely ratified by the governmental bodies they control.[2] It may happen, to be sure, that political decisions in a local com-

---

[1] The phrase comes from the title of Harold Lasswell's pioneering book *Politics: Who Gets What, When, How* (New York: McGraw-Hill, 1936).
[2] C. Wright Mills in *The Power Elite* (New York: Oxford University Press, 1956) offers the best-known example of such interpretations of American politics.

munity are made by a group of influential local citizens rather than by a city council or a mayor or a school board. Nonetheless, one is reasonably safe in looking for the substance of American politics in the legislatures, executives, and courts of the nation, the fifty states, and localities. The politics of which we have been talking consists of the attempts to influence either the making of decisions within these governmental bodies or the selecting of the men and women who will make them.

This struggle for influence, this "politics," is not unorganized, however confusing it may seem to be. Large political organizations attempt to mobilize influence on behalf of aggregates of individuals. In the Western democracies the political party is unquestionably the most important and pervasive of these political organizations. It is not, however, the only one. Interest groups such as the American Farm Bureau Federation and the AFL-CIO mobilize influence. So also do smaller factions and cliques, charismatic individuals, and nonparty political organizations such as Americans for Democratic Action and the American Conservative Union. We cannot, therefore, use the term *politics* to refer only to the activities of the political parties. Even though a substantial portion of American politics goes on within and through the political parties, a substantial portion also goes on outside them. Interest groups rather than parties, for example, bring certain issues and policy questions to legislatures and administrative agencies. Nonparty organizations also support candidates for office with money and manpower, sometimes even more effectively than the parties do. Thus the terms *politics* and *political* include not only the activity of the political parties but also that of other political organizers.

At this point it may help to step back and survey the entire political system in order to understand the place of parties and other political organizations in it (Figure I.1). All these political organizations work as intermediaries between the millions of political individuals and the distant policy makers in government. They build influence into large aggregates in order to have a greater effect on the selection of policy makers and the policies they will make. At the same time they codify and simplify information about government and politics as it moves back to the individual. In a very real sense, therefore, these political organizers are the informal agents by which individuals are represented in the complex democracies of our time. They are in the broadest sense both the builders and the agents of majorities.

In any political system the political organizations develop an informal division of labor. The political parties concentrate on contesting elections as a way of aggregating influence. Others, especially the interest groups, pursue the avenues of direct influence on legislators or administrators. Still others seek mainly to propagate ideologies or build support on specific issues of foreign or domestic policy. Indeed, the nature of the division of labor among the various political organizations says a great deal about any

FIGURE I.1   Political Organizations as Organizing Intermediaries in
the Political System

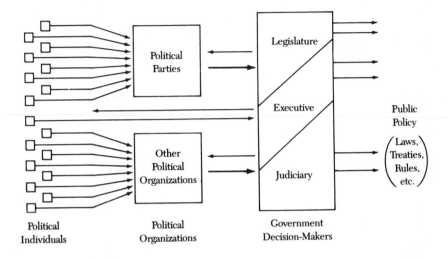

political system and about the general processes of mobilizing influence
within it. The division also speaks meaningfully about the political parties.
It is a commonplace, for example, that among the parties of the democracies the American political parties are to an unusual extent occupied with
the single activity of contesting elections. The parties of Western Europe,
on the other hand, have been more committed to the spreading of ideologies and the disciplining of legislators. And those of countries such as India
have been more involved with the transmitting of political values and information to a citizenry lacking other avenues of political socialization and
communication.

The division of labor among political organizations is, however, neither
clear nor permanent. There is always an overlapping — and hence a competition — among political organizations over the performance of their
activities. That competition is most obvious when it takes place within the
party system, the competition of one party against another. But it takes
place as well between parties and other political organizations — for example, in the competition of parties and powerful interest groups for the attention and support of legislators or for the right to name a candidate in a
primary election. Furthermore, the extent to which any one kind of political organization controls or participates in any one kind of organizing activity may change radically over time. Certainly no one would argue that
the American political parties today control as much of the business of
campaigning as they once did.

All of this competing for a role in American politics implies another kind of competition. The political organizations compete among themselves for political resources: money, skills, expertise, the efforts of men and women. All of these resources are necessary for the fueling of organizational activity, but none of them is in particularly abundant supply in the American society. Then with those resources at hand they compete for the support of individual citizens — that is, they seek to have them attach their loyalties to the goals and leadership of the organization. In sum, the parties and other political organizations compete for scarce resources with which to mobilize the political influence necessary to capture the scarce rewards the political system allocates. They compete first for the capacity to organize influence and then for the influence itself.

Despite these excursions beyond the subject of political parties, however, this *is* a book about political parties. The broader survey of politics and political organizations has merely been background for two themes that will recur throughout the remainder of the book. The first is that the political party is not the unique political organization we have conventionally thought it is. On the contrary, it is frequently difficult to distinguish from other political organizations, and the difficulty of coming to a clear, agreed-on definition of a political party illustrates that point only too well. When one undertakes any exercise in definition, as we do for the parties in the first chapter, the temptation is always to err on the side of the distinctiveness, even the uniqueness, of the phenomenon one is trying to define. It may well be that the distinctions between parties and other political organizations are not, after all, so great as one might imagine. Parties do have their distinctive qualities — and it is important to know them — but there is little point in denying their similarity to many other political organizations.

Second, the broad perspective is essential background for assessing the role and position of the political parties in the American democracy. American writers about the political parties have not been modest in their claims for them. They have celebrated the parties as agents of democracy and even as the chosen instruments through which a democratic citizenry governs itself. Some have gone a step further to proclaim them the originators of the democratic processes which they now serve. E. E. Schattschneider opened his classic study of the American parties this way in 1942:

> The rise of political parties is indubitably one of the principal distinguishing marks of modern government. The parties, in fact, have played a major role as *makers* of governments, more especially they have been the makers of democratic government. It should be stated flatly at the outset that this volume is devoted to the thesis that the political parties created democracy and that modern democracy is unthinkable save in terms of the parties.[3]

[3] E. E. Schattschneider, *Party Government* (New York: Rinehart, 1942), p. 1.

Other scholars, and many thoughtful Americans, too, agree that the American democracy presumes the two-party system of today.

Yet, the major American parties have changed and continue to change — both in the form of their organization and in the pattern and style of their activities. Political parties as they existed fifty years ago scarcely exist today, and the political parties we know today may not exist fifty years hence. In this book a vigorous case will be made for the proposition that the political parties have lost their preeminent position as political organizations and that competing political organizations now perform many of the activities traditionally regarded as the parties' exclusive prerogatives.[4] If this is indeed the case, we must face the question of whether political parties are indeed indispensable and inevitable shapers of our democratic politics.

These two suspicions — that the parties may be less distinctive and their activities less pervasive than we have thought — add up perhaps to no more than a plea for modesty in the study of the American political parties. It is perfectly natural for both young and experienced scholars to identify with the objects of their study and thus to exaggerate their importance. Medievalists often find the late Middle Ages to be the high point of Western civilization, and most scholars of hitherto obscure painters and philosophers find the object of their study to have been sadly neglected or tragically underestimated. So, too, has it been with the study of political parties.

All of this is not to suggest, out of hand, that the American political parties are or have been of little importance. Their long life and their role in the politics of the world's oldest representative democracy scarcely lead to that conclusion. The plea here is merely for a careful assessment, for an abandoning of preconceptions, old judgments, and "great general truths." Assertions that political parties are essential to or the keystone of American democracy may or may not be true. But simply as assertions they advance our understanding of politics and parties very little. The proof is in the evidence, and the evidence is in a detailed knowledge of what the political parties are and what they do.

[4] See also Anthony King, "Political Parties in Western Democracies," *Polity* 2 (1969): 111–41.

# 1

## In
## Search
## of the Political
## Parties

Consider the American adults who insist, "I'm a strong Republican," and "I've been a Democrat all my life." It is unlikely that they ever worked within the party organization of their choice, much less made a financial contribution to it. They would be hard-pressed to recall its recent platform commitments, and if they did, they would not necessarily feel any loyalty to them. Furthermore, they probably never meet with the other Americans who express the same party preferences, and they would likely find it difficult to name the local officials of their party. In fact, their loyalty to the party of which they consider themselves "members" may be little more than a disposition to support its candidates at elections if all other considerations are fairly equal. Yet, when the interviewers of polling organizations come to their doors, they hesitate not at all to attach themselves to that political party. And we do not hesitate to credit their word, for it is in the nature of the American parties and politics to consider people Democrats or Republicans merely because they say they are.

Are the major American parties then nothing more than great, formless aggregates of people who say they are Democrats and Republicans? Are they nothing more than vague political labels that people attach themselves to? It is perilously easy to conclude so, but the American political parties are also organizations. It *is* possible to join them, to work within them, to become officers in them, to participate in setting their goals and strategies — much as one would within a local fraternal organization or a machinists' union. They have characteristics that we associate with social organizations: stable, patterned personal relationships and common goals. In other words, they are more than aggregates of people clinging in various degrees of intensity to a party label.

The act of defining the political party, and the American parties in particular, is hampered by the fact that the nature of the political party, like beauty, often rests in the eye of the beholder. The definition is usually a personal perception; it seems to depend on what one is looking for, what one hopes to see, what consequences one wants parties to have. (See, for example, the range of definitions in the box.) Any one person's definition is likely to be rooted in a particular time and orientation and therefore not likely to reflect the diversity that marks the parties. But, whatever the reason, neither political scientists nor politicians have achieved any consensus at all on what sets the political party apart from other political organizations.

Despite the absence of consensus, however, the most common definitions fall into three main categories. Those whose approach is ideological define the parties in terms of commonly held ideas, values, or stands on issues. That approach has not engaged many observers of the American

---

## A Variety of Definitions of the Political Party

"Party is a body of men united, for promoting by their joint endeavors the national interest, upon some particular principle in which they are all agreed."

Edmund Burke, *Thoughts on the Cause of the Present Discontents* (1770)

". . . We may define 'political party' generally as the articulate organization of society's active political agents, those who are concerned with the control of governmental power and who compete for popular support with another group or groups holding divergent views."

Sigmund Neumann, *Modern Political Parties* (Chicago: University of Chicago Press, 1956), p. 396; italics omitted.

". . . Any group, however loosely organized, seeking to elect governmental office-holders under a given label."

Leon D. Epstein, *Political Parties in Western Democracies* (New York: Praeger, 1967), p. 9.

"An 'established political party' is hereby declared to be a political party which, as to the state, at the last general election for state and county officers, polled for its candidate for governor more than two per cent of the entire vote cast for governor in the state."

*Missouri Statutes* (V.A.M.S. § 120.140, par. 2.)

" 'Party' or 'political party' means any political organization which elects a state committee and officers of a state committee, by a state convention composed of delegates elected from each representative district in which the party has registered members and which nominates candidates for electors of President and Vice President, or nominates candidates for offices to be decided at the general election."

*Delaware Statutes* (15 Del. C. § 101)

political parties, for ideological homogeneity or purpose has not been a hallmark of the major American parties. Most of the attempts at definition vacillate between two other options. One of these is a tendency to view the political party as a hierarchical organization or structure that draws into its orbit large numbers of voters, candidates, and active party workers. The other approach is to view the political parties largely in terms of what they do — what their role, function, or activities in the American political systems are. Proponents of this approach frequently identify American political parties with election campaigns. To those latter two approaches we now turn.

## THE POLITICAL PARTY AS A SOCIAL STRUCTURE

Large organizations or social structures are people in various roles, responsibilities, patterns of activities, and reciprocal relationships. But which people, what activities, what relationships are we talking about when we speak of the two major American parties? The party leaders and officials, the hundreds of anonymous activists who work for candidates and party causes, the people who vote for the party's candidates, its actual dues-paying members, the people who have an emotional involvement in the fortunes of the party, the men and women elected to office on the party's label? All of them? Some of them?

The major American political parties are in truth three-headed political giants, tripartite systems of interactions, that embrace all these individuals. As political structures they include a party organization, a party in office, and a party in the electorate ( Figure 1.1).

### The Party Organization

In the party organization one finds the formally chosen party leaders, the informally anointed ones, the legions of local captains and leaders, the ward and precinct workers, the members and activists of the party — that is, all those who give their time, money, and skills to the party, whether as leaders or followers. These are the men and women who make and carry out decisions in the name of the party. The organization operates in part through the formal machinery of committees and conventions set by the laws of the fifty states and in part through its own informal apparatus. Here one finds the centers of party authority and bureaucracy, and here also one observes the face-to-face contacts and interactions that bespeak organization of any kind.

### The Party in Government

The party in government is made up of those who have captured office through the symbols of the party and of those who seek to do so. The chief

FIGURE 1.1   The Three-Part Political Party

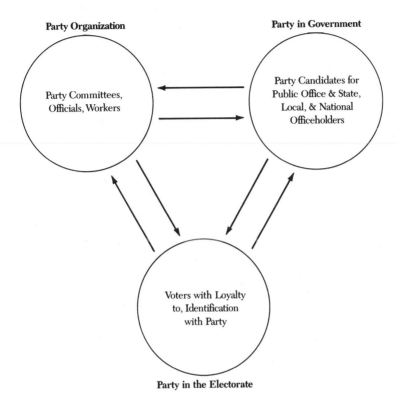

Party Organization

Party in Government

Party Committees, Officials, Workers

Party Candidates for Public Office & State, Local, & National Officeholders

Voters with Loyalty to, Identification with Party

Party in the Electorate

executives and legislative parties of the nation and states are its major components. Although in many ways they are not subject to the control or discipline of the party organization, they do in the broadest sense speak for the party. Their pronouncements are the most audible party statements and carry the greatest weight with the public. A party's president or leader in the Senate claims more attention than its national chairperson.

### The Party in the Electorate

The party in the electorate is the party's least well defined part. It comprises the men and women who affiliate casually with it, show it some degree of loyalty, and even vote habitually for it, even though they do not participate in the party organization or interact with its leaders and activists. Its individuals are not subject to the incentives and disciplines of the party organization. They are, in effect, the regular consumers of the party's candidates and appeals. As such, they make up the majorities necessary for effective political power in the American political system. But their association with the party is a passive one — accepting here, rejecting there, always threatening the party with the fickleness of their affections.

In their three-part structure, therefore, the major American parties include mixed, varied, and even contradictory components. Each party, for example, is a political organization with active, even disciplined participants. It is also an aggregate of unorganized partisans who may begrudge the party organization even the merest public gesture of support or loyalty. The party thus embraces the widest range of involvement and commitment. It is a reasonably well defined, voluntary political organization and at the same time an open, public collection of loyalists.

Perhaps the most telling characteristic of the major American parties, therefore, is the relationship that their clientele — the party in the electorate — has to them. The other political organizations, such as interest groups and ad hoc campaign organizations, usually work to attract supporters beyond their members and workers; but this wider clientele remains outside the political organization. Not so with the political party. The party in the electorate is more than an external group to be wooed and mobilized. State laws usually permit it a voice in the selection of the parties' candidates in the direct primary, and in many states it helps to select local party officials such as the ward and precinct committeeperson. Consequently, the major American party is an open, inclusive, semipublic political organization. It includes both a tangible political organization and its own political clientele (as well as the party in government, of course). In this combination of exclusive organization and inclusive clientele, of organization and electorate, the political party stands apart from the other political organizations on the American scene and apart from parties elsewhere.

Finally, each major party differs from state to state in the relationships and interactions among its three sectors. The Republicans and the Democrats are so decentralized and so diverse that virtually each state party has its own distinctive mix of the three. Party organizations, for example, differ in form from state to state; in some the party organization dominates the party in government, whereas in others the reverse is the case. Also, party electorates differ in composition and in the bases of their loyalties; in some states the two parties in the electorate divide roughly along social class lines, but in others they do not. Indeed, much of the distinctive quality of a state party is a reflection of the form and composition of each of the party sectors and of their relationship with each other.

## THE PARTY AS A CLUSTER OF ACTIVITIES

From a discussion of the political parties as social structures, we move to a definition of them in terms of activities. We move from what they are to what they do. In varying degrees the competitive political parties of every democracy perform three sets of activities. They select candidates and contest elections, they propagandize on behalf of a party ideology or program, and they attempt to guide the elected officeholders of government. The degree of emphasis that any particular political party puts on each of these individual activities varies within and between countries, but no party completely escapes the necessity of any of them.

## Parties as Electors

It often appears that the American parties are little more than regular attempts to capture public office. Electoral activity so dominates the life of the American party that its fever chart follows almost exactly the cycles of the election calendar. Party activity and vitality reach a peak at the elections, and between elections the parties go into a recuperative hibernation. The parties live to mobilize voter support behind their candidates in elections, for only by winning elections do they maintain the confidence and allegiance of their three sectors. Party activity is goal oriented, and in American politics most of the general goals as well as the goals of the individual sectors depend ultimately on electoral victory. It is, in fact, chiefly in the attempt to achieve their often separate goals through winning public office that the three sectors of the party are brought together in unified action.

## Parties as Propagandizers

Second, the American parties carry on a series of loosely related activities that perhaps can best be called education or propagandization. There is, of course, a school of thought which argues that the American parties fail almost completely to function on behalf of ideas or ideologies. The Democrats and Republicans, to be sure, do not espouse the all-inclusive ideologies of a European Marxist or proletarian party. But they do represent aggregates of interests and do stand for different policies on selected issues. At the least the American parties do represent the interests of and the stands congenial to the groups that identify with them and support them. In this sense they become parties of business or labor, of the advantaged or disadvantaged. Moreover, the events of the 1960s and 1970s suggest that ideology in a purer sense is coming to the American parties. In presidential nominating politics alone one merely needs to mention the Goldwater conservatism of 1964 and the McGovern liberalism of 1972.

## Parties as Governors

Finally, the successful candidates of the American parties organize the decision-making agencies of government. The legislatures of forty-nine states (the exception is nonpartisan Nebraska) and the United States Congress are organized along party lines, and the voting of their members shows to varying degrees the effects of party discipline and cohesion. To be sure, that cohesion on controversial issues is irregular, sporadic, and often unpredictable in most legislatures. The congressional Democrats, for example, cannot generally count on their southern contingent to support civil rights bills or much welfare legislation. Yet, in the aggregate an important degree of party discipline does exist. In executive branches presidents and governors depend on their fellow partisans for executive talent and count on their party loyalty to bind them to the executive programs. Only the American judiciary largely escapes the organizing and directing touch of the parties.

These, then, are the chief overt activities of democratic political parties generally and of American parties in particular. They are the activities that the parties set out consciously to perform. Large sections of this or any other book on the American parties must be devoted to them.

To list these activities of the parties, however, is not to suggest that the American parties monopolize any or all of them. The parties compete with the nonparty political organizations over the ability and the right to perform them. The American parties, having organized the legislatures, battle constantly — and often with little success — against interest groups and constituency pressures in order to firm up party lines for votes on major bills. In attempting to nominate candidates for public office, especially at the local level, the party faces an often insurmountable competition from interest groups, community elites, and powerful local personalities, each of whom may be sponsoring pet candidates. In stating issues and ideologies, they are often overshadowed by the fervor of the minor (third) parties, the ubiquitous interest groups, the mass media, pundits, publicists, and political action groups.

These patterns of party activity also affect the party structure and its three sectors. For example, the emphasis on the electoral activities of American parties elevates the party in government to a position of unusual power, even dominance. It frequently competes with the party organization for the favor of the party in the electorate. In parties more closely allied with issues and ideologies — such as those of continental Europe — party organizations often are able to dictate to legislative parties.

On the other hand, individuals from all three sectors of the party may unite in specific activities. Activists of the party organization loyal to an officeholder may unite with that person, with other individuals of the party in government, and with individuals in the party electorate to return him or her to public office. When the election is won or lost, they will very likely drift apart again. Therefore, one finds within the parties these functional clusters or nuclei, these groups of individuals drawn together in a single concerted action.[1] Small and informal task groups cut across the differences in structure and goals that characterize the three party sectors. In American politics, therefore, alliances and coalitions are more common within the parties than between them.

## THE UNPLANNED CONSEQUENCES OF PARTY ACTIVITY

The goal-seeking behavior of any individual or organization has unintended consequences. Congress, by pursuing its legislating activities, may be said to be either resolving or aggravating great areas of social conflict, depending on the observer and his location. Similarly, interest groups, in pursuing their particular goals in the legislative process, are also providing an informal, auxiliary avenue of representation. The same search for the unplanned consequences of party activities is an old tradition in the study of the American parties. It produces rich insights into the contributions of the parties to the American political system. Yet it can be frustrating, its findings imprecise and elusive.

When we say that a political party is picking a candidate or organizing an election campaign, we are talking about overt, intended, observable party activity. Not so when we say that the same party is organizing consensus, integrating new groups into society, or giving voice to political opposition. These latter statements describe the activities we *impute* to the parties. They are statements about the *consequences* of party activity rather than the activity itself. As such they depend on what meaning, results, or outcomes of action we as individual observers see. Some of our observations are more easily verified by empirical evidence than others. It is surely easier to show that the parties contribute to the political socialization of young Americans than it is to demonstrate that they settle social conflict, because it is easier to observe the process and results of socialization. Perhaps the distinction can best be made by narrowing it to a fine point: it is much easier to prove or establish the activity itself than the results or consequences it brings about.

Not surprisingly, then, scholars of the American political parties have seen and recorded wildly differing sets of these unintended consequences. They have usually referred to them as "functions," but that semantic convention is virtually the extent of their agreement. It is perhaps foolish to compound the confusion, but what follows is a brief list of some of the most readily identifiable — and thus most frequently mentioned — of these functions or unplanned consequences of party activity.

1. The parties participate in the *political socialization* of the American electorate by transmitting political values and information to large num-

<hr/>

[1] On the party as a series of task-oriented nuclei, see Joseph A. Schlesinger, "Political Party Organization," in James G. March (ed.), *Handbook of Organizations* (Chicago: Rand McNally, 1965), pp. 764–801.

bers of voters and future voters. They preach the value of political commitment and activity, and they convey information and cues about the confusing political system. By symbolizing and representing a political point of view, they offer uninformed or underinformed citizens a map of the political world. They help them form political judgments and make political choices, and in both physical and psychological terms they make it easier to be politically active.

2. The American parties also contribute to the *accumulation of political power*. They aggregate masses of ineffectual political individuals and groups and thereby organize blocs powerful enough to govern or to oppose those who govern. For the confused and confounded citizen they simplify, and often oversimplify, the political world into more comprehensible choices. By using his or her attachment to the party as a perceptual screen, the voter has a master clue for assessing issues and candidates. So both within the individual and in the external political world, the political party operates to focus political loyalties on a small number of alternatives and thus to accumulate support behind them.

3. Because they devote so much effort to contesting elections, the American parties dominate the *recruitment of political leadership*. One needs only to run down a list of the members of the cabinet or even the Supreme Court to see how many entered public service through a political party or through partisan candidacy for office. Furthermore, the orderly contesting of elections enables the parties to routinize political change and especially change of governmental leadership. More than one commentator has noted the disruptive quality of leadership changes in those countries in which no stable political parties contest in regular elections. And because the American parties pervade all governmental levels in the federal system, they may recruit and elevate leadership from one level to another.

4. Finally, the American parties are a *force for unification* in the divided American political system. The decentralization, even fragmentation, of government is an incontestably crucial fact of American politics. To the fragmentation of the nation and the fifty states, multiplied by the threefold separation of powers in each, the two great national parties bring a unifying centripetal force. They help to hold together the disparate fragments of government by bringing similar traditions, interests, symbols, and issues to all the parts. They unify with an obviously limited efficiency: for example, they often fail to bind president and Congress together in causes that can transcend the separation of powers. But they do constitute a force for unity, a political adhesive, in a set of institutions that divides.

There are two chief difficulties with these lists of party functions. First, there is not much agreement among them, a result not only of scholars' different perceptions of the parties but also of their disagreement over what the word *function* means. Some use it to denote the obvious activities of the parties (e.g., their contesting of elections), and others use it, as we do in this text, to describe the unintended consequences or happy by-products of the intended activities of the parties. For yet another group *function* suggests a contribution the party makes to the operation of the broader political system.[2] Second, there is the problem of defining or formulating the functional categories so that they can be observed and measured. If, as some writers have argued, one function of political parties is to organize social conflict or to articulate important social interests, how do we verify by our own observations whether all parties or some parties do in fact perform those functions? For reasons having to do with both of these problems, this book will look largely at party activity itself, at the more easily observable, intended activity rather than its unintended consequences.

## THE SPECIAL CHARACTERISTICS OF POLITICAL PARTIES

Perhaps it is time to end these excursions into related topics and narrow the search for political parties. The goal is not a memorable, vest-pocket definition. We seek an understanding of what characterizes the political parties and sets them apart from other political organizations. We need, in other words, a firm grasp of what the political parties are and what they do.

All political organizations exist to organize and mobilize their supporters either to capture public office or to influence the activities of those already in public office. That much at least they all have in common. But if the term *political party* is to have any meaning at all, there must also be differences between parties and other political organizations. Far too much has been made of the differences between the major American parties and other political organizations, especially the large national interest (or pressure) groups. But the differences are there nonetheless, even if they are really only differences among species of the same genus.

Above all, the political party is distinguished from other political organizations by its concentration on the contesting of elections. Although the major American parties do not monopolize the contesting of elections, their preeminence in this activity cannot be questioned. Other political organizations do attempt to influence American electoral politics. In many localities interest groups encourage or discourage candidates, work for them within parties, contribute to campaign funds, and get their members to the polls to support them. Other nonparty organizations may raise funds, organize endorsements, and recruit workers for some candidate's campaign for public office. The parties, however, are occupied with the contesting of

[2] Theodore Lowi has brought together a number of descriptions of party functions in his article "Toward Functionalism in Political Science: The Case of Innovation in Party Systems," *American Political Science Review* 57 (1963): 570–83.

elections in a way and to a degree that other political organizations are not. Their names and symbols, indeed, are the ones the states recognize for inclusion on most ballots.

Not only commitment to electoral activity, but its organizational consequences characterize the political party. Since the party chooses to work toward its goals largely in elections, it must recruit an enormous supportive clientele. Organizations that attempt to influence legislative committees or rule making in administrative agencies may succeed with a few strategists and the support of only a small, well-mobilized clientele. The political parties, in order to win elections, must depend less on the intricate skills and maneuverings of organizational strategists and more on the mobilization of large numbers of citizens. Party appeals must be broad and inclusive; the party cannot afford either exclusivity or a narrow range of concerns. It is at the opposite pole from the "single-issue" group or organization. To put it simply, the major political party has committed itself through its concentration on electoral politics to the mobilization of large numbers of citizens in large numbers of elections, and from that commitment flow many of its other characteristics.

Furthermore, the major American political parties and similar parties elsewhere are characterized by a full commitment to political activity. They operate solely as political organizations, solely as instruments of political action. Not so the interest groups and most other political organizations. They move freely and frequently from political to nonpolitical activities and back again. The AFL-CIO, for example, seeks many of its goals and interests in nonpolitical ways, especially through collective bargaining. It may, however, turn to political action — to support sympathetic candidates or to lobby before Congress — when political avenues appear the best or only means to achieve its goals. Every organized group in the United States is, as one observer has suggested, a potential political organization.[3] Still, the interest group almost always maintains some sphere of nonpolitical action.

Political parties are also marked by an uncommon stability and persistence. The personal clique, the faction, the ad hoc campaign organization, and even many interest groups seem by contrast almost political will-o'-the-wisps, which disappear as suddenly as they appear. The size and the abstractness of the political parties, their relative independence of personalities, and their continuing symbolic strength for thousands of voters assure them of a far greater political longevity. Both major American parties can trace their histories over a century, and the major parties of the other Western democracies have impressive, if shorter, life spans. It is precisely this enduring, ongoing quality that enhances their value as reference symbols. The parties are there as points of reference year after year and

---

[3] David B. Truman, *The Governmental Process* (New York: Knopf, 1951).

election after election, giving continuity and form to the choices Americans face and the issues they debate.

Finally, the political parties are distinguished from other political organizations by the extent to which they operate as cues or symbols — or even more vaguely as emotion-laden objects of loyalty. For millions of Americans the party label is the chief cue for their decisions about candidates or issues. It is the point of reference that allows them to organize and simplify the buzzing confusion and strident rhetoric of American politics. As a potent reference symbol, the party label organizes the extensive confusion of American politics *within* the individual American citizen. That is, it organizes his perceptions and structures his choices; it relates his political values and goals to the real options of American politics.

To summarize, the major American political parties exist, as do other political organizations, to organize large numbers of individuals behind attempts to influence the selection of public officials and the decisions these officials subsequently make in office. The parties are set apart by:

— The extent to which they pursue their organizing through the contesting of elections.
— The extensiveness and inclusiveness of their organization and clienteles.
— Their sole concentration on political avenues for achieving their goals.
— Their demonstrated stability and long life.
— Their strength as cues and reference symbols in the decision making of individual citizens.

No one of these characteristics alone sets the political party apart from other political organizations, but when they are taken together and the matter of degree is considered, they do set the major political party apart from other types of political organizations.

But, to reemphasize a point previously made, the differences between parties and other political organizations are often slender. Interest groups certainly contest elections to some degree, and the larger ones have achieved impressive stability and duration and also considerable symbolic status. They, too, can recruit candidates and give political clues and cues to their members and fellow travelers. Groups such as the student organizations that attempted to elect peace candidates in the 1970 congressional elections differ from the parties chiefly in size and influence. They participated in the elections, propagated ideologies, tried to influence and organize officeholders. Like the parties, they achieved symbolic status for members and like-minded voters and operated exclusively in the political realm. However, they did not, and in most localities could not, offer their names and symbols for candidates to use on the ballot. It is only that difference and the whole question of size and degree that separate their activities and political roles from those of the parties.

So similar are the parties to some other political organizations that they resemble them more closely than they do the minor or third parties. In other words, there are political parties and political parties. These minor political parties, called minor because they are not electorally competitive, are only nominally electoral organizations. Not even the congenital optimism of candidates can lead Socialists or Prohibitionists to expect substantial victories at the ballot. Lacking local organization as most of them do, they resemble the major parties less than do the complex, nationwide interest groups. And their membership base, often related to a single issue, may be just as narrow, just as exclusively recruited, as that of most interest groups. In structure and activities, groups such as the United States Chamber of Commerce and the AFL-CIO resemble the Democrats and Republicans far more than do the Vegetarians and the Socialist Workers.

## THE RISE OF AMERICAN PARTIES

To see the special role and character of political parties there is no better place to look than at their origins and rise to importance. In the United States their history is one of an almost 200-year alliance with an emerging popular democracy. The American parties grew up with and in response to the gradual growth of the adult suffrage and to all of the changes it brought to American politics.[4]

In the first years of the Republic the vote was limited in every state to those free men who could meet the property-holding or tax-paying requirements. Furthermore the framers of the new Constitution of 1787 had intentionally limited the power of individual voters at elections. The president was to be chosen, not by a direct vote of the electorate, but indirectly by a group of notables making up the electoral college. And even though the House of Representatives was entrusted to a direct popular vote, the Senate was not. Its members were to be chosen by the respective state legislatures. (Those respective state legislatures, taking the same cue, also decided to select the members of the electoral college themselves.) It was in short, a cautious and limited beginning to democratic self-government.

In their first years the American parties grew out of and matched this politics of a limited suffrage and indirect elections. They began, in fact, largely as caucuses of like-minded members of the Congress. They involved only the men and the issues of politics in the nation's capital. These congressional caucuses nominated presidential candidates and mobilized groups of political figures supportive of and opposed to the administration

---

[4] There are, of course, a large number of histories of the American political parties or of some particular party. Most, however, devote virtually all of their pages to the candidates and platforms of the parties. Few discuss the parties *qua* parties. For three that do, see William N. Chambers, *Political Parties in a New Nation* (New York: Oxford University Press, 1963); Everett C. Ladd, Jr., *American Political Parties* (New York: Norton, 1970; and William N. Chambers and Walter D. Burnham (eds.), *The American Party Systems* (New York: Oxford University Press, 1967).

of the time. Party organization back in the states and localities did not develop until about 1800 with "committees of correspondence." These were the first reachings out of the infant parties to the voters "back home," and through them officeholders organized and communicated with the electorate. Early in the nineteenth century the efforts at local organization resulted in the development of some free-standing local party organizations in a few counties and cities. But the development of parties back in the states went slowly and sporadically at least until the 1820s.

So matters stayed for the first thirty or forty years of the Republic. In fact, one of the infant parties, the Federalists, virtually disappeared shortly after the defeat of its last president, John Adams, in 1800. The Jeffersonian Republicans, the new party of agrarian interests and the frontier, quickly established its superiority and enjoyed a twenty-year period of one-party monopoly. So thorough was the domination by the time of James Monroe's presidency that the absence of party and political conflict was dubbed the "Era of Good Feelings." Despite the decline of one party and the rise of another, however, the nature of the parties did not change. It was a time during which government and politics were the business of an elite of well-known, well-established men, and the parties reflected the politics of the time. In both of his successful races for the presidency (1816 and 1820) Monroe was the nominee only of the Jeffersonian caucus in the Congress.

The early politics of the country began, however, to undergo sharp changes in the 1820s. The states began to expand the electorate by removing the property requirements for suffrage; by the 1830s the removal had been accomplished. The result was a tremendous increase in the electorate between 1820 and 1840. (See Table 1.1.) Simultaneously the electoral col-

TABLE 1.1   Popular Vote and Vote Turnout for Presidential Elections: 1824–40

|  | 1824 | 1828 | 1832 | 1836 | 1840 |
|---|---|---|---|---|---|
| Total popular vote | 356,038 | 1,155,350 | 1,217,691 | 1,505,000 | 2,412,000 |
| Turnout (percentage of adult white males) | 26.9 | 57.6 | 55.4 | 57.8 | 80.2 |

*Sources*   Data on the popular vote come from *Historical Statistics of the United States.* The calculation of turnout percentages is reported in William N. Chambers, "Election of 1840," in Arthur M. Schlesinger, Jr., and Fred L. Israel, *History of American Presidential Elections*, vol. 1 (New York: Chelsea House, 1971), p. 687.

lege ceased to function as it had at first, and presidential politics were transformed. As Ladd has written:

The framers of the Constitution envisioned the president selected by an electoral college of wise and dispassionate men chosen by the several state legislatures; the electors, equal in number to the membership of Congress, would consider the needs of the Republic and exercise their independent judgment. The presidency was thus to be doubly insulated from the people. But one layer of intended insulation was ripped away after the election of just one president — Washington — with the pledging of electors: the majorities in the state legislatures began choosing electors pledged to a particular candidate for the presidency, thus transforming the electoral college from a body for independent judgment to a vehicle for carrying out the wishes of popularly elected state legislative majorities. Then in the 1820s another large step in democratizing the presidency was taken, as all the states except South Carolina shifted from legislative designation to popular election of the slates of electors.[5]

With these changes in the electorate and in the method of electing a president, there were bound to be changes in the politics of that election.

The impact was immediate. The caucus nominations fell under increasing criticism as the work of a narrow-based and self-perpetuating elite. But quite apart from criticism, the caucus system began to decline from its own infirmities. The attempt of the Jeffersonians to nominate a presidential candidate in 1824 was a shambles. The chosen candidate of the caucus, William Crawford, ran fourth in the race, and since no candidate won a majority in the electoral college, it was left to the House of Representatives to choose among John Quincy Adams, Henry Clay, and Andrew Jackson. The House chose Adams over Jackson, the front runner in the election. Jackson in turn defeated Adams in 1828 as the new nation teetered on the edge of a new party politics.

The "new" party politics — the modern political party — emerged by 1840. First, the nonparty politics of the Era of Good Feelings finally gave way to the two-party system that has prevailed ever since. Andrew Jackson took the frontier and agrarian wing of the Jeffersonians into what we now think of as the Democratic party. The National Republicans, whose candidate in 1832 was Henry Clay, merged with the Whigs, and bipartyism in the United States was born. Second, and just as important, the parties as political institutions began to change. The Jacksonian Democrats held the first national nominating convention in 1832 — at which, appropriately, Jackson himself was nominated for a second term. (The Whig and Anti-Masonic parties had both held more limited conventions a year before.) The campaign for the presidency also became more "popular" as new campaign organizations and tactics brought the contest to more and more people. As a consequence Jackson came to the White House for a second

---

[5] Ladd, *American Political Parties*, pp. 59–60. (Emphasis removed.)

term with a popular mandate as the leader of a national political party. Larger numbers of citizens were voting (see Table 1.1) than had ever voted before.

At the same time, party organization in the states had a new burst of growth and conventions increasingly replaced caucuses as the way of nominating candidates for state and local office. By the middle of the century, therefore, party organization was developing throughout the nation, and the party convention became a more and more common way of picking party candidates. And also by 1840 the Whigs and the Democrats established themselves as the first truly national party system, one in which both parties were established and competitive in all the states.

Modern political parties — parties pretty much as we know them today — had thus arrived by the middle of the nineteenth century. They were in fact the first modern parties in western history, and their arrival reflected above all the early expansion of the electorate in the United States. The comparable development of parties in Great Britain did not occur until the 1870s, after the further extension of the adult male electorate in the Reform Acts of 1832 and 1867.

Just as the parties were reaching their maturity, they and American politics received another massive infusion of voters from a new source: immigration from Europe. Hundreds of thousands of Europeans — the great majority from Ireland and Germany — came to the country before the Civil War. So many immigrated, in fact, that their very coming and their entry into American politics became a political issue. The newcomers found a ready home in the Democratic party, and a nativist third party, the American party (the so-called Know-Nothing party), sprang up in the 1850s. The tide of immigration was only temporarily halted by the Civil War. New nationalities came after that interruption in a virtually uninterrupted flow until Congress closed the door to mass immigration in the 1920s.

The American cities offered industrial jobs to the newcomers from abroad, and they settled heavily in them. It was there in the cities that a new party organization, the city "machine," developed in response to their problems and vulnerabilities. The machines were more than impressively efficient party organizations. They were social service mechanisms that helped the new arrivals cope with a new country and all of the threats and adventures of urban, industrial society. They softened the hard edge of poverty, they smoothed the way with government and the law, and they taught the immigrants the ways and customs of their new life. Moreover, they were in many instances indistinguishable from the government of the city; theirs was the classic instance of "party government" in the American experience because their leaders ran the city governments. As such they were the vehicle by which the new urban working class won control of the cities away from the largely Anglo-Saxon, Protestant elites that had prevailed for so long. So the parties again became the instrument of the aspirations of new citizens, just as they had in the 1830s. And in doing so they achieved the high point of political party power and influence in American history.

The American parties — simply as political organizations — thus reached their zenith, something of a "Golden Age" indeed, by the beginning of the twentieth century. Party organization now existed in all the states and localities; it positively flourished in the industrial cities. Parties achieved an all-time high in discipline in the Congress and in most state legislatures. They controlled campaigns for public office — they held rallies, did the door-to-door canvassing, and got the voters to the polls. They controlled access to a great deal of public employment. They were an important source of information and guidance for a largely uneducated and often illiterate electorate. Indeed they rode the crest of an extraordinarily vital American politics; the latter half of the nineteenth century, we often forget, featured the highest voter turnouts in the history of American presidential elections. The parties suited the needs and limitations of the new voters and the problems of mobilizing majorities in the new and raw industrial society. If ever a time and a political organization were well matched, this was it.

To be sure, the democratic impetus was not spent by the turn of the century. The electorate continued to expand — with the enfranchisement of women, with the delayed securing of the vote for blacks, and with the lowering of the voting age to eighteen. The move to direct, popular elections and away from the indirections the Founding Fathers favored also continued its inexorable course. The Seventeenth Amendment decreed the direct election of senators, and by the 1970s the movement to substitute direct election of the president for the electoral college reached its greatest support and credibility. Just as important for the parties, however, were the changes wrought in them in the name of the continuing commitment to egalitarianism and popular democracy. Sleek, powerful, and even arrogant at the end of the nineteenth century, the parties fell under attack by the Progressive reformers. The reformers enacted the direct primary to give the citizenry a voice in party nominations, and large numbers of state legislatures wrote laws to define and limit party organization. The business of nominating a president was made more popular by the enacting of presidential primaries in the states, and activists within the parties reformed their national conventions. All in all, by the 1980s Americans had a pair of parties and a party politics born and shaped in the triumph of the democratic ethos and its expectations.[6]

The reforms of the twentieth century were to some extent intended to

[6] On the reform of the parties, see Austin Ranney, *Curing the Mischiefs of Faction* (Berkeley: University of California Press, 1975).

diminish the power and position the parties had achieved by the end of the 1800s. To that extent they succeeded. For these and a number of other reasons the heyday of the American parties passed. The theme of the decline of the parties runs through all commentaries on the American parties these days, and it will certainly run through this one. Even so, the parties remain to a considerable extent what they were eighty or a hundred years ago: the preeminent political organizations of mass, popular democracy. They developed and grew with the expansion of the suffrage and the popularizing of electoral politics. They were and remain the invention by which large numbers of voters come together to control the selection of their representatives. They rose to prominence at a time when a new electorate of limited knowledge and limited political sophistication needed the guidance of their symbols. Thus it was that the modern American political party was born and reached its time of glory in the nineteenth century. When one talks today of the decline of the parties, it is the standard of that Golden Age against which the decline is measured.

## THE PARTY IN ITS ENVIRONMENT

It is in the nature of a book on political parties to treat them more or less in isolation, to lift them from their context in the political system for special scrutiny. Yet, useful as isolation is, it may give the impression that the political parties are autonomous structures, moving without constraint within the political system. In a too-determined search for the parties alone there is a danger of overlooking the many forces in their environment that shape both their form and their activities.

It is possible on the other hand to let analysis and logic run riot and to imagine a party environment that includes virtually every other structure and process in the political system and a great deal outside it. But despite the superficial truth that every social structure or process is related to every other one, clearly some influences on the party are more powerful and insistent than others. It will suffice to limit this discussion to them.

### Electorates and Elections

As the preceding section indicates, the expansion of the American electorate shaped the very origin and development of the parties as political organizations. Furthermore, each new group of voters that enters the electorate challenges the parties to readjust their appeals. The parties must compete for the votes and support of new voters, and the necessity of doing so forces them to reconsider their strategies for building the coalitions that can win elections.

Similarly, the nature of American elections, too, is bound up with the rise and continuing fortunes of the parties. The move from indirect to direct elections transformed both the contesting of elections and the parties that contested them. And should we finally come to a direct election of the American president, that change, too, would have its impact on the parties.

The election machinery in a state may indeed be thought of as an extensive regulation of the parties' chief political activity. At least it is often difficult to determine where the regulation of the party ends and electoral reform begins. Consider, for example, the direct primary. It is both a significant addition to the machinery of American electoral processes and a sharp regulation of the way a party selects the candidates who bear its label in an election. Even the relatively minor differences in primary law from one state to another — such as differences in the form of the ballot or the time of the year in which the primary occurs — are not without their impact on the parties.

The collective electoral institutions of the nation and of the fifty states set a matrix of rules and boundaries within which the parties compete for public office. The various components of these institutions are not neutral, for they give strategic advantages to some of the contestants. The basic American commitment to plurality elections within single-member districts, as decades of scholars have suggested, works in favor of the large competitive parties and against the small weak ones. Similarly, population inequality and gerrymandering in constituencies distort the strength and composition of the party electorates.

### The Political Institutions

Very little in the American political system escapes the influence of American federalism and the separation of powers. No single factor seems to affect the American legislative parties, for example, so much as the separation of the legislature from the executive. Among the party systems of the world, the legislative parties in parliamentary systems have the greatest discipline in voting and the strongest ties to the party organization. The institutions of the parliamentary form lead to the legislative party's cohesive support of (or opposition to) a cabinet drawn from one legislative party or the other. The political parties in American legislatures are under much less pressure to support or oppose a completely separate chief executive. Indeed, support for and opposition to executive programs often cut sharply across party lines.

The decentralization of American federalism has also left its imprint on the American parties. It has ingrained in them local political loyalties and generations of local, often provincial, political traditions. It has spawned an awesome range and number of public offices to fill; thus it has created an electoral politics that in size and diversity dwarfs that of all other political systems. By creating local rewards, local traditions, even local patronage systems, it has created and sustained a whole set of semiautonomous local parties within the two parties. The establishment of these local centers of power has worked mightily against the development of strong, permanent national party organs. The strong centers of influence within the party organizations are still at the state and county levels.

## Statutory Regulation

No other parties among the democracies of the world are so bound up in legal regulations as are the American parties. The forms of their organization are prescribed by the states in endless, often finicky, detail. The statutes on party organization set up grandiose layers of party committees and often chart the details of who will compose them, when they will meet, and what their agenda will be. State law also defines the parties themselves, often in defining the right to place candidates on the ballot. A number of states also undertake to regulate the activities of parties; many, for example, regulate their finances, and most place at least some limits on their campaign practices. So severe can these regulations be, in fact, that in some states the parties have developed elaborate strategies to evade the worst burdens of regulation.

## The Political Culture

It is one thing to specify such tangibles in the parties' environment as regulatory statutes, electoral mechanisms, and even political institutions and electorates. It is quite another, however, to pin down so elusive a part of the party environment as its political culture. The political culture is the all-enveloping network of the political norms, values, and expectations of Americans. It is, in other words, their conglomerate view of what the political system is, what it should be, and what their place is in it. Furthermore, it varies regionally and among different strata or political subcultures of the American population. Party campaign tactics that the big city takes for granted often outrage the nearby country cousins.

The feeling that party politics is a compromising, somewhat dirty business has long been a major and persistent component of the American political culture. Since the advent of public opinion sampling, the indicators of that hostility toward partisan politics have multiplied. For example, a number of polls have found that American parents prefer that their sons and daughters not choose a full-time political career. Politics as a vocation, in their estimation, compares unfavorably with even the semiskilled trades.[7] In the spring of 1975 the Gallup Poll asked a national sample of college students to rate the "honesty and ethical standards" of people in a number

---

[7] See William C. Mitchell, "The Ambivalent Social Status of the American Politician," *Western Political Quarterly* 12 (1959): 683–99.

of vocations. Although only 2 percent rated college teachers and 5 percent rated medical doctors "low" or "very low," 53 percent gave those ratings to political officeholders. Only "advertising practitioners" scored below the officeholders, and then by only one percentage point.[8]

A more systematic review of American attitudes toward the party system points similarly to a low level of popular support for the parties. More seriously, it documents a recent decline in support in such specifics as holding a loyalty to a party or keeping party labels on the ballot. Furthermore, the decline began before Watergate and thus reflects more basic, perhaps more intractable, causes. In 1973, for example, a national sample of adults was asked to pick among four possibilities in identifying which "part of the government" they most often trusted "to do what's right." The Congress and the Supreme Court were each choices of more than 30 percent of the sample, and almost 24 percent chose the president. Only 1.3 percent chose the political parties. All in all, Jack Dennis concludes, support for the American parties has dipped to "dangerously low levels."[9]

Suspicion of things partisan, however, is only one element in a multifaceted political culture that shapes the American parties. The views of Americans on such broad points as representative democracy itself are relevant. A Burkean view of representation, which holds that the representative ought to decide public questions on the basis of his own information and wisdom, certainly retards the development of party discipline in American legislatures. More detailed public attitudes govern even such matters as the incentives for party activity and the kinds of campaign tactics a party or candidate chooses. Indeed, the whole issue of what we consider fair or ethical campaigning is simply a reflection of the norms and expectations of large numbers of Americans.

### The Nonpolitical Environment

Much of the parties' nonpolitical environment works on them through the elements of the political environment. Changes in levels of education, for example, affect the political culture, the skills of the electorate, and levels of political information. Great jolts in the economy alter the structure of political issues and the goals of the electorate. Educational levels and socioeconomic status also seem related to elements of the political culture. The study in Wisconsin just mentioned suggests that less-educated Americans accept party loyalty and discipline more easily than the better educated do. Even general social values are quickly translated into political values. Acceptance of a Catholic candidate for the American presidency

[8] *Minneapolis Tribune,* May 19, 1975.
[9] Jack Dennis, "Trends in Public Support for the American Party System," *British Journal of Political Science* 5 (1976): 187–230.

had to await changes in social attitudes about religion in general and Catholicism in particular.

Whether the impact of the nonpolitical environment is direct or indirect, however, may be beside the point. The impact is strong and often disruptive. The advent of a recession, for example, may have important repercussions on the parties. It may make money raising more difficult; it will certainly make patronage positions more attractive and perhaps even shift the incentives for recruiting the workers on which the party organizations rely. It will also certainly define a very important issue for the electorate. If the crisis is especially severe, as was the Great Depression of the 1930s, it may even fracture and reorganize the pattern of enduring party loyalties.

What began in this chapter as a search for the distinctiveness of the parties has thus concluded by looking at how they become what they are. To be sure, it is important to have a firm grasp of what we mean when we refer to a political party — especially to understand its peculiar three-part nature. It is important also to understand the nature and role of the party as a political organization, especially as the one variety of political organization attuned to the politics of mass electorates. But the search for the parties is, paradoxically, a search for more than the parties. It is incomplete without a grasp of the context, the environment, in which they are set and by which they are shaped.

# 2
# The American Two-Party System

The powerful personalities and the eccentric issues that often mark the American minor parties have an uncanny ability to divert our attention from the routines of American electoral politics. Amid the sometimes portentous gravity of our politics it may lighten the spirit to reflect on a political party devoted to the moral superiority of the vegetable. And in a politics traditionally divorced from systematic public philosophy, many Americans have understandably been attracted by the ideology and conscience of parties such as the Progressives and the Socialists. It excites us, too, that each new minor party comes as a potential David to challenge the two Goliaths of American politics.

What had since the 1920s been little more than colorful or interesting, however, became a matter of considerable seriousness in 1968. In the presidential election of that year George C. Wallace captured almost 10 million votes and came close to throwing the entire election into the unpredictable hands of the House of Representatives. Had he not been struck down by an assassin's bullet midway in the 1972 preconvention campaign he might well have exceeded his 1968 accomplishment. How is it, then, that we refer so glibly to the American two-party system? Why do we acknowledge only two parties and cavalierly disregard the whole array of smaller ones? Like our deceptively simple references to political parties, our references to party systems flow easily — and vaguely. But the mathematics of "two" and the components of a "system" are by no means self-evident.

The conventional terminology we use to describe party systems is based on two related major premises: that parties are primarily electoral organizations and that their electoral activities are carried out in direct competition with other electoral parties. The designation of a one-party, two-party, five-party, or any other multiparty system simply indicates the number of political parties able to compete for office with some prospect of success. Hence the mathematics rests on a distinction between the competitive major parties and the noncompetitive minor parties. What is called the party system is composed, therefore, only of the electorally competitive parties.

For all its elegant simplicity (and to some extent, because of it) this conventional classification of party systems has a number of significant shortcomings:

— It focuses solely on one dimension of the competition among political organizations. Consequently, it overlooks the possibility that the major parties compete ideologically or programmatically with minor parties, even though they do not compete electorally.
— By focusing only on the political parties, it ignores the full range of competition among all kinds of political organizations. Even in the business of nominating and electing candidates for public office, a party may face competition from a local interest group or political elite.
— By classifying parties exclusively by electoral competition, it ignores any differences in organization the parties may have and centers its measurement on the size of the party's electorate.
— Finally, it tends to ignore the implications of the word *system*. It overlooks the relationships and interactions one expects in any system and settles merely for the presence of competitive parties and their presumed competings in elections.

But so ingrained in both everyday use and in the scholarly literature is this concept of the party system that one has little choice but to work within its terms.[1]

## THE NATIONAL PARTY SYSTEM

Despite local deviations to one-partyism, the American party system is and has been a two-party system for the last 150 years. Beyond all subtle variations in competition, there is the inescapable, crucial fact that almost all partisan political conflict in the United States has been channeled through two major political parties. They rise and fall, they establish their own seats of strength, they suffer their local weaknesses, but they endure. Perhaps even more remarkable is the fact that one does not easily find another democracy in which two parties have so long and thoroughly dominated politics. Even in Great Britain three parties — the Conservatives, Liberals, and Labourites — have sustained some degree of competition for most of this century.

One cannot argue, though, that the American two-party system is as old as the Republic. The period before 1836 was one of instability in the party system. The Federalists established a short period of superiority during

[1] For a sophisticated critique of the traditional classification and analysis of party systems, see Giovanni Sartori, *Party and Party Systems* (Cambridge: Cambridge University Press ,1976).

## The American Major Parties

The list of the American major parties is short and select. In almost 200 years of history only five political parties have achieved a competitive position in American national politics. Three lost it; the Democrats and Republicans maintain it to this day.

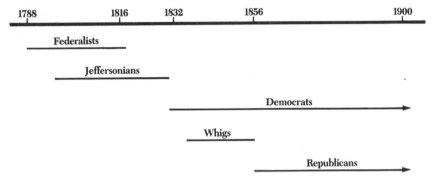

1. *The Federalists.* The party of the new Constitution and strong national government, it was the first American political party. Its support was rooted in the Northeast and the Atlantic seaboard where it attracted the support of merchants, landowners, and established families of wealth and status. Limited by its narrow base of support it quickly fell before the success of the Jeffersonians and the Virginia presidents.

2. *The Jeffersonians.* Opposed to the nationalism of the Federalists, it was a party of the small farmers, workers, and less privileged who preferred the authority of the states. Like its founder, it shared many of the ideals of the French Revolution, especially the extension of the suffrage and the notion of direct popular self-government. (At various times it was known by names such as the Republican and the Democratic-Republican party, both of which confuse it unnecessarily with contemporary parties.)

3. *The Democrats.* Growing out of the Jacksonian wing of the Jeffersonian party, it was initially Jackson's party and the first really broadly based, popular party in the United States. On behalf of a coalition of less privileged voters it opposed such commercial goals as national banking and high tariffs; it also welcomed the new immigrants and opposed nativist reactions to them. (On the post–Civil War period, see Chapter 6.)

4. *The Whigs.* They, too, had roots in the old Jeffersonian party: in the Clay-Adams faction and in enmity to the Jacksonians. Opposed in its origins to the strong presidency of Jackson, its greatest leaders, Clay and Webster, were embodiments of legislative supremacy. For its short life the Whig party was an unstable coalition of many interests, among them nativism, property, and the new business and commerce.

5. *The Republicans.* Born in 1854 as the great conflict approached, it was the party of northern opposition to slavery and its spread to the new territories. It was, therefore, also the party of the Union, the North, Lincoln, the

freeing of the slaves, victory in the Civil War, and the imposition of Reconstruction. From the Whigs it also inherited a concern for business, mercantile, and propertied interests. (On the post–Civil War period, see Chapter 6.)

Thus all of the five major parties in American history had originated before the Civil War; three had also expired by its beginning.

---

the presidency of George Washington but faded quickly with the rise and success of the Jeffersonian Republicans (see box). The Jeffersonians rode their success to a brief period of dominance that culminated in the non-party (or one-party) politics of Monroe's two terms. But as the caucus system crumbled in the 1820s, new national parties emerged, and by 1836 a stable two-partyism was established. For the almost 150 years since then one party — the Democratic party — has sustained a place in the party system. In opposition the Whigs survived until the 1850s and were replaced almost immediately by the infant Republican party. Both the Democratic and Republican parties were briefly divided by the events of the Civil War, but old party lines and labels survived the war and, indeed, survive to this day.

So, the two-party drama is long, the cast of characters short. It has not in truth been quite that cut and dried. Minor parties have briefly pushed themselves into competitiveness but, significantly, never for two presidential elections in a row. The Democratic and Republican parties have of course also changed in their issues and appeals and in the coalitions that are their "parties in the electorate." But all of those hedges do not hide the fact that for more than 120 years the Democratic and Republican parties have together been the American two-party system.

The longevity of the two major parties, exceptional in itself, is almost overshadowed by the closeness of their competition. Of the twenty-three presidential elections from 1888 through 1976, the Republicans won twelve and the Democrats eleven.[2] Of those twenty-three elections only six were decided by a spread of more than 20 percent between the popular vote of the two major parties — that is, in seventeen of them a shift of 10 percent or less of the vote would have given the other party's candidate the lead. And in only four of those twenty-three presidential elections did the winners get more than 60 percent of the total popular vote: Warren G. Harding in 1920, Franklin Roosevelt in 1936, Lyndon Johnson in 1964, and Richard Nixon in 1972. Ten of the twenty-three were decided by a spread of less than 7 percent of the popular vote, and so close have presidential elections been generally that Dwight D. Eisenhower's 57.4 percent of the popular vote in 1956 was widely called a landslide. The shade over 61 per-

---

[2] However, the Democrats led the popular vote in twelve elections, losing the election of 1888 in the electoral college despite Grover Cleveland's lead in the popular vote.

cent with which Lyndon Johnson won in 1964 also set a new record for a president's percentage of the popular vote.[3] The 1960s also saw two of the closest presidential elections in American history. John F. Kennedy in 1960 polled only .2 percent of the popular vote more than did Richard Nixon, and Mr. Nixon in turn led the popular vote by only .7 percent in 1968.[4]

As close as the results of the presidential elections have been, the elections to Congress have been even closer. If we move to percentages of the two-party vote for ease of comparison, we quickly note the remarkable balance between the aggregate votes cast for Democratic and Republican candidates for the House of Representatives from all over the United States during the last 50 years (Table 2.1). From 1928 through 1978 in none of the biennial elections to the House of Representatives was there a difference greater than seventeen percentage points in the division of the two-party vote. The median percentage spread between the candidates of the two parties for the House from 1928 through 1978 was 7.3; it was 10.8 for the presidential candidates in the same period. Perhaps even more telling, in every year except 1948, 1960, 1968, and 1976 the margin between congressional candidates was smaller than that between the presidential aspirants.

The fineness and persistence of party competition in national politics is apparent, therefore, in even the quickest survey of recent electoral history. Even more impressive, perhaps, is the resilience of the major parties. Although from time to time the parties have lapsed from closely matched competitiveness, in the long run they have shown a remarkable facility for restoring balance. The Democrats recovered quickly from the failures of the 1920s, and the Republicans confounded the pessimists by springing back from the Roosevelt victories of the 1930s. And despite the catastrophes of 1964, the Republicans gained forty-seven seats in the House in 1966 and won the presidency in 1968 and 1972.

But is this aggregate record of winning and losing in national elections what we mean by a two-party system? Well, yes and no. It does express the vote support for national candidates running on national issues under national party labels. Indeed the struggle for the presidency every four years is undoubtedly the one occasion on which we actually do have na-

---

[3] The reader may be confused here about political record keeping. Note that this 61.1 percent for Lyndon Johnson was the percentage of the total popular vote. Other relevant records in presidential elections: greatest electoral college vote, Franklin Roosevelt in 1936 with 523 votes; greatest percentage of two-party vote, Calvin Coolidge in 1924 with 65.2 percent.

[4] A persuasive case can, in fact, be made that Nixon actually led Kennedy in the popular vote; the different conclusion depends on how one counts the votes cast for the unpledged electors in Alabama. For a statement of the problem see Lawrence D. Longley and Alan G. Braun, *The Politics of Electoral College Reform*, 2nd ed. (New Haven: Yale University Press, 1975), pp. 5–6.

TABLE 2.1   Percentage of Two-Party Vote Won by Republican
Candidates for the Presidency and House of Representatives: 1928–78

| | Presidential Election | | House Election | |
| | | Percentage spread between Republican and | | Percentage spread between Republican and |
| Year | Percentage Republican | Democratic candidates | Percentage Republican | Democratic candidates |
|---|---|---|---|---|
| 1928 | 58.8 | 17.6 | 57.2 | 14.4 |
| 1930 | | | 54.1 | 8.2 |
| 1932 | 40.9 | −18.2 | 43.1 | −13.8 |
| 1934 | | | 43.8 | −12.4 |
| 1936 | 37.5 | −25.0 | 41.5 | −17.0 |
| 1938 | | | 49.2 | −1.6 |
| 1940 | 45.0 | −10.0 | 47.0 | −6.0 |
| 1942 | | | 52.3 | 4.6 |
| 1944 | 46.2 | −7.6 | 48.3 | −3.4 |
| 1946 | | | 54.7 | 9.4 |
| 1948 | 47.7 | −4.6 | 46.8 | −6.4 |
| 1950 | | | 49.9 | −0.2 |
| 1952 | 55.4 | 10.8 | 50.1 | 0.2 |
| 1954 | | | 47.5 | −5.0 |
| 1956 | 57.8 | 15.6 | 49.0 | −2.0 |
| 1958 | | | 43.9 | −12.2 |
| 1960 | 49.9 | −0.2 | 45.0 | −10.0 |
| 1962 | | | 47.4 | −5.2 |
| 1964 | 38.7 | −22.6 | 42.5 | −15.0 |
| 1966 | | | 48.7 | −2.6 |
| 1968 | 50.4 | 0.8 | 49.1 | −1.8 |
| 1970 | | | 45.6 | −8.8 |
| 1972 | 61.8 | 23.6 | 47.3 | −5.4 |
| 1974 | | | 43.0 | −14.0 |
| 1976 | 48.9 | −2.2 | 42.8 | −14.4 |
| 1978 | | | 45.6 | −8.8 |

*Source*   Data for 1900 through 1960 from Donald E. Stokes and Gudmund R. Iverson,
"On the Existence of Forces Restoring Party Competition," *Public Opinion Quarterly*,
vol. 26 (Summer 1962), p. 162. Reprinted by permission. Data for 1962 through 1978
from *Statistical Abstract*, 1979.

tional parties and a national party system. But on the other hand, such measures are only aggregates, and they obscure the considerable one-partyism in various parts of the country. That is to say, statements about national competitiveness gloss over the issue of how unevenly the competitiveness is spread over the states and localities of the nation. Furthermore, they focus on national electorates, ignoring the fact that organizationally the national parties are only loose coalitions of virtually autonomous state parties. Thus, in several ways the American two-party system is an aggregate, a composite, of the party systems of the fifty states.

## THE FIFTY AMERICAN PARTY SYSTEMS

All but obscured in the incredible closeness of both presidential elections and the aggregate vote for the House of Representatives is the one-partyism not apparent when one examines only national totals. For example, it was not until 1964 that Georgia cast its electoral votes for a Republican and Vermont voted for a Democrat for the first time since the Civil War. And although one may talk of the aggregate closeness of the biennial elections of the House, the aura of competitiveness vanishes in part if one looks at the individual races. Significant numbers of congressmen win election to the House of Representatives with more than 60 percent of the total vote — in 1978, in fact, 72 percent of them did. In that year, in fact, 47 of them (11 percent) were elected without any competition whatsoever.

If we are to discuss the varying degrees of competitiveness of the fifty state party systems, however, the practical problem of defining *competitiveness* can be postponed no longer. Logically competitiveness suggests either an assessment of the quality of past competition or a prediction of the possibilities of competitiveness in the near future. In both cases the problems are considerable. First of all, we must decide whether to count vote totals and percentages or simply the offices won. Do we regard a party that systematically garners 40 or 45 percent of the vote, but never wins office, any differently than we do one that hovers around the 20 to 25 percent mark? If we are to make distinctions between parties such as these, where do we draw the fine line between competitiveness and noncompetitiveness? At 30, 35, 40, or 45 percent? A considerable number of scholars settles for the 40 percent figure. Then, too, we must decide whether and how to discriminate between the party that averages 40 percent of the vote and wins office occasionally from the party that averages 40 percent and never wins.

Finally, the classifier of parties and party systems on the basis of competitiveness must determine which offices to count — the vote for presidential candidates, for governors and senators, for statewide officials (such as the attorney general), for the state legislature, or a combination of them. A state may show strikingly different competitive patterns between its national and its state and local politics. Arizona in the 1950s, for example, voted twice for Eisenhower, elected a Republican governor in three of the five elections, and voted twice for a Republican senator, Barry Goldwater. Yet, during those years the Arizona state senate ranged from 79 to 100 percent Democratic, and the lower house varied from 63 to 90 percent Democratic.[5]

In categorizing the party systems of the American states, one can dismiss the possibility of multiparty systems. To be sure, there are a few examples of them in the American experience. In Minnesota, Wisconsin, and North Dakota in the 1930s and 1940s, remnants of the Progressive movement — the Progressive party in Wisconsin, the Farmer-Labor party in Minnesota, and the Non-Partisan League in North Dakota — competed with some success against the major parties. But in all three cases the heavy pressures of the national two-party system forced them to disband and send their loyalists into the two major parties. In these and a few other instances of statewide multipartyism in the recent American past, the period of multipartyism was brief and ended with a return to two-partyism.

The range of party systems among the fifty states, then, extends only the short way from the one-party system to the competitive two-party system. Drawing on the work of two other scholars, Austin Ranney recently divided the fifty state party systems into four categories: one-party Democratic, modified one-party Democratic, modified one-party Republican, and two-party (see Table 2.2). No states fell into a one-party Republican category. The Ranney rankings are based on a composite index of the popular vote for Democratic gubernatorial candidates, percentages of seats held by Democrats in the state legislature, and percentages of all the gubernatorial and state legislative terms the Democrats controlled. The resulting averages of those percentages yielded scores from 1.000 (complete Democratic success) to .000 (total Republican success); the scores are reported with the rankings in Table 2.2. The rankings are based wholly on state offices; they do not take into account the state's vote in presidential or senatorial elections. To some extent, therefore, they are isolated from the abnormal patterns of national politics that accompanied Lyndon Johnson's sweep in 1964 and George Wallace's incursions in 1968.[6]

[5] These data come from the *Book of the States* (Chicago: Council of State Governments) for the 1950s and 1960s.
[6] Austin Ranney, "Parties in State Politics" (Chap. 3) in Herbert Jacob and Kenneth Vines (eds.), *Politics in the American States,* 3rd ed. (Boston: Little, Brown, 1976), p. 61. The Ranney categories are based on those of Richard Dawson and James Robinson, "Inter-Party Competition, Economic Variables, and Welfare Policies in the American States," *Journal of Politics* 25 (1963): 265–89. For other data and measures, see Paul T. David, *Party Strength in the United States, 1872–1970* (Charlottesville: University of Virginia Press, 1972), updated with later data in the *Journal of Politics* for August 1974, May 1975, May 1976, and August 1978; Joseph A. Schlesinger, "A Two-Dimensional Scheme for Classifying the States According to Degree of Inter-Party Competition," *American Political Science Review* 49 (1955): 1120–28; Davd G. Pfeiffer,

TABLE 2.2  The Fifty States Classified according to Degree of
Interparty Competition: 1962–73

| One-party Democratic | Modified one-party Democratic | Two-party | | Modified one-party Republican |
|---|---|---|---|---|
| Louisiana (.9930) | North Carolina (.7750) | Nevada (.6057) | Pennsylvania (.4705) | North Dakota (.3463) |
| Alabama (.9520) | Maryland (.7647) | California (.6020) | Utah (.4647) | Idaho (.3445) |
| Mississippi (.9145) | Virginia (.7543) | Alaska (.5760) | Arizona (.4377) | Colorado (.3390) |
| South Carolina (.8935) | Tennessee (.7443) | Connecticut (.5670) | Illinois (.4245) | Kansas (.3380) |
| Texas (.8780) | Florida (.7410) | Montana (.5553) | Wisconsin (.4245) | South Dakota (.3373) |
| Georgia (.8710) | Hawaii (.7313) | New Jersey (.5437) | Indiana (.4160) | Vermont (.3307) |
| Arkansas (.8645) | Oklahoma (.7297) | Washington (.5420) | Iowa (.4113) | Wyoming (.3205) |
| | New Mexico (.7107) | Nebraska (.5127) | New York (.4053) | |
| | Missouri (.7085) | Oregon (.5075) | Maine (.4045) | |
| | Kentucky (.7037) | Minnesota (.5037) | Ohio (.3693) | |
| | West Virginia (.6945) | Delaware (.4947) | New Hampshire (.3600) | |
| | Rhode Island (.6860) | Michigan (.4903) | | |
| | Massachusetts (.6730) | | | |

*Source*   From Austin Ranney, "Parties in State Politics," in Herbert Jacob and Kenneth
N. Vines, eds., *Politics in the American States: A Comparative Analysis*, 3rd ed., p. 61.
Copyright © 1976 by Little, Brown and Company (Inc.). Reprinted by permission.

Useful as they are, such indices again do not fully reveal the complexities of party competition. One rarely finds competitiveness evenly spread
through the politics of any one state. For example, Illinois in 1960 gave a
bare .2 percent more of its popular vote to Kennedy than Nixon, yet more
than half of its congressmen were elected in that same year by 60 percent

"The Measurement of Inter-Party Competition and Systemic Stability," *American Political Science Review* 61 (1967): 457–67; and Mark Stern, "Measuring Interparty
Competition: A Proposal and a Test of a Model," *Journal of Politics* 34 (1972): 889–
904. Despite the welter of measures and indices reported here, two scholars have found
that there is a very high order of correlation among the results of the various measures.
See Richard E. Zody and Norman R. Luttbeg, "An Evaluation of Various Measures of
State Party Competition," *Western Political Quarterly* 21 (1968): 723–24.

TABLE 2.3 Size of Democratic Contingent in Forty-nine American State Legislatures: 1978

| Percentage Democratic | Upper House | Lower House |
|---|---|---|
| 0–19 | 0 | 0 |
| 20–39 | 5 | 3 |
| 40–59 | 13 | 14 |
| 60–79 | 15 | 18 |
| 80–100 | 16 | 14 |
| | 49 [a] | 49 [a] |

[a] The total is only 49 because Nebraska has a nonpartisan legislature.
*Source* Data from *Book of States,* 1978–1979.

or more of the vote. Or to concentrate on variations within state politics, gubernatorial elections generally reflect a more intense competitiveness than do elections to the state legislature. Some fifty governors were elected or reelected in 1974 or 1976, and 70 percent of them were elected with less than 60 percent of the vote.[7] Yet the state legislatures that were elected in the same period revealed a partisan composition that belied the competitiveness in the election of governors. Only in 28 percent of the houses of the state legislatures did the percentage of Democratic legislators fall between 40 and 59 percent (Table 2.3). To be sure, some of the lack of partisan balance in the American legislatures may be a result of very skillful drawing of district lines. Yet with all allowances made, the patterns of competitiveness these data suggest are not the same patterns indicated by the data from gubernatorial elections of the period.

Thus it is difficult to speak even of a *state* party system. On close inspection each one is an aggregate of different competitive patterns. It is not at all unusual for a party — even one that wins most statewide elections — to have trouble filling its ticket in some local elections. Powerful officeholders can use a long term and the advantage of office to build a personal following independent of party strength. For the rest of their careers they may insulate themselves from the normally competitive politics in their states. In fact, nothing dampens two-party competition more effectively than the power of incumbency, especially when it is exercised in a small and homogeneous constituency.

[7] The data on the governors were drawn from the 1974 *Statistical Abstract of the United States.*

## THE CAUSES AND CONDITIONS OF TWO-PARTYISM

The rarity of the two-party system among the democracies and its dominance in American politics have stimulated a very considerable explanatory effort. The question is an obvious one: Why should this one nation among so many others develop the two-party system? In the interests of an orderly attack on the problem, the most frequent explanations have been divided into four groups: the institutional, dualist, cultural, and consensual.

### Institutional Theories

By far the most widespread explanation of the two-party system associates it with electoral and governmental institutions. In part it argues that single-member, plurality electoral systems produce two-party systems and that multimember constituencies and proportional representation result in multipartyism. Plurality election in a single-member district means simply that one candidate is elected and that the winner is the person who receives the largest number of votes. There are no second, third, and fourth seats for the trailing parties. In a system of proportional representation, on the other hand, a party polling 20 percent or so of a nation's votes may capture close to 20 percent of the legislative seats. The main purpose of proportional representation is to guarantee minorities representation roughly equal to their strength. That same 20 percent would win very few, if any, seats in the American plurality electoral system.[8] The American election system, therefore, offers no reward of office to any but the plurality winner, and, so the theory goes, the discouragement from repeated losses weeds out the chronic minority parties.

Many of the institutional theorists also argue the importance of the single executive. The American presidency and the governorships, the main prizes of American politics, fall only to parties that can win pluralities. On the contrary, a cabinet in a European nation may be formed by a coalition that includes representatives of minority parties. In the palmiest days of multipartyism in the French Third and Fourth Republics, for instance, a party winning 10 or 15 percent of the national vote did at times capture the premiership. In countries with a single national executive, the indivisible nature of the office favors the strongest competitors. Beyond the loss of the executive office, moreover, the minor party is denied the national leadership, the focus of the national campaign, and the national spokesmen that so increasingly dominate the politics of the democracies. The necessity to contend for a national executive, in other words, works against

---

[8] Large numbers of states do have multimember districts for one or both houses of the state legislature. The fact that these districts have not altered the two-party system suggests that plurality election is more important than single-member districting in sustaining two-partyism.

the local or regional party, even those that may elect candidates in their own local bailiwicks.[9]

## Dualist Theories

The dualists maintain that an underlying duality of interest in the American society has sustained the American two-party system. V. O. Key suggested that the initial sectional tension between the eastern financial and commercial interests and the western frontiersmen stamped itself on the parties in their incipient stages and fostered a two-party competition. Later the dualism shifted to the North-South conflict over the issue of slavery and the Civil War, and then to the present urban-rural or socioeconomic status divisions.[10] A related line of argument points to a "natural dualism" within democratic institutions: party in power versus party out of power, government versus opposition, pro and anti the status quo, and even the ideological dualism of liberal and conservative. Thus social and economic interests or the very processes of a democratic politics — or both — reduce the political contestants to two great camps, and that dualism gives rise to two political parties.

## Cultural Theories

This school of explanation in many ways smacks of the older, largely discredited national character theories. It maintains that the United States and Britain have nurtured two-party systems because of their "political maturity" or their "genius for government." More modestly, it attributes the two-party systems to the development of a political culture that accepts the necessity of compromise, the wisdom of short-term pragmatism, and the avoidance of unyielding dogmatism. Americans and Britons, in other words, are willing to make the kinds of compromises necessary to bring heterogeneous groups of voters into two political parties. Then as they develop the dual parties, their political cultures also develop the attitudes and norms that endorse the two-party system as a desirable end in itself.

## Social Consensus Theories

Finally, the American party system has been explained in terms of a wide-sweeping American social consensus. Despite a diverse cultural heritage

[9] The institutional theorists are best represented by Maurice Duverger, *Political Parties* (New York: Wiley, 1954), and E. E. Schattschneider, *Party Government* (New York: Rinehart, 1942).
[10] See, for example, V. O. Key, *Politics, Parties and Pressure Groups*, 5th ed. (New York: Crowell, 1964), pp. 229ff.; and James C. Charlesworth, "Is Our Two-Party System Natural?" American Academy of Political and Social Science *Annals* 259 (1948): 1–9.

and society, Americans early achieved a consensus on the fundamentals that divide other societies. Virtually all Americans have traditionally accepted the prevailing social, economic, and political institutions. They accepted the Constitution and its governmental apparatus, a regulated but free enterprise economy, and (perhaps to a lesser extent) American patterns of social class and status.

In the traditional multiparty countries such as France and Italy, substantial chunks of political opinion have favored radical changes in those and other basic institutions. They have supported programs of fundamental constitutional change, the socialization of the economy, or the disestablishment of the Church. Whether because Americans were spared feudalism and its rigid classes or because they have had a fortuitously expanding economic and geographic frontier, they have escaped the division on fundamentals that racks the other democracies and gives rise to large numbers of irreconcilable political divisions. Since the matters that divide Americans are secondary, so the argument goes, the compromises necessary to bring them into one of two major parties are easier to make.[11]

In appraising these explanations of the American two-party system, one has to ask some searching questions. Are the factors proposed in these explanations *causes* of the two-party system or are they *effects* of it? The chances are that they are, at least in part, effects. Certainly two competitive parties will choose and perpetuate electoral systems that do not offer entrée to minor parties. They will also channel opinion into alternatives, reducing and forcing the system's complexities into their dual channels. The two-party system will also create, foster, and perpetuate the political values and attitudes that justify and protect itself. It will even foster some measure of social consensus by denying competitive opportunities to movements that challenge the great consensus of the status quo.

Although these factors may be effects of the two-party system, they are also certainly causes. But if they are, why has the two-party system been such a comparatively rare phenomenon? If single-member constituencies and plurality elections explain American two-partyism, why did they not produce a similar outcome in Third Republic France? Moreover, American society is not the first to have an overriding duality of interests in its politics. The socioeconomic class division between "haves" and "have-nots" has plagued no small number of democracies without leading to a two-party system. The implication seems clear that no one of these theories alone can explain the virtual uniqueness of the American party system.

At the risk of fence straddling, one may venture to suggest that all four

---

[11] See Leslie Lipson, "The Two-Party System in British Politics," *American Political Science Review* 47 (1953): 337–58.

explanations illuminate the development of the American party system. No one of them need exclude the impact of any other. Their unique combination has produced a unique two-party system. At the root of the explanation lies the basic, long-run American consensus on fundamental beliefs. No deep rifts over the kind of economy, society, or government we want have traditionally marked our politics. More than one European observer has remarked on the resulting nonideological character of American politics. Consensus has been fostered by American education and social assimilation, aided by two major parties inhospitable to challenges to that consensus. It is not easy now, of course, to talk confidently of a consensus in American life. But if the consensus has broken down to some extent, it has done so well after the American two-party system was established and deeply entrenched.

Lacking cause for deep ideological divisions and disagreeing on few fundamentals, Americans were easily formed into two conglomerate, majority-seeking political parties. The institutions of American government — such as single-member constituencies, plurality elections, and the single executive — were free to exert their power to limit the parties to two without having to repulse countervailing pressures of social division. So, too, in the absence of deeply felt ideologies, a pragmatic opposition to the party in power was easily able to develop a dualism of the "ins" and "outs." And once the two-party system was launched, its very existence fostered the values of moderation, compromise, and political pragmatism that ensure its perpetuation. The system created deep loyalties within the American public to one party or the other and deep loyalties to the genius of the two-party system itself.

## EXCURSIONS INTO ONE-PARTYISM

To argue the existence of only two competitive parties is not to argue that their competitiveness is spread evenly over the country. There are substantial statewide and local pockets of one-partyism in the United States. The states of the Deep South until recently spent very close to their own "four score and seven" years as the country's most celebrated area of one-party domination. Much the same could be said in the past of the rock-like Republicanism of Maine, New Hampshire, and Vermont. And scattered throughout the country today are thousands of one-party cities, towns, and counties, in which the city hall or county courthouse comes perilously close to being the property of one party. Just as important, therefore, as the question of the causes of the two-party system is the question of the causes of one-partyism within it.

One-partyism set within the context of broad, two-party competitiveness often reflects a "fault" in the distribution of the electorates of the competitive parties. Since the 1930s the major American parties, especially in national elections, have divided the American electorate roughly along lines of socioeconomic status and issues — a point that will be developed later. Suffice it here to note that Democratic loyalties have been far more common among ethnic, racial, and religiously minority groups, the urban workers, and lower socioeconomic status (SES) groups in general. The Republicans, on the other hand, have drawn a disproportionate number of loyalists from higher status and rural groups.

So, one-partyism may result from a maldistribution of the characteristics that normally divide the parties. The local constituency may be too small to contain a perfect sample of SES characteristics and thus of competitive politics. Hence the noncompetitiveness of the "safe" Democratic congressional districts of the older, lower-middle-class neighborhoods of the cities and the "safe" Republican districts of the more fashionable and spacious suburbs. In other words, the more heterogeneous are its people, the more likely the district is to foster competitiveness.

One-partyism, alternatively may result from some potent local basis of party loyalty that overrides the SES dualism. In the classic one-partyism of the American South, regional loyalties long overrode the factors that were dividing Americans into two parties in most of the rest of the country. Reaction to the Republican party as the party of abolition, Lincoln, the Civil War, and the hated Reconstruction was so pervasive, even three generations after the fact, that the impact of the SES division was precluded. It was thus a one-partyism based on isolation from the factors that normally produced two-party competitiveness.

Empirical studies of one-partyism suggest, however, that its causes are far more complex than these two logical possibilities. Competitiveness has been associated with general socioeconomic diversity in the constituency — especially with urbanism and its industrialism, higher income levels, and ethnic diversity. Yet the relationships are not always strong or dramatic, and one recent study finds no such relationships at all.[12] We are thus left more or less to conjecture. Perhaps a homogeneous district cut

[12] Charles M. Bonjean and Robert L. Lineberry, "The Urbanization-Party Competition Hypothesis: A Comparison of All United States Counties," *Journal of Politics* 32 (1970): 305–21. For a further introduction to the study of the correlates of competitiveness in the American party system, see the Ranney chapter in Jacob and Vines, *Politics in the American States*, 3rd ed.; V. O. Key, *American State Politics* (New York: Knopf, 1956), pp. 227–46; Heinz Eulau, "The Ecological Basis of Party Systems: The Case of Ohio," *Midwest Journal of Political Science* 1 (1957): 125–35; David Gold and John R. Schmidhauser, "Urbanization and Party Competition: The Case of Iowa," *Ibid.* 4 (1960): 62–75; Phillips Cutright, "Urbanization and Competitive Party Politics," *Journal of Politics* 25 (1963): 552–64; Thomas W. Casstevens and Charles O. Press, "The Context of Democratic Competition in American State Politics," *American Journal of Sociology* 68 (1963): 536–43; and Robert Golembiewski, "A Taxonomic Approach to State Political Party Strength," *Western Political Quarterly* 11 (1958): 494–513. The reader who explores this literature should be aware both of the varying definitions of competition and urbanness and of the difference between competitiveness of states and competitiveness of subdivisions (e.g., counties) within states.

from the middle range of SES factors tends to be more competitive than an equally homogeneous district at either the top or the bottom of the SES spectrum. Alternatively, in some localities the patterns of competitiveness may have little to do with patterns of national SES politics or with any other characteristics of the electorate. They may instead reflect the influences of local personages, of powerful officeholders, of local traditions, or of local political conflict such as that between a dominant industry and its disgruntled employees.

One may also look at these pockets of one-partyism another way. The American party system is made up of two electorally competitive parties, which is really to say that it is formed by two parties competing to enlist a majority of the American electorate. The active, initiating sectors of the party — the party organization and the party in government — recruit and enlist the support of the electorate with assorted appeals. If these two parties were fully competitive in every constituency in the country, they would approach a fifty-fifty division of the electorate. They must, however, compete at various disadvantages, and frequently in some area or locality one party works at a disadvantage that it never manages to overcome. The result is the ability of the other party to maintain a one-party domination. The understanding of one-partyism, then, requires an understanding of the various kinds of competitive disadvantages a party may face.

The competitive disadvantages begin with stubborn party loyalties. Voters are not easily moved from their attachments to a party, even though the reasons for the original attachment have long passed. Also, a party trying to pull itself into competitiveness may find itself caught in a vicious circle of impotence. Its inability to win elections limits its ability to recruit resources, including manpower, because as a chronic loser it offers so little chance of achieving political goals. It may even find itself without an effective appeal to the electorate. The Republican party in the South, for example, found for many years that the Democrats had preempted the salient political issues in that region.

Today the would-be competitive party finds disadvantage taking another form: the formation of party loyalties among lines determined by national or statewide political debate. If the Democratic party is identified nationally with the aspirations of the poor and minority groups, its appeal in a homogeneous, affluent suburb may be limited. Increasingly, national politics thus may rob the local party organization of the chance to develop strength based on its own issues, personalities, and traditions. To the extent that party loyalties and identifications grow out of national politics, patterns of competitiveness (and the lack of it) may be out of the control of the local party organizations.

There are, to be sure, other sources of competitive disadvantage. The dominant party may shore up its supremacy by carefully calculated legislative districting. In the past the southern Democrats stifled potential competitiveness by artificially restricting the electorates to middle-class whites. In other instances majority parties have supported nonpartisanship in local elections as a way of drawing on their one-party consensus. In addition to these institutional buttresses to one-partyism, of course, powerful party organization and sedulous canvassing can maintain superiority. Finally, the normal processes of socialization and social conformity work to the disadvantage of a party trying to become competitive. That force of conformity, a number of observers have argued, works especially against competitiveness in the closely knit, socially sensitive world of American suburbia.

## THE "ALSO-RANS": THE THIRD PARTIES

Periodically a new minor party flashes onto the national scene, getting attention from both scholars and journalists all out of proportion to its electoral impact. But attention aside, only seven minor parties in all of American history have so much as carried a single state in a presidential election (see box). More important, perhaps, no minor party has come close to winning one. The best minor party records so far were set in 1912 by Teddy Roosevelt and the Progressives with 17 percent of the electoral vote and 30 percent of the popular vote. That candidacy was, in fact, the only minor party candidacy ever to run ahead of one of the major party candidates in either electoral or popular vote.

In between the peaks of third-party influence are the valleys. In 1964, for example, the leading minor party, the Socialist Labor party, attracted only 45,168 voters, and altogether the minor parties polled only one-fifth of one percent of the popular vote. And after the George Wallace phenomenon of 1968 — almost 10 million votes for Wallace alone — minor party strength ebbed once again. The total minor party vote for president in 1976 was 820,642 (Table 2.4), or just about one percent of the total popular vote for president. More telling, perhaps, the independent, nonparty campaign of Eugene McCarthy drew almost as many votes as all the minor parties combined: 756,631.

The very looseness with which we customarily use the term *third party* to designate all minor parties may indicate that third place is as good (or bad) as last place in a two-party system. But it would be a serious mistake to treat the minor parties as indistinguishable. They differ in origin, purpose, and function, and American political history affords a rich variety of their activity to illustrate those differences.[13]

[13] The literature on American third parties is rich and varied. Among the best contributions are John D. Hicks, *The Populist Revolt* (Minneapolis: University of Minnesota Press, 1931); Richard Hofstadter, *The Age of Reform* (New York: Knopf, 1955); David A. Shannon, *The Socialist Party of America* (New York: Macmillan, 1955); K. M.

## The Big Little Parties

In order to put the minor parties in some perspective, we need some point of calibration. That is to say, we need some measure by which we can compare them and their electoral strength to that of the major parties and by which we can separate the stronger and weaker minor parties. If we take as a measure the ability to draw at least 10 percent of the popular vote for president, only four qualify (numbers 3, 4, 5, and 7 below). If we choose as a more liberal but certainly modest test of strength the ability to carry one state — just one — at a presidential election, only seven minor parties in American history qualify.

1. *Anti-Masonic party.* 1832: 7 electoral votes. A party opposed to the alleged secret political influence of the Masons; later part of an anti-Jackson coalition that formed the Whig party.

2. *American (Know-Nothing) party.* 1856: 8 electoral votes. A nativist party opposed to open immigration and in favor of electing native born Americans to public office.

3. *People's (Populist) party.* 1892: 22 electoral votes. An outgrowth of a movement of agrarian protest opposed to the economic power of bankers, railroads, and fuel industries and in favor of a graduated income tax, government regulation, and currency reform (especially free silver coinage).

4. *Progressive (Bull Moose) party.* 1912: 88 electoral votes. An offshoot of the Republican party, it favored liberal reforms such as an expanded suffrage, social reforms, conservation of resources, and antimonopoly laws.

5. *Progressive party.* 1924: 13 electoral votes. A continuation of the 1912 Progressive tradition with the candidacy (Robert La Follette) of a man who had been one of its founders and leaders.

6. *States Rights Democratic (Dixiecrat) party.* 1948: 39 electoral votes. A southern splinter of the Democratic party, it ran as *the* Democratic party in the South on a conservative, segregationist platform.

7. *American Independent party.* 1968: 46 electoral votes. The party of George Wallace; traditionalist, segregationist, and opposed to the authority of the national government.

Although it is true, first of all, that most minor parties are parties of *ideology and issue,* they differ in the scope of that commitment. The narrow, highly specific commitment of the Prohibition and Vegetarian parties is apparent in their names. In the 1840s the Liberty party and its successor, the Free Soil party, campaigned largely on the single issue of the abolition

Schmidt, *Henry A. Wallace: Quixotic Crusade 1948* (Syracuse: Syracuse University Press, 1960); George Thayer, *The Farther Shores of Politics* (New York: Simon and Schuster, 1967); Marshall Frady, *Wallace* (New York: World, 1968); and Daniel A. Mazmanian, *Third Parties in Presidential Elections* (Washington: Brookings, 1974).

TABLE 2.4   Popular Votes Cast for Minor Parties in 1972 and 1976
Presidential Elections

| Parties: 1972 | Vote: 1972 | Parties: 1976 | Vote: 1976 |
|---|---|---|---|
| American | 1,099,482 | Libertarian | 173,011 |
| People's | 78,756 | American Independent | 170,531 |
| Socialist Workers | 66,677 | American | 160,773 |
| Socialist Labor | 53,814 | Socialist Workers | 91,314 |
| Communist | 25,595 | Communist | 58,992 |
| Prohibition | 13,505 | People's | 49,024 |
| Others and scattered | 40,431 | U. S. Labor | 40,043 |
| | | Prohibition | 15,934 |
| | 1,378,260 | Socialist Labor | 9,616 |
| | | Others and scattered | 51,404 |
| | | | 820,642 |

*Source*   *America Votes 10* and *America Votes 12*, edited and compiled by Richard M.
Scammon and, in the latter volume, Alice V. McGillivray.

of slavery. At the other extremes are the parties having the broadest ideological commitments — the Marxist parties and the recent profusion of
conservative parties. For example, the Libertarian party, the leading minor
party of 1976, advocates a complete withdrawal of government from most
of its present programs and responsibilities. In the middle ground between
specific issues and total ideologies, the examples are infinitely varied. The
farmer-labor parties of economic protest — Greenback, Populist, and Progressive parties — ran on an extensive program of government regulation
of the economy (especially of economic bigness) and social welfare legislation. The Progressive party of 1948 — at least that part of it separate
from the Communist party — combined a program of social reform and
civil liberties with a foreign policy of friendship with the Soviet Union
and reduction of Cold War tensions.

The minor parties differ, too, in their *origin*. Some were literally im-
ported into the United States. Much of the early Socialist party strength
in the United States came from the freethinkers and radicals who fled Europe after the failures of the revolutions of 1848. Socialist strength in cities
such as Milwaukee, New York, and Cincinnati reflected the concentrations of liberal German immigrants there. Other parties — especially the
Granger and Populist parties and their successors — were parties of in-
digenous social protest, born of social inequality and economic hardship
on the marginal farmlands of America. Other minor parties began as splin-
ters or factions of one of the major parties. The Gold Democrats of 1896,
the Progressives (the Bull Moose party) of 1912, and the Dixiecrats of

1948 come to mind. So great were their objections to the platform and candidates of their parent parties that the Progressives and Dixiecrats contested the presidential elections of 1912 and 1948 with their own slates and programs.

Recent presidential elections have seen the entry of a new variety of minor party: the "nonparty." Found chiefly in the southern states, these nonparties have been dissident movements within the Democratic party that have refused to run as separate parties on the ballot. They have exploited two other strategies instead. In some instances they have attempted to run their own candidate (rather than the one chosen by the party's national convention) as the official presidential candidate of the Democratic party in the state. The only four states which J. Strom Thurmond carried in 1948 for the Dixiecrats were those (Alabama, Louisiana, Mississippi, and South Carolina) in which he, rather than Harry Truman, was the candidate of the Democratic party. George Wallace also captured the Alabama Democratic label in 1968, displacing Hubert Humphrey as the Democratic candidate in that state. In other cases these party movements have run unpledged slates of presidential electors. In 1960 unpledged slates ran in Louisiana as a States Rights party and in Mississippi as the Democratic party (although there was another Democratic party ticket pledged to Kennedy). In 1964 another unpledged Democratic slate of electors ran in Alabama and prevented the Johnson-Humphrey ticket from appearing on the Alabama ballot.

Finally, the third parties differ in their *tactics*. For some their mere existence is a protest against what they believe is the unqualified support of the status quo that the major parties afford. Operating as a political party also offers a reasonably effective educational opportunity. The publicity of the ballot is good, and with it often goes mass media attention the party could not otherwise hope for. Many of these parties have indeed freely accepted their electoral failures, for they have by their very nature chosen ideological principles over electoral success. They have refused to make the pragmatic compromises that working within a major party entails.

But other minor parties do have serious electoral ambitions. Often their goal is local, although today they find it difficult to control an American city as the Socialists did, or an entire state as the Progressives did. More realistically today, they may hope to hold a balance of power between the major parties in the manner of the Liberals in New York. In the 1965 mayoral election, for instance, John Lindsay's vote on the Republican ticket was less than that of his Democratic opponent; his vote reached the necessary plurality only with the addition of the votes he won in the Liberal party column. Or a party may, as did the Dixiecrats of 1948 and Wallace's American Independent party of 1968, play for the biggest stakes of all: the presidency. Both parties hoped that by carrying a number of states, most likely southern states, they might prevent the major party tickets from winning the necessary majority of votes in the electoral college and thus throw the stalemated election into the House of Representatives. The Wallace effort of 1968 faltered because Richard Nixon carried a number of large states, although by small margins in the popular vote.

It is certainly these parties of electoral opportunity that have generally enjoyed the minor party successes of recent years. The more traditional, stable parties of ideology, which Norman Thomas and the Socialists so long typified in American politics, do indeed seem in decline. But it is more individuals than parties of electoral opportunity that challenge the major parties. George Wallace's American Independent party was little more than a vehicle for his ambitions and perhaps not much more than the degree of organization required by the states for a place on the ballot. With his retirement it has slipped into ineffectuality. In fact, after running on the American Independent ticket in 1968, Wallace backed away from its leadership and was contesting within the Democratic party for convention delegates when he was shot in 1971. In a similar vein Eugene McCarthy, a Democrat in 1968, flirted with third party and independent possibilities in the 1970s. The loosening of party loyalties to the two major parties, and the ease with which a popular candidate becomes known through television and the other media, make such careers and the parties allied with them increasingly feasible.

The variety is endless, but what have the minor parties contributed to American politics? For better or for worse they have influenced, perhaps even altered the courses of a few presidential elections. By threatening — about once a generation — to deadlock the electoral college, they have probably kept alive movements to reform it. But beyond their role as potential electoral spoiler, can they count any significant accomplishments? The answer, to be candid, is that they have not assumed the importance that all the attention lavished on them suggests.

One line of argument has persistently maintained that the minor parties' early adoption of unpopular programs has ultimately forced the major parties to adopt them. Its proponents point to the platforms of the Socialist party in the years before the 1930s. The issue is whether or not the Socialists' advocacy of such measures as a minimum wage for twenty or thirty years had anything to do with their enactment in the 1930s. There is unfortunately no way of testing what might have happened had there been no Socialist party. But the evidence suggests that the major parties grasp new programs and proposals in their "time of ripeness" — when large numbers of Americans have done so and when such a course, therefore, is politically useful to the parties. In their prior maturing time, new issues need not depend on minor parties for their advocacy. Interest groups, the mass media, influential individuals, and factions within the major parties may perform the propagandizing role, often more effectively than a minor party. More than one commentator has noted that the cause of prohibition in the United States was far more effectively served by interest groups such as the Anti-Saloon League than by the Prohibition party.

## WHITHER THE AMERICAN TWO-PARTY SYSTEM?

George Wallace's lawyers stood before the United States Supreme Court in early October of 1968 to plead that the Court strike down Ohio election law and permit Wallace's name to be printed on the ballot in that state as a presidential candidate. It was a scene awash in irony. Wallace had often excoriated the Court for its willingness to invalidate the laws of states, and now his attorneys were making substantially that request. The Ohio law in question had been passed in 1948 in order to prevent the third-party candidacy of Henry Wallace in that state. The law required a new and unestablished party to collect a number of signatures equal to 15 percent of the votes cast in the last statewide election — a percentage that required the Wallace forces to muster 433,000 signatures in 1968. In addition, the Ohio law required those petitions to be submitted in early February, a time far earlier than most campaigns are mobilized. Finally, it prohibited independent, nonparty candidates.

In its defense the state of Ohio did not deny its intentions. The law was intended, the state freely conceded, to work to the disadvantage of any other than the two established parties. The state argued that it had a legitimate interest in preserving the existing two-party system, in preventing a division of the vote among a number of parties, and ultimately in making sure that minority candidates would not win elections. The discrimination against third parties was, in other words, the avowed policy of the state of Ohio. The argument did not sway the Supreme Court, and by a vote of six to three the Court struck down the Ohio law for violating the equal protection clause of the Fourteenth Amendment. Justice Black, speaking for the Court, asserted that the Ohio law imposed an unconstitutional burden on the rights of voting and association and that it discriminated against supporters of minor parties. Thus with the help of the Supreme Court did George Wallace place his name on the Ohio ballot in November of 1968.[14]

The lessons of the story of Wallace against the State of Ohio are many. To some extent, at least, it marked the end of argument that it is constitutionally proper to support and preserve the two-party system with electoral law that discriminates against thirty-party competitors. It also signaled the extraordinary success of Wallace in surmounting the obstacles that separate the minor party from effective, competitive status in American politics. Victory over Ohio law gave him access to his fiftieth state ballot in November 1968. Over and beyond all these points, however, Wallace's success

---

[14] *Williams* v. *Rhodes,* 393 U.S. 23 (1968).

suggests answers to the question of the future of third parties in American politics.

The Wallace campaign of 1968 can first of all be viewed as a triumph over virtually all the obstacles that state laws place in the way of minor parties. To be sure, a number of states presented no particular barriers; a mere 300 signatures sufficed to get his name on the ballot in Colorado. But heroic efforts were necessary in states such as Ohio and California. California law requires far fewer signatures than Ohio — actually only a few more than 66,000 — but it requires that those supporters reregister as voters and as new members of the American Independent party. That is to say, they must go through the formal step of ceasing to be Democrats or Republicans and listing themselves on the voter rolls of California as members of the new party. In other states the petitions for a place on the ballot must contain the signatures of at least one voter in every congressional district — in addition, of course, to the requirement for the total number of signatures. Still other states impose elaborate and complicated procedures for collecting and submitting the petitions.

Second, Wallace in 1968 surmounted what had become extraordinary financial problems for most third parties. Most of them had been squeezed into oblivion by their failure to raise sums large enough to engage in the costly campaigning of the day. Campaigns based on the mass media, on armies of advertising and public relations specialists, and on polls and surveys cost increasingly large sums of money. The Wallace campaign astounded observers of American political finance by raising and spending some $7 million, by far the largest sum ever spent by a minor-party campaign in American history. So successful were Wallace fund-raising activities that he left the 1968 campaign with a surplus estimated to be in excess of $1 million.

George Wallace also solved — if only in part — the problem of a minor party's becoming a national party. Almost all the effective minor party activity of the past century has been intensely local. Each of the minor parties has been concentrated in one state or region, or in a city or two. Socialists came from Germany in the middle of the nineteenth century and established Socialist enclaves in cities such as New York, Milwaukee, and Cincinnati. Regional agricultural depressions gave rise to Populism and other similar movements of the plains and prairies. Traditionally, third parties have fed on local loyalties, interests, and appeals, but those appeals have increasingly lost out in a mobile society that receives the same political messages via the same radio and television networks, the same magazines, and the same press services and syndicated columnists. In this nationalization of American life, a political party's national image and national leaders increasingly dominate the responses of voters — to the obvious disadvantage of a regional or local party that has no national visibility or candidates to give it a national presence. Although the only states

George Wallace carried in 1968 were five in the Deep South, he did indeed carry his message to all the states as a national political figure of consequence.

What, then, can we predict for minor parties in American politics? There will continue to be a few local third parties that reflect special local conditions, especially quirks in local election laws. The classic instance, of course, is that of the New York minor parties — the Liberals, the Conservatives, and now a new Right to Life party. They exist because they can nominate the candidates of a major party to run under their party labels. New York election law thus makes them important brokers in New York elections; as the Right to Life party indicates, it also creates a major opportunity for single-issue electoral politics. But for national impact minor parties will generally ride the coattails of a well-known, charismatic candidate. That appears to be the lesson of George Wallace, and it is also the lesson of the American Independent party after George Wallace (see box). It also appears to be the lesson of attempts to found racial and ethnic parties. Separate black parties developed in a number of southern states shortly after the passage of the Civil Rights Acts of the 1960s, but blacks in the South now increasingly organize within the Democratic party (in "caucuses" or "conferences" within it) or in nonparty citizen or community organizations. Only the National Democratic party of Alabama persists as a statewide black party. Similarly, La Raza Unida, the Chicano party, has failed to become an important electoral force.[15]

Although the future of the minor parties seems uncertain, one can with confidence point to a second general trend in the American party system: the increasing competitiveness of the major parties. It is probably safe to say that in national and statewide politics we are in a period of the most intense, evenly spread, two-party competitiveness in the last 100 years. There are no regions of the country, and very few states, that can be thought of as one-party areas. Even the once-solid Democratic South is solid no more. Republicans Barry Goldwater in 1964 and Richard Nixon in 1972 carried Alabama, Georgia, Louisiana, Mississippi, and South Carolina; in 1968 George Wallace carried all but South Carolina and added Arkansas to them.

To take the longer view, presidents have been increasingly winning with popular vote percentages that vary less and less from one state to another. Table 2.5 indicates that the standard deviations of the presidents' popular vote in the states from the national average have been diminishing in this

[15] On the black parties see Hanes Walton, Jr., *Black Political Parties: A Historical and Political Analysis* (New York: Free Press, 1972); more generally on black politics in the South, David Campbell and Joe R. Feagin, "Black Politics in the South: A Descriptive Analysis," *Journal of Politics* 37 (1975): 129–59. For an account of the early Texas successes of La Raza Unida, see Neal R. Peirce, *The Megastates of America* (New York: Norton, 1972), pp. 558–63.

## A Minor Party at the Crossroads

A great many of the dilemmas and problems of a modern minor party are summed up in the following report on the American Independent party by Christopher Lydon of *The New York Times.* It appeared in that newspaper on Sunday, August 29, 1976.

"The American Independent Party, rebuffing efforts to modernize its conservative image, entered the Presidential campaign today under the banner of Lester G. Maddox, a segregationist former Governor of Georgia, on a platform pledging income tax repeal, isolationism and the virtual elimination of the Federal bureaucracy.

"The party, which was the main ballot-line vehicle of Alabama Gov. George C. Wallace's presidential candidacy in 1968, had flirted this year with the idea of a high-priced promotion of some better-known conservative from the right wing of the Republican party.

"In the end, however, the small band of American Independent Party veterans preferred to reclaim control of what they know will be only a fringe movement and a small nuisance to the Democratic and Republican nominees this fall.

"Conservative exiles from the Republican Party who had hoped to reshape the American Independent Party and sell it hard as an alternative to the Republicans, left angrily today after Mr. Maddox's nomination foiled them last night.

" 'This party has turned inward, backward, and downward,' said William A. Rusher, publisher of the National Review and proponent of what he calls the New Majority Party. 'They've written themselves off,' he said of the American Independent Party. . . .

"But the party's leaders who rejected Mr. Rusher's takeover were equally angry that he had failed to deliver them a national celebrity, or at least an elected official, as their candidate.

"Months ago Mr. Rusher had led American Party officers to believe that Ronald Reagan might lead their ticket if the former California Governor lost the Republican nomination. Until two weeks ago, Mr. Rusher held out the hope of enlisting such people as Senator Jesse A. Helms of North Carolina, a Republican; Phyllis Schlafly, an antifeminist crusader; or Ellen McCormack, who ran an anti-abortion campaign in the Democratic Presidential primaries this spring.

"None of those figures apparently welcomed either the long odds against third party candidates or the extremist tinge of the American Independent Party. . . ."

TABLE 2.5 The Growth of National Two-Party
Competitiveness: Standard Deviations of
Presidential Popular Vote in the States, 1896–1976

| Year | Standard deviation[a] | Year | Standard deviation[a] |
|------|------------------------|------|------------------------|
| 1896 | 17.5 | 1940 | 13.4 |
| 1900 | 14.0 | 1944 | 12.3 |
| 1904 | 18.8 | 1948 | 9.8 |
| 1908 | 14.9 | 1952 | 8.5 |
| 1912 | 15.8 | 1956 | 8.3 |
| 1916 | 13.4 | 1960 | 5.8 |
| 1920 | 16.1 | 1964 | 10.3 |
| 1924 | 16.0 | 1968 | 9.7 |
| 1928 | 13.5 | 1972 | 6.9 |
| 1932 | 14.0 | 1976 | 6.6 |
| 1936 | 12.6 | | |

[a] The standard deviation is a measure of the distance of dispersal of items from the average. It discriminates, therefore, among the dispersals of the following three series: 3, 6, 9; 4, 6, 8; and 5, 6, 7. Even though the means (averages) and the medians of the three series would be identical (6), the standard deviations would decline in the order in which the three series are listed. The data used in the table are the percentages of total vote in each state won by the winning candidate.

century. In other words, presidents are no longer carrying some states by fat margins while losing others in a similarly lopsided way. As the overwhelming votes of the one-party states are eliminated, presidential candidates tend to amass more nearly uniform vote percentages all across the country. Competitiveness, then, is spreading increasingly across the fifty states.

This spread of major party competitiveness reflects the same nationalization of life and politics in the United States that threatens local minor parties. It is increasingly difficult for one major party to maintain its dominance on the basis of appeals and traditions quite different from those in the rest of the country — as, for example, the Democrats did in the South from 1875 to 1950. Furthermore, the social and economic conditions that support one-partyism are disappearing. Fading especially are the political monopolies of powerful groups that once dominated the politics of a single state from a base in cotton, copper, oil, silver, or organized labor. As Americans move about the country, as industry comes to formerly agrarian states, as more and varied people move to the urban centers, each state becomes a better sample of the diversity of life and interest that undergirds the national competition between the two parties. National mass media and national political leaders also bring the symbols and dialectics of Democratic–Republican conflict to all corners of the country. Thus the party electorates are increasingly recruited by the appeals of national candidates and issues — regardless of whatever special appeals the local party organization makes.

State party organizations and leaders, conversely, cannot hold out against the political issues and images that engulf the rest of the country. They cannot easily set up their own competitive subsystem. As a result, a creeping competitiveness accompanies the end of one-partyism at the state level. First, the states become competitive in national elections, and then the old one-party ties and fears slowly break down, and competition seeps down to local elections. Pennsylvania, for example, became competitive in presidential politics in the 1930s after forty years of domination by the GOP; by the 1950s and 1960s the state was competitive in state and local politics. In the 1960s and 1970s the same process was under way in a number of southern states.

Ironically, the increasing degree of two-party competition has created a set of vexing problems for the American parties. By eliminating pockets of one-party strength, the new competitiveness eliminates a source of stability in the party system. When a party holds noncompetitive strongholds of its own, it can survive even a catastrophic national loss through victories and continued office holding in its own areas of strength. Without those one-party strongholds to fall back on, a losing party in the future may find its loss more sweeping and devastating. Also the spread of two-party competitiveness expands the scope of party competition and thus makes extra demands for the resources the parties must employ. When one-party areas could be written off in a presidential campaign and election, the area of political combat was reduced. Now the parties must mobilize and organize more resources than ever before, for a presidential campaign has to be fought in fifty rather than in thirty states.

Withal, the reign of the existing parties, and more generally, of the American two-party system seems secure. Their support may not be what it was, but their resilience is still remarkable. Talk of the imminent decline of the Republicans after Watergate and the losses of 1974 and 1976 was silenced by the party's resurgence in the 1978 elections. Changes in the parties and in their appeals, it appears, will have to take place within the party system as we have known it for more than a century.

# II

# THE POLITICAL PARTY AS AN ORGANIZATION

It is often easier to see the political activity than the actor. The tense excitement of a bitterly fought election, the carnival antics and revival-meeting fervor of national conventions, the wrangling between partisan blocs in a state legislature — these and the other activities of the political parties could not be more obvious. But there is a palpable actor behind the activity — a political party with characteristics not unlike those of large national corporations, trade unions, and fraternal societies. The political party is no mere bundle of activities, no disembodied ideology, no unseen hand in the political process. It is a definable, observable social structure that must itself be organized in order to organize political interests.

Within the political party, two of the sectors — the party organization and the party in government — have stable relationships and a rough division of labor and responsibility. Both have, in other words, the characteristics we associate with an organization of any kind. It is a bit misleading, therefore, to call only one of them the party organization, but such are the semantic vagaries of American politics. In justification of that usage, however, it is true that the party organization alone has the organizational capacity to plan and initiate the major share of party activities. It also has the most systematic network of relationships and roles of all the party sectors. It is the sector that speaks in the name of the party, governs it, and under law is responsible for it. It is the sector in which active partisans work to set the goals of the party and to mobilize and deploy its resources. In that sense it is that part of the party most concerned with its governance and with setting its priorities.

In concrete terms, the party organization is the formal apparatus of the precincts, wards, cities, counties, congressional districts, and state that results from the legislation of the state itself. In this way the party organization is the party for the purposes of the state; state laws set up these committees and recognize them collectively as the political party. In addition, each party has set up a national committee, which peaks the pyramid of committees the state has created. The party organization is thus the totality of the machinery operated by party officials, leaders, members, and activists. The three chapters that follow will describe it.

The public life and activities of the party organization — its espousal of ideas and recruitment of candidates, for instance — will receive treatment in chapters beyond these. But party organizations have a "private life" in addition to their public life. It involves the kind of internal relationships and behavior one might find in any complex organization. The three chapters of this part will also examine that private life, especially:

— *The formal structure of the organization:* its committees and machinery; the selection of its leadership.
— *The centers of power:* the relative centralization or decentralization of power within the organization; the locus of final authority within it.
— *The patterns of decision making:* the processes by which decisions are made, especially the degree of intraorganizational democracy.
— *Cohesion and consent:* the maintenance of unity, discipline, and morale within the organization.
— *The recruitment of resources:* the ability of the organization to attract people, money, and skills and the incentives it uses to do so.
— *The division of labor:* the various roles and relationships among people within the organization.

The private life of the party is far less obvious than the public. But although we may separate them, the two are obviously related. To a considerable extent the internal, organizational characteristics of the party affect its capacity to carry on the external, public activities.

A comparison with the large business organization is, if not pressed too far, a valid one. The party organization competes for political resources — manpower, knowledge, and money — against the powerful inducements of the other political organizations. Its rewards or incentives bring together varied groups of men and women who seek their special, and often differing, goals through the medium of party action. What are rewards and incentives from the "mobilizing" viewpoint of the party organization are merely the goals and ends for which their activists have come together in the party. Many of the party organization's activities, therefore, may be viewed in terms of its attempts to win those goals and thereby reward the faithful for their investment of resources, loyalties, work, and support.

Ultimately, the most important questions about the party organizations concern their effectiveness, vitality, and capacity. These characteristics can be summed up as *strength,* and the strength of the party organization has two dimensions: its ability to hold its own in its relationships with the two other sectors of the party, and its ability to function efficiently and consistently in mobilizing resources and making decisions. The party organization, that is, must function successfully within the political party and within the broader political system.

In its relationships with the party in government and the party in the electorate, the party organization rarely achieves any permanent supremacy within the American political party. All three sectors of the party struggle for control of its symbols and its political capabilities. All three have goals — at times competing goals — and each seeks control of the party as a "means" to its own particular ends. Rarely are the party organizations able to dictate to the party in government. It is far more common for them to be dependent on and even submissive to it. They must also conduct an almost endless wooing of their own party electorate, for even the loyal voter is often willing to split his ticket.

In addition to these strained and often dependent relations with the other sectors of the party, the organization confronts formidable problems in maintaining its internal vitality. Contrary to popular impression, party organizations are not unified, omnipotent monoliths. They have within them men and women of different values and goals, and they have always been plagued with dissidents and competing factions. They or parts of them often display amazing degrees of organizational apathy, ineptness, and even organizational disintegration. It is not unusual, for example, to find entire county organizations of the Democratic or Republican party in total desuetude.

In both these dimensions of the problem of strength and vitality, there are, of course, many variations within the American parties. The next few chapters will illustrate the varieties of party organization. The basic fact remains that by the standards of political parties of most Western democracies, the American party organizations are comparatively weak and insubstantial. And to a considerable extent the problem is in the very nature of the animal. The party organization is an expression of some very special qualities of the American political party. To understand its special problems and substantial limitations, one should perhaps compare it with party organizations found among the other democracies of the world.

At the risk of considerable oversimplification, one can say that among democratic political parties two types of organization appear most frequently: the cadre and the mass membership. In the cadre party, of which the major American parties are prime examples, the organizational machinery is run by a relatively small number of leaders and activists. These officials and activists perpetuate the apparatus of the organization, make decisions in its name, and pick the candidates and strategies that will enlist large numbers of voters. In the mass membership party, on the other hand, the party organization grows out of and is more continuously responsible to the party membership. In these parties substantial parts of the party electorates are involved in the party organization as dues-paying members

TABLE II.1    Comparison of Cadre and Mass Membership Party
Organizations

|  | Cadre | Mass membership |
|---|---|---|
| Members | Generally few | Many dues-paying members |
| Activities | Predominantly electoral | Ideological and educational, as well as electoral |
| Organizational continuity | Active chiefly at elections | Continuously active |
| Leadership | Few full-time workers or leaders (avocational) | Permanent professional bureaucracy and full-time leadership (vocational) |
| Position in party | Usually subordinate to party in government | Generally some influence over party in government |

and even as participants in year-round activities. The party organization
has, therefore, a continuous responsibility to its membership, often providing such benefits as insurance and leisure-time activities. In a mass membership party the three sectors are drawn together, with the party organization often occupying a central, dominant position. What we think of as
the party in the electorate becomes an integral, even guiding, part of the
party organization, with rights of picking officers and voting on policy questions. Because of its great power in the selection of candidates — no primary elections limit them — these organizations of the mass membership
parties exert far greater control over the party in government. In short, the
mass membership party resembles a continuous, participatory organization; the cadre party, on the other hand, is far more a momentary, pragmatic coalition of interests and people brought together in a temporary
way to win elections ( see Table II.1 ).[1]

Thus American party organizations are what they are because American
political parties are what they are. The American cadre-style party organization expresses the organizational needs of parties that are preoccupied
— indeed obsessed — with contesting elections. It reflects the organizational needs of parties that must appeal to majorities rather than to 10, 20,
or 30 percent of the electorate. It reflects the needs of parties that have not
traditionally been concerned with ideology, with vast political causes, or
even with taking specific stands on political issues. Finally, it reflects a

[1] Maurice Duverger in his *Political Parties* (New York: Wiley, 1954) inaugurated the
distinction between the cadre and mass membership parties. A third edition of the volume was published in New York by Barnes and Noble in 1969. For an expansion of
that analysis and an excellent comparison of the American parties with those of other
Western democracies, see Leon D. Epstein, *Political Parties in Western Democracies*
( New Brunswick: *Transaction,* 1979).

political system in which the electorate is already organized by a wealth of interest groups and other nonparty political organizations. To state these points the other way, the party organization of the American parties does *not* reflect the politics of a multiparty system, the politics of a deeply ideological political system, or a political system in which the parties have monopolized the organization of political interests.

So there is an insubstantial and even unimpressive quality about party organization in the American parties. Perhaps for this reason the early classic studies of party organization were written in Western Europe rather than the United States.[2] But the American party organizations are nonetheless there, and they command our attention. Despite their weaknesses and episodic failures, they are at the very center of the political party. More than any other sector, they control its life, its name, and its symbols. Any study of the American political parties slights them at great peril.

[2] The major examples are the Duverger book cited in the preceding footnote; Robert Michels, *Political Parties* (Glencoe, Ill.: Free Press, 1949, but first published in 1915); and Moisei Ostrogorski, *Democracy and the Organization of Political Parties*, first published in 1902 and now available in an edition of two volumes edited and abridged by Seymour Martin Lipset (New York: Anchor, 1964).

# 3

# The Party Organization: State and Local

The semantics of American politics often reflect its most tenacious myths. The entire popular vocabulary touching party organization suggests almost menacing strength. "Machines" headed by "bosses" keep the local "captains" toeing a "party line." Their power or strength has become, in a lately fashionable idiom, their "clout." And yet, even the most cursory experience with American party organization suggests that all the puffery hides a vastly less imposing reality.

In many ways the myth of monolithic party organization — and its related vocabulary and idiom — is itself a part of the greater American fear of politics and politicians. In what has become virtually a conspiratorial theory of American politics, the party organization or "machine" is the prime conspirator or corrupter in a wider net of political intrigue. The truth about American party organization is, therefore, difficult for many Americans to accept, for it involves not only a recognition of reality about the parties but also the modification of some dim views of politics in general. Perhaps because they carry no such preconceptions, foreign observers have found it easier to see American party organization as it really is. Recognition of the truth may surprise them, but it forces no major reorientation of political beliefs.

One of the latest in a long series of distinguished foreign commentators on the American polity, H. G. Nicholas, cut quickly through the major myth of party organization in the early 1950s:

Englishmen who have viewed American elections from three thousand miles across the Atlantic have generally been impressed by the elaborateness of the organizations involved as well as by the magnitude and professionalism of it all. The very language of American politics suggests a planned, powerful, smooth-running and disciplined instrument. Surely, these Englishmen have decided, an American party is the counterpart in the field of politics of the corporation in the

60

field of American business — a great, synthetic, efficient, productive mechanism, smoothly controlled from above and ordering the movement of millions below.

.I have discovered in the last few weeks that such an image quickly vanishes when confronted with reality. Even a cursory inspection of the American political scene at election time reveals a wholly different condition of affairs. Far from order, there is a rich and riotous confusion; in place of impersonal "machines," there is every kind of spontaneous organism. The disciplined ward heelers turn out to be an unseemly scramble of enthusiastic volunteers; the symmetrical pyramid we have heard about — from precinct to ward to county to state to nation — is an untidy cairn composed of stones of every conceivable size, with mortar either inadequate or nonexistent, and with an apex whose location shifts according to wherever you happen to be standing at the moment. . . .

The American party organization is a phoenix, burning itself out after each election, soaring with a new (or at least a rewelded) pair of wings after each primary. The effort this must involve for all concerned is something that appalls the visitor; the energy that is given to it excites his admiration; the complexities that result therefrom befuddle his poor comprehension.[1]

So it is that things are seldom what they seem in American party organization. Our main problem may be that we are always shifting among three levels of reality: the party organizations as they are stipulated in state legislation, the party organizations as they are in real life, and the party organizations as large numbers of Americans imagine them to be. Neither the pages of statute books nor the fears of many Americans accurately mirror the reality of party organization.

## THE FORMS AND OUTLINES OF ORGANIZATION

Although the United States Constitution makes no mention or even oblique reference to political parties, the constitutions and statutes of the fifty states bulge with detailed prescriptions defining the nature of party organizations and the duties they are to perform. The states have, in fact, enacted such a kaleidoscopic variety of legislation on the parties that it defies summary or classification. In scope and extent the laws range from those of Oregon, which specify the structure in detailed and full-blown provisions of more than 5000 words, to those of Georgia, which dispose of the parties in a few extended sentences. In between are all grades and degrees of statutory specificity — laws that permit the parties to determine the composition of the state central committee and those which not only spell it out but set the dates and places of its meetings, those which require legislative district organization and those which don't, those which leave the running of the parties to the parties and those which even set the agendas of their

---

[1] H. G. Nicholas, "A Briton Considers Our Bewildering Party Apparatus," *The Reporter*, November 25, 1952, pp. 28–29. Copyright 1952 by Fortnightly Publishing Company, Inc. Reprinted by permission.

periodic meetings. Despite the variety of state approaches, however, the cardinal fact remains that the definition and regulation of political party organization in the United States have been left entirely to the states.

This mass of state legislation on the parties covers an extensive range of subjects. Virtually every state has attempted to define the ways in which parties and their candidates are admitted to the ballot. They usually set vote minima — 5 or 10 percent of the vote cast in the last gubernatorial election, perhaps — or alternatively they prescribe the number of signatures on petitions required for access to the ballot. And virtually all assign specific tasks to the parties: the replacement of candidates who die during the campaign or the selection of presidential electors, for instance. Yet in many ways the most important statutory provisions are those which outline the organizational form the parties must assume and the procedures they must observe as they organize or reorganize. Often the parties in practice modify or embellish that statutory structure, but they never fully escape its imperatives. An examination of the party organization must begin with it.

The party organizations created by the states have one dominant characteristic in common: They match the voting districts and at least some of the constituencies of the state. They form great step pyramids of the myriad, overlapping constituencies of a democracy committed to the election of vast numbers of officeholders (Figure 3.1). At the bottom they are usually built on the smallest voting districts of the state. The basic functionary in the party organization is the local committeeperson representing a ward, a precinct, or a township.[2] Then, in a confusion of layers, the ward and city committees, county committees, and sometimes even state legislative and congressional districts are piled on top of each other.[3] At the apex of the pyramid there is invariably a state committee, usually called a state central committee in the idiom of these statutes. The degree to which this entire structure is actually specified by the statutes differs from state to state. State statutes generally ordain the county and the state committees; some then mandate the other levels, whereas others leave the full articulation of the organizational hierarchy to the parties themselves.

## The Elected Committeeperson

Usually the local committeeperson (or captain or chairperson) is chosen from the precinct, the smallest voting district in the states. Occasionally he or she is selected from the ward (especially in larger cities) or from the

[2] Terminology for local party officials is in transition. The majority of party organizations seem to have replaced "committeeman" and "committeewoman" with "committeeperson." Most state statutes, however, hold to the former usage.

[3] Within the same state the various intermediate committees may cover geographical areas of varying sizes and thus occupy different positions in the organizational pyramid. Congressional districts, for example, may be smaller than a city or larger than a county, depending on the density of population.

FIGURE 3.1    A Typical Pyramid of Party Organization
in a State

township (in rural areas). Since there are more than 100,000 precincts in the United States, a fully staffed, two-party system would assume the participation of at least some 200,000 men and women. In truth, of course, many of the local committee positions are either vacant or only nominally occupied.

The local committeepersons are generally selected in one of three ways. Most are chosen at local party caucuses or at the primary elections of the party, but in a few instances higher party authorities appoint them. In those states choosing them at the primaries, any voter may place his or her name in nomination for the party position with a petition signed by a handful of local voters. If, as it often happens, there are no nominees, the committeeperson may be elected by an even smaller handful of write-in votes. In other states the statutes direct or permit the party to hold local caucuses in the wards and precincts to which any voters of the area who declare themselves attached to the party's principles may come. These party loyalists then elect the committeepersons in the caucus; they also generally elect delegates to county and/or state conventions.

The duties of the local party officials are not often fully spelled out in the statutes. Naturally, in areas where local parties are active, they develop organizational responsibilities that the statutes never mention. The fabled local committeemen or ward heelers of the American political machine knew the local voters, catered to their needs and problems, introduced the party candidates to them, propagandized the parties' issues — all with the ultimate purpose of turning out a bloc of votes for the party on election day. In the less active local parties that are common today the committee-persons may do little more than occasionally attend meetings and campaign for a party candidate.

## The Local Committees

A welter of party committees rises above the local committeepersons. Collectively, they often make up the city, town, village, legislative, county, and congressional district committees or elect the delegates who do. In a few cases, however, these committees or some of them are chosen at county conventions or by the party's candidates for public office. Regardless of this profusion of committees and the various mechanics of their formation, the chief committee is generally the county committee, although in some states the congressional district committees assume a comparable importance.

The dominance of the county committee in most parts of the country is not difficult to explain. The county as a political division elects not one but a considerable number of public officials. And those officials often control the one major remaining source of political patronage: the county courthouse. Furthermore, many other constituencies — such as congressional districts, state legislative districts, and judicial districts — are defined largely in terms of counties. Then, too, in much of America, life and trade are drawn to the local county seat from the surrounding area. Finally, the statutes of most states reinforce the key position of the county committees. Often their members form other parallel committees, and often, too, they send their chairmen or delegates to form the state central committee.

In some metropolitan areas, however, the local party structure is more complex and more diverse. In the Bronx in New York the Democratic county committee is composed of some 3750 local committeepersons. All of them in each state legislative district (for the state assembly) elect district leaders, who in turn elect the county leaders. Typically, the Democrats of neighboring Brooklyn and Queens have somewhat different organizational structures. In other metropolitan centers, the city committees of the large central city assume an unusual importance.

The states, however, do more than create the bare bones of a party structure. They also regulate its activities and its internal processes. Something of the detailed nature of this regulation may be seen in Minnesota's strictures on the operation of its ward and precinct party caucuses. Minnesota statutes specify very precisely:

— The full details of the public announcement of the caucus that must be made at least twenty days in advance.
— The minimum length of the caucus (one hour).
— The length of time during which the caucus must receive nominations (one-half hour).

— The procedures for challenging the presence of any of the participants.
— The use of the secret ballot in all caucus elections.
— The use of *Robert's Rules of Order* (revised edition) in the caucus deliberations.

Other states spell out equally detailed standards for party operation. They may require that local committees meet within thirty or forty-five days after the primary elections, that they notify the secretary of state or the county clerk of the election of officers within a set time, that they not permit the voting of proxies, that they observe a fixed order of business at their meetings, or that they hold their conventions in certain types of public buildings. Again, the variety of rules is endless, but the point is clear: Under the laws of the states, the political parties are not in the usual sense merely private organizations.

## The State Central Committees

The state central committees of the fifty states are created in almost as many ways as human ingenuity can devise. In some states the lawmakers have left the composition to the decision of the parties, but in most they have decided the matter themselves. Basically, the differences center on two points: the lower party unit from which the state committee members are chosen and the ways in which they are chosen. The unit represented may be the county, the congressional district, the state legislative district, the state convention, cities, or a mixture of them. The methods of choice include election at the party's primaries, election by a lower committee, ex officio representation, or selection by a party convention. The possible number of combinations of the two factors is enormous, and state practice confirms that fact. (See, for example, the state committees outlined in the box.)

The activities of these state committees often are set down in what is almost painful detail. California statutes, for example, provide that the chairman of the state central committee shall serve a two-year term, that he cannot succeed himself, and that the office must be held alternately by residents of the northern and southern halves of the state. It is common to assign the committees responsibility for calling and organizing party conventions, for drafting party platforms, for supervising the spending of party campaign funds, and for selecting the party's presidential electors, representatives to the national committee, and national convention delegates and alternates. Regarding the main business of running a party organization and supporting candidates in the primaries and general elections, state statutes are generally silent, except to say occasionally that the parties may make whatever rules are necessary for the conduct of party business. Some do, however, forbid or permit the committees to endorse candidates in the

### The Composition of Six State Central Committees

*Illinois:* One representative from each congressional district chosen at the primary election.

*South Carolina:* One representative per county chosen at a county convention, plus the state chairman and vice-chairman chosen at the state convention.

*California:* Although the two major parties differ in the composition of state central committees, generally speaking the committee is composed of delegates to the party's state convention, party candidates and public officials, state party representatives to the national committee, the chairman of each county committee, and a large number of additional members appointed by county chairmen, party candidates and public officials, and state convention delegates.

*Oregon:* At least two members from each county, with additional members from counties for each 15,000 registered voters affiliated with the party.

*New York:* Two representatives elected at the primary from each state assembly district.

*Wisconsin:* At least two members from each congressional district chosen by the state convention.

primary. But on such "political" political activities, more commonly the state statutes are silent.

A number of states assign to statewide conventions many of the powers and responsibilities that other states leave to the state central committees. They may ordain that the state convention write the platform, select the national committeepersons from the state, nominate presidential electors, and choose delegates and/or alternates to the party's national convention. Indeed, some states provide that the state convention select the state committee itself. Furthermore, in a small number of states the state convention of the party actually nominates candidates for some statewide offices, a reminder of the power of conventions in the days before the direct primary.[4]

Such, then, are the formal organizational structures created for the parties in the states. Three general observations about them are in order. First, state legislators view the parties almost exclusively as electoral organizations. The organizational layers relate to voting districts and the constituencies in which public officials are chosen, and the duties assigned to them

[4] No genuinely comprehensive summary of state statutory provisions on party organization seems to be available. The provisions of the laws of any state can be found easily in the state's codified statutes; the material on party organization is usually located under the general heading "elections." For some summarization see *State Party Structures and Procedures: A State by State Compendium* (New York: National Municipal League, 1967), mimeo.

are almost exclusively concerned with the contesting of elections. The political party organization — as one views it in the statute books of the states — is clearly an auxiliary to the state's regulation of nominations and elections. Indeed, the dominant concern in its creation too often seems to be its usefulness in helping the state administer the electoral processes rather than its viability as a healthy, ongoing party organization.

Second, it is clear from the statutes that state legislators have also viewed the parties as skeletal organizations — as cadre parties — run by a small number of party officials. There is little evidence that they have entertained the possibility of membership parties, or even of parties attracting the concerns and labors of many activists. Indeed, they assume the contrary. By opening the election of local committeepersons (and of other party officials) to the electorate of the primary election, they have defined the parties' voters as a quasi-membership group. By legislative fiat they have tried to democratize the parties, to open them to the ultimate participation and authority of all voters. The party that results is thus no private association whose participating members choose its leaders and chart its affairs. It is the semipublic, easily permeable hybrid of which we have already spoken.

Finally, although the formal organization of the parties appears to be hierarchical, it is not. The state party hierarchies have more aptly been described by V. O. Key as "a system of layers of organization." [5] In some states, for example, the state central committee's members are chosen directly by the voters; the committee, therefore, does not grow out of the committees below it. And even when the linkage between the layers of organization is direct, the links move from bottom to top. Such a system would hardly appear to be ideally designed to produce the centralization of power at the apex that the very concept of hierarchy presumes. There is, in other words, no interlinked chain of command. Basically, the party organization is a system of party committees close to and growing from the political grass roots. The result is to build into the party organizational structure a great deal of localism and decentralization.

## THE SUBSTANCE AND REALITIES OF PARTY ORGANIZATION

These elaborate statutory parties, with their many layers of committees and their armies of committeepersons, conform to the mental images most Americans have of the party organizations. These are the machines, the organizations, the bosses, the ward heelers, and the party cabals of which the great party juggernauts are said to be made. Where statutes and public expectation see active legions of committeepersons and layer on layer of

---

[5] V. O. Key, *Politics, Parties and Pressure Groups*, 5th ed. (New York: Crowell, 1964), p. 316.

impressive organization, however, there is often only sporadic activity by a handful of dispirited party regulars.

Disciplined, effective party organization does exist, to be sure. The classic urban political machine is the best example. Its heyday was the turn of the twentieth century, and its promised land was the burgeoning American city. Its annals are replete with the colorful histories of Tammany Hall in New York, the knaveries of the Prendergasts in Kansas City and Frank ("I am the law") Hague in Jersey City, the cheeky threats of Chicago's "Big Bill" Thompson to punch the King of England on the nose, and the genial rascality (and mail fraud conviction) of Mayor James Curley of Boston.[6] In the last twenty years, however, urban machines have met a series of stunning defeats. The first was the triumph of Mayor Robert Wagner over the organization Democrats in New York in 1961, and the most recent was the victory of Mayor Jane Byrne over the Chicago Democratic machine's candidate to succeed Richard Daley in the 1979 primary. In between those dates all manner of problems beset other urban machines. Some, such as the one in Pittsburgh, were upset by middle-class reformers; others, such as the one in Philadelphia, were replaced by more effective practitioners of the old ethnic politics of the cities.

The recent history of the Daley organization in Chicago tells one a good deal about the present and future of the urban machine. Bolstered by control over some 35,000 patronage jobs and access to another 10,000 in the private economy, the Cook County Democratic organization and Mayor Richard Daley controlled public employment, nominations and elections, and the making of public policy in the city. The key was in turning out a disciplined vote in primaries and elections that would support the choices of the machine; conventional wisdom had it that the organization could deliver 350,000 disciplined voters, the vast majority of whom were the holders of party patronage and their families, friends, and relatives (see box). But the machine gradually lost control of that vote. The decline may have started with the violence surrounding the Democratic national convention in 1968 and the unflattering publicity it brought the mayor and his colleagues. Certainly, too, the machine suffered important defections, and its image was tarnished by convictions for corruption. But most important, probably, it failed after Mayor Daley's death to sustain the level of city services. A series of electoral defeats that had begun while Daley was alive culminated after his death in the upset victory of Byrne over Michael Bilandic, chosen by the machine as Daley's successor.

Irritation over the failure of the city to remove the winter's heavy snows and maintain other city services led in part to the undoing of the Chicago machine. But an assortment of accumulated grievances also contributed.

[6] The antics of Mayor Curley were in fact immortalized — and somewhat romanticized — in the novel by Edwin O'Connor (and its movie version), *The Last Hurrah* (Boston: Little, Brown, 1956).

## Three Views of the Daley Machine

"The money comes from countless sources. From the patronage army, it goes into ward offices as dues, and part of it is turned over to party headquarters. Every ward leader throws his annual $25-a-head golf days, corned beef dinners, and picnics. The ticket books are thrust at the patronage workers, and they either sell them or, as they say, 'eat them,' bearing the cost themselves. . . .

"Contractors may be the biggest of all contributors. Daley's public works program has poured billions into their pockets, and they in turn have given millions back to the party in contributions. Much of it comes from contractors who are favored, despite the seemingly fair system of competitive bidding."

Mike Royko, *Boss* (New York: Signet, 1971), pp. 74–75.

". . . At least once a week, Daley meets with his 'director of patronage' to peruse every application for every city job, right down to the lowliest ditch digger's. If and when the mayor stamps his approval, the successful job winner almost by definition joins The Machine (or organization) and assumes the responsibility of working one of Chicago's 3,412 voting precincts come election time. That sort of quasimilitary arrangement continues to produce virtual blitzes at the ballot box. . . .

"One of the most withering experiences in a ward boss's life comes on election night when he must bring his tally downtown to party headquarters at the Sherman House Hotel. Somewhat in the manner of a schoolboy presenting his report card to a stern father, each of the 50 meets alone with Daley to submit his precinct-by-precinct vote. According to one insider who has observed the ritual, Daley sits at a desk and silently studies the tallies. If they please him, he rises and vigorously pumps both of the successful committeeman's hands. If they displease him, Daley gives the miscreant a blistering tongue-lashing. On one such occasion, the mayor was so incensed with a non-producer that he reached across his desk and began shaking him by his necktie."

From "Chicago's Daley: How to Run a City," *Newsweek*, April 5, 1971, p. 82.
Copyright 1971 by Newsweek, Inc. All rights reserved. Reprinted by permission.

". . . What surprises is the pertinacity of a holdout — a former Congressman, now Alderman, named Roman Pucinski, who has gotten the notion that he should be Mayor himself.

". . . Since it's open season on Pucinski, a helpful precinct captain offers an example of the would-be insurgent's general hopelessness in the political arts. The man's emotions are deeply engaged by the story he tells, for it involves his own sister, a nun who recently died. Although she had been the head of a large convent in Pucinski's ward, the man tells me, the Alderman never went to her wake. 'What kind of a politician is that?' he asks, incredulous still. 'She *controlled* 170 votes!' "

From Joseph Lelyveld, *The New York Times*, March 27, 1977.
© 1977 by The New York Times Company. Reprinted by permission.

The vote for Byrne was especially heavy in the black wards, a sign of the many tensions between the machine and racial minorities in the city. Young voters also appear to have rejected the organization in large numbers. Thus at a primary with an unusually large turnout — almost 60 percent in an off-year primary election — the machine could not turn out a vote of sufficient size for its somewhat colorless candidate. So far, Chicago's experience squares with the experiences of other city organizations. (Some of the Democratic county organizations in New York City have recently lost as many primaries as they have won.) What was different in Chicago was that Mayor Byrne at no time rejected the Democratic organization and its modus operandi. She committed herself, in fact, to lead the machine and revitalize it.[7]

Urban machines such as those in Chicago depend fundamentally on the distribution of patronage jobs. These appointments win the indispensable loyalty and the service of the workers in the machine itself. Their efforts in turn produce the party "vote" — their own votes and those of friends, family, and neighbors. Local party workers also win voter loyalties by coping with the problems of their constituencies. Often those problems are personal — unemployment or a delinquent son — as well as public or governmental. The machine and its men earn political gratitude by finding a social welfare agency for the troubled, jobs for the jobless, contracts for the local merchant, or even the storied Christmas basket or delivery of coal for the needy. Among the more imaginative party organizations, the services of the machine are strictly up to date. A newspaper account of the Democratic bosses of Brooklyn recently reported that one especially deft leader had within the week "obtained school crossing guards for Our Lady of Peace parochial school, arranged for the admission of a retarded child into a specialized school, and managed an interdepartmental transfer of an employee of Merrill, Lynch, Pierce, Fenner and Smith, a stock brokerage."[8]

The classic urban machine has always been the acme of party organization in the United States. It is part electoral organization, part "informal government," part social service agency, and part ladder for upward social and economic mobility. In these ways and in its highly structured, articulated, and bureaucratized army of workers, it resembles the local organization of a European mass membership party. But there are, of course, differences. The American machine has no membership base, and it has few, if any, ideological concerns. Its focus on the immediate needs of its constituents has driven the urban machine to look almost completely inward and to ignore the issues and ideologies of the political world beyond. It is

---

[7] For two informed pictures of the Daley-Chicago organization, see Mike Royko, *Boss: Richard J. Daley of Chicago* (New York: Signet, 1971); and Milton Rakove, *Don't Make No Waves, Don't Back No Losers* (Bloomington: Indiana University Press, 1975).

[8] *The New York Times,* June 1, 1970.

provincially concerned with the city, and its politics are almost completely divorced from the issues that agitate our national politics.[9]

Yet, the machines of the big cities have never been and are not now typical of party organization in the United States. The other extreme — virtually unrepresented in the scholarly or popular literature because it offers so little to study — is virtual disorganization. In these cases, most of the committee positions in the party's county unit are unfilled or held by completely inactive incumbents (who may have been elected without their consent by four or five write-in votes). A chairman and a handful of loyal party officials may meet occasionally to carry out the most essential affairs of the party. Their main activity occurs shortly before the primary elections as they plead with members of the party to become candidates or offer themselves as candidates in order to "fill the party ticket." They are largely without influence or following, for often theirs is a chronic minority party. They meet infrequently, raise little money for election campaigns, and create little or no public attention. The extent of such organizational weakness is difficult to estimate, although it is the rule rather than the exception in much of rural America.

Most American local party organization lies between these two extremes. But "between" encompasses a great organizational distance. It might be accurate, however, to say that the average local party comes closer to the pole of disorganization than to the pole of maximum organization. In some instances, in fact, local party leaders will fight the strengthening of party organization lest new party activists challenge their little arena of power and claim their patronage rewards. More commonly, the incentives with which to staff and maintain the most active party organization are simply not present, or the political culture of the locale does not recognize the propriety of the politics of reward and sanction on which a machine organization rests. Above all, the necessary numbers of voters may not be involved in politics, may not see the importance of a vital party organization and their role in it. Even in a state such as Minnesota — recognized widely for its open and participant politics — the party caucuses in the presidential year of 1976 attracted 7 percent (about 130,000 people) of the citizens who voted in the subsequent elections.[10]

Although it is not easy to locate the "average" city or county organization, it probably shares most of these characteristics:

[9] The literature on the American urban machine is staggering in its size. Among the best pieces are Edward Banfield and James Q. Wilson, *City Politics* (Cambridge: Harvard University Press, 1963); Harold Gosnell, *Machine Politics: Chicago Model* (Chicago: University of Chicago Press, 1939); Raymond E. Wolfinger, "Why Political Machines Have Not Withered Away and Other Revisionist Thoughts," *Journal of Politics* 34 (1972): 365–98; and John A. Gardiner and David J. Olson, *Theft of the City* (Bloomington: Indiana University Press, 1974).
[10] The figure is less than 5 percent if one uses as a base all adults of eighteen years or more living in the state.

— An active chairman and executive committee, plus a few associated activists, who in effect make most of the decisions in the name of the party, who raise funds, who seek out and screen candidates (or approve the candidates who select themselves), and who speak locally for the party.

— A ward and precinct organization in which only a few local committeepersons are active and in which there is little door-to-door canvassing or other direct voter contact.

— The active participation in organizational matters of some of the party's elected public officials, who may share effective control of the organization with its official leadership.

— A distinctly periodic calendar of activities marked by a watchful waiting or general inactivity at other than election times.

Here one does not find the serried ranks of party foot soldiers. The leadership operates not with threats and iron discipline but with pleading and cajoling. There are few incentives and rewards left in the hands of these parties with which to recruit all the effort and manpower the statutory structures seem to assume.

Such a sketch of the "average" local party organization cannot, of course, begin to suggest the many forms that local parties take in the United States. It takes no account, for instance, of the oligarchic rural or small-town machines, in which a few local notables (who may or may not hold party or public office) dominate a political organization with a combination of patronage, local prestige and status, friendship, kinship, and private economic power. (It is one of the most durable — and least supportable — myths of American politics that political muscle, and even corruption, is always urban.)

A sketch of the "average" takes no account either of urban party organizations operating at a level of considerable effectiveness, albeit a level or two below that of the prototypic machine. A recent study of parties in the Detroit area defined the precinct committeeperson's three "critical" tasks to be the registration of new voters, the canvassing of the already registered (by phone or personal visits), and the roundup of voters on election day. Only 17 percent of the Democratic precinct leaders and 25 percent of the Republican leaders performed all three tasks, but another 38 percent of the Democrats and 22 percent of the Republicans carried out two of the three.[11]

[11] Samuel J. Eldersveld, *Political Parties: A Behavioral Analysis* (Chicago: Rand McNally, 1964), pp. 349–50. David Olson has made one of the few systematic attempts at categorizing county party organizations in his article "Toward a Typology of County Party Organizations," *Southwestern Social Science Quarterly* 48 (1968): 558–72.

## THE EXTRALEGAL ORGANIZATIONS

The forms and types of party organization just discussed operate largely within the formal outlines set down in state statutes. But the parties have made organizational embellishments that go beyond the words and sometimes even the clear expectations of many state statutes.

The embellishments are of two kinds, auxiliaries to party organizations and alternatives to them. Among the auxiliaries, women's organizations and caucuses have sprung up in a number of states. In addition to helping the regular organization in fund-raising and organizational work, they promote increased participation in party affairs by women and support candidates sympathetic to women's rights and other feminist issues. And a good many parties have experimented with youth organizations; at various times in the recent past both parties have had both national youth organizations and groups of college youth affiliates. However, with the advent of the eighteen-year-old suffrage and reform attempts to involve young people in the party itself, the youth auxiliaries have declined in membership and vigor. Finally, racial minorities in a number of states have organized within the state parties. The Alabama Democratic Conference, a black group, has worked within the Democratic party of that state for more than a decade, and another black organization, the Mississippi Freedom Democratic party, recently gave up its separate existence and reentered the state's Democratic party.

However, partisans in a number of states have effected greater transformations in party organization than the mere addition of auxiliaries. They have proposed, in effect, an alternative to the regular party organization.

### The Democratic Reform Clubs

Democratic reform clubs were formed in New York to break the power of Tammany Hall. They draw an educated, upper-middle-class and avocational party activist committed to liberal policies and to the reorientation of organizational politics to issues and ideology. In their organizational reform they have attempted to substitute a club-style membership for the usual cadre organization of the regular party. Within the party they have sought to replace both the traditional reliance on patronage and the hierarchical authority of the party leader (i.e., "boss"). More than anything else, however, theirs is a rebellion against the essentially issueless politics of personal reward and ethnicity that typified big city politics for so long. And in New York, at least, it has succeeded. The New Democratic Coalition still includes at least seventy-five such clubs in the city, and in 1979, for the first time, both the mayor, Edward Koch, and the leader of Tammany Hall (i.e., the Democrats of Manhattan), Miriam Bockman, come from the club movement. Similar groups sprang up in Pennsylvania, Ohio, and Illinois, the most persistent and long-lived of them being the Independent Voters of Illinois (IVI).[12]

## The Wisconsin Voluntary Organizations

In the 1920s the conservative wing of the Wisconsin Republicans, repeatedly the losers in primaries to the La Follette progressive wing, formed a separate, extralegal party organization to represent its ideology and support its candidates in the GOP primary. When the Progressives left the Republican cover in the 1930s and formed their own state party, the "regular" Republicans found it easier to operate through their voluntary party organization than through the carefully regulated statutory organization. The Democrats, casting about for a more effective party organization, followed suit in the 1940s and 1950s. Both parties operated through these duplicating voluntary organizations until 1974, keeping a separate and docile statutory organization to perform the mandated statutory duties. In 1974 the Wisconsin legislature brought developments full circle by abolishing the statutory committees and vesting in the voluntary committees the functions that state statutes require to be performed.[13]

## The California Clubs

The splendid profusion of club-style party organizations in California began in the 1930s when liberal Republicans founded the California Republican Assembly to revive the faltering Republican party. A conservative competitor, the United Republicans of California, sprang up in the early 1960s to oppose the liberals of the CRA, but conservatives captured the CRA just a short time later. In 1965 the liberal Republicans repaired to a new set of organizations, the California Republican League. On the Democratic side, the older of the organizations, the liberal California Democratic Clubs, was founded in 1953 with the remnants of the 1952 Stevenson supporters. In both parties these clubs have featured some separate local organizations, a hard core of dues-paying members, and a series of tumultuous conventions at which the clubs' ideologists have endorsed candidates for support at their party's primary. But in both parties their

---

[12] See James Q. Wilson, *The Amateur Democrat* (Chicago: University of Chicago Press, 1962). On New York reform politics see the bittersweet account of Edward N. Costikyan, *Behind Closed Doors* (New York: Harcourt, Brace, 1966).

[13] For an account of the Wisconsin voluntary organizations in their flower, see Leon D. Epstein, *Politics in Wisconsin* (Madison: University of Wisconsin Press, 1958). By the late 1950s the two parties' voluntary organizations had enrolled some 20,000 dues-paying members.

influence appears to have run its course, and by the middle 1970s they can together claim no more than 15,000 or 20,000 members.[14]

Finally, although not many states have equaled this degree of extra-legal party organization, some state parties have in a limited way grafted membership organizations onto the regular statutory organization. In other states, the outlines of party statutory organization are sufficiently loose to permit the parties to shape an organization as they please.

The development of these voluntary organizations speaks volumes about the inadequacy of the conventional statutory party organization within which the parties must operate. The voluntary clubs have arisen in part because the inflexible statutory organization cannot accommodate the new middle-class style of organization with its emphasis on ideological and avocational activists and greater participation by dues-paying members. Furthermore, most reflect the problems that statutory party organizations have in controlling their party's primary. In Wisconsin the old statutory party conventions were required to convene *after* the primary, and in California the statutory party organizations are forbidden to make endorsements in the primary. In other ways, too, the voluntary organizations provide a release from state regulation of parties; in Wisconsin, for example, the voluntary structure enabled the parties to elude the state's severe restrictions on campaign spending by statutory organizations. Finally, the voluntary organizations are often instruments of a factional warfare that is almost always ideological. Fervent ideologists have used them to fight other ideologists or nonideologists within the party.

## THE LOCUS OF POWER

It remains to ask what in reality is the locus of power within these party organizations. Is the hierarchical chain of authority really maintained? Most scholars feel that in most states it is not, that the major locus of organizational authority is the county committee. Many state party organizations are in fact federations — and loose ones at that — of semiautonomous or autonomous local baronies and baronial county chairmen.

The Democratic party of Ohio exemplifies these loosely knit, decentralized state party organizations. Writing of it in the early 1960s, one observer noted,

There was, in fact, no statewide Democratic party in Ohio. The state's Democratic party was an aggregation of city machines which had little or no interest in statewide elections unless the candidate was from their city. Ray Miller, the

[14] For a brief account of the history of the California clubs (and for overviews of big state politics generally), see Neal R. Peirce, *The Megastates of America* (New York: Norton, 1972), pp. 584–85.

Cuyahoga County (Cleveland) Democratic boss, explicitly maintained that his organization was an independent entity with neither legal nor moral ties with a state Democratic party.[15]

This kind of decentralization is often accentuated by factionalism within the party — regional factions, those centering on personages, liberal-conservative factions, or those reflecting ethnic or class differences. Every state party has such factionalism; its effect depends on its relative strength.

In their recent study of state parties Malcolm Jewell and David Olson have in fact erected a typology of state parties primarily on the strength and nature of factions within them. Leaving aside the electorally ineffective parties (the authors call them the "electorally passive" parties), they find that active party organizations fall into three categories: cohesive, bifactional, and multifactional. It is not that the cohesive parties have no factions, but that they are able to unite their partisans despite them.[16] To a very great extent, therefore, the cohesive parties are those of centralized power within the state. The bifactional and multifactional parties — regardless of the causes or bases of their factionalisms — inevitably are fragmented and decentralized. And that in turn means that power and authority within them reside in the most viable of the local levels: the county organization.

Questions of centralization and decentralization or factional structures are important ultimately for what they mean for the operation of the parties. The cohesive and centralized state party organizations have vastly greater power over candidates for statewide office and far greater capacity for enforcing discipline in their parties in the state legislatures. They can control party finances and through them the conduct of election campaigns. The decentralized alternative undermines the possibility of party cohesion in the legislature and prevents the development of statewide issues or campaigns. Instead of a state politics conducted by a state party organization, the individuals of the party in government triumph at the statewide level and locally there prevails a fragmented politics of local interests and leaders.[17]

To build a powerful state organization is to overcome both the grassroots localism of American politics and the widespread antipathy to strong party discipline. Understandably, it is not easy to succeed. Strong and skillful personal leadership by a governor, a senator, or a state chairman helps. So do political resources. Indiana's Democratic party, for one, has maintained its strength and reputation as one of the country's most pow-

[15] John H. Fenton, *Midwest Politics* (New York: Holt, Rinehart, Winston, 1966), p. 137.
[16] *American State Political Parties and Elections* (Homewood, Ill.: Dorsey, 1978), pp. 112ff.
[17] Duane Lockard, *New England State Politics* (Princeton: Princeton University Press, 1959), pp. 325–26.

erful state organizations by controlling a considerable amount of patronage
— estimates vary from 10,000 jobs on up — and a tradition by which the
grateful patronage holders return 2 percent of their salaries to the party
coffers.[18] It helps also to have a tradition or culture that accepts the notion
of a unified and effective party in the state. Similarly, it makes a difference
whether the state parties are given important political responsibilities. It
is no coincidence that central party organization has flourished in the states
in which primary elections are least extensive — states such as Connecticut and Indiana — and in which party organization determines much more
directly who the statewide and congressional candidates will be. But when
these advantages are neutralized, the result in most states is the usual decentralization of authority and power within the state organization. Only
the county and city organizations are ongoing political organizations with
grassroots support and involvement. They alone develop a base of power
directly in the electorate, and that is very powerful leverage indeed within
a party organization.

One last observation about centralization and decentralization in state
parties should be made. Both journalists and scholarly observers have
noted that the Republicans find it easier to build centralized, cohesive
parties than do the Democrats. Why? Two chief explanations suggest
themselves. The first has it that the Democrats are more often the majority
party, and as such bring together a more mixed and varied coalition than
do the Republicans. The explanation seems plausible, but Jewell and Olson
control to some extent for party competitiveness and still find the difference between the two parties.[19] (It is true, though, that even in a Republican state the Democrats are still the majority party in the sense of
national party loyalties.) The second explanation — one both more elusive
and more intriguing — posits a difference in values and traditions between
the two parties. The Republicans, the argument goes, are more willing
than the Democrats to accept central authority and leadership in the party,
more willing to accede to the need for a unified party stand, and less likely
to dissent and generally kick up a fuss within the party.

## TRENDS AND CHANGES

Party organization will reflect the political culture and the socioeconomic
conditions of the time. As they change, the parties also change. No case
better illustrates that fact than the decline of the city machine in American
politics. Civil service and merit systems have gradually robbed it of the
patronage jobs with which it rewarded its workers and officers. The ethnic

18 Robert J. McNeill, *Democratic Campaign Financing in Indiana, 1964* (published
jointly by the Institute of Public Administration, Indiana University, and Citizens' Research Foundation, 1966).
19 Jewell and Olson, *American State Political Parties and Elections*, p. 114.

minorities who supported it in its dominant days have been increasingly integrated into American life. Greater education and literacy have created a political awareness and sophistication that rebels at being led, sheeplike and docile, to the polls in a "delivered" vote. The values of the times demand participatory rights for individuals in all organizations. The growth of the welfare state, too, has provided freely and openly the welfare services that the urban machine "gave" only to its deserving patrons. And the growth of national, ideologized politics and national candidates has helped to break down the isolated localism and the essentially issueless politics of the machine.

Small wonder, then, that the old-style machine organization has fallen on bad days. One increasingly hears its style and ethics condemned. Its military discipline and central authority — its bossism — do not sit well with middle-class Americans any more. Nor do its issueless politics or patronage ethic. But perhaps all this is only to say that as an organizational mode and style the urban machine has outlived its appointed time. In our tendency to dismiss it, though, we too often forget that the urban machine was once one of the few agencies integrating the newly arrived city dwellers into American life and softening their often desperate condition in strange surroundings. It was also an instrument of popular democracy, the means by which the majorities of the cities first won control of their cities from old, aristocratic, and largely Anglo-Saxon elites.

Where something approaching the old-style urban machine persists today, it is in circumstances not unlike those the new immigrant faced in American cities at the turn of the century. The black, Puerto Rican, Indian, and Chicano newcomers to the cities, for example, face the same (or more severe) problems of poverty, discrimination, political powerlessness, ethnic isolation, and inability to cope with the life of the city. Many of the older political incentives and organizational styles "work" in their neighborhoods. But the shift of local party power to the new minorities has not gone smoothly. The old white groups have tried to hold on to positions of party authority in most cities. Not surprisingly, the decline of the old machines in a number of cities featured the massive desertion of the vote of minorities. Alternatively, the new, middle-class, predominantly white reform politics in other cities has had little to offer the new ghettos, either in style or in goals.

It is not easy to measure the decline of the urban machine or of the full range of conventional American party organization. The Survey Research Center reported, for example, that in the 1976 campaign only 28 percent of American adults had been contacted by someone from one of the parties. Most of the voting electorate, in other words, was reached exclusively, if at all, by the mass media. The candidate projecting his image and message through the media and personal appearances need not depend on the political party as the chief organizer and persuader of voters. Unquestionably this revolution in campaigning has also undermined the power of the party organizations. They are no longer the indispensable instrument for election to office. The candidate may now purchase the information and skills necessary for the campaign from the pollster and the public relations specialist. Several generations ago he would have had no alternative but to get them from the party organization — and at the party's price.

The chief contemporary changes in party organization, therefore, are the development of both candidate-centered campaign organizations and a club-style membership organization to accommodate the middle-class ideologists. What we have today in American party organization is far removed from the hierarchies the state legislatures have stipulated. The statutory models do exist here and there across the United States, but they are not — and probably never were — the norm in American party organization. State and local party organizations are today looser and more flexible. They can more accurately be seen as a coalition of political groupings or as a pool or reservoir of party-oriented personnel. The local party organization may, in other words, be a loose aggregation of:

— The statutory organization (or that part of it actually manned).
— A cluster of related, satellite organizations (the auxiliaries, the clubs, and the personal followings of candidates and office holders).
— Allied, nonparty political organizations (the chamber of commerce, trade unions, other local interest groups, civic organizations, or nonparty liberal and conservative groups).
— Active and potentially active individuals, attracted by candidates, by issues, and by the party itself.

The party is, in other words, a flexible and somewhat undisciplined pool of active groups and individuals. They are recruited to the party for different reasons, and they are activated by different candidates, different issues, and different elections. A hotly contested election of local officials, especially those controlling local patronage, will activate one cluster of partisans, and a congressional campaign in which the chief issue is the environment will activate another. What we have thought of as the party organization is thus a reservoir of organization and activists, from which are drawn (in part) the shifting organizational coalitions that speak and act in the name of the local party.

In searching for change in American party organization, however, it is easy to lose sight of what does not change. Despite recent trends the American parties remain largely skeletal, cadre party organizations, run generally by small numbers of activists and involving the great masses of their supporters scarcely at all. The shift away from the hierarchical organizational forms inherent in the statutes of the states has largely been a shift from a tight, hierarchical cadre organization to a loose cadre organization. For despite the brave appearance of some membership clubs, the American parties are still a long way away from becoming mass membership parties, and they are still some distance from achieving the continuously active, year-round tempos of parties elsewhere in the world. By the standards of those parties, American party organization continues to be characterized by unusual fluidity and evanescence, by failure to generate activity at nonelection times, and by the ease with which a handful of activists and public officeholders dominate it.

# 4

# The
# Political
# Party of the
# Activists

Behind the imposing facades of the statutory party structures are the living, organizational realities of the political parties. The statutes do not reckon with the men and women of the party, their goals and motives, their interactions and relationships, the contributions they make to the organizations, the price they exact for those contributions. Yet the activity and motivations of those men and women are closer to the real world of party politics than all the statutory paragraphs put together.

We may easily accept the bemused cynicism of Will Rogers about the organizational condition of the American parties: "I don't belong to an organized political party, I'm a Democrat." But however disorganized they may be, they *are* purposive, goal-seeking organizations. As the most completely electoral parties in the democracies of the world, they are vastly committed to the winning of elections. Additionally, they may seek any number of short- and long-run goals: the spread of an ideology, the enactment of a set of public policies, or the easing of regulations affecting their activities.

As an organization, therefore, the major political party is a mechanism for uniting adherents in the pursuit of goals. It recruits and mobilizes the resources and skills for political action. In the employment of those resources it works out a division of labor and a hierarchy of authority. Like any other complex organization it has its leaders and followers, its own specialization of role and function, its own internal system of communication. And it is a decision-making apparatus in which choices must be made about the mobilization of resources, the setting of strategies, and the deployment of assets. These internal processes are what the private life of the political party is all about. They are the processes by which the party organization converts the raw materials of people, resources, and expertise into goal-oriented activity.

Goal seeking also goes on within the party organization on a personal, individual level. Individual party leaders, workers, and members are in the party organization for some identifiable, if covert or implicit, set of reasons. There must, in other words, be rewards or incentives — "pay-offs" in the broadest sense of the word — for devoting one's time to party activity rather than to the service of the PTA or the improvement of one's golf game.

## THE SYSTEM OF INCENTIVES

The American political parties have never operated primarily in a cash economy. They have rarely bought or hired the millions of man-hours of labor they need. Even today paid staffs are small or nonexistent in most party organizations, and it is a rare party chairman who draws a substantial salary from the party organization. The great number of Americans active in the parties receive no cash in return for their considerable time and skills. Even the earthy old custom of paying precinct workers on election day is vanishing. What is it, then, that induces party workers to lavish their hours and efforts on the affairs of the parties? If the parties' payments are not made in cash, in which coin are they made? [1]

### Patronage

Patronage, the use of appointive governmental positions to reward past party work and induce future labors, is hardly unique to the American political parties.[2] Even today the municipal services of the Italian cities swarm with the partisans in power. But very probably no other party system over its history has relied as systematically on patronage as the American. The easy confidence of the Jacksonians that no public task was so complex that it demanded experience and their matching conviction that "to the victors go the spoils" set the ethic early in the nineteenth century. From then to the present a vast array of public jobholders — from elevator operators and charwomen in city hall to American ambassadors in foreign capitals — have owed their appointment to political worthiness and the right political sponsorship.

Despite the explosive growth of government bureaucracy in this century, the amount of patronage available to the parties has declined precipitously. The expansion of civil service and merit systems has been the chief reason. What was once a flourishing federal patronage — historians write

---

[1] For a somewhat different categorization of incentives, see James Q. Wilson, *Political Organizations* (New York: Basic Books, 1974).

[2] The concept of patronage here is, therefore, one of appointment to governmental jobs on the basis of political criteria. Other studies use broader definitions that include at least the two categories of patronage and preferment used here. For example, Martin and Susan Tolchin in *To the Victor . . .* (New York: Random House, 1971) work with a definition of patronage that includes "the allocation of the discretionary favors of government in exchange for political support" (p. 5).

of the hordes of ill-mannered job seekers overrunning presidential inaugurations — has by now dwindled to well below 1 percent of the federal establishment. There still remain the United States marshals and attorneys, the collectors of customs, and the rural mail carriers, to mention a few of the classic federal patronage posts, but theirs is a shrinking roster.

Similar declines have come, albeit more slowly, to the states and localities. Any number of states, counties, and cities — the great majority probably — have virtually abolished patronage, moving to merit systems of some sort. In a number of states the governor has no patronage available beyond his own immediate staff. Patronage does, of course, continue to flourish in a minority of states. New York, for example, has some 40,000 positions available for party patronage. But in recent years even some of the vaunted centers of patronage have seen the merit principle make new and severe inroads. Kentucky legislation in 1960 reduced the number of year-round jobs available for patronage from 16,000 to 4000, about 75 percent of them on the highway maintenance crews.[3] Pennsylvania, which had almost 50,000 patronage positions as late as 1970, lost a sizable number in collective bargaining. In 1971 some 17,500 workers, most of them also with the highway crews, negotiated a contract in which the state agreed not to discriminate against any employee on the basis of political affiliations. The contract also forbids the state to require workers to make political contributions or to engage in political activity. Furthermore, in 1976 the U.S. Supreme Court held that patronage dismissals violated the Constitution of the United States. That is, a majority of the justices thought that the dismissal of an otherwise satisfactory employee for political reasons — especially those having to do with a change in parties in power — violated the employee's freedoms of political belief and association.[4]

The unavailability of patronage is, however, only a part of the parties' problem. There are administrative problems as well. A recent survey of county chairmen in Ohio finds that they achieve only a partial return in party work or contributions from their patronage appointees.[5] The problems the parties encounter in using the available patronage jobs are legion. Patronage seekers may not meet the skill requirements of the job; heavy-equipment operators are hard enough to find without adding a set of political credentials. Also, the politics of patronage has always worked best among the depressed and disadvantaged; most patronage positions do not tempt the educated, "respected" middle-class leadership the parties would

[3] Malcolm E. Jewell and Everett W. Cunningham, *Kentucky Politics* (Lexington: University of Kentucky Press, 1968), p. 43.
[4] *Elrod v Burns*, 427 U.S. 347 (1976). In late 1979 a federal district court judge in Chicago extended the logic of *Elrod* to hold that hiring (as well as firing) for political reasons violated the Constitution in that it discriminated against job applicants without the proper political credentials. As of early 1980 an appeal in the case was pending.
[5] W. Robert Gump, "The Functions of Patronage in American Party Politics: An Empirical Reappraisal," *Midwest Journal of Political Science* 15 (1971): 87–107.

like to attract. Furthermore, elected executives may use patronage to build their own political followings rather than the party apparatus. Finally, the parties may not be able to use the patronage available to them. Especially when they win power after years of failure, they do not have the necessary administrative machinery or an adequate list of job seekers.[6]

At the same time pressures have understandably grown for patronage with which to reward the educated, middle-class activists in the parties and campaigns. One solution is the "political non-job."

Happily, political leaders have devised ways to bestow the status symbols of high office without the job itself. At Democratic national headquarters in Washington, where many such split-level appointments are routinely requisitioned and cleared, the new institution is known as "the honorary." Elsewhere it has been dubbed the patronage non-job, and it can range from nomination to a White House advisory committee to an invitation to be an honored member of an Air Force civic inspection tour of California, arranged at the behest of your local Congressman.[7]

But chief executives who make appointments to administrative positions, boards, commissions, legal staffs, and judgeships also find themselves pressed to use these positions for patronage purposes. They can and do so use them, but the political considerations must often be tempered by or balanced against important considerations of ability and professional experience. In any event, the positions are not all that plentiful, and they often go — when used for patronage purposes — to reward workers in the campaigns of the appointing official rather than the workers of the party organization.

### Political Career

Elective political office has the income, responsibility, prestige, and excitement — not to mention the power — that most patronage positions do not. And since the political party offers an efficient, and in some cases the only, avenue to elective office, it is inevitable that the possibility of an elective political career should recruit new party activists or sustain activity after other incentives have worn off. Robert Huckshorn, for instance, finds that between 1962 and 1972 one-third of all the state party chairmen were candidates for elective office after serving as chairman. The offices they sought, moreover, were often important ones: governorships, other statewide office, and seats in the United States Congress.[8]

[6] On patronage see also Daniel P. Moynihan and James Q. Wilson, "Patronage in New York State, 1955–1959," *American Political Science Review* 58 (1964): 286–301; and Frank J. Sorauf, "State Patronage in a Rural County," *American Political Science Review* 50 (1956): 1046–56.
[7] Don Oberdorfer, "The New Political Non-Job," *Harper's* (October 1965), pp. 108ff.
[8] Robert J. Huckshorn, *Party Leadership in the States* (Amherst: University of Massachusetts Press, 1976), p. 37.

There are party organizations with such disciplined control over their primaries that they can and do "give" public office, especially at the state and local level, to loyal party workers. If the party dominates the politics of the area, control of the primaries makes public offices an "elective patronage." The candidate is offered the chance to run and then does little more as the party organization runs up the necessary majorities. That degree of control over nomination and election to office is, however, vanishing along with patronage. The party must increasingly look for candidates with some appeal and qualities beyond their service to the party. The candidates know that, useful though the advantage of party support may be, it is rarely sufficient by itself.

What then does the candidate get from the support of the party? He needs advice, know-how, manpower, and money, and in most parts of the country the party still remains a likely source of them. Service in the party, then, yields the skill, experience, connections, approval, and resources that any candidate needs. It is, of course, possible for the candidate without party ties to seek election, but for every one who does, there are dozens of successful office seekers who have party ties. And for the partisan who already holds office there is no easier way to ensure reelection or to move to a more attractive office than by work in the party. So sedulous are the party's officeholders in currying the support of the party organizations that speculation over their ambitions and "moves" remains a favorite intraparty recreation.

## Preferments

The tangible, material rewards of politics may take forms other than appointive or elective office. The active partisan or the financial "fat cat" may, for example, seek preference in the awarding of public contracts. In this respect, it is no accident that the leaders of the construction industry are so active politically in the states and localities that spend millions every year on roads and public buildings. Preference may take other forms: a tolerant or haphazard application of regulatory or inspection policies, unusually prompt or efficient public services (snow and garbage removal, for example), a forgiving instrument of the law (e.g., the fixed traffic ticket), or the granting of a scarce public service (admission to crowded mental hospitals, for instance). It may also involve the granting of scarce "opportunities" such as liquor licenses or franchises. By "preferment," in other words, one means special treatment or advantage, and it is dependent usually on the party's holding the decision-making positions in government. It is partly in this sense that parties talk of "controlling" city hall, the county courthouse, or the state capitol. (see box).

One particularly unappealing form is the "preferment" given activities that operate on the shady side of the law. It may involve a calculated

### Preferments: An Old and a Recent View

Preferments available to the party faithful change with time. So, too, do the terms that describe them and the justifications that support them. But whether it's "honest graft" or an extended definition of patronage, the incentive is the same.

"There's an honest graft, and I'm an example of how it works. I might sum up the whole thing by sayin': 'I seen my opportunities and I took 'em.'

"Just let me explain by examples. My party's in power in the city, and it's goin' to undertake a lot of public improvements. Well, I'm tipped off, say, that they're going to lay out a new park at a certain place.

"I see my opportunity and I take it. I go to that place and I buy up all the land I can in the neighborhood. . . .

"Ain't it perfectly honest to charge a good price and make a profit on my investment and foresight? Of course it is. Well, that's honest graft."

George Washington Plunkett in William Riordan's
*Plunkett of Tammany Hall* (New York: Dutton, 1905), p. 3.

"This is the stuff of modern political patronage:

"Insurance premiums on government property. For example, Erastus Corning 2d, the Democratic Mayor of Albany, is president of an insurance company that receives $100,000 in annual premiums to insure the property of Albany County.

"Bank deposits of state funds. For example, John J. Lynch, chairman of the Brooklyn Democratic party, is chairman of a bank that has $3-million in state funds deposited by Controller Arthur Levitt. . . .

"Mr. Corning said his company received $100,000 in premiums annually for insuring the property of Albany County. This business was obtained without competitive bidding, because the uniform insurance rates are fixed by law by the State Department of Insurance and no insurance company can undersell another.

"Asked whether there was a conflict between his public and private offices, the Mayor replied in an  interview: "I'm in no way a county official. The question of conflict of interest has never been raised.' "

From Martin Tolchin, *The New York Times,* June 17, 1968.
© 1968 by The New York Times Company. Reprinted by permission.

ignoring of prostitution, bookmaking, the numbers game, or traffic in drugs in return for some form of political support. In other forms it has involved the parties' taking a share of protection money or the proceeds from crime, vice, or the rackets. The prevalence of such an incentive to party effort is understandably difficult to estimate. Perhaps it suffices to say that it is probably less vital than the political cynics think and more important than the Pollyannas admit. The chances are, though, that what nexus there is between organized crime and government goes on through mechanisms other than the political party. And when it touches the party and electoral politics, the influence of crime is probably felt more through campaign contributions than directly in the party organization. In 1960 Alexander Heard estimated ("a guess — that is what it is") that underworld money accounted for 15 percent of the campaign expenditures at state and local levels.[9]

## Socioeconomic Mobility

Political activity offers easy publicity (or notoriety) and contacts for those who seek them: young lawyers trying to build a practice, owners of food and watering spots, insurance and real estate brokers, storekeepers, and the socially ambitious. Party activity opens up the contacts that lead to prosperity in a business or profession, to a new job or business opportunity, even to an elevated social status.

Writes one observer of the Philadelphia organization men:

> One explanation of their motivation would locate the "boys' " essential urge in the factor known as "prestige." The truth is, many intellectuals and many members of the upper class who have come in contact with politicians argue that, for the Irish, Jewish, Italian bright boys who pursue it, politics is a "status-conferring" occupation. The Bill Greens and the Victor Blancs and the Aus Meehans, they point out, could no doubt have earned wealth and even the respect of their fellow-men by selling insurance, practicing law, and the like. But one thing that they could not earn in these ways is "place" in the community. Politics gives them that.[10]

In the tired American phrase, some people join the active ranks in the parties to "get ahead," whether they define getting ahead in terms of upward social or economic mobility.

## Social and Psychological Satisfactions

The personal, nonmaterial rewards of party activity are not easy to identify and certainly not easy to measure. But one can sense the social rewards of politics in the camaraderie of the gang at party headquarters or the court-

---

[9] Alexander Heard, *The Costs of Democracy* (Chapel Hill: University of North Carolina Press, 1960), p. 163. Beyond Heard's estimate it is not easy to find a serious treatment of the relationships between crime and politics. Undoubtedly the subject itself restricts the usual scholarly inquiries. There are broader studies of "corruption" in government and politics, but they often suffer from a broad or imprecise definition of "corruption." A number extend the concept of corruption far beyond mere illegality. For a discussion and bibliography, see John G. Peters and Susan Welch, "Political Corruption in America: A Search for Definitions and a Theory," *American Political Science Review* 72 (1978): 974–84.
[10] James Reichley, *The Art of Government: Reform and Organization Politics in Philadelphia* (New York: Fund for the Republic, 1959), p. 104.

house. It is evident at a party dinner as the workers press around the great
and near great of the party, hoping for a word of greeting or a nod of
recognition. In the new-style political clubs the attractiveness of the social
life and friendship circle is explicit. "Many volunteers are rootless, tran-
sient newcomers searching the city for a means of associating with like-
minded people." But while the parties' clubs rely on the social incentives,
those incentives are probably secondary:

> Although many clubs in various cities offer their members reduced air fares to
> Europe on charter flights, a full schedule of social events, forums featuring pres-
> tigious speakers, and the opportunity to play the political game, and although
> some members join simply to find a mate quickly or get to Paris inexpensively, if
> the clubs should cease to define themselves as organizations devoted to liberalism
> or reformism or similar worthy causes, they could not for long sustain the interest
> of any but the handful who simply enjoy the company of others or like being dis-
> trict leader.[11]

Perhaps one can say more simply that party politics is a splendid vehicle
for gregariousness. Almost all reported research on the motivations of
party activists finds that they say they "like people" or that they "like
politics."

Social satisfactions merge almost imperceptibly into the psychological.
"Like the theater, politics is a great nourisher of egos," writes one observer.
"It attracts men who are hungry for attention, for assurance that somebody
loves them, for the soul-stirring music of their own voices." [12] Party work
may also offer the individual a cause or an enterprise with which to identify, a charismatic leader to follow, a round of activities that can lift him
above the personally unrewarding tasks of the workaday world. The party
may be a small island of excitement in a sea of routine. It may even offer
an occasion for the manipulation or domination of others, a chance to
decide or command, even an avenue for the projection of aggressions and
hostilities.

### Ideology and Policy Issues

Even the most casual soundings of party rhetoric indicate an increasing
identification of partisans as "liberals" or "conservatives." Behind these
phrases lies a potent motivation to party activity: a commitment to clusters
of related attitudes about government and politics, especially about the
proper role of government in contemporary society. On a more modest
and limited scale the spur to activity may be concern for a single issue or
interest (tax cuts, the war in Vietnam, abortions, the maintenance of local

[11] James Q. Wilson, *The Amateur Democrat* (Chicago: University of Chicago Press,
1962), p. 165.
[12] John Fischer, "Please Don't Bite the Politicians," *Harper's* (November 1960), p. 16.

schools) or a single area of policy concern (foreign policy, civil rights, local planning). The "cause" may, indeed, be the reform or rehabilitation of the political party itself.

Just as the importance of the immediate, material, personal rewards of politics has recently declined, that of issue and ideology has increased. Even in Manhattan, long the fief of Tammany Hall, the trend is evident:

There is a "new look" among today's political activists. They are "respectable," solid middle-class citizens. The party "hack" of fiction, films, and the traditional literature is hard to find among the young, well-educated, affluent, and socially acceptable committeemen — and women — of the nineteen-sixties. Concomitantly, both the nature of political motivation and the character of political activity have changed. The contemporary politician considers his party organization an instrument for effectuating policy rather than a haven of personal security. He tends to be more interested in social reform than in catering to individual constituents.[13]

In national politics the country in 1964 witnessed the capture of the Republican national party by conservative partisans whose chief criterion for candidate and platform was frankly ideological. And in 1968 and 1972 the ideological left organized around the presidential candidacies of Eugene McCarthy and George McGovern, deeply affecting the presidential politics of the Democrats.[14]

The party activist may also be drawn to the party by a more general civic commitment. A sense of obligation and duty as a citizen, a belief in the democratic values of citizen participation, may impel him. Scholars who have questioned party workers about their motives for service in the party know the familiar answers. They were "asked" to serve, and they assented because it was their civic duty. Often that response, in whatever words it may be couched, merely masks what the respondent feels are less acceptable motives. Often, however, it is an honest reflection of deeply ingrained civic values. Often, too, it may be combined with honest, if vague, commitments to "good government" and political reform.

### The Party Itself

Two final varieties of incentive, both essentially related to the party per se, must be mentioned. First of all, as a party activist works within the party, the well-being of the party itself becomes an incentive for work. He attaches many of his loyalties and aspirations to the party, and its health becomes an end in itself. The party's wins and losses become issues in and of themselves, and attacks on it are far more than attacks on its policies

[13] Robert S. Hirschfield, Bert E. Swanson, and Blanche D. Blank, "A Profile of Political Activists in Manhattan," *Western Political Quarterly* 15 (1962): 505.
[14] Party ideology will be considered more fully in Chap. 16.

and activities. Second, it may be, as Robert Salisbury suggests in his study of St. Louis politicians, that large numbers of party activists participate "because they were brought up in a highly politicized atmosphere." The party "participant *per* family socialization was probably not exposed to involvement in other kinds of organizations, any more than a devout young communicant of the church would necessarily be taught to carry his devotion into other organizational settings."[15] In other words, party workers may gravitate to the party because they are accustomed to it and because through years of socialization they have invested loyalties in it.

No party organization depends on a single incentive, and very few partisans labor in the party for only one. Most party organizations rely on a variety or system of incentives. A residuum of patronage workers may coexist with workers attracted by policy issues or by a middle-class sense of civic responsibility. The mixture of incentives may vary between urban and rural areas, or between different local political cultures. One study suggests that at least in New York's Nassau County, issues and ideologies are a less potent incentive in the majority than in the minority party.[16] The mix may even vary within the same party organization. Eldersveld reports that in Wayne County, Michigan, the precinct chairmen depend heavily on the rewards of social contacts, whereas the party's higher leadership seeks a combination of immediate economic gain and ideological-philosophical rewards.[17]

For all the subtleties of the mix and variety of incentives, however, general comments about their overall frequency *are* possible. Scholarly evidence on the point comes from sporadic studies of parties in scattered parts of the country, but what evidence there is points to the dominance of ideological or issue incentives. Put very simply, the desire to use the party as a means to achieve policy goals appears to be the major incentive attracting individuals to party work these days.[18] And even though similar data are unavailable for earlier periods, there is ample reason to believe that this generalization was far less true of party workers a generation or two ago.

Indeed, incentives may change even for any individual — that is, the

[15] Robert H. Salisbury, "The Urban Party Organization Member," *Public Opinion Quarterly* 29 (1965–66): 562, 564. For additional intergenerational data see David R. Derge, *Public Leadership in Indiana* (Bloomington: Indiana University Institute of Public Administration, 1969).
[16] Dennis S. Ippolito and Lewis Bowman, "Goals and Activities of Party Officials in a Suburban Community," *Western Political Quarterly* 22 (1969): 572–80.
[17] Samuel Eldersveld, *Political Parties: A Behavioral Analysis* (Chicago: Rand, McNally, 1964), p. 278; see also all of Chap. 11.
[18] Lewis Bowman, Dennis Ippolito, and William Donaldson, "Incentives for the Maintenance of Grassroots Political Activism," *Midwest Journal of Political Science* 13 (1969): 126–39; Charles W. Wiggins and William L. Turk, "State Party Chairmen: A Profile," *Western Political Quarterly* 23 (1970): 321–32.

incentive that recruits people to party activity may not sustain them in that activity. Several studies suggest that a shift in incentive takes place in those party activists attracted by the purposive incentives — those who seek to achieve issue, ideological, or other impersonal goals through their party activity. To sustain their involvement in party work, they tend to depend more on incentives of social contact, identification with the party itself, and other personal rewards and satisfactions.[19] Perhaps an electorally pragmatic party — one traditionally committed to the flexibilities necessary to win elections — has difficulty providing the ideological successes to sustain the worker whose incentive remains ideological for any length of time.

## THE PROCESSES OF RECRUITMENT

The mere existence of incentives for work in the party organization will not automatically produce a full roster of active workers. In the political party, as in any other large organization, the organization itself must recruit actively in order to ensure for itself useful and compatible recruits. For his part, the potential activist may lack either the knowledge of the opportunity or the stimulus to act or both. There must, therefore, be some process of recruitment that will join the opportunity and the stimulus to the incentives in order to attract the activists.

However, the parties find it difficult to undertake this recruitment. Frequently their incentives are not attractive enough to compete even with the modest pleasures of activity in a local service club. They lack any effective mechanism for recruiting new personnel and they may even lack the awareness of the necessity for self-renewal. Furthermore, state statutes often take at least part of the recruitment process out of their hands; open party caucuses and the election of party officials at primaries tend to encourage self-recruitment at the expense of party initiatives and control. Above all, the chronic need for personnel of any kind disposes the parties to accept whatever help is available. Even patronage-rich organizations in job-poor communities tend not to be rigorous in recruiting new activists. Friendship and contacts within the party organization may speed the entry of the new activist more effectively than political skills or promise of performance.

In the absence of regular and rigorous recruitment by the party, opportunities for party work come in a haphazard way. Initially, a certain degree of awareness of and information about the parties is necessary, as are strong political goals and commitments. Then at the time of recruitment there must also be some more immediate occasion or stimulus for

[19] Among others, see M. Margaret Conway and Frank B. Feigert, "Motivation, Incentive Systems, and the Political Organization," *American Political Science Review* 62 (1968): 1159–73.

the individual to enter party work. Sometimes that stimulus is internal, and the individual in effect recruits himself. In other cases the stimulus is external, most often the invitation or persuasion of some individual. Activists tend to ascribe their initial recruitment largely to these external stimuli; two studies of local party workers have set the self-starters at only 10 and 29 percent of the interviewees.[20] In view of the favorable myth of the office seeking the individual, however, it may be that the party activists protest too much.

In sum, then, we have an extensive, informal recruitment system — a complex of interrelated factors that selects out of the American population a particular group of men and women. Its chief elements are:

— The motives, goals, and knowledge of the men and women with the kinds of skills and assets the parties want to recruit.
— The incentives to party activity which the party can offer.
— The external factors that alter the value of the incentive (e.g., the impact of employment levels on the value of patronage) or the ability of the individual to accept it (e.g., laws such as the Hatch Acts, which forbid active party work by United States civil servants).
— The factors that determine the party's recruitment role (e.g., the election of precinct workers at primaries).
— The contacts, opportunities, and persuasions that are the immediate, proximate occasions of recruitment.[21]

The components of this system change constantly, and as they do they affect the supply of personnel entering the organization and thus the organization itself. Recruitment in whatever form, though, is a matching of the motives and goals of the individual with the incentives and expectations of the party organization. The immediate act of recruitment is either the catalyst or the occasion for the matching.

An auxiliary recruitment system may also work within the organization to promote especially successful party workers to positions of greater responsibility. What data we have on the political careers of party activists, however, do not suggest that party workers uniformly inch up a career ladder in the party, position by position. For example, only about one-third of a recent group of county chairmen and cochairmen in Oklahoma had

[20] Phillip Althoff and Samuel C. Patterson, "Political Activism in a Rural County," *Midwest Journal of Political Science* 10 (1966): 39–51; and Lewis Bowman and G. R. Boynton, "Recruitment Patterns among Local Party Officials," *American Political Science Review* 60 (1966): 667–76.

[21] For an alternate but similar recruitment model, see the Bowman and Boynton article cited in footnote 20. C. Richard Hofstetter in "Organizational Activists: The Bases of Participation in Amateur and Professional Groups," *American Politics Quarterly* 1 (1973): 244–76, also concludes that individual participation is based on considerations much broader than simply responses to incentives.

ever held any other party office, and half of them had never held any public or party office at all.[22]

On the other hand, Detroit area party leadership tends to rise almost exclusively through the avenues of party and public office. One group comes up through the precinct positions, another through the auxiliary organizations (i.e., the women's groups, youth organizations, political clubs), and a third and smaller group moves from the race for public office to a career within the party.[23] In general, the way stations of a political career vary with the nature of the political organization. In those party organizations of relatively open access and easy mobility, careers in the party are easily, almost spontaneously, developed. In the disciplined, hierarchical party organization, the party activist works up the hierarchy in carefully graded steps and expectations.

## THE RECRUITS: AMATEURS AND PROFESSIONALS

Since recruitment patterns both change over time and differ from locality to locality, it is not easy to generalize about the activists they recruit into the party organization. Note, for example, the differences between the local committeemen and committeewomen of the Democratic parties of Pittsburgh and Manhattan and how these differences are related to fundamental differences in the incentive patterns:[24]

|  | Pittsburgh (1970) | Manhattan (1959–60) |
|---|---|---|
| Patronage holders | 74% of men, 42% of women | Approximately 5% "on public payroll" |
| Education | 17% attended or graduated from college | 67% attended or graduated from college |
| Age | 15% under 40 | 28% under 35 |
| Occupations | Overwhelmingly governmental | 19% business executives and professional; 24% small businessmen |

This is not to suggest that any single factor in the recruitment (in this case the presence or absence of the patronage incentive) fully explains the differences between the Democratic activists of these two city organizations. Differences of this sort may also reflect the kinds of personnel the organization wants and needs, differences in organizational roles and tasks (as between dominant and minority parties or between machine and club-

[22] Samuel C. Patterson, "Characteristics of Party Leaders," *Western Political Quarterly* 16 (1963): 343–44.
[23] Eldersveld, *Political Parties*, pp. 142–43.
[24] Hirschfield, Swanson, and Blank, "Political Activists in Manhattan"; and Lee S. Weinberg, "Stability and Change Among Pittsburgh Precinct Politicians, 1954–70," *Social Science* 50 (1975): 10–16.

style parties) or even differences in what the local community considers acceptable motives and incentives.

American party activists, despite all the variations of this kind, do have in common two characteristics that set them apart from the general population of adults. First, they tend rather uniformly to come from families with a history of party activity. Study after study indicates that large numbers of party activists had in their immediate family an adult party activist as they were growing up. Second, activists are marked by their relatively high socioeconomic status (SES), whether one measures SES by income, by years of formal education, or by occupation. The highest SES among the active partisans can be found, as one might expect, in the top leadership ranks of the parties. The parties thus attract men and women with the time and financial resources to afford politics, with the information and knowledge to understand it, and with the skills to be useful in it. Only some local organizations, and especially their precinct workers, have been exceptions; in general, only in patronage-oriented, favor-dispensing machines in the center cities are the party workers at all representative of the populations in which they work.[25]

In most parts of the country, however, Republican activists come from higher SES groups than do their Democratic counterparts. The Republicans' higher SES undoubtedly reflects their policy and ideological sympathies for higher income and status groups over the last generation or more. One exception to the general SES ascendancy of the Republicans does appear around the country. In one-party Democratic areas the dominant Democratic party attracts high-status leadership, probably because it is both "respectable" as the party of power and inviting as the party of opportunity.[26]

Within this overloading of high-status activists, one special dominance — that of lawyers — is too obvious to be overlooked and too well known to bear much elaboration. Lawyers are the high priests of the American political cult. Studies of county chairmen in Oklahoma, Kansas, North Carolina, and Wisconsin show a median percentage of attorneys among county chairmen somewhat above 20 percent. Recently more than 40 per-

[25] Minor parties may also be an exception to the relatively high SES of party activists. See, for example, James M. Elden and David R. Schweitzer, "New Third Party Radicalism: The Case of the California Peace and Freedom Party," *Western Political Quarterly* 24 (1971): 761–74.

[26] Patterson, "Characteristics of Party Leaders," pp. 332–52; and William J. Crotty, "The Social Attributes of Party Organizational Activists in a Transitional Political System," *Western Political Quarterly* 20 (1967): 669–81. On the more general SES differences between workers of the two major parties, see Richard J. Heuwinkel and Charles W. Wiggins, "Party Competition and Party Leadership Attributes," *American Journal of Political Science* 17 (1973): 159–69. It is also important to note that although party leaders do come from upper SES groups, by and large they do not come from the very highest, elite SES circles.

cent of the state chairmen around the country were also attorneys.[27] To an extent unduplicated in other democracies the lawyer in American society is the professional political careerist. Lawyers have cultivated skills in oratory and debate, and they are occupationally concerned with the actions of government, schooled in public issues, and practiced in parliamentary procedures. Naturally they appear to many Americans ideally suited for political leadership. The major parties even reserve for them a special type of political reward: the elective or politically appointive judgeship.[28]

Workers in the two parties tend also to vary in religion and ethnic background. In a significant number of localities across the country, the Democratic party organizations have larger percentages of Catholics and Jews, those of the Republican party higher percentages of Protestants. Similarly (and very much relatedly), Democratic workers more frequently than Republicans come from Irish and Southern and Eastern European national and ethnic stock. Republicans come more frequently from Northern and Western European backgrounds and from old Yankee families.[29] These interparty differences again reflect the basic voter coalitions of the two parties. Of course, there is a strong tendency for the activists of both parties to reflect the ethnic, racial, national, and religious composition of a homogeneous area. Although they are thoroughly representative of these groups, their education, income, and occupation (especially of the Republicans) will still be well above the average SES for the area.

So much for the social characteristics of the organizational activists. There remains the tantalizing and elusive question of their personalities and their psyches. On a common sense level, one can say without fear of contradiction that party activists are often gregarious and extroverted. That fact is apparent almost by definition alone, for party activity is not apt to appeal to the introvert or the misanthrope. But Harold Lasswell and others have argued that there is a special "political personality" — that political life attracts men and women with personal tensions that can be easily projected on public objects or with personal needs that can be sublimated or satisfied in political activity.[30] No convincing evidence exists, however, that the parties attract activists with any different or more pressing personality needs than the American population as a whole. One study, in fact, finds that the incidence of "authoritarian personalities" is not high

[27] Patterson, "Characteristics of Party Leaders," p. 339; Crotty, "Social Attributes," p. 677; Wiggins and Turk, "State Party Chairmen," p. 325.

[28] One cannot begin to summarize the literature dealing with lawyers in American politics. As an example, see Heinz Eulau and John D. Sprague, *Lawyers in Politics* (Indianapolis: Bobbs-Merrill, 1964).

[29] For example, see Weinberg, "Stability and Change."

[30] Harold Lasswell, *Psychopathology and Politics* (Chicago: University of Chicago Press, 1931), and also his *Power and Personality* (New York: Norton, 1948).

among party workers. (The few authoritarians do tend to favor both disciplined, hierarchical party organizations and nonideological party goals and activities.) [31]

Beyond social and psychological characteristics, it also matters what goals, expectations, and skills the activists bring to the party organizations. To a considerable extent, the goals and activities of the party and the men and women it recruits reflect each other. In fact, observers of the American party organizations have developed a two-part typology of party activists, based not only on their personal characteristics but on what role they play in the organization and the expectations they have for it. The terminology differs — the "old" style activist may be called the professional or the pragmatist, the "new" style the amateur or the purist (see box). Such types are, of course, abstractions rather than descriptions of specific individuals; they tend, therefore, to be purer and more extreme than one often finds in reality.

The implication of the amateurs and professionals for party organization is clear. A different party emerges with one type — or its predominance — than with the other. The nature of the organization, the way it makes decisions, what it does, and how it does it all differ. Above all, the new or amateur activists are more issue-oriented and insist on participation and agenda-setting within the organization in order to bring those issue concerns to the party. They are less comfortable with the traditional electoral pragmatism of the parties — that is, with the making of compromises in their positions in order to win elections. Indeed, they sometimes bring a new willingness to *lose* elections rather than compromise positions. To the extent that they stamp such a willingness on party organizations, they bring a profound change to the American parties. They also work a change of similar magnitude by bringing to the parties a strong impetus for reform — not only in the internal business of the party but also in its external environment by favoring, for example, the adoption of presidential primaries and the public funding of campaigns.[32]

## VITALITY OF THE PARTY ORGANIZATION

The party organization is an apparatus for recruiting political resources and mobilizing them in the pursuit of political goals. Some do it with strength and vitality; others are ineffective. For decades the American model or "ideal" in local party organization has been the classic urban

[31] Louise Harned, "Authoritarian Attitudes and Party Activity," *Public Opinion Quarterly* 25 (1961): 393–99.
[32] The same dichotomy between amateurs and professionals will also be examined in the national convention delegates in Chapter 12. On amateurs and professionals generally, see Dan Nimmo and Robert L. Savage, "The Amateur Democrat Revisited," *Polity* 5 (1972): 268–76; and C. Richard Hofstetter, "The Amateur Politician: A Problem in Construct Validation," *Midwest Journal of Political Science* 15 (1971): 31–56.

## Professionals and Amateurs: A Typology

|  | Old Style | New Style |
| --- | --- | --- |
| names; "labels" | professional, pragmatic | amateur, purist |
| SES level | above average | well above average |
| incentive | patronage, preferment | issue, ideology |
| governing role in party | "follower" | participant |
| expectations for party | candidate, election oriented | concerned with issues |
| locus of party loyalty | traditional party organization per se | officeholders, party clubs, and other auxiliaries |
| expectations for party leaders | full-time, vocational | part-time, avocational |

machine. Its organizational hierarchy, its full range of year-round services and activities, and its army of eager workers in the wards and precincts have traditionally represented organizational strength. It is an organizational form in which the personal attention, service, friendship, and persuasiveness of the local party worker are directed at the local electorate. All its activities through the year are geared to earning the support of that electorate and thus enabling the activists and office seekers of the party to deliver its vote and achieve their political goals through victory at the polls.

As the last chapter suggested, the ideal has never been the norm. The classic machine organization was never widespread in either of the two major parties in the United States. Its chief and indispensable ingredient, the local ward or precinct worker, has too often been inactive or completely absent. Recent evidence, even in the American cities, has begun to mount:

— Of party activists in St. Louis, some 27 percent did not perform "any significant amount of political or electioneering tasks." [33]
— Only about one-fourth of a group of workers in Massachusetts and North Carolina performed all four "critical" campaign tasks (door-to-door canvassing, telephone campaigning, transporting people to the polls, and talking to voters about the election); only one-half of them performed any three.[34]

[33] Salisbury, "Urban Party Organization Member," p. 557.
[34] Lewis Bowman and G. R. Boynton, "Activists and Role Definitions of Grass-roots Party Officials," *Journal of Politics* 28 (1966): 132–34.

— In the Detroit area only 13 percent of the Democratic precinct workers and 3 percent of the Republicans met criteria of organizational efficiency close to the model of the well-organized political machine.[35]

Were there comparable data on rural and small-town party organization, they would surely suggest even greater disorganization.

However, the organizational problem extends beyond inert or underactive committeepersons. Parties often cannot maintain the nexus of roles and relationships on which the organizational paragon depends. Eldersveld's study of the Detroit parties offers the fullest analysis. Communication lines in the parties, he found,

were not a perfect pyramid; communication was highly voluntaristic and noncoercive. From one-fourth to two-fifths of the precinct leaders did not have contacts with their district leaders, and from 10 to 15 percent seemed almost completely isolated. Further, the content of communication in the party seemed highly preoccupied with "vote getting" and campaign tactics.

Nor were authority relationships pyramided, for

the vast majority of precinct leaders were "little oligarchs," running their operations alone or with "friends and neighbors," with limited contact and involvement in district-level operations, and with limited reasons for self-consciously adjusting their work patterns and plans to perceive district-level demands.[36]

Throughout the Detroit parties, in fact, there was only diversity, whereas the ideal assumed monolithic homogeneity. Local workers entered and remained in party service for a splendid variety of motives. They carried out different tasks, even within the same party. They had differing political values and differing perceptions of political reality — even different views of their own and the opposing party. And they differed greatly in the way they perceived their roles as precinct leaders. The parties "did not communicate one particular role conception to rank-and-file leaders. The party line, if there was one, was confused and poorly communicated." As a result, some 45 percent saw themselves chiefly as vote mobilizers, 24 percent as ideological leaders, 18 percent as welfare promoters for local residents, and 10 percent appeared to have formulated no role at all.[37]

The search for the strong, vital party organization goes on — hampered, however, by the lack of agreement on what the ideal ought to be. For many partisans and observers the ideal remains the classic, turn-of-the-century urban machine. It is an ideal rooted in time and in the methods of campaigning and the electorate of a past era. Moreover, its operations are not acceptable to the new activists and the reformers, and voters can furthermore be reached by means other than the ubiquitous precinct

[35] Eldersveld, *Political Parties*, p. 348.
[36] *Ibid.*, pp. 377, 408.
[37] *Ibid.*, pp. 254, 270. No roles were ascertained for 3 percent of the leaders.

worker. What we need — but haven't found — is some common measure of strength and effectiveness for the political realities of the late twentieth century. In that search one scholar has proposed a two-part test: the extent of full-time staffing of the party organization, and its ability to control and limit competition for nominations to public office.[38]

Although the problem of assessing organizational strength has not been solved, the attempts at it go on. And although the shades of vitality in party organization are not easy to sort out, one can much more easily recognize dormancy or inactivity. So, it is possible to generalize roughly about the conditions under which organizational strength develops:

## Urban-Rural Differences

The close proximity of people in urban residential neighborhoods makes possible the intense political activity, the intricate organizational life, and the stable political loyalties of the highly developed political organizations. So, too, do the problems of the cities and the presence of the unassimilated minorities there. Any kind of intensive campaigning and regular contact with the voters — usual signs of strong and vigorous party organization — make far less sense in rural America. Party nominating and electioneering differ there, and so do the incentives for and the amount of party activity. Not surprisingly, then, the acmes of party organization have been reached in the urban, especially in the metropolitan, centers.[39]

## Differences in Political Cultures

The expectations that citizens have about political party organization differ. The persistent canvassing by committeepersons and their frank questions about voter preferences may be taken as a matter of course in some quarters but not in others. Similarly, patronage and the political organization founded on it may be respectable in some states or localities but not in others. What may seem a benevolent party organization in Chicago may offend a good many sensibilities in down-state Illinois. These differences in political culture tend to follow urban-rural lines, but there are also regional and social-class differences in norms and expectations for the parties.

[38] Ronald E. Weber, unpublished paper, quoted in Malcolm Jewell and David Olson, *American State Political Parties and Elections* (Homewood, Ill.: Dorsey, 1978), pp. 61–62.

[39] See Frank J. Sorauf, *Party and Representation* (New York: Atherton, 1963), especially Chap. 3. For a somewhat different approach to this issue with results not altogether different, see Paul A. Beck, "Environment and Party: The Impact of Political and Demographic County Characteristics on Party Behavior," *American Political Science Review* 68 (1974): 1229–44.

## Differences in Two-Party Competitiveness

Unquestionably the great number of defunct party organizations occur in the long-term minority parties. The Republican parties of the Deep South until the 1950s served for a long time as their classic illustration.[40] Badly demoralized and shorn of both influence and hope, the minority party easily lapses into organizational feebleness. It can provide none of the rewards, tangible or intangible, that induce individuals to give their time, skills, or money to a party organization. Its activists often lack respectability, much less influence in the community.

## Differences in State Statutes

The statutory forms and regulations of some states are more burdensome than those of others. All other things being equal, for example, a party is handicapped by a state requirement that all party functionaries be chosen at the primary. Even within a single state, inflexible statutory provisions limit the local parties that wish to innovate in forms of organization.

## Differences in Primary Laws

In a number of states with efficient party organization (Indiana, Connecticut, and Delaware come to mind) the organizations still nominate candidates for statewide offices and some local ones at conventions. That is, the direct primaries of those states are among the least comprehensive in the country, and in the case of Connecticut the primary did not come into being until 1955. Consequently, the party still had a vital nominating role left to it, a purpose and need for maintaining organizational capacity. Lockard wrote of the Connecticut parties before the primary:

In the absence of a primary the opportunity for political advancement lay with the organization, not through independent appeals to the electorate in a primary election. Local organizations had reason to exist even where there was little hope of winning an election for their party, for there were state conventions biennially in which important decisions were made. In contrast to many states in which the primary has been employed, there has been no appreciable withering away of the party organization in local areas.[41]

V. O. Key, in fact, has argued that the introduction of the direct primary into American politics in this century is primarily responsible for the atrophy of local party organization throughout the country.[42]

---

[40] V. O. Key, *Southern Politics* (New York: Knopf, 1949), Chap. 13.
[41] Duane Lockard, *New England State Politics* (Princeton: Princeton University Press, 1959), pp. 325–26.
[42] V. O. Key, *American State Politics* (New York: Knopf, 1956), Chap. 6.

This list of explanations of organizational strength is not exhaustive. And yet its collective effect surely goes a long way to explain why a number of observers find party organization stronger in the more industrialized states of the Northeast and Midwest and weaker in the South and West.[43] For it is the states of the North and East that are the most urbanized, the most competitive in elections, and the least devoted to debilitating primary elections and regulatory legislation.

## POWER AND DISCIPLINE IN THE ORGANIZATION

Organization implies discipline — at least enough discipline to coordinate its parts and to implement its decisions. It also implies some well-established system of authority for making those decisions. But many Americans have gone beyond these implications and imagined virtually authoritarian control within the party organization. Some leader generally identified as the boss has widely been thought to wield absolute power over its minions. Much like a Renaissance despot, he was said to rule by cunning, bravery, and force of will. The boss, in fact, became something of an American folk hero, feared for his ruthlessness and admired for his rascality and intrepid daring. He has been celebrated in the public arts,[44] and if he had not existed, it might have been necessary to create him, if only to justify the political cynicism of generations of Americans ( see box).

Very few organizational leaders ruled or now rule absolutely by personal magnetism, tactical adroitness, or the use of sanctions. Even in the era of boss rule, the boss's power was shared with influential underlings, and the terms of that sharing were deeply rooted in all of the hierarchical traditions of the organization.

The persistent attacks on "Boss rule" have misrepresented the nature of power in the old machine system. Power was hierarchical in the party, diffused in the way it is diffused in the army. Because the commanding general was powerful, it did not follow that the division generals were powerless. Tammany district leaders were important men, and, right down to the block captain, all had rights.[45]

Yet, it does remain true that in many of the classic political organizations, power and discipline were greatly centralized and largely removed from the control of workers and activists in the wards and precincts. The local leader had his rights, but they were bounded by the greater rights and authority of his superiors.

[43] See Weber's rankings of state party organizations reported in Jewell and Olson, *American State Political Parties and Elections*, pp. 61–62.
[44] For example, note Edwin O'Connor, *The Last Hurrah* ( Boston: Little, Brown, 1956), and Robert Penn Warren, *All the King's Men* ( New York: Harcourt, Brace, 1946).
[45] Nathan Glazer and Daniel P. Moynihan, *Beyond the Melting Pot* ( Cambridge: MIT Press, 1963), p. 227.

## The Boss in Cartoon

American artists at the turn of the century caught for all time the enduring American view of the urban political boss. Thomas Nast's portrait of Tammany joined a moneybag head to the body of Boss Tweed. Walter Clark's image needs no explanation.

Thomas Nast, "The Brains." From *Harper's Weekly*,
October 21, 1871. Metropolitan Museum of Art, New York.

Walter Appleton Clark, "The Boss."
From *Collier's Weekly*, November 10, 1906.

From Ralph E. Shikes, *The Indignant Eye* (Boston: Beacon Press, 1969), pp. 312, 321.

Much of that centralization was possible because the foot soldiers in the ranks accepted the hierarchical system of authority. If they were Catholics, and many were, the party's hierarchy may have seemed as natural and inevitable as that of the Church. Furthermore, goals were clear and simple. If they sought the patronage job, they cared little about what else the party did or did not do. More recently, however, party activists have come to demand a voice in the affairs of the party. A goodly portion of the ideological fervor of the amateurs may be directed at reforming the party's authoritarianism and bossism. They are committed to the norms and imperatives of democracy, at least in part because of a higher level of education and political information. Their commitment to intraparty democracy also follows logically from their desire to move the party to ideology, because the achievement of their own political goals hinges directly on the party's achieving congruent ones. So they must reform the American parties if they are to reform American society.[46]

It is not only participation, however, that is cutting into the discipline of the party organization. Discipline depends also on the ability of the organization to withdraw or withhold its incentives. Much of the discipline of the classic machine resulted from the willingness and ability of party leaders to manipulate the material rewards of patronage and preferment. The recalcitrant or inefficient committeeman sacrificed his public job or his hope for it. The newer incentives, however, cannot so easily be given or revoked. The party is only one among many organizations pursuing policy or ideological goals; and given the party's very imperfect control of its legislators, it may not even be the most efficient means to these ends. The ideologically oriented activist may find substitute outlets for his activities in interest groups or nonparty political associations such as neighborhood associations, the Americans for Democratic Action, or the John Birch Society.

Whether or not irresponsible power has been a fact within the party organizations, the American political culture is almost haunted by the fear that a few men, responsible to no one, will control the selection of public officials and set the agendas of policy making in "smoke-filled rooms." Understandably, the search for mechanisms with which to control that power has been a long and diligent one. The results fall into two broad categories: mechanisms that impose controls from outside the parties and those which look to internal controls.

## External Controls

Political laissez-faire suggests that two competitive parties will set limits to each other's exercise of organizational power by their very competition.

---

[46] Wilson, *The Amateur Democrat,* Chap. 5.

The argument, of course, directly parallels the argument of the self-regulating effects of economic competition in the free marketplace. If one party offers the electorate a shoddy political product or if it overprices its political goods, it will lose its political consumers to its competitor. Indeed, the current spread of two-party competitiveness may make that hope more credible. But one-partyism — the monopoly of the political system — negates the automatic corrective action assumed in laissez-faire theory; and some of the centers of greatest organizational power are without serious two-party competition. Mayor Richard J. Daley and his Democratic machine won reelection in Chicago with 78 percent of the vote in 1975.

The states have generally preferred statutory controls on party power to the unseen hand of competition. However, their disappointments have outnumbered their successes. In those states in which voters at the primary pick precinct committeepersons and other party officials, there are rarely contests for offices. Frequently there is not even a single candidate. And in other states the attempts to regulate the holding of party caucuses and conventions have not always guaranteed access to all qualified comers. At the 1964 Democratic national convention the members of the Mississippi Freedom Democratic party charged that they had not been admitted to the party meetings that elected county convention delegates and that when they were elected delegates, they had not been seated at the convention.

The effect of any of these external controls is extremely difficult to gauge. The most outrageous and blatant uses of party organization power in the United States have occurred in the one-party cities or regions. In many states statutorily protected access has opened the organization both to the competitions of other factions or oligarchies and to reinvigoration by new party personnel. And in all the states the direct primary has at least forced the parties to face the scrutiny of voters on one key decision: the nomination of candidates for office. In addition to these two mechanisms, the mass communications media and the other political organizations — by their watchfulness and readiness to criticize — set other limits on organizational power.

### Internal Controls

In his sweeping "iron law of oligarchy," Robert Michels declared 65 years ago without qualification that majorities within organizations are incapable of governing themselves. Organizations, he argued, are by their nature oligarchic or "minoritarian," for only the active minority has the experience, interest, and involvement necessary to manage the affairs of complex organizations.

Organization implies the tendency to oligarchy. In every organization, whether it be a political party, a professional union, or any other association of the kind, the aristocratic tendency manifests itself very clearly. The mechanism of the organization, while conferring a solidity of structure, induces serious changes in the organized mass, completely inverting the respective position of the leaders and the led. As a result of organization, every party or professional union becomes divided into a minority of directors and a majority of directed.[47]

To the extent that we are all believers in the myths of the bosses, the smoke-filled rooms, and the deals between oligarchs, we are all children of Michels.

The kind of intraparty democracy that Michels lamented, however, has little relevance to the nonmembership, cadre organizations of the American major parties. For who are the participating members, the ineffective majorities, here? The party in the electorate, which the states permit to choose some party leaders, are members in only the loosest sense. Only in isolated parts of the country have the parties developed bona fide membership organizations. There is, in the meaning of Michels, really no inactive majority within the American parties. The party organization is the cadre, and it is made up of activists — active in varying degrees, of course — who are reckoned as being "of" the party simply because they *are* active as workers, officers, leaders, or even hangers-on. Control of party power must, therefore, come largely from within the party cadre. The relevant question is not really so much one of control as distribution of power within the organizational leadership.

The distribution of power within most American party organizations can be described in Samuel Eldersveld's apt term *stratarchy*. It is "the enlargement of the ruling group of an organization, its power stratification, the involvement of large numbers of people in group decision-making, and, thus, the diffusion and proliferation of control throughout the structure." [48] Various levels of party organization operate at least semi-independently of other levels, even superordinate ones. Precinct committeemen, district leaders, even county officials freely define their own political roles and nourish their separate bases of party power. So "although authority to speak for the organization may remain in the hands of the top elite nucleus, there is great autonomy in operations at the lower 'strata' or echelons of the hierarchy, and . . . control from the top is minimal and formal." [49]

What accounts for stratarchy and the failure of top party leaders to cen-

---

[47] Robert Michels, *Political Parties* (Glencoe, Ill.: Free Press, 1949; originally published in 1915), p. 32.

[48] Eldersveld, *Political Parties*, p. 99. The term "stratarchy" comes from Harold Lasswell and Abraham Kaplan, *Power and Society* (New Haven: Yale University Press, 1950).

[49] Eldersveld, *Political Parties*, pp. 99–100.

tralize organizational power in the hierarchy? Weighing against the pressures of a centralized party oligarchy are these factors:

— *Participatory expectations.* Large percentages of the new party activists — accustomed to being beneficiaries of the democratic ethos in their service or fraternal clubs — expect to find it also in their political party. The organization, therefore, may have to tolerate or even "create" intraparty democracy (or consultation) to maintain vitality, to lift morale, and to achieve cohesion.

— *Controls of lower party levels over the higher.* The chieftains of the lower-level party organizations collectively make up the conventions or consultative bodies that select the levels of party officialdom above them. Patterson, for example, brings together data on the percentages of county chairmen from Oklahoma, Kansas, and Wisconsin who were delegates to state conventions (Table 4.1). Clearly, the county chairmen in these states are forces to be reckoned with in the state party organizations. Similarly, precinct workers or delegates often form city or county committees.

TABLE 4.1  **Percentages of County Chairmen Serving as Delegates to State Conventions**

|  | Oklahoma | Kansas | Wisconsin |
|---|---|---|---|
| Democratic delegates to state convention | 89.8 | 71.2 | 95.3 |
| Republican delegates to state convention | 86.7 | 84.3 | 100.0 |

*Source*  Data from Samuel C. Patterson, "Characteristics of Party Leaders," *Western Political Quarterly* 16 (1963): 346.

— *Internal competition.* Party organizations rarely are monoliths. They often embrace competing organizations or factions. Differences in goals and political styles produce continuing competition in the selecting of party officials and the mapping of party activities. In 1956 and 1957 in Wisconsin, at least some county party offices were contested in 39 percent of the Republican organizations and 59 percent of the Democratic.[50]

— *Organizational inadequacies.* This theme is sounded repeatedly in the study of the Wayne County, Michigan, party organizations. The mutual role perceptions of various party leadership levels do not "square"; there is no "neat overlap . . . between role perceptions. This divergence and

[50] Epstein, *Politics in Wisconsin*, p. 90.

lack of unanimity suggest no clear understanding or expectation in the party hierarchy as to specific tasks of those in precinct and executive board positions, either as perceptions by others or among themselves." [51] Communication among levels of the hierarchy is sporadic and discontinuous. Motivational and ideological structures differ widely and even conflict, both among levels in the hierarchy and from area to area in the organization.

Diffusion of power marks all but the exceptional party organizations. Top party leaders engage in much mobilizing and wooing of support within the organization; their consultations with middle-level leadership are endless. Even the ward or precinct leader with a small electoral following and a single vote at an important convention must be cultivated. And, above all, party leaders in the eras after those of "patronage and preferment" no longer command, for their commands no longer carry potent sanctions. They plead, they bargain, they cajole, and they reason — and they even learn to lose gracefully on occasion. They mobilize party power not so much by threats as by the solidarity of common goals and interests.

American party organizations have probably never commanded incentives and rewards at all equal to their organizational goals and ambitions. In that sense, they have been chronically "underfinanced." They never have been able to recruit the kinds of resources they would have to have in order to flesh out the party organization that the state statutes create. The thousands of inactive precinct workers and unfilled precinct positions testify to that poverty of incentive. The parties, therefore, have had no alternative but to establish organizational forms that permitted them to live within their means.

[51] Eldersveld, *Political Parties*, p. 111.

# 5

# National Organizations: The Uncertain Summit

So extreme are the traditional observations on the decentralization of the American parties that one is tempted to dismiss them as empty rhetoric or pure hyperbole. One noted scholar of the American parties has written:

> Decentralization of power is by all odds the most important single character-
> istic of the American major party; more than anything else this trait distinguishes
> it from all others. Indeed, once this truth is understood, nearly everything else
> about American parties is greatly illuminated. . . . The American major party is,
> to repeat the definition, a loose confederation of state and local bosses for limited
> purposes.[1]

Is it possible, one wonders, that these disparate, often disorganized, local party organizations are not subordinated to or coordinated by some higher party unit? Are the local and state organizations free to use the name and traditions of a nationwide political party for their own parochial interests without any control by the national party? Closer examination of the American parties reveals that what seems to be hyperbole is in truth a statement of reality. Power and authority in the party organizations are precisely that diffuse, and this fact colors virtually every aspect of party activity.

State and local party organizations of the major parties pick their own officers, nominate their candidates, take their own stands on issues, and raise and spend their own funds without interference from any manifesta-tion of the national party. Every four years they come together as a na-tional party to select a presidential candidate and write a platform, but they have historically been careful to leave behind only an enfeebled na-tional organization as they break camp. What appears to be a pyramiding of state party committees into a single, integrating national party authority,

---

[1] E. E. Schattschneider, *Party Government* (New York: Rinehart, 1942), pp. 129, 132–33; emphasis omitted.

therefore, is in reality nothing of the kind. Often the national committees serve only as arenas for the bargaining and jockeying among the powerful local and state organizations and presidential candidates within the party. The authors of the leading study of the national committees chose pointedly to title it *Politics Without Power*.[2] Indeed, it has often been said that in reality there are no national parties, that what we blithely call the national parties are merely coalitions of jealous, wary, and diverse state and local party organizations.

"Decentralization" is a highly relative term, for one party system's decentralization may be another's centralization. What standards we have can be found chiefly by looking at the status of national party committees and executives elsewhere. In 1957, for instance, the national executive committee of the Congress party of India refused to renominate almost one-third of the party's incumbent members of Parliament because it wanted instead to recruit younger candidates. Although that degree of control over the nomination of local candidates is rare, it is not uncommon for national parties to influence and even occasionally to overturn local nominations. It is also common for national party committees to attempt to enforce party policy on the party's members in the legislature. Socialist parties in Western Europe have for decades held their parliamentary parties to the party positions laid down by the national party executives, occasionally even expelling the legislator who refused to be so bound. The Democratic and Republican national committees have no such disciplinary powers, no such ability to control local nominations, not even the power to speak on behalf of the party on the issues of the day.

Ironically most other aspects of American life and politics are becoming more centralized. The mass media bring the same reporters, TV images, and columnists and commentators into homes in all parts of the country. Government in the American federal system has by any measure been increasingly centered in Washington in recent generations. Even the other two sectors of the party have been "nationalized" in the past few decades. The party in the electorate responds increasingly to national issues such as the war in Vietnam, to national candidates (especially those for the presidency), and to national party symbols and stands on issues. With that nationalization of politics, attention now centers also on the national parties in government: on the president for the party in power and on the congressional leadership of both parties. Can decentralization in the party organization persist in the face of all these other centralizing trends? It has persisted so far, even though there are already a few indications of greater national — that is, central — authority. Whether they will build into some

---

[2] Cornelius P. Cotter and Bernard C. Hennessy, *Politics Without Power: The National Party Committees* (New York: Atherton, 1964). Although the Cotter and Hennessy book is somewhat out of date on details, the general point of view and interpretation are still valid.

kind of trend we will only know with more experience. But before one turns to those emerging indications, the facts of the long-term decentralization in the parties must be faced.

## THE NATIONAL COMMITTEES AND NATIONAL OFFICERS

Technically, the nominating convention that each party holds midway in the year of a presidential election is the party's supreme national authority. But the convention's role rarely goes beyond the selection of presidential and vice-presidential candidates and the formulation of party platforms. It does ratify the selection of national committee members, and it does specify the structure and powers of the national committee. But since the convention adjourns *sine die* (i.e., without setting a time for a future meeting) until four years later, it can exercise no continuing supervision over the national organizational apparatus of the party.

The national committees of the two major parties were for years similarly composed. The drastic revision of the Democratic body in 1972 changed that (Table 5.1). The Democratic National Committee has now become twice the size of its Republican counterpart. More importantly, the Democrats have abandoned the confederational nature of the committee. Traditionally each state had been represented in both national committees on an approximately equal basis, regardless of the size of its electorate or the extent of its support for the party. States, not populations or number of partisans, were represented, much in the way that the United States and the Maldive Islands are represented equally in the United Nations General Assembly. That representational system overrepresented the state organizations of the smaller states, and it also gave roughly equal weight in the national committees to the winning and the losing parts of the party. The practical consequence was to strengthen the conservative wings of both parties, chiefly the southern and western segments of the parties. The newly restructured Democratic National Committee, however, gives weight both to population and to party support. New York and California each have eighteen members on the committee, and Nevada has four. That altered representation at the least establishes one necessary condition for revivifying the national committee.

Formally, the national conventions select the members of the national committees, but that action merely ratifies decisions made within the states. The state parties differ from each other in making their decisions, and in many states, the two parties choose their national committeemen and committeewomen differently. Among the four main methods — selection by state party convention, by the party delegation to the national convention, by the state central committee, and by election at a primary — the first is the most popular in both parties. In this welter of selection processes one point is worth noting. Although the parties' state organizations

TABLE 5.1   Composition of Democratic and Republican National
Committees: 1978

|  | Members |
|---|---|
| *Democratic National Committee* | |
| Chairperson and next highest ranking officer of opposite sex from each state, D.C., Puerto Rico, Guam, Virgin Islands, Democrats Abroad | 110 |
| 200 members apportioned to states, etc., on same basis as delegates to national convention (at least two per state, etc.) | 200 |
| Chairperson of Democratic Governors Conference and two additional governors | 3 |
| Chairperson of Democratic Mayors Conference and two additional mayors | 3 |
| Chairperson of Democratic County Officials Conference and two additional officials | 3 |
| Democratic leader and one other member from each House of Congress | 4 |
| Officials and representatives of National Committee and its auxiliaries | 10 |
| No more than 25 additional members | 0–25 |
|  | 333–358 |
| *Republican National Committee* | |
| National committeeman, national committeewoman, and state chairman from each state, D.C., Guam, Puerto Rico, and Virgin Islands | 162 |
|  | 162 |

can usually control the selection of committee members when they are
chosen by the state committee and by the state conventions, they are less
effective when the selection is by primaries or by national convention delegates. Especially in states that choose convention delegates in presidential
primaries, the delegation may represent voter support of a momentarily
popular candidate more than it represents the leadership of the state party.
A number of Democratic delegations in 1972, for example, were composed
of party newcomers and mavericks who were pledged to George Mc-
Govern. The old-line party leaders in the state had supported other contenders and thus were not delegates.

The chairmen and other officers of the national committees do not have to be — and often are not — members of the committees. They are elected and removed by the committees. Immediately after the conventions, however, tradition recognizes the right of the parties' presidential candidates to name the national chairmen for the course of the presidential campaign. The committees ratify their choices without question. And since the party of the president will continue to respect his choice of a national party chairman after the election, only the committee of the "out" party in effect selects its own national chairman. The committees generally have much greater freedom to select other committee officials — vice-chairmen, secretaries, and treasurers — many of whom come from the committee itself. In addition, both national committees select executive committees, which include the officers and from ten to fifteen other members of the committee.

Within this apparatus — supplemented, of course, by the national committees' permanent staffs — the chairmen dominate. The full committees meet only two or three times a year, and occasionally even less than that. As Cotter and Hennessy report: ˙

Collectively the national committee is not much more than a categorical group. . . . The national committee members have very little collective identity, little patterned interaction, and only rudimentary common values and goals.

Except for occasional meetings — largely for show and newsmaking purposes — the national committees may be thought of not so much as groups, but as lists of people who have obtained their national committee memberships through organizational processes wholly separate in each state.[3]

The other officers of the party are not especially influential, and the executive committees meet only a little oftener than the full committees. Like the full committees, they are men and women whose concern is state (and even local) organizational work rather than the building of a strong national party apparatus. So, traditionally the national chairman, with the permanent staff, has in effect been the national party organization.

In reality, the role of the national committees is flexible. If theirs is the party of the president, they may be little more than managers of the president's campaigns and builders of his political support. Indeed, during the Nixon years, the president and his staff managed his political matters, and Rogers Morton and Robert Dole, the Republican national chairmen, did little more than serve as liaisons between the president and party leaders around the country. Occasionally a president such as Dwight Eisenhower will shift the burden of distributing the federal patronage to the national committee and chairman. In the party out of power the chairman and committee must often bind up wounds, heal intraparty squabbles, help pay debts from the losing campaign, raise new money, and revivify the party

[3] *Ibid.*, p. 39.

organization around the country. The chairman of the opposition party may also speak for the party and as an alternative to the president's party.

As the role of the committee and its chairman shifts, so, too, do the job specifications for a national party chairman. Within the party of the president, he or she must be congenial to the president, representative of his ideological stance, and willing to be loyal primarily to the president (*see* box next page). Within the opposition party, the chairman will often be congenial to — or at least trusted by — the various factions or segments of the party. Frequently he or she is chosen for ideological neutrality or lack of identification with any of the individuals seeking the party's next presidential nomination. Experience in the nuts and bolts of party organization is also desirable. It is significant that the Republicans after the 1964 defeat replaced Dean Burch, a Goldwater ideologue, with an organizational pragmatist, Ray Bliss, the Ohio party chairman. The Democrats did likewise after their catastrophe in 1972, replacing McGovern's choice, Jean Westwood, with an old party "pro," Robert Strauss. As the job specifications vary, so do the hunting grounds for prospective chairmen. Historically, the parties have most frequently found their chairmen among state party leaders; lately, however, the parties have shown a tendency to select members of Congress (see Table 5.2).

Despite their shifting roles and those of their chairmen, the committees have fairly stable, ongoing structures and activities. Each has its research division, which charts trends and projections in election data. Each has a number of divisions working with a special segment of the party's clientele: women, minorities, intellectuals, and young people. Each is also prepared to offer advice to state and local organizations on running campaigns, maintaining good press and public relations, raising funds, selecting winning candidates, and keeping the party organization in repair. And each has a fund-raising arm with its finance chairman. In fact, staff and programs of the national committees now absorb annual budgets of between $1 million and $3 million.[4]

## THE SUPPORTING CAST OF NATIONAL GROUPS

Clustered around the national committees are a set of more or less formal groups that also purport to speak for the national party or some part of it. Some of them are creatures of the national committees, but their independent voices often undermine the authority of national committee pronouncements and actions.

[4] For a good brief section on the Republican National Committee and its operations, see Charles O. Jones, *The Republican Party in American Politics* (New York: Macmillan, 1965).

## A Democratic Chairman Comes and Goes: 1977

The chairman's lot is not always a happy one, especially if he chairs the national committee of the president's party. Neither he nor the committee ever seems to escape the domination of the president and the White House staff.

All of that seemed apparent at the very outset of the tenure of Kenneth Curtis as the chairman of the Democratic National Committee in early 1977. Former workers in the campaign of President Jimmy Carter were appointed to the positions of executive director, treasurer, and deputy chairman of the Committee. Nonetheless, Curtis bravely told reporters that "he expected to handle 'some of the political activity that's been in the White House' in past Administrations.... Asked if he might find himself in a subordinate role as party chairman, Mr. Curtis replied: 'No, I don't think so. If it turns out that way, I'll go back to Portland and practice law.' "

From Warren Weaver, Jr.,*The New York Times*, January 19, 1977.
© 1977 by The New York Times Company. Reprinted by permission.

Within the year, in fact, Mr. Curtis did return to Maine and the practice of the law. Two newspaper dispatches in December tell some of the story.

"Jody Powell, President Carter's press secretary confirmed rumors that had been circulating for several weeks that Mr. Curtis would leave as a result of widespread dissatisfaction among members of the White House staff about the way the committee was being run....

"... it has been an open secret for weeks in Washington that political advisors in the White House, including Presidential Assistant Hamilton Jordan and his political aide Mark A. Siegel, were unhappy with Curtis's relaxed, easy-going stewardship of the committee....

"Mr. Curtis conceded in a recent interview that 'certain people in the White House' were unhappy with his performance and added that he had never intended to be a 'career party chairman.' "

From Terence Smith, *The New York Times*, December 8 and December 9, 1977.
© 1977 by The New York Times Company. Reprinted by permission.

"Cheerfully conceding that the chairmanship of the Democratic National Committee under a Democratic President was inherently 'a lousy job,' Kenneth M. Curtis insisted today that he had not been 'hounded out of office' by a critical White House staff.

"Appearing at a packed news conference at Democratic headquarters just 24 hours after the White House confirmed that he would be leaving office, the outgoing chairman said:

" 'I tried it for nearly a year and simply decided I'd like to do something else with my life.' A moment later he added: 'It's not the sort of job that you lay down in the street and bleed to keep — not at my stage of political life.' "

*Ibid.*, December 9, 1977

TABLE 5.2    National Committee Chairmen of the Major Parties: 1955–80

| Name | Years | Political position at appointment |
|------|-------|-----------------------------------|
| *Democrats* | | |
| Paul M. Butler | 1955–60 | National committeeman from Indiana |
| Henry M. Jackson | 1960–61 | U.S. senator from Washington |
| John M. Bailey | 1961–68 | State party chairman in Connecticut |
| Lawrence F. O'Brien | 1968–69 | U.S. postmaster general |
| Fred R. Harris | 1969–70 | U.S. senator from Oklahoma |
| Lawrence F. O'Brien | 1970–72 | Former national party chairman |
| Jean Westwood | 1972 | Active in McGovern preconvention campaign |
| Robert S. Strauss | 1972–77 | Democratic national treasurer |
| Kenneth M. Curtis | 1977 | Former governor of Maine |
| John C. White | 1977– | Deputy Secretary of Agriculture |
| *Republicans* | | |
| Leonard W. Hall | 1953–57 | Party leader, former congressman from New York |
| Meade Alcorn | 1957–59 | State party chairman in Connecticut |
| Thruston B. Morton | 1959–61 | U.S. senator from Kentucky |
| William E. Miller | 1961–64 | U.S. representative from New York |
| Dean Burch | 1964–65 | Active in Barry Goldwater campaign |
| Ray C. Bliss | 1965–69 | State party chairman in Ohio |
| Rogers C. Morton | 1969–71 | U.S. representative from Maryland |
| Robert J. Dole | 1971–73 | U.S. senator from Kansas |
| George H. Bush | 1973–74 | U.S. Ambassador to the United Nations |
| Mary Louise Smith | 1974–77 | Cochairman of Republican National Committee |
| William E. Brock | 1977– | Former U.S. senator from Tennessee |

## The Regional Organizations

Within recent years both parties have begun to develop regional party organizations. The Republicans have systematically divided the country into a number of regions. The regional groups, composed chiefly of state party officers and executive directors, meet periodically to discuss issues and election strategy. In the past the Democrats in some areas of the country met more sporadically on their own initiative and outside of the auspices of the Democratic National Committee. The new Democratic Charter of 1974, however, instructs the national committee to create regional organizations. As of the present, however, neither party's regional groups have staffs or ongoing responsibilities. They are therefore a long way from being an intermediate level of organization between the state parties and the national committees.

### The Women's Groups

Both the Democratic and Republican national committees have for a long time had a "women's division" within their structures. In addition, both national parties also have national federations of state and local women's groups: the National Federation of Democratic Women and the National Federation of Republican Women. Even though both federations are officially independent of the national committees, they are in fact housed with them and work closely in support of them. Traditionally, they have always been responsive to the cues of national party leadership, and to find any instances of striking independence on their part would be difficult indeed.

These women's divisions and organizations now face a very uncertain future. They are in many ways monuments to the subordinate position women long occupied in the parties. Women have increasingly entered regular leadership positions in the parties within the past decade. A woman has now chaired each party's national committee for the first time in history (Table 5.2), and both parties showed a marked increase in the number of women at the 1972 and 1976 national conventions. Both parties have also eliminated the designated offices for women — for example, the party vice-chairwoman positions — which for so long confirmed their separate but unequal status. For their part, the more activist women want a role in the regular party organizations, or else they prefer to become active in non-party organizations (such as the National Women's Political Caucus). Certainly they do not have in mind the docile role that the parties' auxiliaries traditionally had.

### The Youth Groups

The Young Republican National Federation and the Young Democrats of America are both national federations of state and local youth groups. Both meet biennially in conventions to elect national officers and to debate and pass resolutions. "Young" in both instances means men and women to the age of thirty-five; indeed, the Democrats did not retreat from a maximum age of forty until 1971. Both parties also have federations of college organizations (College Young Democrats of America and the College Republican National Federation), which are similarly organized. In addition, the Republicans have attempted to set up high school units. But in this proliferation of groups, the first set is clearly the most important. Both the

Young Democrats and the Young Republicans traditionally have been represented on their party's national committee, and the major staff and funding for both is provided in substantial part by the senior party.

Unlike the women, the organized youth of both parties have been neither docile nor compliant. At local, state, and national levels they have often taken stands and supported candidates that embarrassed the senior party organization. The Young Republicans, for instance, had a long infatuation with Goldwater conservatism, continuing in it long after the regular leadership of the party tried to reflect a more centrist position. In the late 1960s and 1970s, their loyalties turned increasingly to the conservatism of Governor Ronald Reagan of California. The Young Democrats often stand to the left of their senior party organization. In 1969, for instance, their national convention called for repeal of all legal limits on abortion, for liberalization of marijuana laws, for recognition of Cuba and Communist China, and for an "immediate and total withdrawal of all American troops in Vietnam." That was, to put it mildly, a far cry from the platform that the Democratic National Convention had adopted a year earlier in Chicago.

The future of the youth organizations in both parties, like that of the women's auxiliaries, has been clouded by recent events. The adoption of the eighteen-year-old vote and the youth activism of the 1960s and 1970s brought thousands of young people into the main business of the parties and made them less willing to accept the status of tutelage which the youth organizations imply. Many of them had brought the Eugene McCarthy campaign to major contention in 1968, and many also went as delegates to the 1972 and 1976 conventions of both parties. In any event, membership in all of the party youth groups has fallen off, and signs of apathy are evident in all quarters. It may, indeed, be no exaggeration to say that the youth and women's groups are in good measure victims of the parties' willingness and ability to involve those very groups in their central business.

### The Party Governors

The state governors inevitably speak with authority in the councils of their national party. They have the prestige both of high office and of electoral success. Many lead or command the support of state party organizations. Many also head state delegations to the party's national conventions, and a few inevitably contend for their party's presidential nomination.

The organization of the gubernatorial presence in the national parties, however, is relatively recent. The Republicans were first. Led chiefly by the liberals after the Goldwater defeat of 1964, the Republican governors wanted primarily to create a counterweight to the party's conservatives. A few years later they established a full-time Washington office with financial help from the party's national committee, but their influence waned after the Republican victory of 1968. Like many of these groups within the national parties, the governors operate most tellingly in the power vacuums of an opposition party. Their declining numbers in the 1970s — there were only seventeen Republican governors by 1979 — also undermined their influence within the party.

By the 1970s the Democratic governors began to press for a role in national party politics. Their ranks bolstered by victories and their party even more disorganized in opposition than is usually the case, they sought a more prominent voice in the decisions of 1972. By 1974 they had achieved that voice and won representation, although in modest numbers, on the national committee. They had also demonstrated their strength in the adoption of the new party charter. Meeting only a month before the national party conference in December of 1974, the governors threw their support behind the compromise reform proposal that ultimately passed in the conference. All in all, their position in the party reflected their political position — a large, strong, and politically successful voice in a disarrayed party of opposition.

### The Party Notables

Both the Democrats and Republicans possess a group of party notables who exert informal but very real power in national party councils. Often they are distinguished citizens, former officeholders, captains of finance or industry, holders of famous names, or long-time contributors to the party coffers. Sometimes — as in the case of a distinguished Democrat, Averell Harriman — they are all those things at once. Sometimes they combine contacts in business or finance or distinguished military careers with service to the party. What the notables have in common, of course, is that they are notable, that they have visibility, entrée to important circles inside and outside of politics, and a vast reservoir of experience in public life or service.[5]

To say that these notables exist in each party and that they are influential, however, is not to say that they are organized or that they self-consciously function as an elite or establishment within the parties. The most concrete charges made about them in the last generation have been made by conservative Republicans against the domination of GOP affairs by an "eastern establishment" which was said to include old and famous names in law, finance, and journalism. Fear of its power dogged the personal ambitions of Nelson Rockefeller, widely seen as its most recent representative.

---

[5] It can be argued that the stars of entertainment, now more active than ever in party politics, constitute a new group of "notables." Shirley MacLaine and Frank Sinatra of the Democrats and John Wayne of the Republicans have been among the best known. They and their colleagues, however, are largely without experience in public office and probably without major influence in the councils of the party.

## The Ideologists and Issue Framers

Those partisans concerned primarily with issues and ideology have not found it easy to organize their concerns within the national parties. Groups with a tangential relationship to the formal organizations of the national parties have, however, sprung up from time to time. For example, the Ripon Society — named for the city in Wisconsin that claims to be the birthplace of the Republican party — in recent years has served as a voice for liberal Republicanism. The society, composed chiefly of young, East Coast academics and professional people, won considerable attention in early 1970 with a demand for the dismissal of Attorney General John Mitchell.[6] At the other end of the Republican spectrum, a group calling itself United Republicans of America continues to raise money for the support of conservative Republican candidates for Congress. The New Democratic Coalition, composed largely of the remnants of the McCarthy crusade, sprang up in the wake of the Democratic fiascoes of 1968, but by the mid-seventies it was replaced by two other liberal organizations: the Democratic Conference and the Democratic Agenda. Both were active in the party's 1978 mid-term convention. After the Democratic loss in 1972 the Coalition for a Democratic Majority attempted to speak for a centrist, perhaps even nonideological, position.

These ideological voices have largely been the work of outsiders, of partisans who have seen the party captured by an ideology, or a lack of ideology, unacceptable to them. On the other hand, the national committees have struggled since the 1950s to create policymaking bodies that could and would define stands on public issues for the broader party.

The most recent of them — the Democratic Policy Council — will serve as an illustration. Composed of sixty-six members, it was established in 1969 by the Democratic National Committee and designed primarily to make statements on national issues. Hubert Humphrey, the party's defeated presidential candidate, became its chairman. It quickly found itself between the stone and the hard place. The former supporters of the Eugene McCarthy and Robert Kennedy campaigns were suspicious of its old-style, centrist liberalism, and the party's congressional contingent was not happy when it took positions to the left of congressional preferences. The life and times of groups such as the Democratic Policy Council are complicated by the fact that they are not merely instruments for enunciating policy. A tip-off to their deeper purposes is found in the fact that they exist only in opposition parties. Their supporters generally intend them to prevent the party's congressional party from acting as the only spokesman of

---

[6] The attorney general was widely quoted as having dismissed the Riponeers as "little juvenile delinquents." A good deal of the society's work is, however, less dramatic and more scholarly than this exchange might suggest. See, for example, its report on the 1968 presidential elections, *The Lessons of Victory* ( New York: Dial, 1969).

the opposition party. That desire to compete with the congressional party stems mainly from disapproval of the relative conservatism of the party's congressmen. In the Kennedy and Johnson years the moderates within the GOP formed an All-Republican Conference with General Eisenhower as its honorary chairman. The Republican congressional leadership accepted membership with good grace if not with enthusiasm, but Senator Barry Goldwater, speaking as a conservative and as a seeker after the 1964 nomination, criticized it as a splinter group and an untimely reincarnation of the citizens' groups that had led to the Eisenhower draft of 1952. Also after the loss of 1976, the Republicans set up a "policy committee" within the ambit of the national committee.

The latest idea in mechanisms for debating national issues and ideologies is the national party conference held midway between the regular nominating conventions. The Democrats held the first two in American party history in the Decembers of 1974 and 1978. Both were held that late in the year, in fact, in order not to intrude on the congressional elections! In both conferences, too, there were strong pressures to forestall policy stands that might embarrass the party's officeholders. In 1974 the party's congressional leadership feared excessively liberal pronouncements. President Carter shared the same concerns in 1978 — as well as a more general concern about criticism of his administration — and the White House and the DNC worked very hard to prevent or moderate criticism. Consequently the two conferences were modest, largely affirmative affairs that excited no great interest in the party. There were complaints that they were too closely managed, and those who saw them as instruments for holding the party in government accountable were inevitably disappointed. Party officeholders, especially those in the Congress, stayed away in droves. And the general lack of enthusiasm extended to the party grass roots. While one-third of the 1,625 voting delegates in 1978 were *ex officio*, the other two-thirds were chosen in the nation's congressional districts where there was often a paucity of would-be delegates and a very low participation rate in selecting them.[7]

None of these subordinate groups or forums has been more than a small supporting character in the drama of American national politics. None of them generates much influence or speaks for large numbers of party voters or activists. But so relatively weak are the national party committees that the presence of even these groups tends to diffuse and disperse the modest aura of authority the committees have. By far the greatest challenge to the authority of the national party organizations, however, comes from the

---

[7] For an excellent report on the 1978 mid-term conference, see Elizabeth Drew, "A Reporter at Large: Constituencies," *The New Yorker* (January 15, 1979), pp. 41ff.

party's powerful members in office — its party in the Congress and in the White House. To the battle for control of the national party we now turn.

## WHO SPEAKS FOR THE PARTY?

Among the political parties of the rest of the world, it is not difficult to find examples of powerful, authoritative national committees. It is the rule that the national committees of political parties dominate the national presence and image of the political party and that they enunciate the ideology and the policy views of the party. The national committee is also the national center of authority within the party organization, maintaining substantial control over such matters as party finance and the running of party campaigns. That model of the highly centralized party is not, of course, even remotely applicable in the United States. Within the two major American parties, the national organizations — the party's national committees — long ago failed in their attempt to speak for the national party to the party's officeholders.

It is no exaggeration to say that national party organizations in the United States have been crippled in a collision with the American presidency. So pervasive has been the influence of the presidency on the national parties that the problem of control can best be divided in two: the situation in the party holding the presidency and that in the party out of power.

### The Party in Power

When the party holds the presidency, the president's program and record of decisions become the party's. It is the president who interprets the party's platform and the mandate of its voters. His preferences, whether embodied in the formal measures of the State of the Union address or tossed off more casually at a press conference, impose a policy on his party. He may consult the party chairman or other party worthies, but no one mistakes the presidential initiative.

The vitiation of the national committee and its apparatus reached new levels in the presidential years of Richard M. Nixon. In the early Nixon years an active and well-financed national committee staff worked closely with the president and the White House staff. Increasingly, however, national Republican strategy was formulated in the White House. The president's immediate political advisors — men like Harry Dent and Murray Chotiner, for instance — and even his immediate staff became directly involved in political party decisions. The White House tapes revealed that John Ehrlichman and H. R. Haldeman were repeatedly involved in the business of the 1972 campaign. That campaign was in fact headed by a Committee for the Re-Election of the President (the so-called CREEP) with another administration figure and old political crony, John Mitchell, at the helm. The national committee and its chairman, Senator Robert Dole, were pushed to the margins of party activity — far enough, indeed, for them to be completely ignorant and innocent of the Watergate activities.

Republican presidents have not been alone, however, in dominating their national committee and chairman. Under John F. Kennedy, the Democratic National Committee and its officers declined in importance as the president, his brother Robert, Lawrence O'Brien, and other Kennedy aides took over the dealing with state party leaders, the mapping of election strategy, the raising of party funds, and the issuing of party statements. Lyndon Johnson's relations with the national committee had two phases. First there was a period of dominance within the committee and its staff by Johnson men, many of them old Texas associates; later the president began to replace committee operations with those of his own White House staff and advisors (chief among them were Marvin Watson, formerly a chairman of the Texas Democratic party, and Kennedy's old advisor, Lawrence O'Brien). Initially in the Carter administration — and perhaps because Jimmy Carter came to Washington as an outsider in the Democratic party — he relied on a strong national chairman, Robert Strauss. After the Strauss chairmanship, however, relationships between the White House and the Democratic National Committee settled into more usual patterns. Carter men held the chief positions at the DNC, and the Carter staff in the White House held the entire apparatus on a short and tight rein.

This White House dominance of the national party does not necessarily please the state and local organizations of the party. Although they want a weak national party and headquarters, they want one that will offer them patronage, campaign help, and organizational advice and services. A vigorously political president, on the other hand, often wants the national apparatus to serve *his* interests. He wants its organizational skills to promote his political future, its pronouncements to assist his program, its dealings with Congress to help his dealings with Congress. He sees in the limited federal patronage an opportunity to achieve the goals of his administration or his political career rather than a set of rewards for workers in the state and local parties. Quite simply, it is not always in the interest of the president that the national committee attend to the wants of local party organization (*see* box).

### The Party out of Power

By contrast, in those four long years after presidential defeat, a national party suffers an almost incessant jockeying for the right to lead. The defeated candidate, the party's legislative leadership, the national chairman, and other party notables all purport to be the voice of the party. This

## The President and the Committee

President Jimmy Carter's relationships with the Democratic National Committee were surprisingly rocky, especially through the first half of his presidential term. As an outsider to both Washington and to his national party, he probably suffered at least in part from inexperience in the intricacies of Democratic politics. In any event, matters came to a head on April 1 (of all days!), 1977. Warren Weaver, Jr. in *The New York Times* of April 2 wrote:

"The Democratic National Committee formally rebuked President Carter today, accusing him of neglecting to consult Democratic state officials on Federal appointments and of sending political fund raisers into the states without notice. . . .

"Democratic observers at the meeting could not recall a comparable example of the committee reprimanding an incumbent President, much less one just beginning his first term with unusually high popularity ratings. . . .

"The resolution said it was 'required' that the following be done:

— The White House solicit recommendations and consult state party leaders before making appointments, and notify them before an announcement is made affecting a resident of their state.

— The White House work with state party officials in developing the activities of the Democratic National Committee.

— The national committee consult state officials before undertaking a fund-raising project in their state and, at the minimum, notify them of such activity."

Eventually President Carter apologized and made up with the committee. This episode may also have encouraged him to tighten White House control over the operation of the DNC. But the events of April, 1977 are interesting on their own account for at least two reasons. First, they document a rare falling-out between an incumbent president and the national committee of his party. Second, they illustrate graphically the decentralization of the American parties. Here was a *national* party committee reminding the president of its own party that he must not ignore the power and perquisites of the state parties — that he must make more concessions to the decentralized nature of the national party.

From Warren Weaver, Jr., *The New York Times*, April 2, 1977.
© 1977 by The New York Times Company. Reprinted by permission.

contention, furthermore, is over much more than policy positions and initiatives. It is also part of the continuing struggle to define the party's strategies and pick its next presidential candidate.

The formal traditions of American politics rather pretentiously label the defeated presidential candidate the "titular head" of his party. Whatever the term may mean, a losing presidential candidate must fight to maintain even a precarious influence in the party. How effective a voice he has in party policy depends on his own base of power within the party. All other things being equal, a candidate who lost by a few hundred thousand votes will maintain control better than one who lost by several million. His political skills, his policy orientations, his control of a state party, his taste for party conflict, even his own ambitions, also affect his power. In 1967 Richard Nixon, a Republican loser once removed, probably came closer to being a spokesman for the Republican party than did its most recent loser, Barry Goldwater. Similarly, Hubert Humphrey and Gerald Ford maintained greater leadership roles after their narrow defeats in 1968 and 1976 than did George McGovern after the landslide of 1972.

More commonly, however, the leadership of the "out" party falls to its leaders in Congress. The congressional party, simply because its legislative responsibilities force it to take policy stands, formulates the party position and challenges the program of the president. Its leaders are often featured in the newspapers and newsmagazines, and they approach something of celebrity status through television interview shows and snippets on the evening TV news. The role is easier to manage, of course, when the party controls the Congress. During the Ford administration even the relatively reserved Democratic leaders, Speaker Carl Albert and Senator Mike Mansfield, were thrust into national attention. But even though the Democrats control both the Congress and the White House in the Carter years, Senator Howard Baker, the Republican leader in the Senate, has assumed a leadership position in the Republican party strong enough to propel his name into consideration for the presidential nomination.

Failing to fill the role of enunciator of policy and issue positions, the national committees might more modestly be expected to function as coordinators of campaigns and party organization. But even in those electoral tasks, the national committees have not found a central role. What role they have generally centers on the presidential election. For that reason the organizational and activity level of the national committee is, like that of most other party committees in the United States, definitely periodic. It comes to life for elections and then sinks back into some degree of inactivity. Presidents and other national party leaders tend to view the national committee as one more party campaign organization, this one for the presidential conventions and campaigns of every four years. For their part, state organizations want a national committee that will render campaign assistance without imposing organizational or ideological control.

Even in the congressional elections the national committees defer in great measure to the powerful campaign committees that each party has organized in each house of Congress. These four party campaign committees — often referred to as the Hill committees — exist for only one purpose: the election of the parties' candidates to the Congress. They assist incumbent senators and representatives by providing speech-preparation services, television and radio tapes and scripts, press releases, legislative histories and roll-call research, photographic services, and campaign literature. For nonincumbent candidates — especially those in closely competitive districts — they provide campaign assistance that ranges from money and research on the record of the opponent to organizational help in the district and advice on the skillful use of press, radio, and television. Whereas the national committee deals with the party's national candidates, national image, and national issues, the Hill committees minimize national issues and candidates if it is prudent to do so in the essentially local elections with which they are concerned. They are thus one more force for decentralization in national party politics.

## THE NATIONAL PARTIES: TROUBLES AT THE SUMMIT

Like so many other groups in American life — the American Bar Association, the American Medical Association, the United States Chamber of Commerce, the large international trade unions, to mention only a few examples — the Democratic and Republican parties have an organizational structure that follows the lines of American federalism. Above the state organizational units the parties have erected a single national committee. But unlike so many federated organizations, the parties' national committees have never surmounted the autonomous power of the state and local organizations. They remain relatively powerless victims of the decentralization of American politics. The hierarchical form of American party organization deceives once again.[8]

The causes of national committee weakness are many. Like all American parties the national committee is a skeletal organization without any base of mass membership. Unlike state and local organizations, however, it lacks even the circles of workers and loyalists that sustain the cadre parties. Furthermore, it must depend on financial levies on the state parties (quotas) to help pay its staff and expenses, and state organizations may fall quickly into arrears on their payments when miffed or disappointed. Also, the national committees lack the full-time attention of their members, whose main concern is often state and local politics. Even the national chairman may be preoccupied with his own business or profession, with his role in state party affairs, or with a cabinet office or a seat in Congress. Even if he devotes full time to the job, the chairman rarely stays long

[8] For a good description of the relationships of the state party chairpersons with their national parties (including the national committees), see Robert J. Huckshorn, *Party Leadership in the States* (Amherst: University of Massachusetts Press, 1976), Chap. 8. Significantly, less than one-fourth of them consider the national party chairman either their primary or secondary contact with the national party.

enough to master the complexities of the national committee operations; from 1955 to 1979 the Republican and Democratic chairmen both averaged about two and a half years on the job.

Furthermore, the national committees have no sanctions over state and local organizations or over rebel congressmen and senators. They cannot control or even greatly influence nominations in the states. Even if the traditions of political localism did not prevent such intervention, the direct primary would. Nor can the national committee control the selection of local party officials; custom and state law prevent it again. And so far the national committee has not been able to develop the power of the purse as a weapon of national party authority. Above all, among the state party organizations there is no consensus, no unity that a national committee might reflect and that it might use as a base of power.

Consequently, therefore, the party in government dominates the national parties even more than it dominates the state and local parties. Incumbent presidents commonly turn them into personal organizations, and in the party that lost the presidential election they serve, however wanly and uncertainly, as an alternative to or a critic of the president and his administration. Thus the national party is in effect a presidential party. It reflects the struggle for the national constituency of the president rather than the local, far less "national" congressional constituencies. It exists to nominate and elect a president. And ironically, it is a national committee's victory in the presidential election that signals its own lesser role as the handmaiden of presidential power.

Is there then no hope of raising the stature and influence of national party committees? They might well expand their role under either one of two conditions. They would certainly be strengthened if they could win control of some of the resources of partisan politics. If the national committee were to control the distribution of party and electoral resources — campaign funds, for example — the present distribution of power within the parties would be sharply altered. But the campaign finance reforms of 1974 channel public funds to the presidential campaigns rather than to the parties themselves. Furthermore, alternative fund-raising schemes have been only fitfully successful. The Democratic National Committee emerged from the 1976 election with a deficit of more than $3.5 million, largely as a result of its failures in raising money for the Carter campaign.[9]

Alternatively, the national party apparatus would certainly be strengthened by the continued turn of party electorates and party activists to a politics of issue or ideology. Already men and women are increasingly brought to political activity by a concern for issues, and those issues and the ideologies related to them are more and more national in scope. Cov-

---

[9] Campaign finance will be discussed at greater length in Chap. 13.

erage by television and the other mass media focuses attention on national events, national issues, national personalities. State parties find it more difficult to isolate themselves from the currents of national politics and to base their appeals on local issues and traditions. Even such general ideological labels as "liberal" and "conservative" have meaning only in issues of national scope, and increasingly they have the same meaning in all parts of the country. Ultimately, if a national party were to be unified behind a national ideology or posture on issues and were to be peopled by activists loyal to it, it would inevitably express that unity in stronger national party organizations.

The centralizing forces are clearly more vigorously at work in the Democratic party in the mid-1970s. The McCarthy bid for the party nomination in 1968 and the McGovern candidacy of 1972 brought new ideologists into the party ranks. The Democrats have also tightened national control over the selection of delegates to the national conventions, a degree of national control over state practice unimaginable several decades ago. The Democrats have also adopted a new constitution (The Democratic Charter) and held their first national mid-term party conferences in 1974 and 1978. All were less vigorous than their original proponents had planned, but they nonetheless may be portents of things to come. Most striking of all, two committees of the party set up in 1968 and chaired finally by Congressmen James O'Hara and Donald Fraser actually included a national membership party for the Democrats in the proposed charter. They envisioned a national party in the European mode with personal membership (with dues from those who could afford them), a vital national organization, and party conferences that would write party policy for the party in government. The charter as it finally passed in 1974 contained none of this, of course. But for the moment the failure may be less important than the fact of the attempt.[10]

In short, there is already within the Democratic party more sentiment in favor of national party strength — or at least against the traditional localism of the parties — than there has ever been. Much or most of it is issue-centered. If it continues to grow, we may well expect increased support for proposals similar to those of the Fraser and O'Hara committees. If it does not grow and still persists, the question of reform and nationalization will continue to divide the party. All of these trends are, to be sure, less evident at the moment within the Republican party. It was the presidential party in the early 1970s, and these reforms are the phenomena of parties out of power. But it is hard to believe that nationalizing

[10] See Chap. 11 for a description of the recent battles in both parties over the nature of representation in the national conventions. See also Austin Ranney, *Curing the Mischiefs of Faction* (Berkeley: University of California Press, 1975), pp. 171–87, for a fuller account of the centralizing trends.

trends can or will strike only one of the two major parties. Both parties must respond in the long run to the same imperatives of the political climate and culture.

## A FINAL NOTE ON PARTY ORGANIZATION

We have come to accept large-scale organization as an important social reality in this century. In business, government, universities, and voluntary organizations, it is a time of complex social structures and of the bureaucrats who have become their symbols. We have every right to include the parties among them, but it is an inescapable fact that the parties, almost alone among our major social institutions, have resisted the development of large, centralized organization.

Even by the standards of the parties of the other democracies, the American party organizations cut an unimpressive figure. They lack the hierarchical control and efficiency, the unified setting of priorities and strategy, and the central responsibility we associate with large contemporary organizations. Instead of a continuity of relationships and of operations, the American party organizations feature only improvisatory, elusive, and sporadic structure and activities. And whereas the party organizations of the rest of the Western democracies have had a permanent, highly professional leadership and large party bureaucracies, the American organizations have generally done without a professional bureaucracy or leadership cadre.[11] One does not make a career in the administration of the American parties. The business of American party organization is largely in the hands of part-time activists, which is perhaps to say that its business and its organizational relationships require no specialists and no full-time professional care.

One is compelled to wonder at the reasons for the stunting of American party organization. In part it results from statutory limits and prescriptions. Traditional fears of political parties and party strength have certainly contributed as well. (There is little in American political values that would welcome an efficient or "businesslike" operation of the parties.) In large part, however, the underorganization of the American parties results from their fundamental character. They have been pragmatic electoral parties, involved chiefly in supporting candidates for public office and active mainly during campaigns. As such they have long been led and dominated, not by career bureaucrats, but by public office seekers and holders. Perhaps, too, the degree of pragmatic flexibility to which Americans have carried their party politics rules out the routine and the fixity of a large

---

[11] On party bureaucracy, see the perceptive article of Charles E. Schutz, "Bureaucratic Party Organization Through Professional Political Staffing," *Midwest Journal of Political Science* 8 (1964): 127–42.

organization. Organization is to some extent routine and unchanging, and it is therefore more compatible with the party of unchanging ideology or principle than with one committed to the adjustments necessary for electoral success. So the electoral preoccupations of the American parties have tipped the scales in favor of parties in government and against the party organizations.

# III

## THE POLITICAL PARTY AS AN ELECTORATE

In very few party systems is the gulf between the party organization and the party in the electorate[1] as great as it is in the American party system. Unlike most of the parties of the European democracies, the American party organizations have not been able to integrate the party's most loyal supporters into the party organization. Throughout the 1960s and into the 1970s the Italian Communist and Christian Democratic parties by themselves enrolled about 10 percent of Italian adults into party membership. On the other hand, membership groups within the American parties are very small and comparatively rare.

Nor have the American parties mounted any substantial programs to educate their loyal electorates into the programs and traditions of the party. American party organizations view even the most sympathetic voters as a separate clientele to be reinforced anew at each election. And those sympathetic voters, for all their protestations of loyalty to the party, also stand apart. They consider their obligations to the party amply filled if they support its candidates in a substantial majority of instances.

This party in the electorate, unlike the party organization, is largely a categorical group. There is no interaction within it, no structured set of relationships, no organizational or group life. And like any categorical group it is an artifact of the way we choose to define it. There is common scholarly agreement, however, that the party in the electorate is characterized by its feelings of loyalty to or identification with the party. In the American political context its people are the men and women who consider themselves Democrats and Republicans; they may even, in the loose usages of American politics, consider themselves "members" of one party or the other. In practical, operational terms they are the partisans who answer

---

[1] The term was popularized by V. O. Key in his *Politics, Parties, and Pressure Groups*, 5th ed. (New York: Crowell, 1964), p. 164. Key, however, attributed the term to Ralph M. Goldman.

either "Republican" or "Democrat" to survey questions such as, "Generally speaking, do you usually think of yourself as a Republican, a Democrat, an independent, or what?" [2]

The size of the American parties in the electorate depends, of course, on the measures of them we employ. The 1976 data of the Survey Research Center (SRC), for example, indicate the following breakdowns of party identifications within the American electorate.[3]

| | |
|---|---|
| Strong Democrats | 14.7% |
| Weak Democrats | 24.8 |
| Independents | 35.8 |
| Weak Republicans | 14.2 |
| Strong Republicans | 8.9 |
| Others (no answer, apolitical, other party, etc.) | 1.6 |
| | 100.0% |

If one groups all the partisan identifiers together, one defines two party electorates that account for almost two-thirds of American adults (62.6 percent). A more reasonable alternative might be to accept only the "strong" identifiers, totaling 23.6 percent of the American adults, as approximations of the two parties in the electorate.

Such estimates of the size of the party electorate, it should be emphasized, are exceptionally arbitrary. One can imagine other acceptable ways of measuring the party in the electorate. One might, for example, identify it with the party's regular voters, regardless of what loyalty they may or may not declare. (In 1976 about 37 percent of the SRC's national sample declared that they had always voted for the same party since they began to vote.) But there are good reasons for preferring the criterion of party identification. Strong party identifiers do tend to be the party's faithful voters. But they are more than straight-ticket voters. They have a degree of loyalty and emotional attachment to the party that substitutes in some measure for the formal act of membership in a party system in which membership is not common. They are also more apt to be active workers in the party. In short, the party identifiers bring fairly predictable votes

[2] The question is the chief one the Survey Research Center of the University of Michigan uses to determine party identification. The Gallup Poll (American Institute of Public Opinion) uses the following similar question: In politics, as of today, do you consider yourself a Republican, Democrat, or independent?

[3] The identifications here were developed in response to the question in footnote 2 and to a follow-up question that separated the partisan identifiers into strong and weak groups. The independents were also broken into the following subgroups on another question: independent Democrats, 11.7 percent; pure independents, 14.4 percent; and independent Republicans, 9.6 percent.

to the party, but in addition they bring loyalty, activity, and even public support to it.[4]

Despite their expressions of party loyalty, the members of the parties in the electorate are fickle and sometimes waver in the support of the party of their choice. The party organizations and candidates know that even their electoral support cannot be taken for granted; other appeals and loyalties may on occasion override even the staunchest party loyalties. And some loyalists — probably a minority — express a loyalty that is little more than an empty formula. They may be Democrats or Republicans in the same sense that many individuals call themselves "members" of a religious denomination even though they have not stepped inside a church for years. And yet for all of this, the members of the party electorates do vote for the candidates of "their" party and support its public positions with a faithfulness far beyond that of the rest of the total electorate. They tend, in other words, to be the party regulars and straight-ticket voters. They are the men and women who, in the argot of Madison Avenue, display the greatest partisan "product loyalty."

For all its uncertainties the party in the electorate does provide the party organization and candidates with a stable, hard core of electoral support. The reliability of this electorate releases the organization and its standard-bearers from the intolerable burden of convincing and mobilizing a full majority of the electorate in every campaign. But the party in the electorate performs additional services for the party. It is a reservoir of potential activists for the organization. Its members may also make financial contributions to the party, or they may work in a specific campaign. Those people who attend party rallies, who talk about politics and persuade friends, or who express any form of political enthusiasm in the community very probably come from its ranks. Its members are most active in perpetuating the party by socializing their children into loyalty to it and possibly activity in it. In sum, they give the party a substance, an image, a presence in the community, and the most involved among them constitute something of an auxiliary semiorganization that supports the work of the loyal party organization.

The party in the electorate is an alarmingly diverse group largely because the simple gesture of loyalty that defines it — a word or two in response to a stranger asking questions — means so many different things to different people. (Notice that we include people in the party electorate on the basis of their own attribution of attachment and not on the basis of actual voting, or activity, or contribution to the life of the political party.) Understandably, the boundaries of the party electorate are indistinct. In-

---

[4] For an examination of the alternatives in identifying party adherents, see Everett C. Ladd and Charles D. Hadley, "Party Definition and Party Differentiation," *Public Opinion Quarterly* 37 (1973): 21–34.

dividuals also move freely in and out of it, either to or from the more active circles of the party organization or the less committed circles of the electorate at large.

But a party in the electorate is more than a categorical group or even a quasi organization. It is also an aggregate of cognitive images. It is, in other words, a system of impressions, or an object of opinion and judgment, *within* large numbers of individual voters. It is a loyalty or identification ordinarily so strong that it assumes a dominant position in the individual's political cosmos. In this sense it is the "party *in* the elector." It acts as a reference symbol, a political cue-giver, and a perceptual screen through which the individual sees and evaluates candidates and issues. Loyalty to a political party is, therefore, often a dominant factor in the subtle calculus by which the American political animal sees, reacts, decides, and acts. And for voters and citizens, the political party of their cognitions may be far more real and tangible than any overt political activity or any observable political organization. For they react to what they believe and perceive. The political party of their perceptions may be only a loosely codified set of judgments and impressions of people, issues, and events, but for them it may be more real than the party of leaders, platforms, and organizations.

Since the American parties are still cadre parties without important membership contingents, the party in the electorate gives the party its mass, popular character. It is to the party in the electorate that people generally refer when they speak of Democrats and Republicans. It is certainly to the party in the electorate that the casual observer refers when he says, for example, that the Democratic party is the party of the disadvantaged or that the Republican party is the party of the small towns. Many of the differences in the programs and the public images of the major parties spring from differences in the segments of the American electorate that they are successful in enlisting. In fact, the interplay between the appeals of the party (i.e., its candidates, issues, and traditions) and its loyal electoral clienteles — each one shaping and reinforcing the other — comes very close to determining who and what the parties are.

All of this is not to suggest that the rest of the American electorate is of less concern to the American party. At no time can a party or its candidates find within its party electorate the majorities needed for election to office. Even though the voters outside the loyal party electorates have lighter commitments to party and issue, competition for their support is keen, for the two American parties are ever aware of the need for majority support. They cannot, as can some of the parties of the parliamentary democracies, fall back on a safely committed and heavily ideological 15 or 25 percent of the electorate. So they must mobilize majorities in part from vast, fluid, heterogeneous, often disinterested voters beyond the parties in the electorate.

The individuals of the American electorate, therefore, range along a continuum from heavy, almost blind commitment to a political party to total lack of commitment, not only to a political party but to *any* political cause or object. The competitive American parties do not ignore or take for granted any segment of that total electorate. The three chapters of Part III examine the electorate's variety and importance. Chapter 6 deals with the amorphous parties in the electorate, asking who are the Democrats and who are the Republicans. It is concerned, as we earlier suggested, with the party electorate as a categorical group. Chapter 7 takes up the party *within* the elector, the party as a set of cognitive images. It deals with the impact of party loyalty or identification on the political behavior of the individual. Chapter 8 focuses on the legal and self-imposed restrictions on the total electorate that limit the parties' attempts to activate their loyalists and recruit new supporters.

# 6

# The
# Loyal
# Electorates

For millions of Americans unconcerned with the intricacies of party organization, the group of party loyalists we call the party in the electorate *is* the political party. Much of the written history of American parties and politics has reinforced that impression. It has recorded the successes of the parties, not in terms of party organization, strategy, or activity, but in terms of the enduring blocs of voters supporting them. Thus the parties have been defined at various times as parties of the East or West, the North or South, the city or country, the rich or poor, the white or black.

This visibility of the party in the electorate, even though it is only a loosely defined categorical group, is one of the major sources of its importance. Its interests and involvements contribute significantly to the public image of the party, and its political goals and values will inevitably be impressed on it. That impact, however, is matched by a second. Within the cognitive mechanism of American voters, loyalty to or identification with a political party has long been the single most important influence on their political behavior. It colors judgments of candidates and issues, and it guides decisions on how to vote.

## TWO-PARTY DIVISIONS IN THE ELECTORATE

In the period since 1860 the two major parties have each enjoyed a time of long-run ascendancy. From 1860 through the presidential election of 1928, Republican presidential candidates won fourteen out of eighteen times. Their supremacy was broken only by the two victories of Grover Cleveland, each won by an eyelash margin, and by the two of Woodrow Wilson. Moreover, Wilson's initial victory in 1912 was built on less than 40 percent of the popular vote, a result of the fact that Teddy Roosevelt's Bull Moose candidacy split a sizable chunk of Republican votes from the regular Republican candidate, William Howard Taft. Furthermore, in this period the Democrats managed to set one record in futility; in the election of 1924 they won only 34.8 percent of the two-party popular vote for president.

Since the 1930s the Democrats have enjoyed a period of similar dominance. Of the twelve presidential elections from 1932 through 1976 the Democrats won eight, losing two to Dwight D. Eisenhower and two to Richard Nixon. Furthermore, in this latter period the Republicans set two records of their own in futility. In 1936 they won only eight electoral votes, the smallest number for a major party in modern times, and in 1964 Lyndon Johnson rolled up a record 61.1 percent of the total popular vote at their expense.

The same two periods of dominance are reflected even more dramatically in party control of the two houses of Congress (Table 6.1). The very fact that the cycles of control of Congress follow those of the presidency so closely lends further support to the conclusion that these are cycles of *party* ascendancy. Since the Civil War, in fact, on only three occasions (1956, 1968, and 1972) did a winning president see the opposing party carry both houses of Congress in a year of his election.

Behind the striking dominance of the Republicans from 1861 to 1930 and the Democrats from 1930 to the present lies the great probability that each party was the majority party in the time of its ascendancy. That is, during the period of its successes the dominant party commanded the partisan loyalties of a majority of Americans. Its loyal, supportive party in the electorate was large enough to guarantee victory in the great percentage of elections. The minority party could win only sporadically by overriding the dominant party loyalties with an uncommonly attractive candidate or an especially salient issue. That the Republicans were such a majority party before 1930 we must take more or less on faith. More precisely, we make that assumption in a projection backward of what we have learned about the American electorate and the power of party loyalty through public opinion surveys since the 1940s.

With an amazing regularity for the past generation, the American adult population has been preferring, identifying with, or expressing loyalty to

---

TABLE 6.1  Partisan Control of the Houses of Congress, 1861–1931 and 1931–79

|  | House of Representatives | | Senate | |
|---|---|---|---|---|
|  | Dems. | Repubs. | Dems. | Repubs. |
| 1861–1931 (37th–71st Congress) | 12 | 23 | 5 | 30 |
| 1931–79 (72nd–96th Congress) | 23 | 2 | 22 | 3 |

TABLE 6.2   Party Identification of American Adults: 1956–76

| Identification | Oct. 1956 | Oct. 1960 | Oct. 1964 | Oct. 1968 | Oct. 1972 | Oct. 1976 |
|---|---|---|---|---|---|---|
| Strong Democrats | 21% | 21% | 27% | 20% | 15% | 15% |
| Weak Democrats | 23 | 25 | 25 | 25 | 26 | 25 |
| Independents | 24 | 23 | 23 | 29 | 35 | 36 |
| Weak Republicans | 14 | 13 | 13 | 14 | 13 | 14 |
| Strong Republicans | 15 | 14 | 11 | 10 | 10 | 9 |
| Others | 3 | 4 | 2 | 2 | 2 | 2 |

*Source*  Survey Research Center of the University of Michigan; data made available through the Inter-University Consortium for Political Research.

the Democratic party.[1] Table 6.2 indicates the persistence of the Democratic party's superiority among the party identifiers.[2] It also illustrates the remarkable stability of party identifications in the United States — a stability so great in recent years that not even a popular president of the minority party, General Eisenhower, could jar it. Nor did Richard Nixon's sweeping victory in 1972 add any loyalists to the Republican ranks. Finally, it should be clear that such data on party identification do not assess patterns of voting but rather the fundamental loyalties to or preferences of party, regardless of the candidates and issues in any specific election campaign.

But more important than the question of how many Democratic and Republican identifiers there are is the question of who they are. From what educational backgrounds, what regions, what occupations, what religions, what social groups come the Democrats and the Republicans? On what bases of interest do the parties attract supporters and voters? Or, conversely, what experiences and values shape the decisions of Americans to align themselves with one party rather than the other? Why do some Americans identify with the Republicans and others with the Democrats?

[1] For the basic procedures and assumptions underlying this concept of party identification, see Angus Campbell et al., *The American Voter* (New York: Wiley, 1960). For a continuation of the analysis represented in *The American Voter*, see Norman H. Nie, Sidney Verba, and John R. Petrocik, *The Changing American Voter* (Cambridge: Harvard University Press, 1976).
[2] The data of the Gallup Poll (American Institute of Public Opinion) are very similar, even though the questions and categories are a little different.

|  | 1960 | 1964 | 1968 | 1972 | 1976 |
|---|---|---|---|---|---|
| Democrats | 47% | 53% | 46% | 42% | 48% |
| Independents | 23 | 22 | 27 | 31 | 29 |
| Republicans | 30 | 25 | 27 | 27 | 23 |

Gallup data for mid-1977 show further Republican erosion to 20 percent. Democratic strength was at 49 percent and Independents at 31.

## THE ACQUISITION OF PARTY LOYALTIES

It is a commonplace among Americans to say that they are Democrats or Republicans because they were born to the party, just as one was born to Methodism, Catholicism, or Christian Science. The processes of political socialization begin early in life as the child begins to become aware of political parties and absorb judgments about them. He soon realizes that one of the parties is the family's party, that it is "good," that it is "our" party. Even in later life many Americans recognize the early origins of their party loyalties:

> I'm a borned Republican, sister. We're Republicans from start to finish, clear back on the family tree. Hot Republicans all along. I'm not so much in favor of Eisenhower as the party he is on. I won't weaken my party by voting for a Democrat. . . .

> I was just raised to believe in the Democrats and they have been good for the working man — that's good enough for me. The Republicans are a cheap outfit all the way around. I just don't like the Republicans, my past experience with them has been all bad.[3]

Even though they do not often consciously indoctrinate their children into loyalty to a political party, parents are the first agents of political socialization in the American culture. Their casual conversations, their references to political events, and the example of their political activity are sufficient to convey their party loyalties to their children. And so stable are the results that the intergenerational similarities in party loyalty persist even when the children reach adulthood (Table 6.3).[4] Furthermore, parents with consistent, reinforcing party loyalties are more likely to produce strong party identifiers among their children. Those without party loyalties or with mixed loyalties produce offspring who are more likely to be independents. Interestingly, too, a number of studies have found that the relationship in party preferences between generations is greater than the relationship in political attitudes. Thus, as one writer has put it, "We have suggestive evidence that the socialization of the individual into a *party* is a much more direct process than the socialization of the logically congruent area of ideology."[5]

That the acquisition of party loyalties comes surprisingly early and easily is also one conclusion of a study of schoolchildren in New Haven,

[3] Angus Campbell, Gerald Gurin, and Warren Miller, *The Voter Decides* (Evanston: Row, Peterson, 1954), p. 92.
[4] Campbell et al., *The American Voter*, p. 147.
[5] Herbert Hyman, *Political Socialization* (Glencoe: Free Press, 1959), p. 74. The high degree of intergenerational similarity in party identifications is reaffirmed and explained in Paul A. Beck and M. Kent Jennings, "Parents as 'Middlepersons' in Political Socialization," *Journal of Politics* 37 (1975): 83–107.

**TABLE 6.3 Intergenerational Similarities in Party Identification: 1976**

| Party identification of children | Party of Mother and Father[a] | | | | |
|---|---|---|---|---|---|
| | Both Democrat | Both Republican | Both Independent | Father Democrat, Mother Republican | Mother Democrat, Father Republican |
| Strong Democrat | 24.0% | 3.6% | 7.1% | 9.9% | 14.4% |
| Weak Democrat | 38.1 | 9.1 | 5.3 | 22.8 | 15.8 |
| Independent | 26.7 | 31.3 | 73.5 | 42.6 | 32.9 |
| Weak Republican | 7.0 | 33.6 | 3.5 | 11.9 | 26.3 |
| Strong Republican | 3.8 | 22.0 | 8.8 | 12.9 | 10.5 |
| Other[b] | .5 | .4 | 1.8 | — | — |
| | (N = 1005) | (N = 550) | (N = 113) | (N = 101) | (N = 76) |

[a] The table omits a number of possible parental combinations involving small numbers (e.g., one parent allied with a minor party or apolitical).

[b] The category "other" includes loyalists of minor parties, apoliticals, and the usual "don't knows" and "no answers."

*Source* Survey Research Center of the University of Michigan; data made available through the Inter-University Consortium for Political Research.

Connecticut.[6] More than 60 percent of the fourth-grade children were able to state a party preference — a percentage, the author notes, close to the percentage the SRC data showed for the twenty-one- to twenty-four-year-old segment of its national adult sample. At this age, however, few of the children support their identification with much information about party leaders, issues, or traditions. Not until they are eighth-graders do they develop the supportive knowledge that permits party identification to become fully operative in the political world. At that age, for example, they begin to associate the parties with general economic interests or groups — with business or labor, with the rich or the poor. So, this abstract party loyalty is much more easily acquired than information about political issues and ideology.

The strong correlation of the child's party identification with that of his or her parents points to the family as a major socializer into party loyalty. It also suggests, of course, that both parents and children have the same experiences that shape party loyalties and that they perceive and react to them with the same values and the same perceptual mechanisms. Some offspring, to be sure, do leave the parties of their parents. Those whose initial identification is weak are more apt to change than those whose first party commitment is strong. But by and large, people hew to the first party loyalty, and the intergenerational agreement persists in the great number of cases.

Despite that stability of the initial party identification, we do know that the process of socialization, including the development of party identification, is no single, one-shot influence. At the least it involves a life-long series of refinements and reinforcements of the initial socialization. It may also be weakened or altered during adulthood by cataclysmic events, such as the Civil War, the Great Depression of the 1930s, or the unrest and upheaval in social values in the 1960s and 1970s. Although changes in occupation alone seem not to affect party identification, a change in life style, peer groups, or basic social attitudes often does. The initial entry into the world of work is one such crucial period. Beneath the stability of the aggregate totals of party identifications in the country, there are individuals moving in some direction across party lines at every moment. In the late 1950s and 1960s, at least, some 10 percent of the American electorate was shifting party identification between one presidential election and the next.[7]

In part the stability of these party loyalties results from the relative absence in the American political system of other agencies of political so-

[6] Fred I. Greenstein, *Children and Politics* (New Haven: Yale University Press, 1965). See also Robert D. Hess and Judith V. Torney, *The Development of Political Attitudes in Children* (Chicago: Aldine, 1967), especially pp. 80–81.
[7] See Douglas Dobson and Douglas St. Angelo, "Party Identification and the Floating Vote: Some Dynamics," *American Political Science Review* 69 (1975): 481–90.

cialization that might challenge the early influences of the family. Schools in the early grades often avoid political studies, and the main conscious educational attempt at political socialization — the high school civics course — may not have the impact planned for it. One recent national study concludes that there is no evidence that the courses have a significant effect on the political orientations of the great majority of high school students.[8] American churches generally steer clear of partisan commitments — contrary, for example, to the willingness of many European churches to support the various Christian Democratic parties of Europe. The American parties themselves engage in very little direct socialization; they do not maintain the youth groups, the flourishing university branches (which may have offices, lounges, and eating facilities), the social or recreational activities, or the occupational organizations that their European counterparts do.[9] Business and worker groups — especially trade unions — do engage in this kind of socialization, but often with a gingerliness one would not find as often in their European counterparts. Indeed, it has long been a maxim of American middle-class gentility that one does not discuss either religion or politics in polite company.

Thus adolescents and young adults find that their party loyalty is supported by a homogeneous political environment of family, friends, and secondary groups into which no new political socializers threaten to intrude. Friends, associates, relatives, and spouses have the same partisan loyalties that they do. In short, most individuals are "anchored in a matrix of politically harmonious primary associations — a result, to some extent, of conscious selection and of the tendency for the social environment to bring together people of like views." [10] But when individuals are not so anchored, they may alter their party identification. For example, when the parents' party identification is not congruent with their general social class characteristics — that is, when the political signals are not harmonious or homogeneous — their children are more apt to develop an identification with the other party.[11]

Party identification in the United States, therefore, has traditionally been acquired early and lingered late. For most Americans it has remained

[8] Kenneth P. Langton and M. Kent Jennings, "Political Socialization and the High School Civics Curriculum in the United States," *American Political Science Review* 62 (1968): 852–67.

[9] The new Democratic Charter promises new Democratic activity in this area. Article Nine sets up a National Education and Training Council and provides: "In order to encourage a lifetime of meaningful political participation for every Democrat, the National Education and Training Council shall attempt to reach every young citizen as they [sic] enter the electorate at 18 years of age." It remains to be seen if the Democrats can carry out those plans.

[10] Herbert McClosky and Harold E. Dahlgren, "Primary Group Influence on Party Loyalty," *American Political Science Review* 53 (1959): 775.

[11] Arthur S. Goldberg, "Social Determinism and Rationality as Bases of Party Identification," *American Political Science Review* 63 (1969): 5–25.

long after the stimuli for its formation were forgotten. But what has always been need not always be. At least one recent study suggests that the processes of initiation into party identification may be changing.[12] A recent national sample of twelfth-graders shows a lower than expected correlation with the party loyalties of their parents. That same group also contained a higher percentage of independents than one finds in the adult American population. It may well be that changes in family life and in the relationships between generations have reduced the effectiveness of the family as a socializer, or it may be that the mass media and other sources of information to which high schoolers are exposed have broken the family's monopoly on political socialization. Either possibility would presage a new set of socialization processes. It would probably also herald greater instability in the patterns of party identification in American politics.

## SOCIAL CLASS AND PARTY IDENTIFICATION

The processes of political socialization do not, however, explain the distribution of party loyalties in the United States. They describe how rather than why the individual acquires his particular party loyalty. And to some extent, explanations of socialization, resting as they do on parental influences, merely push the question back a generation.

The search for an explanation of these party loyalties should very likely begin with social class. It is probably true, as Seymour Lipset has asserted, that the principal generalization one can make about loyalties to the parties of the democratic world is that they are primarily based on social class.[13] We have referred before to social class and to socioeconomic status, and a fuller explanation of the terms is probably overdue. Much of the literatures uses them interchangeably (or almost interchangeably), but the preference here is for the latter term and its conventional abbreviation, SES. Socioeconomic status is simply the relative ranking of the economic and/or social deference the individual can command. But regardless of the rubric one chooses, status differences underlie the party electorates of the mature, industrial democracies with which one can most reasonably compare the United States. The very nature of economic and political development, and thus of the class differences of industrialized economies, seems to transcend the older party lines based on ethnic, racial, religious, or regional differences.

The signs and marks of SES conflict are scattered throughout American history, even in the preindustrial decades. James Madison, one of the most knowing observers of human nature among the Founding Fathers, wrote

[12] M. Kent Jennings and Richard G. Niemi, "The Transmission of Political Values from Parent to Child," *American Political Science Review* 62 (1968): 169–84.
[13] *Political Man* (New York: Anchor, 1963), p. 230.

in his famous tenth paper of *The Federalist* that economic differences are the most common source of faction.[14] Social and economic status differences clearly underlay the battle between the wealthy, aristocratic Federalists and the less privileged Jeffersonians. Then, almost a century later, William Jennings Bryan made the Democratic party the vehicle for the protests of the Grangers, the emerging Socialists, the Greenbackers, the Knights of Labor, and the Populists — all of them composed largely of the discontented and disadvantaged. Bryan ("the Great Commoner") came to the Democratic convention of 1896 as the voice of prairie Populism. He challenged the conservatism of Grover Cleveland in his celebrated attack on the gold standard and hard money: "You shall not press down upon the brow of labor this crown of thorns. You shall not crucify mankind upon this cross of gold." Stirred by the Nebraska prophet, the convention repudiated its conservative leadership and picked Bryan himself as its candidate. Despite his defeat, the Democrats twice (1900 and 1908) returned to him as their presidential candidate for the crusade against corporate wealth, eastern banking interests, and what Bryan liked to call the "plutocracy."

In many ways Bryan and the Democrats of 1896 appear to have been the harbingers of modern American politics. Bryan captured the Democratic party for the rural and agrarian interests in their fight against the new industrial and financial interests. The Republicans became the party committed to the pursuit of industrialization. Woodrow Wilson's "New Freedom" and its reforms reflected the Democrats' identification both with agrarian interests and increasingly with urban, immigrant, industrial have-nots. In the suffusing prosperity of the 1920s many of the class differences between the two parties were greatly muted. But in the elections of 1928 and 1932 they erupted again.[15]

The SES stamp on the parties became more vivid in the 1930s. The migration to the cities and the crushing impoverishments of the Great Depression were the events out of which Franklin Roosevelt rebuilt the Democratic party more firmly than ever as a party of social and economic reform. This intensification of the SES lines between the two parties was his "revolution" in party politics. His New Deal programs — labor legislation, social security, wages and hours laws — solidified the Democratic party's image as the party of the relative have-nots. Even groups such as the blacks, long allied with the Republicans as the party of Lincoln, were lured to the Democratic banner; the strength of SES issues even kept them as allies of southern whites in the Roosevelt coalition. In brief, Franklin Roosevelt buttressed the class divisions of industrialism by adding to

---

[14] See Madison's tenth *Federalist* paper: ". . . the most common and durable source of factions has been the various and unequal distribution of property."

[15] See the excellent account of this section of American party history in Everett C. Ladd, *American Political Parties* (New York: Norton, 1970), Chap. 4.

its conflicts the consequent response of government: the Welfare State. Its programs and expenditures heightened the stakes of socioeconomic status politics.[16]

All of this is not to argue that only socioeconomic status differences divided the major American parties in this century. But the evidence is very strong that it did constitute an important and possibly the overriding difference between them. However, only since the 1940s and the advent of reliable public opinion polling has it been possible to make fairly precise and confident statements about the attitudes, the SES, the party identifications, and the votes of individual Americans. Much of our analysis of electorates before World War II, therefore, rests on indirect evidence.

The relationships between party and SES in the 1970s are apparent in the nature of the two party electorates in 1976 (Table 6.4). The relationship lurks even where it is not obvious. The implications of the partisan differences in educational levels, for example, cannot be taken at face value. There seems little reason to suspect that the intellectually liberating experiences of formal education lead young men and women overwhelmingly to the true path of Republicanism. It seems more reasonable to suppose that the positive relationship between years of education and Republicanism results from the intermediating SES variable (i.e., a higher percentage of upper SES parents send their sons and daughters to college, and the college degree leads to higher SES). Also, given the higher SES of Protestants in the United States, their relationship with Republicanism unquestionably reflects in part those status differences. And there certainly is no need to elaborate the enormous SES differences between whites and blacks in the United States.

Furthermore, to the extent that Americans see themselves in different social classes, those differences relate strongly to their party loyalties (Table 6.5). In the survey reported in the table less than one percent of the respondents put themselves in either an upper or a lower class; they are therefore eliminated from the table. Within that simplified view of social classes in America, however, the partisan differences are abundantly clear. Republicans tend to see themselves as middle class, and Democrats are much more apt to consider themselves working class.

Yet, the lines of SES difference between the American parties are less distinct than their rhetoric and campaigns might lead one to expect. They are certainly less clear than comparable ones in European party systems.

[16] Among the histories of the American parties see Wilfred Binkley, *American Political Parties* (New York: Knopf, 1962); George H. Mayer, *The Republican Party: 1854–1964* (New York: Oxford University Press, 1964); William N. Chambers, *The Democrats: 1789–1964* (Princeton: Van Nostrand, 1964); Arthur M. Schlesinger, Jr. (ed.), *History of United States Political Parties*, 4 vols. (New York: Chelsea, 1973); Everett C. Ladd, Jr., *American Political Parties* (New York: Norton, 1970); Ralph M. Goldman, *The Search for Consensus: The Story of the Democratic Party* (Philadelphia: Temple University Press, 1979).

**TABLE 6.4  Social Characteristics of Party Identifiers: 1976**

| | Strong Democrat | Weak Democrat | Independent | Weak Republican | Strong Republican | Others[a] | Totals |
|---|---|---|---|---|---|---|---|
| *Race* | | | | | | | |
| White | 12.6% | 23.0% | 37.3% | 15.9% | 10.0% | 1.4% | 100.2% |
| Black | 34.1 | 35.7 | 23.5 | 2.7 | 1.7 | 2.2 | 99.9 |
| Other | 4.5 | 39.4 | 36.4 | 9.1 | 1.5 | 9.1 | 100.0 |
| *Occupation* | | | | | | | |
| Professional | 10.2 | 23.1 | 38.8 | 16.9 | 10.6 | 0.3 | 99.9 |
| Manager, official | 12.0 | 18.4 | 43.0 | 13.7 | 12.7 | 0.4 | 100.2 |
| Clerical, sales | 12.7 | 22.9 | 39.5 | 14.2 | 10.5 | 0.2 | 100.0 |
| Skilled, semiskilled | 19.3 | 25.7 | 37.8 | 11.8 | 3.7 | 1.8 | 100.1 |
| Unskilled, service | 17.9 | 29.5 | 31.9 | 12.1 | 6.8 | 1.7 | 99.9 |
| Farmer | 19.3 | 24.1 | 21.1 | 22.3 | 11.4 | 1.8 | 100.0 |
| Other (retired, etc.) | 12.7 | 25.7 | 31.6 | 15.6 | 11.0 | 3.3 | 99.9 |
| *Religion* | | | | | | | |
| Protestant | 14.5 | 22.5 | 33.7 | 17.4 | 10.7 | 1.1 | 99.9 |
| Catholic | 17.4 | 31.9 | 34.5 | 9.1 | 6.1 | 1.1 | 100.1 |
| Jewish | 24.4 | 31.1 | 37.0 | 4.4 | 3.0 | — | 99.9 |

**TABLE 6** *continued*

| | Strong Democrat | Weak Democrat | Independent | Weak Republican | Strong Republican | Others[a] | Totals |
|---|---|---|---|---|---|---|---|
| *Education* | | | | | | | |
| None through 8 grades | 23.2 | 29.3 | 22.4 | 13.6 | 6.7 | 4.8 | 100.0 |
| Some high school | 21.4 | 26.5 | 32.6 | 13.5 | 4.4 | 1.6 | 100.0 |
| High school grad | 12.9 | 25.1 | 39.3 | 13.4 | 8.2 | 1.2 | 100.1 |
| Some college | 9.3 | 20.8 | 43.5 | 15.7 | 9.8 | 0.9 | 100.0 |
| Baccalaureate degree | 7.4 | 18.1 | 39.8 | 16.0 | 18.4 | 0.3 | 100.0 |
| Advanced degree | 12.9 | 28.6 | 32.6 | 15.2 | 10.7 | — | 100.0 |
| *Family Income* | | | | | | | |
| $0–$2999 | 23.2 | 26.8 | 28.0 | 12.4 | 7.2 | 2.4 | 100.0 |
| $3000–$5999 | 19.3 | 30.7 | 27.6 | 9.8 | 10.3 | 2.3 | 100.0 |
| $6000–$8999 | 19.0 | 26.6 | 32.3 | 14.4 | 6.0 | 1.6 | 99.9 |
| $9000–$12,999 | 14.3 | 24.6 | 38.1 | 14.3 | 6.6 | 2.1 | 100.0 |
| $13,000–$19,999 | 11.0 | 24.6 | 45.2 | 11.6 | 6.3 | 1.3 | 100.0 |
| $20,000 and over | 9.9 | 18.5 | 37.4 | 19.9 | 14.3 | — | 100.0 |

[a] Includes respondents who prefer other parties, who are apolitical, or who won't or can't answer.

*Source* Survey Research Center of the University of Michigan; data made available through the Inter-University Consortium for Political Research.

147

TABLE 6.5    Social Class Perceptions of Party Identifiers: 1976

| Respondent's view of own social class[a] | Strong Democrats | Weak Democrats | Inde- pendents | Weak Republicans | Strong Republicans |
|---|---|---|---|---|---|
| Middle class | 35.1% | 40.8% | 48.6% | 51.5% | 70.2% |
| Working class | 64.9 | 59.2 | 51.4 | 48.5 | 29.8 |
|  | (N = 405) | (N = 684) | (N = 980) | (N = 394) | (N = 248) |

[a] Small numbers of respondents indicating "lower," "upper," and "other" classes have been eliminated from the table.

*Source*    Survey Research Center of the University of Michigan; data made available through the Inter-University Consortium for Political Research.

In a comparison of party identifiers in the United States and Norway, Campbell and Valen reported:

In both countries the occupational distribution of identifiers differs among the parties. In the United States, the differences are rather small. The Democratic Party draws 30 per cent of its adherents from the white-collar occupations, 46 per cent from the blue-collar. The Republicans come 36 per cent from the white-collar occupations and 39 per cent from the blue-collar. The occupational differences are very much greater among the various Norwegian parties. Of the Labor Party identifiers 79 per cent are blue-collar workers, 17 per cent are white-collar; among the Conservatives the proportions are 19 per cent and 76 per cent.[17]

Even the two Norwegian parties of the center, whose ideologies are not primarily economic, are more distinctive in their division of occupational groups than are the American parties. Furthermore, SES differences between the two parties are deteriorating at an increasing rate. As recently as 1968 almost 60 percent of the unskilled and service workers identified with the Democratic party; by 1976 it was 47.4. Similarly, the 62.8 percent of those with a grammar school education or less who identified with the Democratic party in 1968 shrank to 52.5 percent in 1976.

So we approach the conclusion of most observers of the American parties: that socioeconomic status and party loyalty are not so closely associated in the United States as they are in a number of the other Western democracies.[18] Both American parties have within their loyal electorates an important number of representatives from upper, middle, and lower status groups. Consequently, they find it difficult to formulate overt class appeals or to enunciate ideologies that reflect sharp class differences. The

[17] Angus Campbell and Henry Valen, "Party Identification in Norway and the United States," *Public Opinion Quarterly* 25 (1961): 514–15.
[18] See Robert R. Alford, *Party and Society* (Chicago: Rand McNally, 1963), Chap. 8.

heterogeneity of their loyalists is perfectly consistent with the parties' pragmatic, relatively nonideological tone, and with their mission as brokers among diverse social groupings. Thus the lines of SES division between the major American parties are indistinct and overlapping, and although SES is one explanation of interparty differences, it is by no means the only one.

The weakness of SES differences between the two party electorates may result partially from the imperfect translation of SES differences into differences in party identification. Among the influences muting the translation of status differences into political ones the following may be the most important:

— *The shifting SES lines of American federalism.* SES lines differ from state to state, and it is difficult and somewhat misleading to make aggregate, national comparisons using identical categories. The distribution of SES groups in Montana, for example, differs greatly from that in New York. Some large and powerful groups in New York — blacks, Jews, and urban unionists come to mind — are considerably less numerous and important in Montana. The Republican parties of the two states, therefore, recruit electorates that greatly differ in SES composition. By the sheer necessity of remaining competitive, the Republicans of New York will amass a more heterogeneous electorate than the Republicans of Montana.

— *The suppression of SES differences.* Some state and local party leaders obliterate SES lines (with decreasing success, probably) by fostering an issueless politics of localism and loyalty to personalities. For years the Democratic parties of the southern states were classic examples of that kind of determinedly non-SES politics. Furthermore, the ascendancy of non-SES issues such as abortion and the war in Vietnam inevitably mutes SES issues and differences. Furthermore, American mores do not encourage the perception of class or socioeconomic status. Many Americans do not see class divisions or conflict in the American society; at most they see themselves as members of a very broad and inclusive middle class.

— *The slowness of SES translation into politics.* The loyalties of party identification tend to respond only slowly to changes in SES. Many party loyalties formed early as a result of family influences, in fact, are responses to SES one or two generations late. The young man or woman socialized into the Democratic party by a working-class parent or an early work experience may cling to that party identification long after entering the business world and reaching the country club. Furthermore, party loyalties shaped as SES responses to depressions, recessions, or prosperity may remain long after the events have passed.

## ALTERNATIVES TO THE SES BASIS OF LOYALTIES

In view of the relatively weak SES divisions between the Democratic and Republican electorates, there must clearly be additional explanations for the distribution of party loyalties in the United States.[19]

### Sectionalism

The greatest challenge to the SES interpretations of American politics came historically from the school that ascribed the primary differences between parties to sectional differences. The sectional theories held that the varying geographic areas or sections of the country had separate, identifiable, and deeply felt political interests, which when honored and favored by a political party united large numbers of otherwise differing voters.[20] Thus the sectional explanations spoke of the Republicans' and the Democrats' building coalitions behind presidential candidates by joining the votes of one section to those of another, or of parties' dominating the loyalties of this or that section of the country.

Unquestionably the most enduring sectionalism in American party history was that of the Democratic party in the South. Even before the Civil War the interests of the South in slavery and in an agriculture geared to export markets had unified it. The searing experience of that war and the reconstruction that followed made the South into the Solid South and delivered it to the Democrats. United by historical experience and by a desperate defense of a way of life, the eleven states of the Confederacy cast their electoral votes for Democratic presidential candidates in every election from 1880 through 1924, except for Tennessee's defection in 1920. Al Smith's Catholicism frightened four of them into the Republican column in 1928, but the Roosevelt economic programs reinforced the region's economic interests — and in no way greatly challenged its way of life — and brought the South back to the Democratic party for the four Roosevelt elections. Only with the successes of the Dixiecrat ticket in 1948 did the South begin to move away from its traditional party loyalties.

Similarly, strong East-West differences have periodically marked American party conflict. In the early years of the Republic, the fading Federalists held to an ever-narrowing base of eastern seaport and financial interests, while the Jeffersonians expanded westward with the new settlers. Jackson, too, pointed his party appeals to the men of the frontier, and the protest movements that thrust William Jennings Bryan into the 1896 campaign

---

[19] Nie, Verba, and Petrocik explore the group and demographic bases of the parties in Chap. 13 ("The Party Coalitions") of *The Changing American Voter.*

[20] For a somewhat different and excellent essay on the nature of sectionalism, see V. O. Key, *Politics, Parties, and Pressure Groups,* 5th ed. (New York: Crowell, 1964), pp. 232–33.

sprang from the agrarian discontent of the western prairies. Many of the Populists' loudest complaints were directed at eastern capitalism, eastern bankers, and eastern trusts. Indeed, the geographical distribution of the presidential vote of 1896 is striking affirmation of sectional voting (Figure 6.1).

Sectionalism can best be identified by its most obvious characteristic: sectional one-partyism. When sectional loyalties have been strong enough to override all the other sources of party loyalty, they have unified the section behind a single party. When the sectionalism has endured, it has reinforced the one-partyism both socially and psychologically. Young voters learned that the dominant party was the party of the section because it was the defender of the style and quality of its life.

The pull of sectionalism has declined steadily within the past several generations. The isolation and homogeneity of life in the sections have yielded to a nationalization of life and interests in the nation. Sectional loyalties, of course, have not completely disappeared. Southern sectionalism awakened in a new guise in 1964 as five states of the Deep South supported Barry Goldwater, the Republican presidential candidate. They were the only states he carried beyond his own home state of Arizona. Then in 1968 George Wallace carried only five states on the American Independent ticket: Alabama, Arkansas, Georgia, Louisiana, and Mississippi. But

**FIGURE 6.1  States Carried by the Democratic Party in the Presidential Election of 1896**

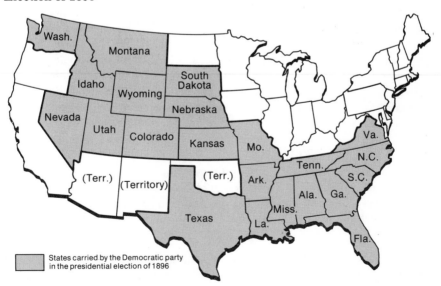

States carried by the Democratic party in the presidential election of 1896

elsewhere sectionalism now appears to have receded into a secondary position in the development of political party loyalties.

In retrospect, it is difficult to say what force sectionalism had even at its zenith. The great difficulty with the sectional explanations is that the term "section" may simply be an obscuring shorthand for a geographic concentration of other identifiable interests — ethnic, racial, or possibly SES. Much sectional voting in the past, for instance, reflected conflicts among crop economies in the various agricultural sections. Thus the central question: Are the sections themselves the basic source of sectional interests, or are they merely categories or concentrations of voters who identify with a party for other reasons? It means little to say that the Midwest supported Franklin Roosevelt in 1936 or that the West backed Eisenhower. To be sure, the South has been more than a descriptive category; its political behavior has been sectional in the sense of unified interests and an awareness of the region and its distinctiveness. But the case for sectional explanations weakens greatly as soon as one looks beyond the South.[21]

## Urban-Rural Differences

For a considerable portion of the twentieth century there was a conventional wisdom that, especially outside of the South, the Democrats were the party of the cities and the Republicans the party of the small towns and countryside. And it was probably so. The big-city political machines were overwhelmingly Democratic, and it was largely in the urban centers that the Democratic blue-collar workers and racial and ethnic groups lived. The Republican commitment to individual self-reliance and a limited role for government appealed to the less complicated ways of rural America. Beginning in the 1960s, however, the urban-rural division between the major parties became progressively blurred and muted. By the 1970s there is only an indistinct division in which, though the largest metropolitan areas show some preference for the Democrats, there are no real differences by party in any of the other urban or rural categories. And what differences remain can clearly be explained on other than urban grounds, especially on the obvious SES ones.

As the United States becomes increasingly urban and metropolitan — almost three-fourths of the American population in 1970 lived in some urban place or urbanized area — the question ceases to be one of urban versus rural America. It becomes one of distinction within the urban sectors, between different kinds of cities and different parts of metropolitan areas. Selective migration out of the older center cities promises to leave them ethnic, racial, and low-SES enclaves and thus inclined to be Demo-

[21] For a study of the end of Southern one-partyism at the level of the individual voter, see Paul A. Beck, "Partisan Dealignment in the Postwar South," *American Political Science Review* 71 ( 1977 ) : 477–96.

cratic. Urban diversity and two-party competitiveness may move to the suburbs and urban fringe areas.[22] But two related points seem clear on urbanism and the division of the two-party loyalties. First, what differences there are along or within urban-rural lines are largely socioeconomic, and as those SES differences in American party loyalties decline, so too will the urban-rural ones. Second, though a case can indeed be made that there are genuinely urban or rural or small-city interests in American politics, they have never stamped themselves on party loyalties.

## Religion

Even when income, education, and occupation are held constant, Catholics and Jews tend to support the Democratic party and non-Southern Protestants the Republican party. Again, however, the statistical relationships are only that; they do not necessarily identify cause. Perhaps despite the holding of some SES factors constant, there remains an SES factor. A Jew of high income, lengthy formal education, and professional occupation (the usual formal characteristics of high SES) may be denied by prejudice the status he might otherwise expect. The same illustration applies to some Catholics, but not with the force it had a generation or two ago when anti-Catholic bias was greater and when Catholic identification with the Democratic party was at its strongest.

Yet, it does appear that religion — both as theology and as group identification — is involved here.[23] A Jewish internationalism and concern for social justice, rooted in the religious and ethnic traditions of Judaism, disposes many Jews to the Democratic party as the party of international concern, support for the state of Israel, and social and economic justice.[24] In the case of American Catholics, the tie to the Democratic party is in great part a tie of personalities and political organization. The political machines of the cities were traditionally led by Catholics, and their patronage and largesse often went to the newly immigrated Catholics from Europe. The roll call of Catholics in Democratic leadership, furthermore, extends beyond the local bosses. Virtually all the national chairmen of the Democratic party in the first sixty years of this century were Roman Catholics. The Democratic party was also the party of the two Catholic candidates for the presidency: Al Smith and John F. Kennedy. The ties of Protestantism to Republicanism are less obvious, probably in part because of the enormous diversity of sects that Protestantism embraces. Very possibly, how-

---

[22] See also Benjamin Walter and Frederick M. Wirt, "The Political Consequences of Suburban Variety," *Social Science Quarterly* 52 (1971): 746–67.

[23] David Knoke, "Religion, Stratification and Politics: America in the 1960's," *American Journal of Political Science* 18 (1974): 331–45.

[24] Lawrence Fuchs, *The Political Behavior of the American Jews* (Glencoe: Free Press, 1956).

ever, the theological individualism of more conservative Protestantism disposes individuals to Republicanism; at least there has been a clear relationship in recent years between Protestant fundamentalism and political conservatism.[25]

## Race

Not too long ago the Republican party, as the party of Lincoln, the Civil War, and reconstruction, was associated with racial equality in the minds of Americans both black and white. In the generation between 1930 and 1960, however, the wheels of racial politics turned 180 degrees. It is now the Democratic party, the Kennedy and Johnson administrations, and Democratic Congresses that blacks see advancing racial equality and integration. Blacks identify with the Democratic party in overwhelming numbers and regardless of any other set of social characteristics. The 1976 SRC data show that 70 percent of black adults identify with the Democratic party and only 4 percent with the Republicans. All other indications suggest that Chicanos, Puerto Ricans, and American Indians also identify heavily with the Democrats.

## Traditionalism

Attachments to a political party need not be associated with an interest, a set of goals, or a group need. It is sufficient for some Americans that their party is the party of their parents, their friends, or their locale. Or that it is the party of their fellow workers or worshippers. For these identifiers it suffices to say, for example, "Everyone around here is a Democrat (or a Republican)." In some sections of the country the prevailing homogeneity of party identification may still reflect the loyalties of the original migrants into the area. Southern Illinois, settled by Democrats from the South, inclines to the Democratic party even today.[26]

## Party Leadership and Personalities

Individuals may identify the political party with a particular leader or group of leaders within it. They may attach themselves to the Democratic party as the party of Franklin Roosevelt or John F. Kennedy, or to the Re-

[25] The 1960 presidential election occasioned a spate of works on the religious factor in American party loyalties and voting behavior. See Scott Greer, "Catholic Voters and the Democratic Party," *Public Opinion Quarterly* 25 (1961): 611–25; and Philip E. Converse, "Religion and Politics: The 1960 Election," in Angus Campbell et al., *Elections and the Political Order* (New York: Wiley, 1966), pp. 96–124.

[26] For a discussion of these traditional loyalties resulting from patterns of migration, see V. O. Key, *American State Politics* (New York: Knopf, 1956), Chap. 8.

publican party as the party of Dwight D. Eisenhower or Barry Goldwater. For them the party is little more than an extension of an attractive, compelling personality, and their loyalty to it is in great part loyalty to that personality. Such an explanation of party identification, however, is probably easily overestimated. President Eisenhower, despite the magnitude of his victories and his personal popularity, made little dent in long-run party loyalties, even of those Democrats who voted for him.

## Issue Involvement

Well-informed citizens who are involved in political issues and ideologies will possibly identify with a political party because of the policy positions it takes. For most of this century, for example, the Democratic party has been more willing than the Republicans to espouse American commitments abroad, beginning with entry into the League of Nations and continuing today over questions of foreign aid. Republicans have on the whole been more chary of foreign involvement, more nationalistic, and more prone to isolationism. Other short-run policy differences may have had an equal impact. The issues of prohibition and the Noble Experiment of the Eighteenth Amendment have by now receded into the mists of American history. But in the 1920s and 1930s the question divided the two parties and probably some of their identifiers. The "drys," who supported the experiment, were largely in the Republican party, and most of its "wet" opponents were Democrats.

In the 1970s party identification seems related most closely to individual stands on the social issues — on those questions concerning government programs that guarantee a minimum standard of living or security for all Americans (Table 6.6). These are the issues of the Welfare State, the ones touching government medical care or insurance, guaranteed levels of income, social security, or welfare programs. Fundamentally they are questions of the redistribution of wealth, for the government taxes income progressively to provide programs of greatest proportional advantage to lower income groups. They are SES issues, one might say, because they propose different benefits for people of different economic status.

So, *this* is a major part of the SES connection in American politics. Clearly much of the partisan rhetoric and conflict of American politics runs along SES lines — whether it is a congressional debate over a poverty program or medicaid, a presidential speech on balancing the budget, or a state or local clash over a sales tax. The American electorate, even in its distribution of partisan loyalties, responds to SES issues. But the response comes not as the response of specific social classes or groups, but from individuals who for one reason or another have come to hold attitudes or views about the role of government and its social responsibility for the less advantaged. Americans develop what appear to be SES sympathies

TABLE 6.6   Opinions of Party Identifiers and Independents on
Government Responsibility for Guaranteeing Jobs and
Standard of Living: 1976

| Opinions on government role in guaranteeing jobs, standard of living | Strong Democrats | Weak Democrats | Independents | Weak Republicans | Strong Republicans |
|---|---|---|---|---|---|
| Positive | 25.1% | 15.1% | 9.4% | 4.7% | 6.1% |
| Slightly positive, neutral, and slightly negative | 52.9 | 59.1 | 58.7 | 52.2 | 43.1 |
| Negative | 22.1 | 25.8 | 31.8 | 43.1 | 50.8 |

*Note*  This table represents a collapsing of a seven-point scale of responses (three positive, one neutral, and three negative) between the two polar positions: that the government should have responsibility for jobs and standard of living, and that each individual should get ahead on his own. The categories on the left above group the center three positions in the middle with the two extreme positions on each side. It is also important to note that almost 32 percent of the national sample was unable or unwilling to express a view on this question.

*Source*  Survey Research Center of the University of Michigan. Data made available through the Inter-University Consortium for Political Research.

that are not necessarily congruent with their own SES. They may reflect some sympathy for the socioeconomic "underdog," some deference to the socioeconomic "overdog," or some identification with an earlier status of their own. They may even be acting on some personal vision of the good society. So, the relationship is not always between socioeconomic characteristics and party identification; it may also be between attitudes and party. And in politics, after all, it is the operational attitude, not the origin, that is important.

The force of issues on party identification is more complex than all of this suggests. For one thing, the attitudes on SES-type issues are for many voters absorbed into broader liberal and conservative ideologies. As one might expect, there is a considerable correlation between self-described liberals and Democrats, and conversely, between conservatives and Republicans (Table 6.7). And second, we clearly see the rising importance of non-SES issues in recent elections — issues of the war in Vietnam, violence and crime, and thus of "law and order," racial and sexual equality, and the new moral issues such as those of abortion and sexual freedom. Most of them cut across present party lines. Many of them have influenced a good many presidential votes in recent years. But so far they have not altered any party loyalties.[27]

[27] Warren E. Miller and Teresa E. Levitin, *Leadership and Change: The New Politics and the American Electorate* (Cambridge: Winthrop, 1976), pp. 213–14.

TABLE 6.7 Relationship between Ideological Self-Perception and Party Identification: 1976

| Voters' description of own position[a] | Strong Democrat | Weak Democrat | Inde- pendent | Weak Repub- lican | Strong Repub- lican |
|---|---|---|---|---|---|
| Liberal | 25.4% | 20.3% | 16.7% | 7.1% | 3.9% |
| Moderate | 22.1 | 25.1 | 29.5 | 25.8 | 12.5 |
| Conservative | 13.4 | 17.0 | 22.7 | 38.2 | 62.3 |
| Don't know, no answer, can't say, etc. | 39.1 | 37.6 | 31.1 | 29.0 | 21.4 |
| | 100.0 | 100.0 | 100.0 | 100.1 | 100.1 |

[a] The three categories represent a collapsing of a seven-point scale on the original question. "Liberal" here embraces three options: extremely liberal, liberal, and slightly liberal. "Conservative" includes answers to three parallel options. "Moderate" reports answers to that single option.

Source  Survey Research Center of the University of Michigan. Data made available through the Inter-University Consortium for Political Research.

## PARTY IDENTIFICATION IN FLUX

Party loyalties in the American electorate are more fluid than ever. The old ties to socioeconomic backgrounds, and even to attitudes or preferences on SES issues, are declining. It becomes harder and harder to say to what party identification relates and from what more basic attachments it springs. Fewer and fewer individuals, indeed, will declare it; the independents in the electorate rise inexorably. There is some evidence that changes in it are occurring more rapidly, and perhaps more casually, than ever. And even among those who still hold to some measure of party loyalty, that attachment seems to affect less and less of their political perceptions and behavior.[28] Furthermore, the consequences of these changes for the American parties can scarcely be exaggerated. Since the stability of the two major American parties has been grounded in the party as a symbol or a cognitive image, the decline of that symbolic strength "within" the American voter poses the most serious threat imaginable to the parties and to their traditionally central position in American politics.

The American party electorate has always been distinctive in that it is a group defined primarily by that loyalty and not by loyalty to an ideology or a class position (in which the party is merely a means to those ends). This very "partisan-ness" and heterogeneity of the American party elec-

[28] This point and its ramifications will be examined in the next chapter.

torates made them staunch allies of the two-party system, as Campbell and Valen have observed:

> The strength of these party attachments and the general weakness in the American electorate of ideological interest both serve to maintain the two-party system. The failure of various attempts to launch third parties appealing to the special interests of the farmers or the urban working class reflects the conserving force of these two attributes of the American party system. Deriving from the two-party system, they have become important factors in its preservation.[29]

What was most important, in other words, was not the composition of the two parties in the electorate but the depth and the durability of the allegiances behind them. It was precisely this willing loyalty on the part of so many Americans that undergirded the stability of the two-party system. As the quantity and quality of that loyalty declines, the change in the parties and in American politics will be fundamental.

The importance of these party loyalties is matched by their complexity. The coalitions that compose the Democratic and Republican electorates at any one time are built from complicated sets of influences. Among them are both SES and non-SES factors, those that relate to specific social interests or philosophies and those that are related to old traditions, to family preferences, or to group solidarity. It is, therefore, too simple to speak in dichotomies of rich and poor, black and white, city and farm. It is too simple even to look for single categories of explanation, single sets of influences. One might with a little imagination see these party electorates as thick sheets of plywood, each drawing strength from many different layers with their grains all running in different directions.

Especially because party loyalties are enduring, one must look not only at the complex influences of the day but also at those of past days. Party loyalists are added to a party's electorate in successive stages, in buildups of layer on layer. To understand those coalitions requires, therefore, a kind of political geology that explores the political strata of the past. Indeed, Walter Dean Burnham finds that issues of the 1964 presidential election — especially those with racial resonances — awakened in New York state some old electoral alignments of the nineteenth century. Beneath a dominant or overt cleavage characterizing the two party electorates at any one time,

> there are also latent or suppressed cleavages which may endure for decades without losing their capacity to influence voting outcomes. . . . [There] is the strong likelihood that American voting behavior in the present era is crosscut with a far richer mixture of overt and latent cleavages, cleavages of "ancient" and "modern" vintage, than has hitherto been supposed.[30]

[29] Campbell and Valen, "Party Identification," p. 524.
[30] Walter Dean Burnham, "American Voting Behavior and the 1964 Election," *Midwest Journal of Political Science* 12 (1968): 32.

Whatever may be the overt configuration of party loyalties at any time, there is no reason to think it will last for all time. It is thoroughly possible that a major American military loss or a crippling international oil embargo would elevate defense or foreign policy issues to a new power in determining party identifications. It is equally possible that a serious depression or a galloping inflation would reawaken and sharpen the old SES divisions. The determinants of party loyalties are themselves shifting, dynamic, and vulnerable to change. When they shift radically, we have those great and rare rearrangements of party loyalties called realignments. Most recently the events of the Great Depression of the late 1920s and 1930s established the SES coalitions that persist, although in weakened form, in the parties today. (Realignments will be discussed more fully in the next chapter.)

Not all the changes in the party electorates, of course, are sharp, fundamental, long-time realignments. Individual voters change their party loyalties at all times of the political season. Estimates have for some time put the figure at more than 20 percent. In 1976, for example, 21 percent reported they had made the change at least once in their lives.[31] Some events in the world, some change in their own lives, some change in the parties, some change in their perception of events or the parties, some new political influence in their lives — to suggest only some of the possibilities — had made them shift their partisan loyalties.

More important than these individual conversions in the short run are the changes new voters bring to the parties in the electorate. Their party loyalties have been shaped by the events and values of their generation, and those events and values may lead to new patterns of party loyalty and behavior. One need only look at the new voters who have entered the American electorate in the last ten or fifteen years. The percentage of voters between eighteen and thirty who call themselves independents is much higher than the percentage for the adult population as a whole (Table 6.8). Also it is clear that those who do pick a party are less inclined to the Republicans than are older voters. Furthermore, it is the younger voters who less and less translate their social class directly into a party choice.[32] Thus, as young voters enter the party electorates — or do not enter them — the shape of American party coalitions is slowly altered. But the result falls short of a realignment. Missing are the massive and radical shifts in party loyalties, the sharp alterations in the coalitions of voters making up the parties in the electorate, that one associates with realignment. Instead we have erosion and weakening in the status quo without the kind of renewal or "fresh start" that realignment brings.

[31] For the late 1950s the estimate was less than 20 percent; Campbell et al., *The American Voter*, p. 48.
[32] See Paul R. Abramson, "Generational Change in American Electoral Behavior," *American Political Science Review* 68 (1974): 93–105.

**TABLE 6.8   Percentage of Partisans and Independents
in Two Age Segments of the American Electorate: 1976**

|              | 18–29 | 30 and over |
| ------------ | ----- | ----------- |
| Democrats    | 35.1  | 41.8        |
| Independents | 48.5  | 31.9        |
| Republicans  | 16.4  | 26.2        |
|              | 100.0 | 99.9        |

*Source*   Survey Research Center of the University of Michigan; data
made available through the Inter-University Consortium for Political
Research.

So, change and yet stability mark the party electorates in the late 1970s.
We have experienced no realignment, and thus there is long-term stability.
But the short-term changes have been dramatic. There has been the persistent rise in the number of independents. The Democrats have lost support in the South as the Republicans gain it there. The simple SES lines
between the parties of a generation ago have deteriorated. Working-class
identification has risen among Republicans, and the Democrats attract
new support from the professional middle and upper-middle classes. And
yet — to complicate matters further — by 1976 the pace of even these
changes had slackened off. SES lines seem to have stabilized, and the
growth of the independents seems to be leveling off for the moment.

In this pause in recent trends the parties thus find themselves with
exceptionally diverse, potentially fluid electorates. They are so diverse
that the parties will in the future surely find it difficult to keep all parts
of them happy. At the very least, the candidates of the parties will find
it a challenge to unite them at any one election.

That the bases and divisions of the party electorates seem less and less
clear is perhaps only an analytical nuisance. That only a shrinking percentage of Americans is willing to join a party electorate is a challenge
to party politics as we have recently known them. But the possibility that
the force of the party "in" the voters is weakening, that the effect of party
loyalties on their political perceptions and decisions matters less, threatens
the very future of the American two-party system. To that question we
now turn.

# 7

# The
# Party within
# the Elector

The hyperactive world of American politics is difficult to understand at best. The contests of parties and candidates, the overlapping layers of party organization, the hyperbole of political charge and countercharge may baffle even the highly politicized and active party workers. The confusion is inevitably greater among the less experienced and involved members of the party electorate. Their best guide to this trackless political world is their party identification. Donald Stokes has written:

> In view of the fact that very few Americans have very deep interest in politics, it is a mild paradox that party loyalties should be so widespread. A partial key to this puzzle is that these identifications perform for the citizen an exceedingly useful evaluative function. To the average person the affairs of government are remote and complex, and yet the average citizen is asked periodically to formulate opinions about those affairs. At the very least, he has to decide how he will vote, what choice he will make between candidates offering different programs and very different versions of contemporary political events. In this dilemma, having the party symbol stamped on certain candidates, certain issue positions, certain interpretations of political reality is of great psychological convenience.[1]

The political party, therefore, exists in two forms for individuals. Obviously they can see the party of the real world — the party of conventions, candidates, campaigns, and organizations. But they also come to depend on a cognitive party — the party of attitudes, goals, and loyalties, the party *within the elector*. This party is an organizing point of view, a screen or framework through which the individual sees political reality and in terms of which he organizes it in his own mind. We all perceive the world about us selectively, and for the committed partisan, the member of the party electorate, party loyalty is the key to the selectivity. Because the party identification will very likely be the most enduring political attachment, it serves as something of a political gyroscope, stabilizing political outlooks against the buffetings of changing political currents.

[1] Donald E. Stokes, "Party Loyalty and the Likelihood of Deviating Elections," in Angus Campbell et al., *Elections and the Political Order* (New York: Wiley, 1966), pp. 126–27.

Before we go on to a discussion of the influence of party identification, three general points ought to be established about the party identification itself. First of all, it is remarkably unchanging, despite all the flux of American politics. The distribution of loyalists between the two parties has been very stable (see Table 6.2). Since 1952 the Democratic identifiers have remained between 40 and 52 percent. And at the level of the individual, SRC data for the 1976 election show that only about one out of five Americans had had different loyalties at any earlier time in their lives.

Second, party identification is the major key to the political behavior of the American adult. Knowing that one fact about a person or a group tells us more about their political perceptions and political activities than does any other fact. It is the single most important influence on the political behavior of the American adult.[2]

Third, party identification, still powerful though it may be, is today less dominant than it was ten or twenty years ago. In fact, the 1972 election was, according to SRC analysis, the first presidential election in its experience in which party identification was no more important than issues in determining the outcome of the election. So, even though party identification was once again the major key to the outcome of the 1976 elections, we are less certain than we once were of its continuing primacy.


## IDENTIFICATION, PARTY, AND POLITICAL ACTIVITY

The stronger the party identification, the greater is the probability that the individual will be active in politics generally and active in a political party in particular. The individuals with the strongest party identifications are more likely

— To evince an interest in coming elections, to express a concern about their outcome, and to think their outcome makes a difference.
— To follow the newspaper, magazine, television, and radio reports about politics or a campaign, and to be present at the events of the campaign themselves.
— To talk with their friends about the election and to try to persuade them to support a party candidate. For example, in 1976 the "strong party identifiers" were almost two times more likely to be "very much interested" in the election campaign than were other American adults.

To put these relationships in more general terms, the men and women whose political interest and activity place them within or very close to

---

[2] This chapter is concerned only with party identification and its influences and impacts. It is by no means an attempt to deal with the entire range of American political or voting behavior.

TABLE 7.1  Perceptions of Party Identifiers and Independents about the Ideological Positions of the Democrats and Republicans: 1976

|  | Strong Demo- crats | Weak Demo- crats | Inde- pendents | Weak Repub- licans | Strong Repub- licans |
|---|---|---|---|---|---|
| *Perceptions of Democrats* |  |  |  |  |  |
| Extremely liberal, liberal | 39.6% | 34.2% | 35.5% | 51.9% | 68.9% |
| Slightly liberal, moderate | 42.0 | 46.5 | 49.3 | 39.1 | 27.5 |
| *Perceptions of Republicans* |  |  |  |  |  |
| Extremely conservative, conservative | 54.1 | 43.1 | 34.6 | 37.0 | 34.2 |
| Slightly conservative, moderate | 33.2 | 36.5 | 49.3 | 54.2 | 59.7 |

*Note*  The percentages in the table are based only on the respondents ranking the parties; excluded are the 41 percent of the individuals unable or unwilling to respond.

*Source*  Survey Research Center of the University of Michigan. Data made available through the Inter-University Consortium for Political Research.

the activists of the party organization come in disproportionate numbers from these identifiers.[3]

Short of activity in the parties, the "strong" party identifiers also see the parties in sharper terms than do the "weak" identifiers and the independents. They describe the parties as more committed to sharply differentiated liberal and conservative positions, and they are more apt to spot "extremism" in the other party (Table 7.1). They also are surer that there are important differences between the parties on specific policy issues.[4] And, not very surprisingly, the party electorates tend to have stronger positive and negative views about the two parties and their abilities to govern for the benefit of the nation.

Such relationships by themselves are no reason to leap to the conclusion that party identification by itself produces greater party activity or a sharper issue image. Party activity — or any political activity, for that matter — appears to be the result of a complicated set of recruitment, access, incentive, and availability factors. That one of these factors is probably loyal commitment to a party seems clear. But it is equally clear that party identification is not the only condition necessary for party activity.

[3] Data on the political activity and involvement of party identifiers can be found in virtually all studies of American voting behavior. Among others, see Angus Campbell et al., *The American Voter* (New York: Wiley, 1960), especially Chap. 6; and Sidney Verba and Norman H. Nie, *Participation in America* (New York: Harper and Row, 1972).

[4] Gerald M. Pomper, *Voters' Choice* (New York: Dodd, Mead, 1975), Chap. 8.

## JUDGMENT OF CANDIDATES AND ISSUES

Party identification and the commitments it involves operate as a screen through which individuals select political information from the welter of political messages that assail them. It also serves as an aid to help one evaluate information. The effect of party identification on judgments of the parties can easily be surmised. But its effect on the individual's perceptions of candidates and political issues bears greater scrutiny.

Party identification provides a perceptual predisposition through which the voter sees the candidates. "The stronger the voter's party bias, the more likely he is to see the candidate of his own party as hero, the candidate of the other party as villain." [5] In the 1960 presidential election, however, competing perceptual predispositions were at work. Catholics tended to perceive John F. Kennedy more favorably than did Protestants. Nonetheless, party identification kept its organizing power. When religious loyalties were held constant, party identification had its effect on the perception of Kennedy. And when party identifications were held constant, the religious loyalty had *its* effect. When one says, therefore, that a candidate is attractive or compelling, he says something about the electorate as well as about the candidate.

The control that party identification exercises in the perception of candidates may, however, be somewhat selective. In any event, that is the conclusion of a study of a sample of Detroit voters.[6] The partisan perception appears to extend to the candidate's political traits but not to such purely personal matters as his personality, appearance, or social characteristics (e.g., his religion). The partisan view of candidates is selective in another sense: It is not without limits. Before the 1972 election, for instance, Democrats joined Republicans in viewing Richard Nixon more favorably than George McGovern.

The impact of party identification on political issues is not as easy to determine as its impact on candidate perception. The candidate is a tangible person, but an issue is an abstraction with far more subtle components. It is easy to show that party identifiers of the two parties take more sharply defined positions on public policies than the nonidentifiers (see Table 6.6). They are also more apt to have an issue or ideological position congruent with the one generally associated with the party of their choice. (That effect, it should be noted, has become less and less apparent as the American electorate has increasingly identified the positions of the parties correctly.) Party identification may, of course, provide that congruence in the first place by guiding some party loyalists to their party's position on

[5] Donald E. Stokes, "Some Dynamic Elements of Contests for the Presidency," *American Political Science Review* 60 (1966): 23. The material of this paragraph is drawn from the Stokes article.
[6] Roberta A. Sigel, "Effects of Partisanship on the Perception of Political Candidates," *Public Opinion Quarterly* 28 (1964): 483–96.

issues. For other party loyalists the congruence is the result of an ideology that predated and governed the choice of party. The explanation, and thus the uncertainty, is in the relationship between the formation of issue stands and party loyalty.

## PARTY IDENTIFICATION AND VOTING

So powerful and stable has party identification been in the voting behavior of American adults that the Survey Research Center organizes its main typology of American presidential elections around the question of the role that party loyalties played in them. Thus the SRC describes three chief election types:

1. The *maintaining* election, in which the party attachments of the recent past prevail without any great change or divergence. The elections of 1948, 1960, 1964, and 1976 would appear to be examples.
2. The *deviating* election, in which the basic distribution of party loyalties is not changed but in which short-run forces (such as an attractive candidate or issues of great salience) cause the defeat of the majority party; the Republican successes of 1952, 1956, 1968, and 1972 are examples.
3. The *realigning* election, in which a new distribution of party loyalties emerges and governs the outcome; the elections of 1928 and 1932 offer the most recent examples.[7]

These latter realigning elections are distinguished by "the presence of a great national crisis, leading to a conflict regarding governmental policies and the association of the two major parties with relatively clearly contrasting programs for its solution." [8]

Implicit in this typology is another useful trichotomy to which we have already referred. Scholars of voting behavior find it useful to break the influences on the voting decision into three main categories: party identification, candidate, and issues. Of the three, party identification has usually dominated not only because it has such depth and endurance but also because it affects perceptions and judgments of the other two. Only very appealing candidates and issues overturn the power of the long-run party identification (in what would be a deviating election). The case of the 1972 presidential election is a classic example. President Richard M. Nixon,

[7] See Angus Campbell, "A Classification of the Presidential Election," in Campbell et al., *Elections and the Political Order*, pp. 63–77. See also V. O. Key, "A Theory of Critical Elections," *Journal of Politics* 17 (1955): 3–18.

[8] Angus Campbell, in Campbell et al., *Elections and the Political Order*, p. 76. For an extended debate on an alternative, four-part scheme, see Gerald M. Pomper, "Classification of Presidential Elections," *Journal of Politics* 29 (1967): 535–66, and Walter Dean Burnham, *Critical Elections and the Mainsprings of American Politics* (New York: Norton, 1970), pp. 32–33.

the candidate of the minority party in party identifications, won over George McGovern, the majority party candidate, on two grounds. He was the more credible and respected of the candidates (in October 1972, of course), and his party's positions on issues such as the war in Vietnam were more acceptable to the majority of voters. It was the first time among recent elections in which the issues weighed at least as heavily as party identification in determining the votes of the electorate.[9]

The stronger the party identification, however, the less likely it is that the voter will be deflected from support of his party by the short-run appeals of candidates or issues (Table 7.2). Even in 1972 strong Democrats voted for McGovern over Nixon by almost three to one. And the stronger the identification, the more likely it is that the voter has supported the party consistently in the past (Table 7.2). Although there is an important conceptual distinction between party identification and party voting, one clearly leads to the other.

The 1960 presidential race between Richard M. Nixon and John F. Kennedy affords a fascinating instance of the clash of party loyalties with another potent set of social loyalties — those of religion. In this sense Kennedy's Catholicism was more than an issue or a candidate; it was the stimulus for another, largely nonpolitical, predisposition. The effect of those loyalties on the perceptions of Kennedy himself we have already assessed. But despite the strength of the religious loyalties, Philip Converse concluded after an examination of voting in the 1960 election that in casting their votes, "Protestant Democrats were more likely to behave as Democrats than as Protestants, and Catholic Republicans were more likely to behave as Republicans than as Catholics."[10]

These observations on the impact of party identification on the voter largely reflect decisions in national or statewide elections. Party identification may have either more or less impact in state and local elections. Where the voter has personal, face-to-face contact with the candidates in a rural county, his evaluation of them may be so strong that it overrides party loyalties. Or some voters may find the application of party loyalties inappropriate to the less partisan campaigns for local office, especially when the office appears to have little policymaking responsibility (e.g.,

[9] A note of clarification is in order. When we speak of the power of party identification here, we speak of its ability to affect large numbers of vote decisions. It is possible for it to be the prime determining force in the sum of the vote decisions and yet at the same time for the majority party to lose an election (as in 1952 and 1956). The margin of such electoral victories is small, and the great majority of voters may still be responding to party cues. In 1972, however, there was both a minority party victory and the eclipse of the total effect of party loyalty in the electorate. On 1972 see Arthur H. Miller, Warren E. Miller, Alden S. Raine, and Thad A. Brown, "A Majority Party in Disarray: Policy Polarization in the 1972 Election," *American Political Science Review* 70 (1976): 753–78.

[10] Philip E. Converse, "Religion and Politics: The 1960 Election," in Campbell et al., *Elections and the Political Order*, p. 123.

TABLE 7.2   Presidential Vote in 1976 and Record of Past Voting among Party Identifiers and Independents: 1976

|  | Strong Demo-crats | Weak Demo-crats | Inde-pen-dents | Weak Repub-licans | Strong Repub-licans |
|---|---|---|---|---|---|
| Vote for President: 1976 | | | | | |
| Jimmy Carter | 58.4% | 39.5% | 23.3% | 13.4% | 2.7% |
| Gerald Ford | 5.4 | 13.1 | 28.3 | 47.7 | 75.8 |
| Other, no answer, etc. | 1.2 | 3.4 | 4.6 | 2.9 | 1.6 |
| Didn't vote | 35.0 | 44.1 | 43.8 | 36.0 | 19.9 |
|  | 100.0 | 100.1 | 100.0 | 100.0 | 100.0 |
| Voted for same party since began to vote: 1976 | 61.5 | 37.9 | 19.1 | 42.0 | 64.8 |
| Voted in "all" past presidential elections: 1976 | 41.8 | 33.6 | 37.9 | 43.2 | 68.0 |

*Source*   Survey Research Center of the University of Michigan. Data made available through the Inter-University Consortium for Political Research.

the local clerk of the court or the registrar of deeds ). On the other hand, voters in local elections may have to rely even more than in national elections on the guidance of party. In a large city, the voter having to make choices on a long ballot of city, county, state, and other officers may have no alternative to reliance on the party label. In these elections his or her information on issues and candidates may be only a fraction of what it is in a presidential election.[11]

## THE MYTHS OF THE INDEPENDENT

That party loyalties should govern so much political behavior in a culture that so warmly celebrates the political independent is too striking a paradox to have escaped attention. That there is some gap between myth and reality is clear, and the problem is with the myth of the independent. But before the myth is finally put to rest, we ought perhaps to be clear what myth we are burying.

If by the term *independent* we mean those Americans who refuse to identify with a political party, then the myth *is* a casualty of survey research. Although it is true that the self-styled independent splits his ticket

[11] For another view of the differential effect of party identification on vote choice, see Barbara Hinckley, Richard Hofstetter, and John Kessel, "Information and the Vote: A Comparative Election Study," *American Politics Quarterly* 2 ( 1974): 131–58.

more frequently, waits longer in the campaign to make his voting decision, and shows a moderate level of interest in government generally, he falls short of the picture of the independent in most other respects. He is less concerned about specific elections than identifiers are, less well informed and less active politically than they are. And he is more apt than they not to vote at a given election (Table 7.2). He is, in short, less politically active and involved than the party identifier, especially the *strong* party identifier, and in many respects less the "good citizen."

There is no reason, however, why we cannot define the political independents in terms of their behavior or activity. In his last work, published posthumously, V. O. Key attempted to reclaim the independents from their current obloquy by dealing not with the self-styled independents but with voters who switched their party vote in a consecutive pair of presidential elections.[12] The picture of the American voter that emerges from American political folklore and the new electoral studies, Key thought, is not a pretty one; it is one of an electorate whose voting decision is determined by deeply ingrained attitudes, perceptions, and loyalties without its having grasped the major political issues and alternatives.

Key's search for electoral "rationality" centers, therefore, on the switchers, the voters who do *not* keep voting for the same party in consecutive elections. Key's switchers, by the usual criteria, come much closer to the image of the independent than do the self-described independents. He finds their levels of political interest no lower than those of the stand-patters who remain firm in their voting allegiances. By his definition, of course, the switchers are not nonvoters. Above all, they are marked by an issue-related rationality that well fits the usual picture of the independent. They agree on policy issues with the stand-patters toward whom they shift, and disagree with the policies of the party from which they defect.[13]

Just as we have been trying to adjust our views of the independent to reality, however, the reality has begun to change! The numbers of self-styled independents among American voters have increased significantly. (Tables 6.2 and 6.8.) Indeed, among the electorate under thirty the percentage of independents approaches 50 percent. There are also signs that recent additions to the group have altered its composition. Many of the new independents are from higher educational and SES levels than the older ones, giving the independents a more heterogeneous social composition.

Independents' behavior and attitudes in presidential elections have shown some inclination to change. They recently have appeared as interested in the general affairs of government and politics as "weak" party

[12] V. O. Key (with the assistance of Milton C. Cummings), *The Responsible Electorate* (Cambridge: Harvard University Press, 1966).
[13] A concept of the independent as ticket-splitter is developed in Walter DeVries and Lance Tarrance, *The Ticket Splitter* (Grand Rapids: Eerdmans, 1972).

TABLE 7.3   Levels of Interest in the Campaign and in Government and Public Affairs among Party Identifiers and Independents: 1976

|  | Strong Demo- crats | Weak Demo- crats | Inde- pen- dents | Weak Repub- licans | Strong Repub- licans |
|---|---|---|---|---|---|
| Respondent "very much" interested in campaign | 58.1% | 31.1% | 27.4% | 31.2% | 63.1% |
| Respondent follows government and public affairs "often" | 49.6% | 32.9% | 34.7% | 31.1% | 60.9% |

*Note*   The data of the table come from two separate questions; in each case only the responses to the question reflecting the highest level of interest are reported.

*Source*   Survey Research Center of the University of Michigan. Data made available through the Inter-University Consortium for Political Research.

identifiers (Table 7.3). And in 1968 the independents voted in the same percentage and were as attentive to the campaign as were the party loyalists. It may have been that the range of options in 1968 — from Eugene McCarthy through George Wallace — drew them, if briefly, into more sustained contact with American politics. In 1976, too, they voted at about the same rate as the "weak" partisans. More generally, we now seem to have

at least *two sets* of independents: "old independents," who correspond to the rather bleak classical survey-research picture, and "new independents," who may have declined to identify with either major party not because they are relatively politically unconscious, but because the structure of electoral politics at the present time turns upon parties, issues, and symbolisms which do not have much meaning in terms of their political values or cognitions.[14]

Even though this second group may not quite meet the criteria for the classic American independent, it comes closer than the independents did earlier. We now find that the American political independents have evolved into a group as diverse as the party identifiers. Taken as a single group, though, they tend increasingly to respond to politics and elections in ways similar to the "weak" party identifiers. So, we have gone from believing in independents as "superior" citizens to describing them as "inferior" citizens, and now to seeing them as increasingly like the rest of the electorate.[15]

[14] Burnham, *Critical Elections and the Mainsprings of American Politics*, p. 127.
[15] William H. Flanigan and Nancy H. Zingale suggest another kind of diversity among independents based on whether or not they lean to one party or the other in their *Political Behavior of the American Electorate*, 4th ed. (Boston: Allyn and Bacon, 1979). See also, Hugh L. LeBlanc and Mary Beth Merrion, "Independents, Issue Partisanship, and the Decline of Party," *American Politics Quarterly* 7 (1979): 240–56.

## THE LOYAL ELECTORATES IN CHANGE

The leaders of the party organizations scarcely know the men and women of the party's loyal electorate. They know them largely in the same way that political scientists do: in some abstract, aggregate profile. They know that members of the party in the electorate see the issues and candidates through party-tinted glasses. They know that the party electorate has a unified and reinforcing view of politics, that it is more likely to vote the party ticket, and that it is easier to lure into activity for the party or a candidate. Party strategists know, in other words, that it is a reliable hard core of party supporters. In a general if vague way, they see — as do political scientists — that party identification is a commitment strong enough to affect other commitments and pervasive enough to color and codify perceptions of political reality.

Much of the strategy of American political campaigning is based on these assumptions about loyal party electorates. The general strategy is often to stimulate and reinforce the party loyalties of one's own partisans while making candidate and issue appeals to independents and partisans of the other party. When in 1968 workers and union members threatened to bolt the Humphrey ticket, labor leaders drove hard to reinforce old labor loyalties to the Democratic party and to hammer at the issues of wages and employment that would reinforce those ties. (As it turned out, they succeeded in bringing back a large number of strays to the Democratic fold by election day.)

Furthermore, the sizes and composition of the two party electorates determine the more specific strategies. It appears that the present pattern of party loyalty, for example, requires the Republicans to minimize party-stimulating appeals, party identifications, and SES issues. Their hope at present rests with attractive candidates and nonclass issues. It is surely not coincidental that both Barry Goldwater in 1964 and Richard Nixon in 1968 and 1972 emphasized a large number of issues that met those specifications: crime and morality, local responsibility for civil rights and racial equality, defense and foreign policy, and the war in Vietnam.

So great has been the controlling and stabilizing force of these two great, unchanging party electorates in American politics that it is hard to imagine what politics would be like without them. But many signs indicate that we may know without having to let our imaginations loose. As the percentage of independents rises, of course, the number of people expressing a party loyalty declines. But the signs of trouble for the parties are more extensive than declining numbers. Party identifications are losing some of their old control over the judgments and decisions of the American voter. Even party loyalists are splitting more tickets and showing more attention to issues.

The nature of the recent changes can best be seen against the backdrop of the traditional stability of American party lines. Because large numbers of people had party identifications, because they rarely changed them, and because those identifications strongly governed their voting decisions, patterns of voting support for the two parties have been extremely stable. In election after election, individual voters voted straight party tickets. And the patterns of party support remained stable geographically. A party's pattern of state-to-state support (and county-to-county support within states) remained steady election after election. And when the votes *have* shifted — enough to tip balances of victory and defeat — they have shifted so evenly as not to alter greatly those overall patterns of support. A party's state-to-state profile of support has been raised or lowered but not greatly changed.

Only periodic party realignments — those shifts triggered by the conjunction of presidential elections and cataclysmic events such as panics, wars, and depressions — jolted this long-term stability. At such times a new pattern and distribution of party loyalties was established, and it persisted until the next realignment. But in the late 1960s and the 1970s we are experiencing instability without realignment. Split-ticket voting is on the upsurge and increasing faster than the growth rate of self-described independents. The comfortably high correlations of presidential vote from one election to another have disappeared. The elections of 1964, 1968, and 1972 saw the parties putting together coalitions that bore little resemblance to the coalitions of their supporters in 1960 and the years before. In visual, maplike terms, the profile of the parties' areas of strengths and weaknesses in those elections differed sharply from earlier ones and from each other.[16]

It is just possible that we are teetering on the edge of party realignment. A strong third-party movement — such as that of George Wallace — has usually preceded realignments in the past. And a great many signs point now to a decline in the number of party loyalists and a decline in the power of loyalties that persist. A number of observers have suggested that the Democrats may build a new coalition by combining the young, the disaffected, the minority groups, the disadvantaged, and a goodly portion of the successful and affluent. The Republicans would thus become the party of a working-class and middle-class conservatism — the party of the middle America or silent majority of whom Republican orators speak.[17]

It is even more likely, however, that we will not have realignment. We may well be seeing nothing more than the declining effectiveness and strength of party loyalties. In the past we ignored the possibility that

[16] On the 1968 election, see Philip E. Converse et al., "Continuity and Change in American Politics: Parties and Issues in the 1968 Election," *American Political Science Review* 63 (1969): 1083–1105.
[17] James L. Sundquist, *Dynamics of the Party System* (Washington: Brookings, 1973).

alignments might stay relatively fixed while their force declined. But it is possible that ultimately many voters will not take their party loyalties — or the very idea of loyalty to a political party — seriously enough to change them. It is, indeed, more than possible that large numbers of Americans will hold, however halfheartedly, to their weakening loyalties or perhaps slip into some degree of independence. Others may well shift their loyalties to another party, but on an individual, ad hoc basis. Instead of the quick, sharp, and dramatic realignments of the past we may have a continuous realignment of individuals within the existing structure of the party electorates as we know them today.[18]

Furthermore, the more we learn about the process of realignment, the less likely it seems that the process is now underway. Conventional explanations of how realignments happened assumed a massive shifting of voters from one party to the other. It was, in other words, an explanation based on the conversion of existing voters. New and careful analysis of the 1928–32 realignment, however, suggests that it — the most recent of our realignments — resulted largely from the infusion of new voters.[19] If it is indeed the case that realignments depend on the first-time party identifications of new voters rather than the conversion of the old ones, realignment under present conditions seems remote. The new voters entering the party system now are largely young voters who show a markedly greater preference for not having a party identification. And those willing to identify with a party do so largely along the lines of the partisans already in the party electorates.

In a subject (and chapter) filled with paradoxes, it may be fitting to conclude with one more. It has often been said that the source of the weakness of the American parties is their refusal to make commitments to ideology, their inability to take distinctive policy stands. They have been pragmatic, brokerage parties, attracting mass followings without programs. Yet, it is precisely this relative absence of political ideology in American politics that has made the parties in the electorate as strong as they are. In the United States it is the political party and loyalty to it that guide the individual. The party itself, not a class-based ideology or some other social loyalty, structures political reality and decisions. In American politics the political party is, therefore, closer to the cognitive and behavioral center of the voter and his judgments. It has many organizational competitors in the recruitment of resources and clienteles, but the major American party is without serious competition as a force in organizing the world *within* the American voters.

[18] Many of these themes are developed more fully in Burnham, *Critical Elections and the Mainsprings of American Politics*, Chaps. 5 and 6.
[19] Kristi Andersen in Chap. 5 of Nie, Verba, and Petrocik, *The Changing American Voter.*

# 8

# The American
# Electorate

Much of the history of the political parties of the Western democracies can be written in terms of their responses to the expansion of the suffrage. The parties began as essentially aristocratic instruments mobilizing very homogeneous and limited electorates and, as the electorates expanded, they have had to alter their organizations and appeals to include virtually all adults. In multiparty systems in the Western world, new parties often rose to represent new groups admitted to the suffrage. The European Socialist and Labor parties, for example, organized the newly enfranchised industrial workers.

The stability of the American two-party system, however, has ruled out such an accommodation of new electorates. The two major American parties have had to expand their hospitality to new groups winning the vote. And since they are overwhelmingly electoral parties, any changes in the size, composition, or activity level of the American electorate affect them profoundly. From the electorate's total dimensions they recruit their own, especially loyal, party electorates and the workers, skills, and money for party organizations and campaigns. And, above all, they seek in it the majorities they must mobilize if they are to win elections.

Unfortunately, it is not entirely clear just who constitutes the American electorate. Obviously it is something less than the total number of American adults. The "something less" is generally the result of two kinds of factors: (1) the restrictions placed on it (or, if one prefers, the definitions of it) by the states, and (2) the unwillingness of the eligibles either to register or to vote. Just how and why these limitations operate, on whom they fall, and the numbers they disenfranchise are not easy matters to settle. It is impossible, for example, to give anything more than an educated guess about the number of Americans who actually meet the legal requirements for voting in presidential elections in the fifty states. That guess is made especially difficult by the fact that the requirements differ from state to state. The task is really the definition of fifty electorates.

If the American electorate — either in its legal or its self-defining (turnout) dimension — were an accurate sample of the adult American population, the issue of its dimensions would be far less important. But the effective electorate is nothing of the sort. It overrepresents some groups in the American society and underrepresents others. Because of the preference of various groups for one party or the other, the composition and possible enlargement of the electorate are matters of differential advantage for the parties. Since American blacks identify largely with the Democratic party at present, for example, various attempts to bring them into the American electorate affect the nature of the parties' loyal electorates and the patterns of their competition.

## THE ELECTORATE: THE PROBLEM OF MEASUREMENT

After every presidential election, commentators on American civic values don sackcloth and ashes to note that as usual a relatively small percentage of American adults stirred themselves to vote. In 1968, for instance, a campaign of unparalleled cost and scope — and one that included the liveliest third-party candidacy in more than forty years — attracted only 61 percent of the "potential electorate" to the polls. Somewhat more lackluster two-way races in 1972 and 1976 attracted only 55.5 and 54.3 percent turnouts. The lowest figures in 1976 were the 33.3 for the District of Columbia and 41.7 for South Carolina; the highest were 71.4 in Minnesota and 69.4 in Utah.[1]

These and similar turnout percentages, regardless of what elections happen to be involved, depend on two categories of data, one fairly reliable and the other highly suspect. Because of the generally accurate counting and reporting of vote totals that prevail in most localities, the figures on actual turnout (the numbers of voters voting) are fairly reliable. However, the base figures of total possible voters (on the basis of which the turnout percentages are calculated) are questionable. Whether the base is called total voters, potential voters, or the potential electorate, it usually turns out to be a total of all persons of voting age in the states (by count of the United States Census Bureau). Thus the widely quoted 54.3 percent turnout for the 1976 presidential election was computed on such a base of some 150,041,000 "potential voters."

Such reckonings of so-called potential voters are essentially misleading because they fail to take into account the restrictions on the suffrage other than that of age. Nor do they consider the number of voters made ineligible to vote by their failure (where required) to go through the administrative processes of registration. The reasonable remedy, therefore, is to substitute for the concept of potential voters some measure of *eligible* voters, but that total is precisely what is so hard to come by.

The outer limits to the American electorate are not hard to determine. The electorate can be no larger than the number of adults of age in the

---

[1] These data and many others in this chapter are from *Statistical Abstract of the United States: 1978*, 99th ed. (Washington: U.S. Bureau of Census, 1978), pp. 518ff.

country and no smaller than the number of actual voters (categories 1 and 3 in Table 8.1). But the intermediate estimate of the eligible electorate (category 2 in Table 8.1), the one so badly needed for accurate estimates of turnout percentages, is the puzzle. Until we have that figure, the easy availability of the larger number of total adults (the potential electorate) will dictate the use of that figure, and we will continue to manufacture inaccurately low (and unflattering) turnout percentages.

The size of the effective American electorate (whether one defines it as the eligible or the actual electorate — categories 2 and 3 in Table 8.1) results from the impact of forces internal and external to the individual. The external influences include the legal restrictions of the states, their application by the administrative machinery of the state, and the informal restrictions of force or economic and social sanction. The internal influences refer to the values and goals, the motivational levels, the role perceptions, the sense of civic responsibility within the individual. The external definitions of the American electorate are clearer because they are more tangible, and we turn to them first.

**TABLE 8.1   Categories of Potential, Eligible, and Actual Voters: Presidential Elections of 1964, 1968, 1972, and 1976**

|  | 1964 presidential election | 1968 presidential election | 1972 presidential election | 1976 presidential election |
|---|---|---|---|---|
| 1. The so-called *potential electorate* (all persons 18 years and older) | 114,090,000 | 120,285,000 | 140,068,000 | 150,041,000 |
| 2. The *eligible electorate* (persons meeting state requirements) | ? | ? | ? | ? |
| 3. The *registered eligible electorate* (where registration required) | ? | ? | ? | ? |
| 4. The *turnout* (persons who actually voted) | 70,645,000 (61.9%) | 73,212,000 (60.9%) | 77,719,000 (55.5%) | 81,556,000 (54.3%) |

*Source   Statistical Abstract: 1978, p. 520.*

## LEGAL DEFINITION OF THE ELECTORATE

The decentralizing influences of the American federalism touch almost
every important aspect of American electoral politics, and the electorate
itself is no exception. The definition of the American electorate over the
past 150 years has expanded through the curiously American interlacing
of national and state action. The chief expansions have been these:

— In the early nineteenth century the states themselves gradually repealed
the property and tax-paying qualifications for voting by which they had
so severely restricted the male suffrage. By 1860 there remained no
states that required property holding and only four that required substantial tax paying as a condition for voting. About a century later the
Twenty-fourth Amendment and the Supreme Court finally ended even
the small poll tax as a requirement for voting.
— By the mid-1870s women began to work through the states for their
right to vote, and in 1890 Wyoming became the first state to grant the
full franchise to women. Progress slowly bogged down, especially in
the eastern states, and women shifted their hopes to the United States
Constitution. The Nineteenth Amendment, forbidding states to deny
the vote on grounds of sex, was finally ratified in 1920.
— The expansion of black suffrage began by state action in some of the
states of New England before the Civil War, but it culminated after
the war with the passage of the Fifteenth Amendment. Congress and
the federal courts from that time to the present have periodically attempted to enforce its clauses on some reluctant states.
— In the 1960s a movement of young people met varied success in their
attempt to lower the voting age to eighteen or nineteen by state constitutional amendment. Then the United States Congress in June 1970
passed a law extending the suffrage to eighteen-year-olds in both state
and federal elections. Less than a half year later the Supreme Court
decided by a five to four vote that the act was constitutional as it applied to federal elections but unconstitutional as it applied to state and
local elections. Congress then passed and sent to the states for ratification an amendment to the Constitution lowering the age to eighteen
for all elections. That amendment, the Twenty-sixth, was ratified by
1971.[2]

None of the major expansions in the American electorate, therefore,
was accomplished without national limitations on the power of the states

_____

[2] The Supreme Court decision was in *Oregon* v *Mitchell*, 400 U.S. 112 (1970). The
chief section of the constitutional amendment states: "The right of citizens of the
United States, who are eighteen years of age or older, to vote shall not be denied or
abridged by the United States or by any state on account of age."

to define the electorate.[3] Undoubtedly, however, it was the intention of the Founding Fathers to vest control over the electorate in the states. At least that outcome was ensured by writing Article I, Section 2, which provides that for elections to the House ". . . the electors in each state shall have the qualifications requisite for electors of the most numerous branch of the state legislature." That was as much as they said on the suffrage in the entire constitutional document. No more was necessary, for senators were to be elected indirectly by state legislatures, and the president and vice-president by a genuinely deliberative electoral college. As for the selection of electors to the electoral college, Section 4 of Article I stipulated that each state was to "appoint in such manner as the legislature thereof may direct, a number of electors. . . ." When the Congress and the states converted the election of senators to a direct and popular election, they wrote into the Seventeenth Amendment the same formula that applies to the House: "The electors in each state shall have the qualifications requisite for electors of the most numerous branch of the state legislature."

So, contrary to the traditions of other countries and even of other federal systems, the formulating of voting requirements was left to the states. The inevitable result was the absence of a uniform national electorate even for national elections. The constitutional authority of the United States government, therefore, has until very recently been limited to the passive role of saying in three amendments that the states shall not deny citizens the vote solely and explicitly on grounds of race or color (Fifteenth), sex (Nineteenth), or failure to pay a tax (Twenty-fourth). Furthermore, the Fourteenth Amendment's equal protection clause ("no state shall make or enforce any law which shall . . . deny to any person within its jurisdiction the equal protection of the laws") has been interpreted by the Supreme Court to prevent a state from discriminating against blacks in defining its electorate. Presumably that same clause would similarly protect ethnic, religious, occupational, regional, or other social groups in the unlikely possibility that a state should deny the suffrage to, say, Presbyterians, Italian-Americans, or government employees.

In recent years, however, the national government, through both the Congress and the Supreme Court, has expanded its role in defining the American electorate. The Congress by ordinary statute — rather than by constitutional amendment — extended the vote to younger voters in federal elections; banned literacy, understanding, and character tests for registration; and waived residency requirements for voting in presidential elections. The newly expanded congressional authority appears to rest on the Supreme Court's interpretation of Article I, Section 4, the section on

[3] For background on the early development of the American electorate, see Chilton Williamson, *American Suffrage: From Property to Democracy* (Princeton: Princeton University Press, 1960).

the control of congressional elections.[4] The Court itself has expanded its own application of constitutional guarantees, that expansion culminating in 1972 in its decision sharply restricting state residence requirements.[5]

Between the constitutional territory of the states and that of the nation there is a tiny no-man's-land, the District of Columbia. For almost all of American history the citizens of the district have remained voteless, even in their own local affairs. However, since the passage of the Twenty-third Amendment to the Constitution in 1961, the voters of the District of Columbia have had three votes in the electoral college. They also elect a nonvoting delegate to Congress and a series of local officials on the authorization of the Congress.

## THE AMERICAN ELECTORATE TODAY

Despite their freedom under the Constitution, the states have developed legal definitions of the suffrage that are surprisingly similar. In part, the negative controls of the constitutional amendments have hemmed them in. So, too, have the political pressures for universal adult suffrage, the examples of other states, and increased supervision by the Congress and Supreme Court. In any event, it is now possible to deal with the state definitions of the suffrage in a small number of categories.[6]

### Minimum Voting Age

As recently as the 1968 elections, all but four states fixed the minimum voting age at twenty-one. But thanks to the 1970 Voting Rights Act and the Twenty-sixth Amendment, the minimum age became eighteen for all elections, beginning in 1972.

### Citizenship

All states now require that voters be citizens of the United States. As surprising as it may seem, in 1900 there were still eleven states that permitted aliens to vote, even though some states required the individual to have

[4] Section 4 of Article I is as follows: "The Times, Places, and Manner of holding Elections for Senators and Representatives, shall be prescribed in each State by the Legislature thereof; but the Congress may at any time by Law make or alter such Regulations, except as to the Places of choosing Senators." Every reader can be his own constitutional expert in deciding whether questions of suffrage are what the Founding Fathers had in mind in writing this section of Article I.

[5] For the citation to this case, see footnote 10. For a full and excellent study of the legal and constitutional issues in defining the electorate, see Richard Claude, *The Supreme Court and the Electoral Process* (Baltimore: Johns Hopkins University Press, 1970).

[6] For a general survey of state laws defining the electorate, see Constance E. Smith, *Voting and Election Laws* (New York: Oceana, 1960).

begun to seek American citizenship. But in 1926 Arkansas, the last state to capitulate, closed off the alien suffrage. More than any other single factor, the end of mass and open immigration into the United States signaled the end of the vote for noncitizens.

## Poll Taxes

Until 1964 five states — Alabama, Mississippi, Texas, Vermont, and Virginia — continued to require the payment of a poll tax (i.e., a head tax or a per capita tax) as a qualification for voting.[7] The tax amounted only to one or two dollars a year, but its disenfranchising effect was often increased by stipulations that it be cumulative, that it be paid well in advance of the election, or that the taxpayer keep the receipt and present it at the polling booth. In 1964 the Twenty-fourth Amendment to the Constitution, however, invalidated tax paying as a condition for voting in national elections. A year later, in the Voting Rights Act of 1965, Congress legislated a finding that poll taxes in *any* election are discriminatory. In interpreting that law the Supreme Court noted that a state violates the Constitution "whenever it makes the affluence of the voter or payment of a fee an electoral standard." [8]

## Residence

For most of the history of the Republic, the states were free to require that citizens live for a certain period of time in the state and locality before they could vote. Most, indeed, devised three-layer residence requirements: a minimum period of time in the state, a shorter time in the county, and an even shorter period in the local voting district. Traditionally the longest residence requirements were those of the southern states (where they disenfranchised migrant and mobile farm labor), but long waits for eligibility were not uncommon elsewhere. In 1970, in fact, the median residence requirement among the fifty states was one year in the state, three months in the county, and one month in the voting district.[9]

Substantial residence requirements began to crumble in the 1950s and 1960s, however, largely in response both to the demands of a physically mobile society and to its rising democratic expectations. States lowered their residence requirements, and many also set up even lower ones for newcomers wishing to vote in presidential elections. Congress in 1970 set-

---

[7] In Vermont's case the poll tax was a qualification for voting only in local town affairs; the state repealed it early in 1966.

[8] The 1966 case was *Harper* v *Virginia State Board of Elections,* 383 U.S. 633 (1966). On the poll tax generally, see Frederic D. Ogden, *The Poll Tax in the South* (University, Alabama: University of Alabama Press, 1958).

[9] *Book of the States 1970–71* (Lexington: Council of State Governments, 1971).

tled the latter issue by establishing a national uniform residency requirement of thirty days within a state for voting in a presidential election. Then, the Supreme Court in 1972 struck down Tennessee's one-year residence requirement for voting in state and local elections, indicating then a strong preference for a thirty-day limit. The Court later accepted a fifty-day requirement, but in doing so it noted that such a period "approaches the outer constitutional limit." [10] Consequently, almost half of the states have dropped residence requirements altogether, and most of the rest have fixed them at one month.

## Disqualifications

Virtually all the states restrict the suffrage for reasons of crime or mental incompetence. Institutionalization for insanity or severe mental illness temporarily removes an individual from the suffrage in all states, and in the great majority of states so do convictions for certain categories of crimes, the most common being felonies and electoral corruption. The disqualification for mental illness is limited generally to the time of illness or incapacity. The disqualification for felonies, however, lasts indefinitely in some states, even after release from prison. Only gubernatorial pardon or some formal administrative or legislative action will then restore the franchise.

## Literacy Tests

Twenty states in early 1965 — before the passage of the Civil Rights Act of that year — required that the applicant for the suffrage demonstrate his or her literacy. Often the test, especially when administered by an election clerk, constituted little more than a test of the ability to scrawl a signature. In other states one proved literacy by filling out application forms for registration. In a few states the test was more substantial. The New York comprehensive test, drafted and administered by educational authorities, included questions to test the reader's understanding of brief expository paragraphs. (In Alaska the applicant could demonstrate his facility in English either by reading or speaking it.) Furthermore, it had been customary for literacy to mean literacy in English; only Hawaii offered an alternative: Hawaiian.

Associated with these literacy tests were tests of understanding or interpretation. Originally the states intended them as alternatives to literacy tests. If individuals could not read or write, they might qualify for the

[10] *Dunn v Blumstein*, 405 U.S. 330 (1972), and *Burns v Fortson*, 410 U.S. 686 (1973). See also Richard J. Carlson, "Election Legislation," *Book of the States 1974–75*, pp. 24–52.

franchise by demonstrating their ability to explain some aspect of the governmental system or some section of the state constitution. In other states such as Louisiana and Georgia, the local voting registrar could permit an illiterate person to register if he was convinced the individual was of "good character." Mississippi, home of the interpretation test, required this ability in addition to literacy and good character. Local voting registrars selected one of the 286 sections of the state constitution for the applicant to read and interpret; the registrar, of course, was the judge of the adequacy of the interpretation.

In the Voting Rights Act of 1970 Congress suspended the use of literacy, understanding, and character tests anywhere as a prerequisite for registration to vote. It reasoned that, regardless of the states' various intentions, the tests had worked discriminatorily against minority groups. The Supreme Court agreed.

### Federal Lands

Traditionally, the states have refused to recognize citizens living on federal reservations — military posts, national parks, and veterans hospitals, for instance — as citizens of the state for the purpose of voting. Only three states — California, Utah, and West Virginia — give them a vote. Hence the great majority of Americans living on one or another of the five thousand separate pieces of land over which the national government exercises exclusive jurisdiction are without a vote. The one exception is the District of Columbia.

### THE SPECIAL PROBLEM OF MINORITIES

Throughout these past paragraphs there runs a repeated theme: the special limits placed on racial and ethnic minorities. Take the case of American blacks. The residence requirements penalized them for poorly paid jobs as itinerant farm laborers, jobs that often prevented them from educating their children. Nor is it unfair to say that black disenfranchisement is a major reason why the poll tax persisted in the South, why residence requirements were more stringent in the South, why criminal disqualifications are broadest in the South, and why literacy, interpretation, and understanding tests were most common in the South.

But beyond all these explicit limitations, blacks traditionally found themselves blocked by the administration of registration and election law. Endless delay, unavailable registrars, niggling technicalities, double standards — these have been their greatest barriers in recent years. The hearings of the United States Civil Rights Commission document the problem with ample detail. Charles C. Humpstone, staff attorney of the Commission on Civil Rights, reported on the leniency of registrars in

Issaquena County, Mississippi, in evaluating the interpretations of white applicants:

> A number of inadequate answers were accepted. For example, one white applicant, asked to interpret section 35, which reads, "The senate shall consist of members chosen every 4 years by the qualified electors of the several districts," wrote only, "equible wrights" . . . and passed.

Mrs. Mary Oliver Welsh of Humphreys County, Mississippi (who was on old-age assistance and receiving government surplus commodities), recounted her attempts to register to vote:

> Well, when I went to register, the registrar asked me what did I come down there for. I told him "to register." He said "Register? For what?" I told him, "To vote." He said "Vote? For what?" And I told him I didn't know what I was coming to vote for. He hollered at me and scared me so, I told him I didn't know what I came to vote for. I was just going to vote. . . . He told me I was going to get in trouble, and he wasn't going to give me no commodities. That's what he said.[11]

These extralegal barriers were in many ways the highest. They were at least the most elusive, the least predictable, and ultimately the most demoralizing. And they, along with physical and economic intimidation, were the hardest to stop.

In the beginning the struggle for the black franchise began in the classic American way as a constitutional issue. For years after the end of reconstruction, in fact, the states and the United States Supreme Court played a grim game of constitutional "hide and seek." The states would devise a scheme of disenfranchisement, the Court would strike it down, and the states would find another — ad infinitum. The states sometimes were careful not to disenfranchise poorer whites along with the blacks — hence their devising of grandfather clauses, which automatically registered all persons whose ancestors could vote at some specific date before the ratification of the Fifteenth Amendment. The manic quality of this constitutional chase is perhaps best illustrated by the white primary cases. The white primary was simply a party primary in which blacks were forbidden to vote; it arose at a time in which the candidate who won the Democratic primary in southern states was assured of victory in the general election against an enfeebled Republican party. It expired finally, but only after twenty-one years of litigation and five cases before the United States Supreme Court.[12]

Court action, however, is not nearly so well adapted to dealing with informal administrative evasions. Increasingly the most useful remedies

---

[11] Hearings before the U.S. Civil Rights Commission, I (held in Jackson, Mississippi, on February 16–20, 1965), pp. 49, 53, 95–96, 131–32.

[12] The end of the white primary is recorded in *Smith* v *Allwright,* 321 U.S. 649 (1944).

are legislative and administrative, a fighting of fire with fire. The civil
rights acts of 1957, 1960, 1964, 1965, and 1970 (some are also called voting
rights acts) all make this kind of an attack on discrimination against the
would-be black voter:

— The *attorney general* has been authorized to seek injunctions against
   individuals preventing blacks from voting in primaries or general elections. In those instances in which he can convince a federal court that
   a "pattern or practice" of discrimination exists in a district, the court
   may order registration and send referees to the area.
— The *Justice Department* has acquired authority to supervise voting
   procedures in states and counties in which less than 50 percent of
   potential voters voted in the recent presidential election. Interpretation tests and other similar qualifications have been suspended, and
   the attorney general may send in federal registrars and election observers. Any changes in voting procedures (such as in election districts)
   must be approved by the attorney general or the United States District
   Court in the District of Columbia.
— *Local registrars* have come under greater regulation and control. They
   must keep voting and registration records for twenty-two months, and
   they must not apply voting requirements unequally. Nor are they permitted to seize on immaterial errors or omissions in the application
   process as a reason for refusing registration.

It is both inaccurate and unjust to treat all the states of the South as if
they were of a single piece. They vary in racial ratios, socioeconomic
characteristics, political traditions, and in the legal and extralegal barriers they raised to black voting.[13] Some of those differences are reflected
in the different registration percentages — both black and white — in
Table 8.2. Also, one should keep in mind that black registration and voting
percentages in the rest of the country were and still are below those of
whites. But whatever the variations and the history, black registrations in
the South now approach those of white Southerners and of blacks elsewhere. Individual attempts to discourage black registrations may continue
sporadically, but the systematic and explicit exclusion of blacks from the
electorate is largely a thing of the past.

The major instrument in the lengthy fight for the black franchise has
unquestionably been the 1965 Voting Rights Act. Its life was extended in
1970 and once again in 1975, the second time with only minimal congressional opposition. Certainly a major part of the changes recorded in Table

[13] Articles on black voter registration in the South by Donald R. Matthews and James
W. Prothro, *American Political Science Review* 57 (1963): 24–44 and 355–67. See also
H. Douglas Price, *The Negro and Southern Politics* (New York: New York University
Press, 1957).

**TABLE 8.2    Registration by Race in States Covered by the Voting Rights Act of 1965: 1960 and 1976**

|              | 1960 | | 1976 | |
|--------------|-------|-------|-------|-------|
|              | White | Black | White | Black |
| Alabama        | 63.6% | 13.7% | 79.3% | 58.4% |
| Georgia        | 56.8  | 29.3  | 65.9  | 74.8  |
| Louisiana      | 76.9  | 31.1  | 78.4  | 63.0  |
| Mississippi    | 63.9  | 5.2   | 80.0  | 60.7  |
| North Carolina | 92.1  | 39.1  | 69.2  | 54.8  |
| South Carolina | 57.1  | 13.7  | 58.4  | 56.5  |
| Virginia       | 46.1  | 23.1  | 61.6  | 54.7  |

*Source    Statistical Abstract of the United States: 1978.*

8.2 result from it.[14] Moreover, in the 1975 extension of the act the Congress broadened the protection to include linguistic minorities, that is, any political subdivision in which more than 5 percent of the adults belong to such a minority and in which more than half of the adults failed to register or vote in the preceding presidential election. Those districts would also be required to provide bilingual election materials and officials. The United States government is thus extending its concern for voting to American Indians, Alaskan natives, Asian-Americans, and Spanish-speaking Americans. In one more way the national government has replaced the authority of the states in defining the American electorate.

## THE CUMULATIVE EFFECT

The voting requirements of the fifty states whittled down the 1976 American electorate well below the 150,041,000 persons of voting age shown in Table 8.1. The true "eligible" total was probably more than 12 million below the figures usually used to compute voter turnout percentages. Most ineligibles were resident aliens, institutionalized, residents on federal lands, or unable to meet even modest residence requirements. Of those

[14] For a full review of progress and problems under the Voting Rights Acts of 1965 and 1970 see the report of the U.S. Civil Rights Commission, *The Voting Rights Act: Ten Years After* (1975). It is uncommonly well organized and well written, especially as the reports of governmental commissions go.

redefined eligibles, however, only 76.7 percent were actually registered to vote. So, we can complete the middle rows of Table 8.1 in this fashion:[15]

| | |
|---|---|
| Persons meeting minimum age for voting | 150,041,000 |
| Persons eligible to register to vote | 138,000,000 |
| Persons actually registered | 105,837,000 |
| Persons voting in 1976 election | 81,556,000 |

Using these data, then, one finds that in 1976 some 59.1 percent of the really eligible voters and 77.1 percent of the registered voters actually voted.

While the total number of individuals of voting age creeps upward, the percentage of them who are registered drops. The percentage registered was 72.3 percent in 1972, but it had sunk to 70.1 percent by 1976. That fact is all the more striking when one realizes that the diminution of residence requirements has increased the eligible electorate in those years. Furthermore, the decline in registrations has also happened while a number of states are making it easier to register. States are increasingly adopting mail registration — eighteen states and the District of Columbia by 1978 — and several of them send registration forms even to those persons who do not request them. (The United States is still some distance from the European countries in which voters are registered automatically without the voter's requesting or aiding the process.) And beginning in 1976 two of them — Wisconsin and Minnesota — began to register voters on election day at polling places.

So, it now becomes clear that there are two equally important points at which the nation loses voters: the failure to register and the failure to vote. In 1976 the percentage of eligible voters not registering was virtually as large as the percentage of registered voters not going to the polls. Much of the focus on the nonvoting issue in recent years, therefore, has centered on the registration process. The United States Senate in 1972 killed a national system of voter registration by postcard in a close vote won by a coalition of Republicans and southern Democrats. The proposal of President Jimmy Carter in his first term to permit national registration on election day also came to naught, even though a careful scholarly study estimated that such a move would increase turnout by 10 percent.[16] It is

[15] The data are largely from the U.S. Census and are reported in *The Statistical Abstract of the United States: 1978*. The datum on "individuals eligible to register" is my estimate based on Census projections. See also U.S. Bureau of Census, "Voting and Registration in the Election of November, 1976," *Current Population Reports*, Series P-20, No. 322. For an attempt at a similar calculus, see William G. Andrews, "American Voting Participation," *Western Political Quarterly* 19 (1966): 639–52.

[16] Steven J. Rosenstone and Raymond Wolfinger, "The Effect of Registration Laws on Voter Turnout," *American Political Science Review* 72 (1978): 22–45.

clear, nonetheless, that the newest frontier in the expansion of the American electorate is the registration process.

## TURNOUT: POLITICAL VARIATIONS

Turnout levels vary widely among the states, even at presidential elections. In 1976 the turnout percentage (i.e., the number of voters taken as a percentage of the total adults of voting age) of Minnesota was almost 40 percentage points higher than the District of Columbia's. Enormous variations, however, also occur between different kinds of elections. That fact itself suggests that there are important political limitations on turnout inherent in the American political system itself. Clearly, the attention and interest of American voters flag as they face the four-year cycle of American politics, and many of them respond only to those elections of greatest prominence. Probably no electorate in the democratic world is more frequently called to the polls than the American. Within a four-year cycle it confronts national, state, and local elections for legislative and executive officeholders (and for the judiciary in a majority of the states), not to mention school boards and assorted other local authorities. Most of these elections are preceded by primaries; initiatives, referenda, and even an occasional recall election further complicate the calendar. So whereas the British voter in a four- or five-year cycle may go only twice to the polls — once for a parliamentary election and once for the election of local officials — civic obligation may call his beleaguered American counterpart to the polls for six to ten primaries and general elections.

### Size of Constituency

In the first place, voter participation varies substantially with the size of the constituency. It is generally greatest in presidential elections and smallest in local elections. Although the voting percentage in presidential elections runs now between 50 and 60 percent (of all the adults of voting age), it is less for the gubernatorial elections that come in the nonpresidential years. The congressional elections, too, draw considerably fewer voters in the years between the presidential elections (see Figure 8.1). And in elections limited to local officials, turnout drops even further.

The reasons for this phenomenon are not hard to imagine. The more intense campaigns for the presidency and the governorships unquestionably spark greater voter interest and involvement. The personalities are famous or at least well-known, and the issues seem more momentous. Furthermore, party fortunes are involved and party loyalties are inflamed — contrary to the case in many nonpartisan local and judicial elections. To put it very simply, one should hardly be surprised that a presidential election in which two national political figures and two national parties

**FIGURE 8.1    Percentage of Adults Voting in Presidential and
Congressional Elections 1920–1976**

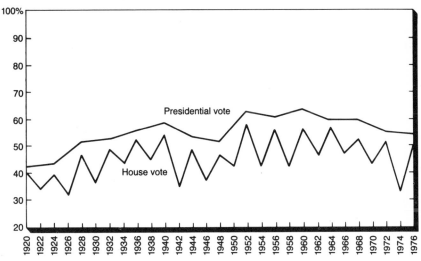

Source Statistical Abstract of the United States, 1974 (95th ed.)

engage in a three-month mass-media campaign draws three or four times
more voters to the polls than does a nonpartisan judicial campaign in
which the candidates talk discreetly and a bit dully of the efficient administration of the courts. The wonder is that it is not eight or ten times
the number.[17]

### The Neglected Primary

Generally throughout the United States, voting in primary elections falls
far short of that in general elections. It is not unusual for primary turnouts to be half or less of the turnouts in general elections — more precisely, only 20 or 25 percent of the adults of voting age (the so-called
potential electorate). Key's work on gubernatorial primaries marked
some of the dimensions of primary voting:

In a sample of 15 nonsouthern states over the period 1926–1952, in three out
of four primaries not more than 35 percent of the potential electorate voted in the
primaries of one or the other of the major parties. That is, the total Democratic
primary vote plus the total Republican primary vote did not exceed 35 percent of
the number of citizens 21 years of age or over. In about one of six primaries the

[17] See, for example, Howard D. Hamilton, "The Municipal Voter: Voting and Non-
Voting in City Elections," *American Political Science Review* 65 (1971): 1135–40.

voters in Democratic and Republican gubernatorial primaries did not exceed 20 percent of the number of citizens 21 and over.[18]

Among primaries for the same office, turnout tends to increase under two circumstances. It increases with competition in the primary and the usually lively campaign that attends a contested primary. It also increases sharply within the dominant party of one-party states. In the southern one-party states, voter turnout in the Democratic primary historically exceeded even the voter turnout of the general election.

### Issues and Referenda

Elections to decide issues — referenda and constitutional amendments, chiefly — do not attract the same turnout as do ordinary elections. Even when these issues are on the ballot of regular elections, fewer voters choose to vote on them than for the candidates at the top of the ballot. Very possibly the absence of a personal clash in these questions reduces their interest and immediacy. Perhaps, too, their frequent complexity confuses many would-be voters. But having made these general statements about issue elections, we should note that voter turnout among referenda fluctuates greatly. An emotionally charged and relatively clear issue such as a referendum on property taxes, equal rights for homosexuals, or the sale of alcoholic beverages will attract far more voters than esoteric questions of bonding authority or reorganizing state administrative agencies.

### The Political Factors

Turnout does vary, therefore, from one kind of election to another. But there are other influences that affect it. Interparty competition in a constituency — whether it is a state or a council district in a city — also increases voter turnout. It does so, furthermore, even when all differences in SES characteristics of the electorate and all historical voting trends in the district are held constant.[19] Understandably, voters seem to be stimulated politically by the excitement of closely contested elections and by the fact that their votes may well affect the outcome. Conversely, there is little appeal in trying to undo a foregone conclusion.

---

[18] V. O. Key, *American State Politics* (New York: Knopf, 1956), p. 134. More recent estimates of primary turnout confirm Key's picture. Even in years in which both gubernatorial primaries are contested, turnout in the median states hovers around the one-third mark (that is, one third of adults of voting age). The study covered the years from approximately 1950 to 1976. Malcolm E. Jewell and David M. Olson, *American State Political Parties and Elections* (Homewood, Ill.: Dorsey, 1978).

[19] C. Richard Hofstetter, "Inter-Party Competition and Electoral Turnout: The Case of Indiana," *American Journal of Political Science* 17 (1973): 351–66. Virginia Gray, however, finds a much weaker relationship between turnout and changes over time in competition in "A Note on Competition and Turnout in the American States," *Journal of Politics* 38 (1976): 153–58.

At the same time the details and curiosities of state election law all work their effect on turnout. Partisan elections stimulate larger turnouts than nonpartisan ones. Some states make voting more difficult with shorter voting hours, less attractive or convenient voting places, and more restricted options for absentees. In some instances the use of voting machines — with their mechanical mysteries and intimidation — may discourage voting.[20]

## TURNOUT: THE PERSONAL EQUATION

All Americans, however, are more or less confronted by the same plethora of elections and the same complexity in local election procedures. The crucial point is that some of them show voter fatigue more quickly than others. It is also true that all American voters are subjected to the same immediate political "causes" of nonvoting (the uninteresting campaign or the obscure issue, for example), and all face the same immediate personal ones (sickness, forgetfulness, bad weather).

Nonvoters in the United States are part of a broader group of political nonparticipants and apathetics — that is to say, they resemble the citizens who abstain from all forms of political activity, whether it be voting, discussing politics, working for a candidate, joining a political party or other political organization, or attending political speeches, rallies, or dinners. Voting turnout is higher among men, higher-income groups, the middle-aged, Jews and Catholics, whites, and those with high-status occupations. Individual social characteristics taken together explain a great deal of the voting and nonvoting in the United States. One recent study, in fact, finds that individual differences in race, age, income, and educational level together explain more than half of the total variation in voter turnout among the American states.[21] Certainly a substantial part of recent dips in voter turnout is age-related. Voters under thirty-five have for a long time voted in below average numbers, and they increased from 28 to 40 percent of the American electorate between 1964 and 1976.

Furthermore, regular voters have, not surprisingly, higher levels of political interest and involvement than nonvoters. They know the candidates and the burning issues. They are also more apt to be strong party identifiers, and they tend to believe that politics and elections are important. They have strongly ingrained beliefs about the duty to vote, and they possess strong feelings of political "efficacy." That is to say, they think that

[20] Norman C. Thomas, "Voting Machines and Voter Participation in Four Michigan Constitutional Revision Referenda," *Western Political Quarterly* 21 (1968): 409–19.
[21] Jae-On Kim, John R. Petrocik, and Stephen N. Enokson, "Voter Turnout Among American States: Systemic and Individual Components," *American Political Science Review* 69 (1975): 107–23, with a supplementary comment following it by Douglas D. Rose. For general works on political participation, including voting, see Robert E. Lane, *Political Life* (Glencoe: Free Press, 1959) and Lester W. Milbrath and M. L. Goel, *Political Participation,* 2nd ed. (Chicago: Rand McNally, 1977).

they can shape the decisions of government and important political outcomes. In fact, by their SES, their own perception of their place and
worth in society, their sense of efficacy within it, and their acceptance
into its group life, regular voters enjoy a secure place in the community.
Conversely, the low-status nonvoters, poorly educated and economically
disadvantaged — and possibly further handicapped by racial or ethnic
prejudice — have feelings of powerlessness, alienation, and anomie. Rarely
sharing in the prosperity or esteem of the community, they believe that
they are not influential in it and that those who are care little about what
they think or want.[22]

Indeed, if one seeks explanations of nonvoting by focusing on the nonvoters rather than the voters, another possibly important point stands out
beyond the fact of alienation and a low sense of political efficacy. Voting
is often a threatening activity for the citizen who decides not to vote. For
adults who know little of politics, of the candidates, or of the issues, the act
of voting exposes their own ignorance and threatens their own sense of
confidence and self-esteem. For the citizen whose political cues are mixed
— who was, for example, raised as a Democrat but has Republicanism
urged on him by a persuasive spouse, or who favors the ideology of one
party but the candidate of the other — the necessity of voting threatens
turmoil. Rather than resolve these conflicts the citizen may escape the difficulties of deciding and not vote at all. Conversely, it may be no exaggeration to say that for many habitual voters it is *nonvoting*, with its attendant
feelings of guilt, that is threatening.

There are myriad other ways of explaining the failure to vote. Despite
the women's movement, for instance, there are still groups and locales in
which concern for politics and public affairs is still considered a male responsibility. There are also ad hoc, personal excuses — illness and infirmity
as an example — at least some of which are valid. Especially when individuals begin to explain (rationalize?) their own nonvoting, one gets a
sense of how complex the psychology of nonvoting really is (Figure 8.2).

## CONSEQUENCES FOR THE POLITICAL PARTIES

The American parties, therefore, must operate within an American electorate that constantly shifts in size and composition — but one that, regardless of its momentary size and composition, is never a sample of either the

[22] On political efficacy, see Angus Campbell et al., *The American Voter* (New York:
Wiley, 1960), pp. 96–110, and on the related subject of political cynicism there is
Robert E. Agger, Marshall N. Goldstein, and Stanley A. Pearl, "Political Cynicism:
Measurement and Meaning," *Journal of Politics* 23 (1961): 477–506. A *New York
Times*-CBS poll in 1976 found feelings of powerlessness much more strongly associated
with nonvoting than was distrust of or disillusionment with government, *The New York
Times* (Nov. 16, 1976). For a more impressionistic view, see Arthur T. Hadley, *The
Empty Polling Booth* (Englewood Cliffs: Prentice-Hall, 1978).

## FIGURE 8.2   Nonvoting and the Public Service Ad

The advertisement below appeared as a full page in the *New York Times* the day before the 1977 local elections in that city (Monday, November 7, 1977). It carried no title or heading, and indeed, it hardly needed one. Barney's is a clothing store in New York City.

THE NEW YORK TIMES, MONDAY NOVEMBER 7, 1977

I only vote for President.
The polls are too far away.
I don't want to be called for jury duty.
I had to work late.
I was too tired when I got home.
It's raining.
I didn't know I had to register.
I have a headache.
I hate making decisions.
Whenever I vote, they lose.
I forgot.
Tuesday's my bowling night.
I hate waiting on lines.
The voting booth gives me claustrophobia.
I didn't know where to vote.
My company doesn't give me off.
I was out of town.
There's no one to watch the kids.
I broke my glasses.
The polls were closed when I got there.
I hate crowds.
The Knicks were playing.
I'm moving anyway.
My car broke down.
Everyone knows who's gonna win.
I had a doctor's appointment.
When was the election?
I already voted in the primaries.
I had to study for a test.
It was my vacation day.
My vote won't make the difference.

## A collection of the classics from Barney's.
Polls will be open tomorrow from 6:00 AM to 9:00 PM

Courtesy of Barney's, New York

full American adult population or that segment of it eligible to vote. Much of the strategy of the parties in pursuing their goals, especially the contesting of elections, must take account of those facts.

## Long-range Consequences

The long-run consequences for the parties of changes in the electorate spring from basic changes in its legal definitions. Since electorates in democracies expand rather than contract, the changes invariably result from the addition of new groups to the eligible electorate. At the moment, the American parties are absorbing two major groups: previously disenfranchised American blacks and young citizens between eighteen and twenty-one. Despite the increasingly competitive efforts of Republicans, these new electorates will be Democratic ones at least in the foreseeable future.

All the SES characteristics of the black electorate predispose it to the national Democratic party. So, too, does the national Democrats' support of black equality and aspirations. About two-thirds of the black electorate identifies with the Democratic party, and the black vote in both 1964 and 1968 was more than 90 percent Democratic. It was 84 percent in 1972 and 88 percent in 1976. The major impact of the expansion of black voting opportunities after 1965 was, of course, felt more dramatically in some states. In Texas, for example, the combination of the abolition of the poll tax and the passage of the 1965 Voting Rights Act — plus some vigorous registration drives among blacks and Chicanos — added well over 400,000 voters between 1964 and 1968. Not accidentally, perhaps, the Humphrey-Muskie ticket carried Texas in 1968.[23]

The impact of the youngest voters entering the electorate for the first time is more complex. They are somewhat more Democratic than the rest of the population, and they are also much more frequently ideological liberals, regardless of party preference. But they are also more likely to be independents, to split their tickets, and indeed, not to register or vote in the first place. In 1972 the class of newly eligible voters was larger than ever (aged eighteen to twenty-four) because of the lowering of the minimum voting age beginning in that year. More than 25 million young voters entered the electorate at that time, and approximately half of them voted. That eighteen- to twenty-four-year-old group preferred George McGovern over Richard Nixon by a margin of 51 to 49 percent. Nixon won 66 percent of the votes of those twenty-five and over. However, President Carter took only 51 percent of the under-twenty-five two-party vote in 1976.[24]

[23] On black voting and nonvoting, see Donald R. Matthews and James W. Prothro, *Negroes and the New Southern Politics* ( New York: Harcourt, Brace, 1966).
[24] The voting data come from Gerald M. Pomper, *Voter's Choice* (New York: Dodd, Mead, 1975), p. 93. The 1976 data are from the Survey Research Center of the University of Michigan.

Long-run consequences for the parties also stem from changes in the composition or distribution — rather than the size — of the American electorate. Population growth and migration offer an example. The parties of Alaska, Arizona, California, Colorado, Florida, Maryland, and Nevada all faced increases in state populations in excess of 25 percent between 1960 and 1970. Similarly the aging of the American population creates a larger group of over-sixty-five voters in each successive presidential election. Again, the important point is that these shifts and growths are differential — the groups (and their goals) added in each case are not a sample of the entire American electorate.

One more striking datum should suffice to conclude these remarks about the consequences of participation and nonparticipation for the parties. There were still some 45 million adults of voting age in 1976 who were not registered to vote — whether for reasons of disqualification or their own unconcern. We have every reason to suspect they are heavily Democratic in their inclinations. Legislation to begin national election day registration thus became a partisan issue in the Congress in 1977, with liberal Democrats supporting it and conservative Democrats and Republicans in opposition.

### Short-range Consequences

In addition to the long-range consequences of changes in the basic structure of the eligible electorate, the political parties must react to the short-range consequences of changes in turnout from election to election. Since increases or decreases in turnout are unlikely to benefit all parties and candidates equally — because nonvoters as a group have different political characteristics from voters (Table 8.3) — these matters, too, have potent political consequences. The increasing or decreasing of voter turnout and the exploiting of variations in turnout between various elections frequently become focal points in party strategy. The somewhat innocent campaigns of Boy Scouts and the League of Women Voters to "get out the vote" sometimes miss this point. Getting out the vote may be tantamount to getting one party or candidate into office.

The conventional wisdom of American politics has it that big turnouts favor the Democrats. With the general truth of that maxim there is little room to quarrel. The greatest percentage of nonvoters in the United States comes from the groups ordinarily disposed to the Democratic party. It is for this reason that effective registration or get-out-the-vote campaigns help the Democrats more often than not. The truth of the maxim explains the money and manpower that organized labor spends in registration campaigns. It explains the ancillary maxim that rainy weather is Republican weather. And it also suggests why in some states Republicans prefer an electoral calendar in which the gubernatorial elections are held in the non-

**TABLE 8.3**   Comparison of Voters and Nonvoters in the 1976
Presidential Election

|                                               | Presidential Voters | Presidential Nonvoters |
| --------------------------------------------- | ------------------- | ---------------------- |
| Percentage male                               | 44.3%               | 33.6%                  |
| Percentage white                              | 90.1%               | 85.3%                  |
| Median age                                    | 45                  | 34                     |
| Median education                              | high school grad    | high school grad       |
| Percentage "very much" interested in campaign | 44.1%               | 21.2%                  |
| Percentage identifying as "independent"       | 33.4%               | 42.6%                  |

*Source*   Survey Research Center of the University of Michigan. Data made available through the Inter-University Consortium for Political Research.

presidential years and, therefore, in a smaller electorate a bit more favorable to Republican candidates.

Despite the general truth of the maxim linking big turnouts with the Democrats, the relationship is a more subtle and complicated one. Dwight D. Eisenhower, for example, won the presidency as a Republican in two high-turnout elections, and what's more, the nonvoters in 1956 were disposed also to the Republican candidate (Table 8.4). The Eisenhower success seems to force a clarification. High turnout works to a Democratic advantage only in elections in which party loyalty is a chief or overriding factor. A heavy turnout may be stimulated by a candidate (Eisenhower) or issues (as in 1972) that work to Republican advantage. Especially since the nonvoter is less partisan, he may be more responsive to the momentary, dramatic appeal of issue or candidate. Therefore, the maxim works best in elections or party systems in which the SES factors underlie the division of party loyalties and in which party loyalties remain the chief key to the decisions of voters.

Party strategists cannot fail to consider the likely voting electorate as they prepare their campaigns. They nourish the often fragile hope that turnouts can be affected selectively and differentially, and they attempt, therefore, to mold the size and makeup of the participating electorate itself in the campaign. When they must contest a primary election, they may hope by discreet and selective campaigning to minimize the turnout, for (generally) the smaller the turnout, the larger will be the proportion of it accounted for by the party's own loyal electorate. In general elections the strategists may try to concentrate campaigns in areas of known party strength and thus maximize that turnout. And individuals planning a con-

TABLE 8.4   Postelection Preferences of Nonvoters: 1952–76

|                              | 1952 | 1956 | 1960 | 1964 | 1968 | 1972 | 1976 |
|------------------------------|------|------|------|------|------|------|------|
| Would have voted Democratic  | 52%  | 28%  | 51%  | 80%  | 45%  | 35%  | 57%  |
| Would have voted Republican  | 48   | 72   | 49   | 20   | 41   | 65   | 43   |
|                              | 100  | 100  | 100  | 100  | 86 [a] | 100 [b] | 100 [b] |

[a] Fourteen percent would have voted for George Wallace's American Independent party.
[b] The 1972 and 1976 data are the preferences of respondents who did not intend to vote in the election; the SRC apparently did not try to question nonvoters after the election after 1968.

*Source*   Angus Campbell et al., *The American Voter* (New York: Wiley, 1960), p. 111. (Campbell's table has been updated by SRC data.)

gressional career always confront the fact that they will seek reelection by different electorates in alternate elections — the large turnout of the presidential election followed by the smaller turnout of the mid-term elections two years later.

## THE BROADER ISSUES

The democratic ethos assumes the desirability of full popular participation in the affairs of democratic self-government. The case for democracy itself rests on the wisdom of the widest possible sharing of political power and political decision-making within the society. And it is precisely this ethos that is offended by the relatively low voting percentages of American adults. The affront to the democratic ethos seems all the greater in view of the fact that voting percentages are higher in countries that Americans would like to think have less stable and responsive democracies.

Widespread nonvoting also casts some doubt on the effectiveness with which the political parties — the political organizations primarily concerned with contesting elections — manage to involve the total eligible electorate. Presumably the parties, heralded so often as the instruments of democratic politics, should maximize political participation in the American society. The political parties themselves are, after all, the political organizations that developed to mobilize the new democratic masses and all of whose capabilities are directed to recruiting large political aggregates. Much of the case for their superiority as political organizations rests on that ability.

The record of the parties in mobilizing and involving the American electorate is clearly a mixed one. We can point to many examples of effective competition for the support of new groups entering the electorate. The two parties of the South in various areas, despite the strength of old racial mores, have recently made room for black voices in party councils and have made more moderate appeals to the new black electorate. Furthermore, one can hardly blame the parties for the legal limits on the suffrage or for the poverty, illiteracy, and alienation in American society.

Even so, the hands of the parties are not completely clean. They often appear not to relish the challenges of new voters, especially those of low status. The experience of political power has made them (and especially their parties in government) sympathetic to the comfortable status quo of two-party competition. Party leaders and officeholders themselves have been largely recruited from high-status groups in American society and easily accept prevailing norms and institutions. They do not welcome the uncertainties that a radical alteration in the electorate would bring. The party in government, which will have to make the changes in the formal definition of the electorate, has won office with the support of the electorate as it now exists, and it is understandably not anxious to alter it greatly. Furthermore, some state party organizations in one-party areas have entrenched themselves in power largely by restricting the electorate; in many southern states the Democratic party until recently stayed in power with the aid of an artificially homogeneous suffrage. Not unexpectedly, then, the history of women's suffrage and the end of black disenfranchisement indicate that the parties were not in the vanguard of either movement to expand the electorate.

Do the parties also carry a share of the responsibility for the voluntary disenfranchisement of the American nonvoter? They have been blamed for suppressing participation by failing to interest large numbers of Americans in the dialectics and personalities of politics. E. E. Schattschneider, for example, argued that to 35 million nonvoters the rituals and choices of American politics are virtually meaningless.[25] The trouble with the Schattschneider thesis is its assumption that nonvoters are rational, informed, and careful surveyors of the political scene who decide they find it irrelevant to their goals. All that we know about the American nonvoters indicates quite the contrary. However, our data on the nonvoter suggest only what he is, not how he happened to become what he is. Thus it is possible to argue that the political parties are one of a number of important political and social institutions that fail to educate and involve various sectors of the American society.

The American parties, therefore, work within an artificially homoge-

---

[25] E. E. Schattschneider, *The Semi-Sovereign People* (New York: Holt, Rinehart and Winston, 1960), Chap. 6.

neous "active" electorate. That electorate reduces the totality of political conflict and the range of political interests the parties must respond to. In every way the parties' political job is easier because of the cumulative restrictions (regardless of how they are imposed) on the American electorate. The parties find it easier to be moderate and pragmatic because the electorate to which they respond is largely settled in and committed to the present basic social arrangements. Compromise and tactical movement come more easily when the effective electorate is homogeneous and in agreement on fundamentals. In brief, although it has been fashionable to say that the moderate, pragmatic, nondoctrinaire American parties are the result of an electorate agreed on the fundamental questions, it is probably also true that the pragmatic, majoritarian parties in a two-party system do not easily draw into their ambit the low-status, alienated, dissident individuals who are not a part of that moderate consensus.

# IV

# THE POLITICAL PARTIES IN THE ELECTORAL PROCESS

The contesting of elections unites, however briefly, the disparate and fragmented American parties. The choice of a presidential candidate and the following campaign bind the state and local parties into a fleeting semblance of a national party. A statewide election similarly focuses the activities and energies of local organizations and leaders within the state. Furthermore, any election joins the three party sectors into a grand coalition of the party elites and the party clienteles. The contesting for public office is the one time in the life of the party when all its various sectors are united in the pursuit of their varied goals.

The pursuit of victory in elections unites the party for a number of reasons. The election is the event that elevates the business of politics to a visibility that stimulates even the less concerned members of the electorate. The contesting candidates personify and simplify the difficult choices of American politics. Furthermore, the recruitment of resources for the party organization depends on the party's establishing the likelihood, or at least the possibility, of electoral victory. In the long run the incentives that lure resources to the party flow only to those parties that win. Only from electoral victory come the patronage job, the triumph of an interest or an ideology, and even the social and psychological rewards of politics.

The American parties are parties that must win elections; therefore, they must be able to mobilize majorities in the electorate. The conventional references to the American parties as electoral parties are, however, a little too glib and hackneyed. For one thing, these references imply that the parties carry out their electoral activities with ease. To the contrary, the party organizations find it difficult to control the selection of candidates, take stands on issues, fix campaign strategies, even raise money. Those aspects of the contesting of elections are controlled, in the name of the whole party, by its candidates — its party in government and the candidates hoping to join it. In many parts of the country the party candidates, in fact, have organized their own campaigns, recruited their own workers, hired their own campaign advice, and raised their own campaign funds. If it is true that the party in government controls the central, most visible activities of the party (at the expense of a frustrated party organization), can the party organizations reasonably achieve the goals their activists set?

At the same time that the party stages an internal competition over the control of its electoral strategies, it also faces the competition of other political organizations. They also seek their political goals increasingly in the electoral processes. Over the past twenty years the nonparty political organizations — the interest groups, party factions, personal followings, voluntary campaign committees, ideological organizations — have taken aggressive, overt roles in the nomination and election of candidates. It is not uncommon now to read newspaper accounts of the electoral activities of trade unions, ad hoc campaign organizations such as the Ford for President Committee, public relations firms, reform groups such as the National Women's Political Caucus, and even a nebulously defined Kennedy family organization.

Such fundamental issues of control and competition in elections — both within the party and within the broader company of all the political organizations — raise questions to which generalizations about the parties must ultimately be addressed. For these kinds of competition go a long way in determining what the parties are and what they do in the political system. Throughout the coming chapters runs another theme close to those same basic questions: the impact of political institutions on the forms and activities of the parties. For nowhere are the effects of political institutions on the parties clearer than in the electoral processes. The direct primary, for example, touches every attempt the parties make to control the nomination of candidates. In fact, it is the primary that so often turns the control of nominations from the party organization to the candidates themselves or to other political organizations.

In the chapters of this section, we will observe two sets of distinctions for the sake of orderly exposition. The first is the common one between the nominating of the parties' candidates and the contesting of the general election.[1] Even though the distinction between the two parts of the electing business can be arbitrary and misleading, it is analytically useful. The use of the distinction does not deny that it is a single process we are de-

---

[1] Within the last several years Louisiana has broken the tradition of separate nomination and election steps. For races other than those for the presidency and Congress, it now holds a single election. All candidates of all parties run in it and are designated by party on the ballot. If one candidate wins a majority of the vote, he or she is elected to the office. If not, the top two candidates, regardless of their party, face each other in a runoff election.

scribing. Elections may be lost or won in the earliest informal steps to encourage candidates, and the nature of the nomination often depends on the ultimate chances for electoral victory.

The special chapters set aside for the nomination and election of the American president reflect the second distinction. The contest for the presidency is a special case and must be so treated. Although the direct primary dominates the formal nominating machinery for almost all American public offices, the convention it replaced still functions in the nomination of presidential candidates. And the special election machinery of the electoral college sets the presidential election apart from the simpler plurality elections that prevail elsewhere in American politics (Table IV.1).

Thus Chapters 9 and 10 describe the modal patterns of American electoral machinery and politics. Chapters 11 and 12 deal with the fascinating and peculiar processes by which presidents are chosen. The final chapter of this part discusses the recruitment of the most important resource for the contesting of elections: money.

**TABLE IV.1   Comparison of Steps in the Nomination-Election Processes in the United States**

|  | Prenomination | Nomination | Election |
|---|---|---|---|
| *Presidential elections* | Selection of delegates to national convention by state party action or presidential primary | By national party convention | By plurality vote within the states, and majority of votes in electoral college |
| *Other American elections* | Access to primary ballot by petition, request, or party action | By direct primary or (in a few cases) by convention | By plurality vote at a general election |

# 9

## The Naming of the Party Candidates

Few Americans realize how indigenously American the direct primary is. Having devised it and adopted it almost universally for the nomination of candidates, they seem unaware that the rest of the world has not followed their lead. The point is important, not because American political naïveté is unusually great, but because it points up the peculiar and even unique aspects of American politics and political parties. No other single fact goes so far to explain the differences between the American parties and those of the other Western nations as the direct primary. It has forced on the parties a different set of strategies in making nominations, in contesting elections, and in attempting eventually to maintain responsibility over their successful candidates in office.

In the irresistible advance of the direct primary in the twentieth century no state has been untouched. The great majority of states employ it in all nominations, and the rest use it in most. For the present it suffices to say that by the direct primary (or more simply the primary) we mean a special election in which the party electorate chooses candidates to run for public office under the party label. At a subsequent general election, the total electorate then makes the final choice from among the nominees of the parties.

Even though the nomination does not formally settle the electoral outcome, its importance is great. The major screening of candidates takes place at the nomination; the choice is reduced to two in most constituencies. Especially in areas of one-party domination the real choice is made at the primary.

For the parties themselves, the consequences of the nomination processes bulk large. The images of the candidates of a party are to some extent its images; the candidates' reputations and stands on public issues become the party's. Furthermore, the candidate with whom the party goes into the election campaign determines to a great extent its ultimate chances for victory. The nomination of candidates, moreover, offers the party a major opportunity for uniting its wings and factions behind acceptable candidates. In short, it is crucial to a political party who its candidates are, both for the winning of elections and for the building of internal unity and cohesion.

## ADVENT OF THE DIRECT PRIMARY

At the beginning of the twentieth century the direct primary had come into use only in scattered communities in scattered states. For the first 110 years of the Republic, first the party caucus and then the party convention dominated the nomination of candidates for public office. Each gave way successively under the criticism that it permitted, if not encouraged, the making of nominations by self-picked and irresponsible party elites. Finally, the primary triumphed on the belief that in a democracy the greatest possible number of "party members" ought to take part in the nomination of the party's candidates. The history of the evolution of nominating methods in the United States, above all, is a story of the progressive victory of the values and symbols of democracy.

Formal systems of nomination developed in the United States along with and as a part of the development of the party system. In fact, parties as parties (rather than as legislative associations) developed and evolved largely as nominators of candidates for public office. At the end of the eighteenth century, local caucuses met to select candidates, and frequently caucuses of like-minded partisans in legislatures met to nominate candidates for governorships and other statewide offices. Similar congressional caucuses met to nominate presidential and vice-presidential candidates. But whatever their form, the caucuses were self-selected. There was no machinery, no procedure, for ensuring even the participation of all the powerful in the party. The Jacksonians attacked the caucus relentlessly as an aristocratic device that thwarted popular wishes, and "King Caucus" was indeed an ample target.

In 1832 the Democrats met in a national convention for the first time and, appropriately enough, nominated Andrew Jackson for the presidency. From then on, the convention system quickly triumphed along with Jacksonian popular democracy, the values of which it shared. It dominated the making of nominations for the rest of the nineteenth century. Broadly representative at its best, the nominating convention was composed of delegates chosen by the local party organizations. But even though they were representative in form, the large and chaotic conventions were scarcely that in reality. Both in the picking of delegates and in the management of the conventions, the fine, guiding hands of party leaders were too obvious and oppressive. Party insurgents, unhappy with bossism at the conventions and with the alliance of the bosses and "the interests," belabored the convention system with moral fervor and political cunning.

### La Follette and the Primary

No one has captured the rhetoric and fervor of the movement for the direct primary as well as its leader, Robert M. La Follette, governor and then United States Senator from Wisconsin. Writing in his autobiography in the chapter "Struggle with the Bosses," La Follette reports a speech of his in February, 1897, at the University of Chicago. Here are some excerpts from the conclusion:

"Put aside the caucus and convention. They have been and will continue to be prostituted to the service of corrupt organizations. They answer no purpose further than to give respectable form to political robbery. Abolish the caucus and the convention. Go back to the first principles of democracy; go back to the people. Substitute for both the caucus and the convention a primary election . . . where the citizen may cast his vote directly to nominate the candidate of the party with which he affiliates. . . . The nomination of the party will not be the result of 'compromise' or impulse, or evil design — the 'barrel' and the machine — but the candidates of the majority, honestly and fairly nominated."

Robert M. La Follette, *La Follette's Autobiography*
(Madison: R. M. La Follette, 1913), pp. 197–98.

The Progressives led the movement and their journalistic handmaidens, the muckrakers, furnished the often shocking, often piquant, corroborative details.[1]

The cure offered by the Progressives, the direct primary, comported easily with their democratic norms. For it was an article of faith among them that to cure the ills of democracy one needed only to prescribe larger doses of democracy. Appropriately it was one of progressivism's high priests, Robert M. La Follette, who authored the country's first statewide primary law in Wisconsin in 1902 (see box). In the next fifteen years all but four states had adopted the primary, at least in part. In 1955 Connecticut capitulated and became the last state to adopt it.

Although the primary was designed to reform the nominating processes by "democratization," many of its supporters saw in it an instrument for crippling the political party itself. For them the primary was an attempt to cut back the power of the parties by striking at their chief activity as a party organization: the nomination of candidates. The party organization had done the nominating under the caucus and convention systems, but primaries took from it the control of who would run under the party

[1] For the story of the convention system and the early years of the direct primary, see Charles E. Merriam and Louise Overacker, *Primary Elections* (Chicago: University of Chicago Press, 1928).

name and symbols. Regardless of the motives of the enactors of the primary laws, there is little doubt that they badly hurt the power of party organizations.

The quick success of the direct primary happened during the years of the greatest one-partyism in American history. In the early years of the twentieth century sectionalism was pervasive, and one party or the other dominated the politics of many states. One-partyism made the nomination of the dominant party crucial. Although the failings of the conventions might be tolerated when a real choice remained in the general election, they could not be borne when the nomination of one party was equivalent to election. The convention could choose the weariest party hack without fear of challenge from the other party. And so the Progressives, who fought economic monopoly with antitrust legislation, fought political monopoly with the direct primary.

## VARIETIES OF THE DIRECT PRIMARY

The primaries of the fifty states are usually divided into three categories. These three differ chiefly in the way they define the party electorate that can vote in them.

### The Closed Primary

Found in thirty-nine states (and the District of Columbia), the closed primary requires that voters declare their party affiliation so that they may vote only in the primary of their own party. In most of these states voters specify their party affiliation when they register. Then at the primary election they are given only the primary ballot of their party so that they may choose among their fellow partisans who seek nomination. They may always change their party affiliation on the registration rolls, but most states require that this be done sometime ahead of the date of the primary. Iowa and Wyoming permit a change of party registration at the polls.

In the other closed primary states, voters simply declare their party "membership" — or, more accurately, their party attachments or preference — when they go to the polling place. They are then given the primary ballot of their party. In some states their declarations can be challenged by one of the party observers at the polls; they may then be required to take an oath of party loyalty. Some states require the voter to affirm that he has voted for the candidates of the party in the past; some demand that he declare himself sympathetic at the moment to the candidates and principles of the party; and others ask nothing at all. Needless to say, the secrecy of the ballot makes it impossible to challenge the worth of such pledges.

### The Open and Blanket Primaries

In the eight states of the open primary — Idaho, Michigan, Minnesota, Montana, North Dakota, Utah, Vermont, and Wisconsin — the voter votes in the primary without disclosing any party affiliation or preference. On entering the polling booth voters are given either ballots for every party (one of which is selected in the privacy of the booth) or else a consolidated ballot on which the part with the party of the voter's choice is selected. A voter may not, however, participate in the primary of more than one party.

The distinctions between open and closed primaries are easy to exaggerate. Too simple a distinction ignores the range of nuances and varieties within the closed primary states, which after all do account for 82 percent of the states. Take the case of Illinois. Voters do not register as members of a party; at the polling place they simply state their party preference and are given the ballot of that party, no questions asked. Because Illinois voters must disclose a party preference before entering the voting booth, their primary is generally considered "closed." One would be hard put, however, to argue that it is in operation much different from an open primary.[2]

The blanket primary, found in Alaska, Louisiana, and Washington, goes one step in freedom beyond the open primary. Not only does the voter not need to disclose any party affiliation, but he is free to vote in the primary of more than one party — that is, he may choose among Democrats seeking nomination for one office, among Republicans seeking another nomination (Figure 9.1). In more puritanical days it was called the "free love" primary.

Among these forms of primary the party organizations clearly prefer the closed primary with party registration prior to the primary. It pays a greater respect to the right of the party itself to make nominations by limiting the party's primary electorate to its own party electorate. And prior registration of party affiliation gives the parties an added bonus: published lists of their partisans. Yet it is not quite that simple. Party registration is at best an approximation of party loyalties at the moment. People are slow to change their party affiliations and the party totals lag behind the pattern of voting at the moment. Furthermore, the registration figures of the major or leading party tend also to be swollen by conformists and by a few "political rationalists," who register in it solely to vote in its crucial primary.

But the parties would gladly accept these uncertainties in preference to

[2] There are some authorities who distinguish between open and closed primaries on the question of whether there is or is not party registration (rather than freedom to choose one's party in the secrecy of the polling booth). Their criterion inevitably yields a larger number of open primaries.

## FIGURE 9.1   The Washington "Blanket" Primary Ballot: 1970

### SAMPLE

# PRIMARY ELECTION BALLOT

THURSTON COUNTY, WASHINGTON                              TUESDAY, SEPTEMBER 15, 1970

INSTRUCTIONS:  To vote for any candidate place an X in the ☐ at the right of the name of such candidate.

| FEDERAL | LEGISLATIVE | COUNTY |
|---|---|---|

**FEDERAL**

**UNITED STATES SENATOR**   Vote for One
| | |
|---|---|
| HENRY M. JACKSON | Democrat ☐ |
| R. J. (BOB) ODMAN | Republican ☐ |
| JOHN (HUGO FRYE) PATRIC | Democrat ☐ |
| WILLIAM H. DAVIS | Republican ☐ |
| CARL MAXEY | Democrat ☐ |
| HOWARD S. REED | Republican ☐ |
| BILL PATRICK | Republican ☐ |
| CHARLES W. ELICKER | Republican ☐ |
| MRS. CLARICE PRIVETTE | Democrat ☐ |
| | ☐ |

**REPRESENTATIVE IN CONGRESS**
THIRD CONGRESSIONAL DISTRICT   Vote for One
| | |
|---|---|
| KEN STEVENS | Republican ☐ |
| JULIA BUTLER HANSEN | Democrat ☐ |
| R. C. (SKIP) McCONKEY | Republican ☐ |
| | ☐ |

**JUDICIAL**

**JUDGE, STATE SUPREME COURT**
POSITION NO. 1  (6 year term)
Non-Partisan   Vote for One
| | |
|---|---|
| ROBERT T. HUNTER | ☐ |
| VAUGHN E. EVANS | ☐ |

POSITION NO. 2  (6 year term)
Non-Partisan   Vote for One
| | |
|---|---|
| MARSHALL A. NEILL | ☐ |
| | ☐ |

POSITION NO. 3  (6 year term)
Non-Partisan   Vote for One
| | |
|---|---|
| CHARLES F. STAFFORD | ☐ |
| WILLIAM C. GOODLOE | ☐ |
| | ☐ |

POSITION NO. 4  (Unexpired 2 Year Term)
Non-Partisan   Vote for One
| | |
|---|---|
| MORELL E. SHARP | ☐ |
| CHARLES T. WRIGHT | ☐ |
| | ☐ |

**JUDGE, COURT OF APPEALS, Div. 2, Dist. 2**
POSITION 1  Non-Partisan   Vote for One
| | |
|---|---|
| HAROLD J. PETRIE | ☐ |
| | ☐ |

**JUDGE, SUPERIOR COURT**
POSITION NO. 3  (Unexpired 2 Year Term)
Non-Partisan   Vote for One
| | |
|---|---|
| FRANK E. BAKER | ☐ |

**LEGISLATIVE**

**STATE REPRESENTATIVE (22nd District)**
POSITION NO. 1   Vote for One
| | |
|---|---|
| HAL WOLF | Republican ☐ |
| CHARLES (CHUCK) A. LINDBERG | Democrat ☐ |
| ELMER KEISKI | Democrat ☐ |
| | ☐ |

POSITION NO. 2   Vote for One
| | |
|---|---|
| MARY STUART LUX | Democrat ☐ |
| WILLIAM M. AMBURGEY | Democrat ☐ |
| BURTON R. JOHNSON | Democrat ☐ |
| FLOYD CONWAY | Republican ☐ |
| | ☐ |

**COUNTY**

**ASSESSOR**   Vote for One
| | |
|---|---|
| DEL PETTIT | Democrat ☐ |
| JOHN M. (JACK) COWAN | Republican ☐ |
| BERTRAN (CARL) NELSON | Democrat ☐ |

**AUDITOR**   Vote for One
| | |
|---|---|
| C. WESLEY LEACH | Republican ☐ |
| AMY BELL | Democrat ☐ |

**CLERK**   Vote for One
| | |
|---|---|
| MARK CANTERBURY | Republican ☐ |
| MARY SULLIVAN GOLDENBERGER | Democrat ☐ |
| MARY WOOD | Republican ☐ |
| | ☐ |

**CORONER**   Vote for One
| | |
|---|---|
| HOLLIS B. FULTZ | Republican ☐ |

**PROSECUTING ATTORNEY**   Vote for One
| | |
|---|---|
| JERRY BUZZARD | Republican ☐ |
| SMITH TROY | Democrat ☐ |

**SHERIFF**   Vote for One
| | |
|---|---|
| DONALD E. ROBERTS | Democrat ☐ |
| PAT HALL | Democrat ☐ |
| TONY SEXTON | Republican ☐ |
| DON REDMOND | Democrat ☐ |
| CLARENCE A. VAN ALLEN | Republican ☐ |
| FRED G. ANDERSON | Republican ☐ |
| | ☐ |

Compiled by:  **C. WESLEY LEACH**
Thurston County Auditor
Supervisor of Elections

**COUNTY**

**TREASURER**   Vote for One
| | |
|---|---|
| GEORGE M. HASKETT | Democrat ☐ |
| W. R. (DICK) CHAPMAN | Republican ☐ |
| | ☐ |

**JUDGE—Thurston County Justice Court District**
Non-Partisan   Vote for One
| | |
|---|---|
| FRANKLIN K. THORP | ☐ |
| | ☐ |

**COMMISSIONER**
THIRD DISTRICT   Vote for One
| | |
|---|---|
| WES ESTES | Republican ☐ |
| HOMER HEDGEPETH | Democrat ☐ |
| | ☐ |

**SPECIAL ELECTION**
THURSTON COUNTY, WASHINGTON
Tuesday, September 15, 1970

INSTRUCTIONS:  To vote for or against the proposition, place an X in the appropriate ☐ following the proposition.

**PROPOSITION NO. 1**
County Courthouse and Building Bonds
$8,500,000.00

Shall Thurston County, Washington, contract an indebtedness in the sum of not to exceed $8,500,000.00 and issue its negotiable general obligation bonds therefor, to be payable by annual tax levies to be made without limitation as to rate or amount, and to mature in from two to not more than thirty years from date of issue, for County capital purposes only, other than the replacement of equipment, to construct, equip and furnish a new County Courthouse, health facilities and juvenile home on sites presently owned by the County, all as provided in Resolution No. 4080 of the Board of County Commissioners of Thurston County, passed and approved July 31, 1970?

| | |
|---|---|
| BONDS, YES | ☐ |
| BONDS, NO | ☐ |

N. P. BANK NOTE CO. ◆ OF OLYMPIA

what they regard as the more serious perils of the open primary. (The blanket primary enjoys even less favor.) Party leaders levy two charges against the open primary: crossing over and raiding. The terms are sometimes used synonymously, but a distinction can be made between them. Crossing over is the participation by voters in the primary of the party they do not generally support or feel a loyalty to. It is a drifting across party lines in search of the excitement of a primary battle. Raiding is an organized attempt on the part of one party to send its partisans into the primary of the other in order to foist the least attractive candidates on it.

That crossing over happens in open primary states is beyond doubt. Take the case of primary contests in Wisconsin, cradle of the open primary and home of an especially rambunctious political tradition. It is also the state in which the open primary has been most thoroughly studied. Survey data on two gubernatorial primaries in the 1960s put the crossover vote at between 6 and 8 percent of the primary voters. It was, however, much higher in the state's presidential primaries of the same period: an average of about 25 percent of the voters in the 1964, 1968, and 1972 presidential primaries. Crossing over was doubtless kept to a minimum in the gubernatorial primaries by the need to stay in one's party's primary to decide other party contests. Since the presidential primaries involve only the one contest, no such constraint was present in their cases.[3]

As for organized raiding, there is little evidence to suggest that it is more than a worrisome myth. Every party fears that voters drifting to the other party's primary will develop a habit of voting that will carry over to the general election. Furthermore, the party must also be on guard lest the migration from its own primary permit its contests to be settled by unrepresentative or irresponsible minorities. In other words, the party has every reason to encourage its loyalists to stay and vote in their own primary.

## PRIMARIES: RULES OF THE GAME

The distinctions discussed in the last few pages concern the basic form of the primary election. The following paragraphs elaborate on its implementation.

### Access to the Primary Ballot

First of all, the states must deal with the problem of how a candidate gets on the primary ballot. Most states permit access to the ballot by petition (called nomination papers in some areas). State statutes fix the number

[3] Austin Ranney, "Turnout and Representation in Presidential Primary Elections," *American Political Science Review* 66 (1972): 21–37; and David Adamany, "Cross-over Voting and the Democratic Party's Reform Rules," *American Political Science Review* 70 (1976): 536–41.

of required signatures, generally either a specific number or a percentage of the vote for the office in the last election. In some cases it is sufficient for the would-be candidate to present himself to the clerk of elections and pay a usually modest fee. Finally, a few states put candidates on the ballot if they have formal party support. In Colorado, for example, any seekers after nomination who poll 20 percent or more of the endorsement vote at party conventions are automatically placed on the primary ballot.

Even such mundane matters as access to the primary ballot have consequences for the parties. The easier the access, the easier it is for crank or dissident candidates to engage the party-supported candidate in a costly primary battle. Such arcane matters as the number of signatures a petition must have, therefore, may materially affect the number of primary contests in the state.[4]

### Cross-filing

Until 1959 California, alone among the states, permitted candidates to enter both major party primaries, a practice called cross-filing. In 1946, while it was in full flower, Earl Warren won both party nominations for governor; in the general election Earl Warren, Republican, ran without Democratic opposition. Bowing to criticism that cross-filing destroys a party's responsibility for its candidates and, in fact, destroys the basic assumption of nominations by a political party, the state legislature abolished it. The closest remaining practice is New York's willingness to permit cross-filing if — and the "if" is a big one — the second party approves. Since the two major parties do not approve, New York has had no instances of candidates running on both Democratic and Republican tickets. The major parties are, however, friendly to the idea of their candidates running also on the ticket of an appropriate minor party. So, one sees the quest for the two-way nomination on Democratic and Liberal party ballots or on the Republican and Conservative party tickets.

### Run-off Primaries

Finally, some states have tried to cope with the issues of primaries that are settled by less than a majority of the voters. In those cases in which

---

[4] Access to the ballot is, along with all other aspects of election law, receiving greater attention by the United States Supreme Court these days. The effect of the scrutiny doubtless will in the long run be to make candidacy easier. For example, in 1972 the Court invalidated a Texas law requiring candidates to pay both a flat fee for candidacy and a share of the cost of the election. The total charges had run as high as $9000 for a candidate. *Bullock* v *Carter* (405 U.S. 134, 1972). In March of 1974 the Court also overturned the California scale of filing fees. It did not prohibit filing fees per se, but the justices ruled that states using them must provide an alternative means of access to the ballot (such as a petition) for candidates unable to pay the fee. *Lubin* v *Panish* (415 U.S. 709, 1974).

candidates are nominated by only 35, 40, or 45 percent, most states simply hope that the general election will produce a majority winner. But the District of Columbia and nine states, all from the South and its borders, have run-off primaries if the winner in the regular primary wins less than 50 percent. In these second primaries the two candidates with the highest vote totals face each other. This southern institution reflects the period of Republican impotence in which the Democratic nomination was in effect election and in which intense Democratic factionalism often produced three, four, or five serious candidates for a single office. Much more recently, another center of one-party domination, New York City, has begun run-off primaries if no candidate in the primary wins 40 percent of the vote. Iowa and South Dakota have approached the same basic problem with a fresh solution. If no primary candidate gets 35 percent of the votes cast, a party convention meets and selects the party's candidate.

### The Nonpartisan Primary

Although of lesser importance in a book on American political parties, the nonpartisan primary is the means of nominating most judges, thousands of local officials, and even the legislature of Nebraska. As the nominating system that must accompany the nonpartisan election, the nonpartisan primary puts all candidates for the office on one ballot on which no party designations appear. The two candidates receiving the highest number of votes at the primary become the candidates for the nonpartisan general election. Although there are no party labels on the ballot, the party affiliations of various candidates may be well known. Party organizations may openly endorse and support candidates, especially in nonpartisan mayoralty and city council elections. In those cases the distinction between a partisan and nonpartisan primary may remain only for the voters who have inadequate political information.

## THE LINGERING CONVENTIONS

The convention as a device for nominating candidates faded quickly under early inroads by the direct primary. But decline has not meant death, and as of now the convention as a nominating device retains firm control over a significant number of public offices.

Many states exempt the minor parties from the direct primary. The states are not anxious to incur the financial expense, and realism suggests that minor-party nominations are not especially important anyway. Moreover, parties such as the Prohibition and Socialist Labor parties have difficulty enough finding even one candidate to run the futile race. Depending on state law, their candidates may be chosen by party convention or simply by petition. In the one-party days of the South it also became common to give Republican parties the option of making their nominations in party conventions rather than in the primary.

Furthermore, a minority of states still keeps some offices (usually statewide ones) out of the direct primary. In Delaware, nominations for statewide offices are still made in state party conventions. In other states such as Michigan, candidates for specific statewide offices are so chosen. Until very recently, New York parties chose their statewide candidates in state conventions, in which the ideological and geographic factions of the parties were propitiated and possibly even unified. In 1967, however, New York replaced convention nominations with a system that permits the state committees of the parties to designate their candidates. Other would-be candidates may then challenge the committee's choices in a statewide primary.

Connecticut, the last state to embrace the primary, did so without a conspicuous show of affection. The Connecticut primary is like New York's, a challenge primary, and it combines convention with primary. Each party holds conventions to nominate candidates, and if no other candidate challenges the party nominee, the latter goes directly on the ballot of the general election without an intervening primary. In the event of a challenge, a primary is held, but the challenger must have sought nomination in the convention, must have amassed at least 20 percent of the convention votes, and must later have filed nomination petitions. The first statewide primary took place in 1970, fifteen years after the adoption of the Connecticut primary.

Why has the convention survived in some of the states? It remains in a few states having strong, centralized party organization and a political culture more accepting of the role of parties as robust, self-contained political organizations. As Lockard has written of Connecticut:

> Why such protracted and successful resistance? Connecticut is not immune to political innovation. Although it may be known as "The Land of Steady Habits," it has nonetheless adopted an imposing array of progressive legislation, particularly in matters of labor law and social welfare. Still, matters of party concern are different — at least in Connecticut. For Connecticut parties are different from those of most other states; they are strong, centralized, and highly competitive with each other. The character of Connecticut party leadership — the power it has and the generally responsible manner in which it uses its power — constitutes the main reason why advocates of the primary made so little progress in Connecticut.[5]

In other words, strong, centralized parties can protect the sources of their strength, for in politics, too, "them that has, gets." Convention nomination enables them to bargain within the party to reconcile internal differences

[5] Duane Lockard, *Connecticut's Challenge Primary: A Study in Legislative Politics* (New York: McGraw-Hill, 1960), p. 1.

within it and to maintain a control over candidates and officeholders. It is no coincidence that in a state such as Connecticut, in which parties as parties still control nominations, party cohesion in the state legislature is just about the strongest in the United States.

## THE THREAT OF THE DIRECT PRIMARY

The direct primary does not often substantiate the parties' worst fears, but occasionally it does. In 1962 a political novice from Cleveland with the promising name of Kennedy (Richard D.) managed to win the Democratic nomination for Ohio congressman-at-large in an eleven-cornered primary contest. Not only was he a novice with no support in the Democratic party, but he had run in the primary on a frankly segregationist program. A shocked Democratic party announced that it would not support him in the general election, and Democratic Governor DiSalle said he could not vote for him. Only nominally a Democratic candidate, Mr. Kennedy lost badly in the general election to Robert A. Taft, Jr., the Republican nominee.

Even though such a disaster befalls a party only rarely, the primary often causes it any number of lesser inconveniences, disruptions, and problems. Consider the threats it makes to the well-being of a political party organization:

— For the party that wants to influence nominations, the primary greatly escalates the costs of politics. Supporting candidates in a contested primary is almost always more expensive than holding a convention.

— The primary diminishes the power of the party organization to reward its faithful with nomination for public office. It thus makes less certain one of the rewards by which the party can induce service in its ranks.

— By curbing party control over nominations, the primary denies the party a powerful lever for ensuring the loyalty of its officeholders to the party program. For if the party cannot control or prevent the reelection of the maverick officeholder, it really has no effective sanction for enforcing loyalty to its programs. (The power of European parties to deny renomination to their recalcitrant parliamentarians contributes substantially to their maintenance of party discipline in parliament.)

— The primary permits the nomination of a candidate (1) hostile to the party organization and leadership, (2) opposed to their platforms or programs, or (3) out of key with the public image the party wants to project — or all of the above! At the worst it may permit the nomination of an individual under the party label who will be, intentionally or not, a severe embarrassment to it.

— The primary creates the distinct possibility that the party will find itself saddled with an unbalanced ticket for the general election. In the hypo-

thetical case of an electorate divided into $X$ (50 percent), $Y$ (30 percent), and $Z$ (20 percent) — letting $X$, $Y$, and $Z$ represent regions, races, religions, ethnic or national groups — the voters at the primary may select all or most of the candidates from $X$. (We are assuming considerable bloc voting, but that assumption, after all, lies behind party attempts to balance tickets.) Party leaders unquestionably would think that a sprinkling of $Y$s and $Z$s would make a stronger ticket.
— Party activists also fear that the primary may produce a losing candidate for the party. The nominee may have appealed to only a shade more than half of the dedicated 20 or 30 percent of the electorate that votes in the party's primary. Such a candidate may be poorly equipped to make the broader appeal necessary in the general election.

In addition to all these specific threats is the more general fear that the primary exacerbates party rifts, splits, factions, feuds, or whatever the headline writers choose to call them. It pits party worker against party worker, party group against party group.

A genuine primary is a fight within the family of the party — and, like any family fight, is apt to be more bitter and leave more enduring wounds than battles with the November enemy. In primaries, ambitions spurt from nowhere; unknown men carve their mark; old men are sent relentlessly to their political graves; bosses and leaders may be humiliated or unseated. At ward, county, or state level, all primaries are fought with spurious family folksiness — and sharp knives.[6]

The resulting wounds are often deep and slow to heal. The cost to the health and strength of the party is considerable. Furthermore, there is also substantial evidence that the candidate winning a contested primary will fare less well in the election.[7]

Not even the gloomiest Cassandra expects all these misfortunes to result from any given primary or even a series of them. But they are distinct possibilities for any party, especially the relatively weak and passive one. The parties recognize the danger, but they recognize, too, the futility of a direct assault on the primary. So in the best American tradition of join-

[6] Theodore H. White, *The Making of the President 1960* (New York: Atheneum, 1961), p. 78.
[7] The search for the effects of a contested (and thus "divisive") primary has led to a very substantial scholarly literature. On the effects on the party organization see Donald B. Johnson and James R. Gibson, "The Divisive Primary Revisited: Party Activists in Iowa," *American Political Science Review* 68 (1974): 67–77, and John Comer, "Another Look at the Effects of the Divisive Primary," *American Politics Quarterly* 4 (1976): 121–28. The research reports on the effect in the general election are divided. For the argument that it does lessen the chances of victory in the election, see Robert A. Bernstein, "Divisive Primaries Do Hurt: U. S. Senate Races, 1956–1972," *American Political Science Review* 71 (1977): 540–45. For the opposite view see James E. Piereson and Terry B. Smith, "Primary Divisiveness and General Election Success: A Reexamination," *Journal of Politics* 37 (1975): 555–62.

ing 'em if you can't beat 'em, some parties have set out to control the primary. Others have lacked the will or the strength to do so. Still others have lost ground to local political cultures that disapprove of a party role in the primary. The result is a range of party responses to the primary that extends from no response at all to complete party domination.

## THE PARTY ORGANIZATION FIGHTS BACK

One axiom and a corollary deriving from it govern party strategy in the primary. The axiom is simple to the point of truism: The surest way to control the primary is to prevent competition with the party's choice. And the corollary is equally clear: The party must act as early as possible in the preprimary jockeying of would-be candidates if it is to choke off unwanted competition.

Within some party organizations a powerful party leader or a few party oligarchs make the preprimary decisions for the party organization (see box). Or it may be a party executive committee or candidate selection committee. If their sources of information are good, they will know who intends to run and who is merely considering the race. They may arbitrate among them, or they may coax an unwilling candidate into the primary. If they command a strong and winning organization, their inducements to the nonfavored to withdraw may be considerable. They may be able to offer a patronage position or a chance to run in the future. Any would-be candidate understands the risks in running against a party choice. It is true that some politicians have begun and made political careers by "bucking" a party choice in a primary, but they are not legion.

This informal and often covert selection of candidates — communicated to the party faithful by the "nod" or by the "word" — has been replaced within more and more parties by representative, publicized party conventions. A few states have formalized them; but in those cases state law usually prevents an unqualified endorsement. Colorado laws provide that all candidates who polled more than 20 percent of a convention endorsement vote shall go on the primary ballot in the order of their vote percentage. Utah directs the parties to nominate two candidates for each office. Conversely, a few states attempt by law to minimize the possibility or the power of endorsing conventions. California in 1963 prohibited party organizations from "officially" endorsing candidates for office. And other states, such as Wisconsin, have achieved substantially the same result — with greater subtlety — by requiring party conventions to meet after the primary is safely past.

In most states, however, party endorsing bodies act informally and extralegally — that is, without the laws of the state taking notice of them. In Minnesota, for example, both the Republican party and the Democratic-Farmer-Labor party (the state's version of the Democratic party) hold

## One of the Last of the Slatemakers Slates a Slate

Journalists flocked around Mayor Richard Daley of Chicago to watch his attempts and those of his cohorts to determine party nominations in 1972. Perhaps it was out of a sense that they were watching one of the last of a breed engage in an old and dying tribal ritual. From two reports, these excerpts:

"In Illinois, neither major party bothers with the expense and possible disruption of a state nominating convention. Instead, the state organizations create 'slating committees' to recommend their party's slates of candidates. Committee recommendations are reviewed by the state central committees, usually a formality, and those favored become the organization candidates.

"These candidates are still not officially nominated until they are selected by voters in the primary, but here in Illinois, the party organizations are rarely troubled by serious primary opposition."

From Seth S. King, *The New York Times*, December 7, 1971.
© 1971 by The New York Times Company. Reprinted by permission.

"Slatemaking follows a highly stylized script. Each election year in December, the 'slating committee' — composed of the party's district committeemen, state legislative leaders and a few key Daley observers — repairs to the downstate capital of Springfield to interview prospective candidates. But the Springfield sessions are only warm-ups for the main event: after a few days the Democratic pols pack up and move to the smoky Emerald Room in Chicago, where they are joined by the Cook County panjandrums . . . [including] His Honor himself.

"There, some two dozen office seekers arrive to pay court, hoping to be chosen for jobs ranging from U.S. senator to county coroner. Often the screening boils down to three key questions: How much money can you bring to the campaign? Will you support the entire ticket? How will you distribute patronage?"

From "How Congress Packs It In," *Newsweek*, December 20, 1971, p. 29.
Copyright 1971 by Newsweek, Inc. All rights reserved. Reprinted by permission.

conventions to endorse candidates for statewide office and Congress. In some parts of the state, chiefly the urban areas, they also endorse local candidates and candidates for the state legislature. The instruments of endorsement, the conventions, grow out of the local ward and precinct caucuses mandated by state law. The required vote for endorsement, set by party rule, is 60 percent within both the GOP and the DFL. The party endorsement, however, is strictly unofficial. The endorsee must still go through regular procedures to get on the primary ballot, and the ballot does not note the endorsement.[8]

8 On Minnesota, see G. Theodore Mitau, *Politics in Minnesota*, 2nd ed. (Minneapolis: University of Minnesota Press, 1970).

If a primary contest does develop despite all plans and strategies, the party then falls back on its resources in conventional ways. It may urge party committeepersons to help the anointed candidates circulate nominating petitions and leave the other candidates to their own devices. It may make available money, know-how, party workers, and the party bureaucracy to the chosen ticket. It may print advertisements announcing the party endorsees or issue handy little reference cards, which the forgetful voter can take right into the polling booth. On the day of the primary the party organization may help to get the party's voters to the polls. Whether the party organization acts overtly or covertly in the primary campaign depends both on the local political culture and on the candidates' own appraisals of it. The party and/or the candidates may feel that voter sensitivity to party intervention (i.e., "bossism") may dictate that the candidates appear untouched by party hands.[9]

Of the frequency of party attempts to manage or influence American primaries, it is impossible to write authoritatively. Practices vary not only from state to state but within states, and descriptions of local party practice are hard to come by. One is probably safe in generalizing that the most common nominating activity is the recruiting of candidates to seek the nomination. County party leaders in Wisconsin and Oklahoma have freely conceded that they encourage qualified candidates to seek office. Yet they have not widely attempted to perform the more demanding recruitment activities; only 10 percent of the Wisconsin chairmen, and less than that in Oklahoma, have tried to dissuade some would-be nominees.[10] The result is that in most parts of the country the political party is only one of a number of agencies seeking out and supporting men and women to run for office. It shares their recruitment with local business, professional, farm and labor groups, with civic and community associations, with ethnic, racial, and religious organizations, with political interest groups, and with officeholders.[11]

There are, however, those party organizations that *do* control the recruitment of candidates and the other preprimary processes. Generally

[9] There have always been dark intimations of another party tactic in the primary: "dummy candidates." They are candidates induced by the party to enter an already contested primary in order to divert and divide the support of the unendorsed candidates. The tactic has undoubtedly been employed in American politics, but probably with an incidence far below some suspicions.

[10] Leon D. Epstein, *Politics in Wisconsin* (Madison: University of Wisconsin Press, 1958), p. 93; Samuel C. Patterson, "Characteristics of Party Leaders," *Western Political Quarterly* 16 (1963): 348.

[11] Lester G. Seligman, "Political Recruitment and Party Structure: A Case Study," *American Political Science Review* 55 (1961): 77–86. The interaction may also be reciprocal and complex. J. David Greenstone has illustrated Democratic party influence on trade union endorsements for congressional seats in his "Party Pressure on Organized Labor in Three Cities," in M. Kent Jennings and L. Harmon Zeigler (eds.), *The Electoral Process* (Englewood Cliffs: Prentice-Hall, 1966), pp. 55–80.

they are the parties that also intervene in the primary itself. A study of legislative elections in Pennsylvania constituencies in the late 1950s found that party organizations regularly attempted to influence the primary in 74 percent of the primaries. In 56 percent of them the interventions in the primary were public and explicit.[12] Such determined attempts to control the primary are not necessarily the norm in other parts of the country, however. County chairmen in Kansas, Nebraska, North Dakota, South Dakota, and Iowa disclosed a few years later that they are not a part of Pennsylvania-style activities in the primaries. Some 40 percent of them said they never openly supported a candidate in a primary contest, and about two-thirds of them declared that their party organizations never endorsed candidates before a primary.[13] Just what kind of party relationship to the primary was or is now typical across the United States is anyone's guess.

The role the party organization takes before and during the primary election appears to be a function of a number of factors. First of all, all data point to a greater party role in urban and metropolitan areas. The political ethos of the cities seems to be more tolerant of party action in the primary; furthermore, the cities are also the sites of the strong and virile party organizations.[14] Second, at least one study indicates that party intervention into the primary is most probable in areas of two-party competitiveness. In one-party areas the majority party may tend to be smugly confident or may be dominated by incumbent officeholders. The minority party tends to be helpless, and primary contests within its ranks are rare.[15] Finally, in the states of the Great Plains, at least, it appears that party control of the primary is more common within the Democratic party, even when one controls for urban-rural differences.[16] That finding suggests differences between the two parties in intraparty expectations and ethos. Commentators on the styles and images of the two parties have often noted the more aggressively partisan style of the Democrats and the "nonpartisan," middle-class style of the Republicans. Very possibly these differences affect their approaches to the direct primary.

## CANDIDATES AND VOTERS IN THE PRIMARIES

What the parties can accomplish in the primaries depends to a considerable extent on the candidates and on the electorate. They are often the

[12] Frank J. Sorauf, *Party and Representation* (New York: Atherton, 1963), Chap. 5.
[13] Marvin Harder and Thomas Ungs, *Notes Toward a Functional Analysis of Local Party Organizations* (paper delivered at 1964 meeting of Midwest Political Science Association).
[14] Sorauf, *Party and Representation*, Chap. 5; Harder and Ungs, *Notes Toward a Functional Analysis*.
[15] Patterson, "Characteristics of Party Leaders."
[16] Harder and Ungs, *Notes Toward a Functional Analysis*.

parties' unwitting allies. To put it simply, the primaries are more "manageable" because candidates do not often contest them and because the vast majority of voters do not vote in them. Very possibly one or both of these conditions is of the party's making; the absence of candidates, for example, may reflect the skill of the party's preprimary persuading and dissuading. Regardless of cause, however, the result tends to be a nomination politics of a limited scope more easily controlled by aggressive party organization.

### The Candidates

Simple countings will confirm that in every part of the United States large numbers of primary candidates win nomination without contest. Kirk H. Porter referred to it as the "deserted primary" after finding that in 1944 there had been no contest in either primary for any county office in well over half of Iowa's counties.[17] A number of more recent studies of primary contests in state legislative races suggest that matters have changed little since then. For example, in the 1958 primaries for Pennsylvania legislative elections, 66.2 percent were without contest. Forty-five percent of the legislative primaries in Ohio in 1948 were not contested.[18] In Wisconsin from 1966 through 1972, 58.9 percent of state legislative primaries were not contested. Competition, however, appears to be much more plentiful for the more prestigious statewide offices. In a survey of gubernatorial primaries in thirty-five nonsouthern states from 1950 to 1976, Jewell and Olson found that the majority of states had contests for the gubernatorial nominations in both parties more than 80 percent of the time.[19]

In the aggregate, competition in American primaries (measured by the number of contestants) is greater under certain rather predictable circumstances: (1) Competition tends to flourish in primaries of the dominant party. In other words, competition tends to increase as the party's electoral prospects do, and aggregately it is greatest between the two parties of a district when they are closely matched. (2) Competition also prospers in primaries in urban areas. It tends to increase with increases in the percentages of voters living in urban or metropolitan places. (3) Competition thrives in primaries in which there is no incumbent officeholder seeking nomination. (4) Finally, competition increases in the absence of effective party control or endorsement.

[17] Kirk H. Porter, "The Deserted Primary in Iowa," *American Political Science Review* 39 (1945): 732–40.
[18] Sorauf, *Party and Representation*, p. 111; V. O. Key, *American State Politics* (New York: Knopf, 1956), p. 178.
[19] That is to say, the median percentage of years in which the individual states had contests in both parties' primaries was 81.3 percent. Malcolm E. Jewell and David M. Olson, *American State Political Parties and Elections* (Homewood, Ill.: Dorsey, 1978), p. 143.

There are also other factors influencing competition: the attractiveness of the office and the ease of getting on the ballot, for example. But the chief factor probably is the party's prospects for victory in the general election; large numbers of Americans do not fight for the right to go down to almost certain defeat. As for the power of the incumbent to discourage competition, it is one of the ironies of the primary. The primary puts a premium on the popular appeal and exposure that often only the well-known incumbent can muster. As a result, it fosters the conditions that diminish its own effectiveness.

### The Voters

If candidates are scarce at the primaries, so are voters. All evidence points overwhelmingly to one cardinal fact about the voting behavior of the American electorate at primaries: it does not vote. Even the study of gubernatorial primaries (1950–76) that identified a relatively high incidence of contested races found modest turnout levels. In these instances of races in both of the major party primaries the total voter turnout in the thirty-five states (outside the South) ranged from 95 to 32 percent of the total two-party vote in the subsequent general election. The median was 56 percent. Turnouts for uncontested primaries or those involving only local races and the normally placid judicial races often fall considerably below half of that at the following election.[20]

Even though the primary electorate is small, it does have some special characteristics of its own. A substantial sector of it generally comes from party loyalists and activists. Primary voters, as one might expect, also have higher levels of political interest and higher educational attainments. Conventional political wisdom has also held that primary voters represent more extreme ideological positions than the party's full electorate. Ranney and Epstein's recent studies in Wisconsin, however, disprove the wisdom for that state.[21] Yet it is probably true that primary voters generally are more concerned with ideologies and issues than nonvoters. So although the ideological position of the primary voters may not differ, the intensity of their commitment to it may.

Even this generally interested electorate often lapses into unpredictable voting behavior. For large numbers of voters in the primary, the choice is more difficult than that at the general election. Since all the candidates come from the same party, party loyalties cannot guide the voter's decision. Nor can any reaction to "ins" and "outs." The primary campaign is brief,

---

[20] *Ibid.*
[21] Austin Ranney and Leon D. Epstein, "The Two Electorates: Voters and Non-Voters in a Wisconsin Primary," *Journal of Politics* 28 (1966): 598–616; Austin Ranney, "The Representativeness of Primary Electorates," *Midwest Journal of Political Science* 12 (1968): 224–38.

the candidates are not well known, and the issues, if any, are often unclear. Therefore, the voter's choice is not so well structured or predictable; the presence of an incumbent in the race may be the only continuing, stabilizing element. Consequently, many voter decisions are made right in the polling booth; the effect of the ballot position and the success of the famous names indicate that. Small wonder, then, that parties are never confident in primaries and that public opinion pollers prefer not to predict primary outcomes.

To all of the generalizations on competition and voter turnout in American primaries, there is, however, one great exception: the South. From the end of Reconstruction to the years right after World War II it was securely and overwhelmingly a one-party Democratic section. Despite recent Republican advances, the Democratic party remains dominant in state and local politics. For most offices, therefore, winning the Democratic nomination is tantamount to winning the office itself. The effective competitive politics of the southern states have thus centered in the Democratic primary. In every state of the South, with the exception of North Carolina, the turnout in the Democratic primary has even recently been greater than the Democratic vote in the general election. Sometimes, indeed, it has even been greater than the two-party vote in the election! Voting in the Democratic primaries has, furthermore, been structured in ways unknown in the rest of the country. The Democratic parties of the Southern states have developed a fairly stable, identifiable factionalism, different factions centering around specific interests, regions, and personalities. The Democratic factions best known in the rest of the country are those centering around great family dynasties — the Byrds in Virginia, the Talmadges in Georgia, and the Longs in Louisiana. To the extent that voters can identify candidates as representatives of one faction or another they have a set of cues and a source of political information quite rare for a primary election.

## THE DIRECT PRIMARY AFTER SIXTY YEARS

More than sixty years have now passed since the incorporation of the direct primary into American politics. Thousands of candidates have waged the necessary primary campaigns, and millions of weary voters have puzzled over obscure choices and no choices whatsoever. What difference has it all made? Has the primary democratized the nomination process by taking it out of the hands of party oligarchs? And has it materially increased popular participation in the selection of candidates for public office?

Basically, the democratic hopes behind the direct primary falter on the lack of competition and low voter turnout. There must be participation — both by candidates and by voters — if there are to be meaningful choices based on meaningful alternatives. But the primary by its nature tends to diminish both. The need for broad public appeal, the cost of a contest, and the sheer difficulty of getting on the primary ballot discourage candidacies. And the multiplicity of primaries with their unstructured, confusing, and unclear choices probably also reduces both the quantity and quality of voter participation. Clearly, if mass participation in the nominating processes was a goal of the reformers who initiated the primary, their hopes have not been realized.

The 1976 primaries for the United States House of Representatives in all the nonsouthern states summarize the amount of choice afforded American voters in one set of primaries (Table 9.1).[22] In only 41.1 percent of the primaries was there any competition at all. More significantly, in only 20.3 percent of them was there competition enough to prevent the winner from winning by a two-to-one margin. Table 9.1 also pinpoints the presence of incumbents as a major inhibitor of primary competition. (It also indicates again the tendency for a greater degree of competition in Democratic primaries.) All in all, the opportunities for popular choice in these congressional primaries were considerably limited.

Second, if one purpose of the primary was to replace the caucuses and conventions of the party organizations as nominators, the primary fails when it falls under the sway of those organizations. If the party cannot eliminate primary competition, it can often defeat it. It often commands the money, symbols, and organization essential for primary victory. The party organization also often commands the chief political loyalty of a major share of those who vote in the primary. If only 30 or 40 percent of registered voters vote in the primary, some 15 or 20 percent will be sufficient to nominate. Parties count on the fact that a substantial part of that group is likely to be loyalists who respond to the cues of party leaders or endorsements. So, strong party organizations able to mobilize voters, money, and manpower are still very effective determiners of primary outcomes.[23]

For a variety of reasons, however, the parties control the primaries only imperfectly. The sheer size of the task deters many of them. The Jacksonian tradition of electing every public official down to the local coroner has confronted them with too great a number of contests. The expense of supporting so many candidates — not to mention the expenditure of organizational energy — forces many organizations to be selective in their primary interventions. In other instances parties stand aside because a role in the primary threatens their internal harmony and cohesion. They may be paralyzed by the fear that their activity in the primary will open

[22] The data here and in Table 9.1 are from the 323 congressional districts of the non-South. The inclusion of the 112 districts of the South would further diminish the percentages.
[23] For example, Phillip Cutright and Peter H. Rossi, "Party Organization in Primary Elections," *American Journal of Sociology* 64 (1958): 262–69.

**TABLE 9.1   Competition in Primaries for the House of Representatives:
The Non-South in 1976**

| Primaries | Uncontested | Degree of Primary Competition | | |
| --- | --- | --- | --- | --- |
| | | One candidate | Some competition | Close competition[a] |
| Democratic with incumbent | — | 127 (58.8%) | 74 (34.3%) | 15 (6.9%) |
| Democratic without incumbent | — | 51 (34.9%) | 32 (21.9%) | 63 (43.2%) |
| Democratic uncontested | 5 | — | — | — |
| Republican with incumbent | — | 91 (82.7%) | 14 (12.7%) | 5 (4.5%) |
| Republican without incumbent | — | 128 (56.4%) | 33 (14.5%) | 66 (29.1%) |
| Republican uncontested | 30 | — | — | — |
| Total | 35 (4.8%) | 397 (54.1%) | 153 (20.8%) | 149 (20.3%) |

[a] "Close" here means that the winner won by less than a two-to-one margin over the closest competitor.

*Source*   Richard Scammon (ed.), *America Votes 12* (Washington: Governmental Affairs Institute, 1977).

new wounds or heat up old resentments. Still others are stymied by local political cultures that resist party activity as a violation of the spirit of the primary.

Yet, to argue that the primary has not fulfilled the most optimistic hopes is not to argue that it has had no effect. In competitive districts — especially when an incumbent has stepped down — voters often do play the kind of role the reformers envisioned. And even for the strong party organization, the primaries set tangible limits. Many no longer find it possible to whisk any "warm body" through the nomination process. The direct primary perhaps can best be thought of both as creating a veto body that passes on the work of party nominators and as affording an opportunity for interparty dissidents to take their case to the party's electorate.

Finally, let us consider the more general impact of the primary on the political parties. V. O. Key argued that the primary leads to one-partyism by drawing both the voters and the attractive, prestigious candidates increasingly to the primary of the dominant party. Little by little the majority party becomes the only viable instrument of political influence and the minority party atrophies, a victim of "the more general proposition that institutional decay follows deprivation of function." [24] The burden of opposition is then shifted to contests within the primary of the majority party. However persuasive the argument, it is as yet unproved. One-partyism has receded in recent years, and much of it that remains can be explained in terms of changes in the characteristics of the American electorate. It is more likely that the direct primary has caused a general atrophy in party organization in dominant as well as minority parties. Strong, centralized party organization remains in states in which conventions either nominate candidates or make systematic, crucial, preprimary endorsements.

Furthermore, the direct primary has unquestionably altered the distribution of power within the party. When one speaks of party control of nominations, one means control by the party organization, and any weakening of that control obviously weakens the organization and enhances the power of the party candidates and the party in government. Their ability, especially as incumbents, to defy the organization's wrath and to win primary battles frees them from its discipline and, indeed, often calls them to positions of party leadership. In fact, the inability of party organization in the United States to control the party in government (as it does in so many other democracies) begins with the failure to control its nominations. The direct primary undercuts the ability of the party organization to recruit to public office those partisans who share its goals and accept its discipline.[25]

The goal of the Progressives and the other proponents of the primary was to substitute the party electorate for the party organization as the nominator. With the primary they thwarted the organization's quest for its own goals. Instead of achieving any genuine mass control of party nominations, however, they largely moved the control from the elites of the organization to the elites of the party in government. They succeeded in multiplying the party oligarchies rather than in democratizing them.

[24] V. O. Key, "The Direct Primary and Party Structure," *American Political Science Review* 48 (1954): 24; the same argument reappears in his *American State Politics*, Chap. 6.

[25] Leo Snowiss notes differences in ideologies, voting records, political ethos, and party loyalty among congressmen nominated under various degrees of party organization control. See his "Congressional Recruitment and Representation," *American Political Science Review* 60 (1966): 627–39.

Finally, the direct primary has buttressed the prevailing decentralization of power in the American parties. As long as the candidates or incumbents can appeal to a majority of local primary voters, they are free from the control and discipline of a state or national party. Even so powerful a president as Franklin Roosevelt in 1938 met his greatest political defeat in trying to purge a number of Democratic senators and representatives in their local Democratic primaries; only one of his conservative targets was defeated. The primary plays on local loyalties and appeals to the local electorate, and the vast number of them are extremely difficult for a centralized party organization to control.

If the advocates of the direct primary wanted to aim beyond the nomination process and strike the parties themselves, they found their target. In many instances the direct primary has weakened the parties' control of nominations, robbed their organizations of an important raison d'être, and liberated their officeholders. It has in many important ways made the American political parties what they are today.

# 10
## The
## Campaign
## for
## Election

The formidable Democratic party organization of Pennsylvania had long had a reputation for winning primaries and general elections. At the outset of the campaign in the gubernatorial primary of 1966, few observers gave any chance to Milton Shapp, a Philadelphia industrialist who was challenging the organization's candidate, a thirty-four-year-old lawyer and state legislative leader, Robert B. Casey. But in what was billed as a battle of "exposure versus organization," the Shapp campaign employed some 7000 spot radio commercials, thirty-four half-hour television shows on prime time, an assortment of thirty or so pamphlets and leaflets, more than sixty campaign headquarters across the state, and a single mailing of one large brochure to a million and a half voters (estimated cost: $75,000). The total cost of the primary campaign, financed in large part from Shapp's personal fortune, ran over a million dollars. Shapp won the primary.

The use of polls, direct mailings, and television — even campaign pictures with well-known athletes, who were paid up to $500 for the picture taking — continued into the general election. Shapp lost that contest, however, to Republican Raymond Schaefer. After it was all over, a reflective Robert Casey observed about the campaign he had lost:

Politics is changing tremendously. The old ways no longer work. From that election, I learned that these days you need a combination of two things. First, the traditional grass-roots effort, the telephoning and the door-knocking. But more than that, you have to do what he did. You have to use the new sophisticated techniques, the polling, the television, the heavy staffing, and the direct mail. You can't rely any more on political organizations. They don't work any more. These days, who wants a job in the courthouse or with the highway department? Why, the sons of courthouse janitors are probably doctors or professional men. You can't give those jobs away any more. We're at the tag end of an era in Pennsylvania.[1]

[1] *National Observer*, September 26, 1966.

To those reflections one can add two postscripts. The Shapp campaign in 1966 was managed by a young professional campaign manager, Joe Napolitan, who went on in 1968 to help run the Humphrey presidential campaign. And in 1970 Shapp finally succeeded in winning the Pennsylvania governorship, without the help of Napolitan, again defeating Casey in the primary.

Stories such as this one — typifying the clash of the old and new campaigning — were news in the 1960s and the early 1970s. They heralded a great change, a watershed, in the contesting of American elections that we now increasingly take for granted. It is clear now to us that the new professional managers, media specialists, pollsters, and advertising and public relations men have become a new and powerful force in American political campaigning. It is equally clear that they are replacing the party organization as the major planner and executor of campaigns. As one urbane former candidate has put it:

> With mass media which use a common language that everyone can read, people no longer need party workers to advise them how to vote. When a citizen can see and hear the candidate on a screen at home, and read news, written by the best journalists from a variety of points of view, about the candidate's public and private life, he does not heed what is told him by the precinct captain on his block. The media have done to the campaign system what the invention of accurate artillery did to the feudal kingdom — destroyed the barons and shifted their power to the masses and the prince. A candidate now pays less attention to district leaders than to opinion polls.[2]

The argument, briefly, is that the party organization has become technologically obsolete — that it has been superseded by newer, more efficient, and more timely avenues and techniques of campaigning. Thus, the argument goes, the party organization has lost an important measure of control over the contesting of American elections and, ultimately, over its candidates elected to public office.

These new campaign politics, however, take place within a limiting context of legal regulation and definition. Prior to a discussion of campaigning and changes in it, therefore, it is necessary to discuss the shape of the electoral process itself. The strategies of the electoral game make sense only if one first understands the game itself.

## THE ELECTORAL INSTITUTIONS

Each part of the legal framework, each rule of the electoral game, places a strategic limitation on the campaign. Each adjustment in any one rule

[2] Stimson Bullitt, *To Be a Politician* (New York: Anchor, 1961), p. 65.

may affect one party or candidate more than another. Thus the framework is much more than a neutral presence in the campaign and election.

Political parties around the world have not been slow to realize the possible advantages to be gained by careful, selective tinkering with election law. The major American parties have been no exception. But Americans have generally tinkered more with the size and shape of the electoral districts; gerrymandering is a peculiarly American art form. The rest of the American electoral rules have remained surprisingly stable, even though they have been complicated by the usual state-to-state variations. The kind of repeated electoral tinkerings common in Europe — the shiftings to systems of proportional representation and back again, and the experiments with second, run-off elections, for instance — have not been common here.

### The Secret Ballot

The American ballot is now uniformly secret, but it was not always so. Until the late nineteenth century the oral vote was common in many states and jurisdictions. The voter simply stated to electoral officials which candidates he preferred. During the nineteenth century the oral vote was gradually replaced by ballots printed by the parties or candidates. The voter brought the ballot of his candidate or party to the polling place and deposited it in the box. Since the ballots were by no means identical, his vote was often apparent to observers.

The secret ballot was introduced as a way of curbing election corruption, especially vote buying. With the secret ballot, the corrupter could never be sure the vote would be delivered. Named the Australian ballot after the country of its origin, it quickly swept the day. By the beginning of the twentieth century its success was complete, and it remains the practice today. It is a ballot printed at public expense by public authorities, and it lists all candidates for office on its single, consolidated form. It is distributed only at the polling places and only to bona fide voters, who then mark it in the seclusion of a voting booth.[3]

Increasingly, especially in large American cities, the voting machine is replacing the paper ballot. It does not, however, alter the basic form and premises of the Australian ballot. Only the mechanics of voting are different. The voter faces the machine within a small, draped enclosure and votes by moving levers next to the names of candidates or parties he chooses. A master lever formally records the votes and at the same time

---

[3] Jerrold Rusk also finds that the introduction of the Australian ballot was accompanied by a sharp increase in split-ticket voting. See his article, "The Effect of the Australian Ballot Reform on Split Ticket Voting: 1876–1908," *American Political Science Review* 64 (1970): 1220–38.

opens the drapery for the voter to leave. The advantages of the voting machine, its makers assert, are its long-run reduction of election costs and its speed and accuracy in counting votes. It also thwarts certain forms of ballot box stuffing and dishonest counts.

### Forms of Ballots

The ballots in use in the United States fall into two main types. About twenty states use the *office-block* ballot, which groups the names of the candidates according to the offices they seek (Figure 10.1). In the majority of states the *party-column* ballot prevails; it is so named because the candidates of each party are listed together in a vertical column. The names of all candidates for the same office fall in horizontal rows (Figure 10.2). Thus only in the party-column ballot are the candidates of each party grouped so that the voter can perceive them as a party ticket. By their very nature, of course, nonpartisan elections employ the office-block ballot.

All evidence indicates that the parties are correct in their belief that the party-column ballot encourages straight-ticket voting (i.e., voting for all of a party's candidates for all the offices being filled at the election). But the amount of straight-ticket voting also hinges on the presence or absence on the ballot of a single square or circle (or a single lever on machines) by which the voter can, in one fell swoop, cast a vote for the entire ticket. These squares or circles are more commonly employed on party-column ballots, but some states combine them with the office-block ballot. Thus, the format of the ballot can affect the way the voter sees the electoral contest and the nature of choices in it.

Three other aspects of ballot form deserve mention. Almost every ballot makes some provision for voters to write in the names of persons not listed on the ballot. But the success of write-in candidates is so rare that it is hardly a real question in American politics. Senator J. Strom Thurmond of South Carolina, to be sure, was elected initially in 1954 as a write-in candidate, but one political scientist has referred to that election as "one of the seven wonders of American politics," noting that "nothing of the sort had ever happened before in the history of the country." [4]

Second, the order in which candidates' names appear in the office groupings on office-block ballots may affect the outcome of the election. American voters have shown a notorious disposition to vote for the first name on a list of candidates.[5] The issue of ballot position is actually greater in the

---

[4] William Goodman, *The Two-Party System in the United States*, 3rd ed. (Princeton: Van Nostrand, 1964), p. 440.
[5] Donald S. Hecock and Henry M. Bain, *Ballot Position and Voter's Choice* (Detroit: Wayne State University Press, 1957); Delbert A. Taebel, "The Effect of Ballot Position on Electoral Success," *American Journal of Political Science* 19 (1975): 519–26.

**FIGURE 10.1** The Office Block Ballot: The Nebraska General Election Ballot, November 1978.

# SAMPLE BALLOT

## General Election, November 7, 1978

### Senatorial Ticket

**FOR UNITED STATES SENATOR**
Vote for ONE

- ☐ J. J. Exon .................... Democrat
- ☐ Don Shasteen ............. Republican
- ☐ _____

### Congressional Ticket

**FOR REPRESENTATIVE IN CONGRESS FIRST DISTRICT**
Vote for ONE

- ☐ Hess Dyas ................... Democrat
- ☐ Doug Bereuter ............. Republican
- ☐ _____

**FOR REPRESENTATIVE IN CONGRESS SECOND DISTRICT**
Vote for ONE

- ☐ John J. Cavanaugh ......... Democrat
- ☐ Hal Daub ................... Republican
- ☐ _____

**FOR REPRESENTATIVE IN CONGRESS THIRD DISTRICT**
Vote for ONE

- ☐ Marilyn Fowler ............. Democrat
- ☐ Virginia Smith ............. Republican
- ☐ _____

### State Ticket

**FOR GOVERNOR**
Vote in ONE Square Only

- ☐ Gerald T. Whelan, Governor / Orval Keyes, Lieutenant Governor } Democrat
- ☐ Charles Thone, Governor / Roland A. Luedtke, Lieutenant Governor } Republican
- ☐ _____ Governor / _____ Lieutenant Governor }

**FOR SECRETARY OF STATE**
Vote for ONE

- ☐ Clarence Davis, Jr. ......... Democrat
- ☐ Allen J. Beermann ......... Republican
- ☐ _____

**FOR AUDITOR OF PUBLIC ACCOUNTS**
Vote for ONE

- ☐ Darl Naumann .............. Democrat
- ☐ Ray A. C. Johnson ......... Republican
- ☐ _____

**FOR STATE TREASURER**
Vote for ONE

- ☐ E. J. McBride ............... Democrat
- ☐ Frank Marsh .............. Republican
- ☐ _____

**FOR ATTORNEY GENERAL**
Vote for ONE

- ☐ Thomas J. Garvey .......... Democrat
- ☐ Paul L. Douglas ........... Republican
- ☐ _____

**FOR PUBLIC SERVICE COMMISSIONER SECOND DISTRICT**
Vote for ONE

- ☐ James F. Munnelly ..... Democrat
- ☐ Frank C. Skrupa ..... Republican
- ☐ _____

### Non-Political Ticket

**FOR MEMBER OF THE STATE BOARD OF EDUCATION FIFTH DISTRICT**
Vote for ONE

- ☐ Sara Freeouf
- ☐ Dorothy Weyer Creigh
- ☐ _____

**FOR MEMBER OF THE STATE BOARD OF EDUCATION SIXTH DISTRICT**
Vote for ONE

- ☐ Margaret Lockwood
- ☐ _____

**FOR MEMBER OF THE STATE BOARD OF EDUCATION SEVENTH DISTRICT**
Vote for ONE

- ☐ George Gengenbach
- ☐ Arlene E. Hart
- ☐ _____

**FOR MEMBER OF THE STATE BOARD OF EDUCATION EIGHTH DISTRICT**
Vote for ONE

- ☐ Bernard F. Costello
- ☐ William C. Ramsey
- ☐ _____

**FOR MEMBER OF THE LEGISLATURE _____ DISTRICT**
Vote for ONE

- ☐ _____

**FOR REGENT OF UNIVERSITY OF NEBRASKA FIRST DISTRICT**
Vote for ONE

- ☐ Leo Hill
- ☐ Edward Schwartzkopf
- ☐ _____

**FOR REGENT OF UNIVERSITY OF NEBRASKA SECOND DISTRICT**
Vote for ONE

- ☐ Harlan M. Nelson
- ☐ Kermit Hansen
- ☐ _____

**FOR JUDGE OF THE SUPREME COURT SECOND DISTRICT**
Shall Judge Donald Brodkey be retained in office?

- ☐ Yes
- ☐ No

**FOR JUDGE OF THE SUPREME COURT FIFTH DISTRICT**
Shall Judge Leslie Boslaugh be retained in office?

- ☐ Yes
- ☐ No

**FOR JUDGE OF THE WORKMENS COMPENSATION COURT**
Shall Judge Theodore W. Vrana be retained in office?

- ☐ Yes
- ☐ No

**FOR JUDGE OF THE DISTRICT COURT _____ DISTRICT**
Shall Judge _____ be retained in office?

- ☐ Yes
- ☐ No

**FOR JUDGE OF THE SEPARATE JUVENILE COURT _____ COUNTY**
Shall Judge _____ be retained in office?

- ☐ Yes
- ☐ No

**FOR JUDGE OF THE COUNTY COURT _____ DISTRICT**
Shall Judge _____ be retained in office?

- ☐ Yes
- ☐ No

**FOR JUDGE OF THE MUNICIPAL COURT CITY OF LINCOLN**
Shall Judge Janice L. Gradwohl be retained in office?

- ☐ Yes
- ☐ No

FIGURE 10.2    The Party-Column Ballot: a Sample Ballot from the New Hampshire General Election, November 1978.

| | REPUBLICAN | DEMOCRATIC | LIBERTARIAN NOM. PAPERS | INDEPENDENT NOM. PAPERS | INDEPENDENT NOM. PAPERS |
|---|---|---|---|---|---|
| For Governor Vote for any ONE | Meldrim THOMSON, Jr. ORFORD | Hugh J. GALLEN LITTLETON | Mabel G. EVERETT MILFORD | Ralph BREWSTER SOMERSWORTH | Wesley POWELL HAMPTON FALLS |
| For United States Senator Vote for any ONE | Gordon J. HUMPHREY SUNAPEE | Thomas J. McINTYRE LACONIA | Craig FRANKLIN NASHUA | | |
| For Representative in Congress Vote for any ONE | James C. CLEVELAND NEW LONDON | Edgar J. HELMS CONCORD | | | |
| For Councilor Vote for any ONE | Paul M. MAYETTE HAVERHILL | John A. MARRO LITTLETON | | | |
| For State Senator Vote for any ONE | James A. SAGGIOTES NEWPORT | | | | |
| For Representative to the General Court Vote for any ONE | George I. WIGGINS SUNAPEE | John W. McCUSKER | | | |
| For Sheriff Vote for any ONE | John W. McCUSKER CLAREMONT | John W. McCUSKER CLAREMONT | | | |
| For County Attorney Vote for any ONE | Edward J. TENNEY, II CLAREMONT | W. Howard DUNN NEWPORT | | | |
| For County Treasurer Vote for any ONE | Peter R. LOVELY, Sr. NEWPORT | Peter R. LOVELY, Sr. NEWPORT | | | |
| For Register of Deeds Vote for any ONE | Zella Eastman LaFORGE NEWPORT | Zella Eastman LaFORGE NEWPORT | | | |
| For Register of Probate Vote for any ONE | Bernice M. Sawyer MacWILLIAMS | Bernice M. Sawyer MacWILLIAMS NEWPORT | | | |
| For County Commissioner First District Vote for any ONE | Sam J. NAHIL CLAREMONT | | | | |
| For County Commissioner Second District Vote for any ONE | Remington B. WOODHULL NEWPORT | Remington B. WOODHULL NEWPORT | | | |
| For County Commissioner Third District Vote for any ONE | Dana E. OLDEN CHARLESTOWN | | | | |

SUNAPEE

primaries, in which a number of names in the same party compete for voter attention. Some states respond to the problem by asking candidates to draw lots for first place; others list incumbents first. Others rotate names; if there are three candidates, for example, each occupies first place on a third of the ballots. In the general election the issue is really one of *party position* — first place for its candidates on the office-block ballot or the left column on the party-column ballot. Most often the states give the preferred position to the majority party in the state.

Finally, the American ballot is and has always been a long ballot. Its length, to be sure, cannot be controlled merely by electoral or ballot law. It reflects the American tradition of electing, rather than appointing, a great number of state and local officials — judges, coroners, surveyors, sheriffs, jury commissioners, superintendents of public instruction, assessors, public utilities commissioners, clerks of the courts, party committeepersons, auditors, and comptrollers. An observable effect of the long ballot, especially in the office-block form, is voter fatigue.[6] Many voters, either

---

[6] Jack L. Walker, "Ballot Forms and Voter Fatigue: An Analysis of the Office Block and Party Column Ballots," *Midwest Journal of Political Science* 10 (1966): 448–63.

tiring or despairing, do not vote in contests at the bottom of the ballot. Partial voting (drop-off) of this sort can be as high as 20 or 30 percent of the voters at a given election.

## Structure and Rules of the Choice

Overwhelmingly, American elections are governed by the twin principles of single-member constituencies and plurality election. In other words, we elect only one person per constituency to a city council, to the House or Senate, to the local mayoralty. The candidate who gets the most votes, even if it is not the majority of 50 percent plus one, is elected. Even in those cases of multimember districts — two-, three-, or four-member state legislative districts or at-large elections of local councils or commissions — the principle is not altered.[7] One casts the same number of votes as there are officials to be elected from the district, and the plurality principle still governs. In a two-member state legislative district, for example, each voter casts two votes; the two candidates with the greatest number of votes (i.e., the plurality) are the winners. The effect is little different from that of a single-member district.

The American states have experimented scarcely at all with the systems of *proportional representation* (PR) that so often enchant the other democracies of the world. In these systems, which are of necessity based on multimember constituencies, the voter casts his vote for a party slate of candidates. The parties then share the seats according to the percentage of the votes they polled. In a five-member legislative district, for example:

| Party A | 58% of vote | 3 seats |
| Party B | 21% of vote | 1 seat |
| Party C | 16% of vote | 1 seat |
| Party D | 5% of vote | — |
| | 100% of vote | 5 seats |

The possible combinations and modifications are virtually limitless in PR systems, but those endless complexities need not concern us here.[8] What is important is the political result of proportional representation of any form. First, it encourages minor political parties by giving them a share of the elective offices. Ten or 20 percent of the vote will rarely win any public offices in the plurality elections of American politics, but in a num-

---

[7] For a good survey of the effects of various types of district, see Howard D. Hamilton, "Legislative Constituencies: Single-Member Districts, Multi-Member Districts, and Floterial Districts," *Western Political Quarterly* 20 (1967): 321–40.
[8] For an excursion into some of the complexities, see Wolfgang Birke, *European Elections by Direct Suffrage* (Leyden: Sythoff, 1961). See also Douglas W. Rae, *The Political Consequences of Electoral Law* (New Haven: Yale University Press, 1967).

ber of European countries it wins parliamentary seats and cabinet positions for a number of parties. Second, proportional representation strengthens the hand of the party vis-à-vis its candidates. In strict party list systems especially, the party fixes the order of the party list. To return to the illustration of the five-man district under simple PR, the leadership of parties A, B, C, and D draw up party lists of five candidates. By placing a candidate first on the party list the leaders of parties A, B, and C virtually place him in public office; by placing him fifth they consign him to defeat. The prevailing single-member, plurality structure of American elections, on the contrary, reinforces both the two-party system and the independence of candidates and officeholders.

In a few instances, however, American states and localities have experimented with various exotic electoral systems. New York City adopted a variety of proportional representation from 1938 to 1947, with a resulting growth and representation of minor political parties (Table 10.1). The system was abandoned in 1947 after tension with the Soviet Union made the representation of the local Communist party intolerable for many New Yorkers. Perhaps the classic case of electoral exoticism has been Illinois' cumulative voting system. Since 1870 the lower house of the Illinois legislature has been elected from three-person constituencies. In order to facilitate representation of the minority party (of the two major parties), the voter is permitted to cast his or her three votes in any one of four different ways: all three for one candidate, one and a half for each of two, one for each of three, and two for one and one for another. Before the election (and the primary), party committees in each of the constituencies deter-

**TABLE 10.1   Effects of Proportional Representation in the New York City Council Elections: 1945**

| Party | Percentage of vote | Council seats | |
|-------|-------------------|---------------|---|
| Democratic | 59 | 14 | (61%) |
| Republican | 15 | 3 | (13%) |
| American Labor | 10 | 2 | (9%) |
| Communist | 9 | 2 | (9%) |
| Liberal | 7 | 2 | (9%) |
| | | 23 | (100%) |

*Source*   Belle Zeller and Hugh A. Bone, "The Repeal of Proportional Representation in New York City — Ten Years in Retrospect," *American Political Science Review* 42 (1948): 1132.

mine whether the party in the district will offer one, two, or three candidates for the three seats. They often decide cumulatively to contest only a total of three seats (one party offers two candidates and the other party only one), leaving the voters of the district no choice in the general election. The nature of the choice in the system, in other words, has encouraged the parties to adopt cautious, minimizing strategies that reduce competition between the two parties in the name of securing representation for both of them.[9]

## Date of the Election

In 1845 Congress chose to use its constitutional power to determine the dates of presidential and congressional elections (Article I, Section 4; Article II, Section 1). It provided that all states would select their presidential electors on the first Tuesday after the first Monday of November and that the same date would be used for electing members of Congress unless a state's constitution provided otherwise. For many years Maine chose to hold congressional elections in September, but all fifty states now use the November date. Since considerations of economy dictate that the states hold state and local elections at the same time, they have widely accepted the same date. So a uniform election date prevails, even though the rationale for the date, chosen originally to follow the fall harvests, seems less and less convincing in an urban nation. No such uniformity on primary dates exists, however. Some come in April and May, some not until September. Consequently, the total campaign for public office may be six months or more in some states and two or less in others.

### Election Day

The states and localities set the hours and places of elections. In most communities the polls remain open for about twelve or thirteen hours; they open between 6 and 8 A.M. and close at 7, 8, or 9 P.M. The polls usually are located in some public building — a school, a firehouse, a city hall — although they may be found in barbershops, auto showrooms, and private homes in some communities.

In each voting district, usually called the precinct, the administration of the polling place is in the hands of a group of publicly appointed judges, inspectors, or commissioners, as they are variously called. They check the

---

[9] The possibilities of cumulative voting have spurred a sizable scholarly literature, including: George S. Blair, *Cumulative Voting* (Urbana: University of Illinois Press, 1960); Jack Sawyer and Duncan MacRae, "Game Theory and Cumulative Voting in Illinois: 1902–1954," *American Political Science Review* 56 (1962): 936–46; and James Kuklinski, "Cumulative and Plurality Voting: An Analysis of Illinois' Unique Electoral System," *Western Political Quarterly* 26 (1973): 726–46.

voters' registration, give them ballots or see them into the voting machine, and make sure their votes are cast. Often they remain after the polls have closed to count the ballots, although centralized counting exists in some jurisdictions. The parties or candidates usually have the right to appoint poll watchers to oversee the administration of the balloting and the counting of the ballots.

Voting machines, of course, greatly facilitate the counting of ballots. Final totals are simply read off a set of dials. But in many precincts the job is still a laborious one, often extending into the small hours of the morning. Weary polling officials, often after twelve hours of work at the polls, must decipher unclear marks and apply the often complicated state law on what constitutes an invalid ballot. For example, does a check mark suffice as a substitute for an X? In some states it does, and in some it does not. In a few close cases the count may be challenged, and a partial or total recounting of the ballots may result. The 1962 Minnesota gubernatorial election was in doubt for four months while a special three-man court supervised bipartisan counting officials in a recount of every paper ballot cast in the state. The Democratic candidate finally emerged a ninety-one-vote winner. That and other recounts have testified to three conclusions about the marking and counting of ballots. There has been little or no dishonesty documented, first of all. Second, honest errors in counting and recording do occur: for example, 10s become 100s, digits are inverted, the two parties' totals are reversed. Third, a significant number of voters do not correctly mark their ballots. In the 1962 election in Minnesota, for example, 389 voters voted (invalidly) for two candidates for governor, more than enough to decide the outcome that hinged on ninety-one votes.[10]

### Absentee Voting

Most states have some provision for voting by people unable to come to the polls because of illness, travel, service in the armed forces, studies, or an occupation that takes them away from home. There is, however, little uniformity in the details of the provisions for absentee voting. Some states permit it only for specific reasons, some permit it only for certain elections, and some permit it only if the person has left the boundaries of the state. Congress had been under pressure to ensure the serviceman's right to an absentee ballot in the face of the reluctance of some states to provide one, and in 1975 it granted citizens living overseas the right to register and vote in federal elections in the state in which they last lived.

---

[10] On recounts, see Ronald F. Stinnett and Charles H. Backstrom, *Recount* (Washington: National Document Publishers, 1964); Samuel J. Eldersveld and A. A. Applegate, *Michigan's Recounts for Governor, 1950 and 1952: A Systematic Analysis of Election Error* (Ann Arbor: University of Michigan Press, 1954).

## POLITICAL CONSEQUENCES OF ELECTORAL LAW

Perhaps the chief impact of American political institutions on the politics of campaigning has been to focus attention on the candidates rather than on the parties. The American electoral process is relatively free from institutions such as parliamentary-cabinet government or proportional representation, which encourage the voter to see electoral contests in terms of the greater fortunes and future of political parties. On the contrary, such details of electoral law as the office-block ballot tend to structure the electoral choice as a series of contests between individual candidates and not as a single, multifaceted campaign between two great parties. Nonpartisan elections have even further reduced the visibility of the party in elections.

The specific components of the electoral system, therefore, do more than ensure efficiency or good government, the preservation of democratic norms, or protection against vote frauds. They carry grave consequences for the parties and for campaign politics in general. They may affect the voting behavior of the electorate in the following ways:

— All evidence suggests that the office-block ballot discourages *straight-ticket voting* and that the party-column ballot encourages it.[11] So, too, do other electoral details, such as the presence of a party circle or square on the ballot.
— *Voter fatigue* ( or roll-off ), the tendency to vote in only some of the contests on the ballot, appears to be in large part the result of the ballot itself. It is greater in areas using the office-block ballot, and it tends to be greater the longer the ballot. The arrangement of the face of the voting machine will also affect it. Studies in the Minneapolis area show, for example, that in those eighteen communities with voting machines in the election of November 1966, only 33.9 to 78.3 percent of the voters voted on a constitutional amendment up for ratification; but in seventeen communities with paper ballots the percentages varied between 92.2 and 100.[12]
— Every ballot form discourages *write-in voting*, but some discourage it more than others. It is especially difficult on most voting machines; and even so small a detail as whether or not the state permits the use of stickers as a way of writing in a candidate's name may be significant.

Such impacts on the voting responses of the electorates to whom the parties and their candidates must appeal obviously affect the parties and campaign strategies.

[11] Angus Campbell et al., *The American Voter* ( New York: Wiley, 1960), p. 276.
[12] *Minneapolis Star*, April 11, 1967. The story reports research findings by the Citizens' League of Hennepin and Ramsey Counties. Following that report, the 1967 Minnesota legislature required local governments to put reminders on the machines to alert voters to the amendments. In a subsequent referendum in 1970 the average in voting machine communities went up to 84 percent. It remained at 96 percent in the others.

The electoral system, however, may have an impact on the parties and campaign strategy beyond its effect on the voters. The states may limit the access of minor parties and their candidates to the ballot by requiring them to file petitions with large numbers of signatures. Electoral systems such as Illinois' cumulative voting, rare though they may be in the United States, drastically alter the nature of the campaign and choices in it. That system, paradoxically, has increased the party role in the election by forcing it to decide what number of the three seats in the constituency to contest while effectively reducing the amount of two-party competition. Even ordinary multimember constituencies invite a party of limited strength to concentrate its voting strength on a single candidate by voting for him and no other candidate (a practice widely referred to as bullet voting).

Most important, the details of American electoral law often do not touch the parties or candidates equally. If voting machines confuse less well-educated, lower SES voters, and if office-block ballots encourage greater voter fatigue (roll-off) among less-educated voters,[13] then the disadvantages may accrue more to the Democratic party. And if the state refuses absentee ballots to travelers, whether on business or pleasure, the disadvantages may strike mainly the Republicans. Any ballot form that facilitates party-ticket voting works to the advantage of the majority party in the constituency. And prime ballot position helps the incumbent and the majority party; so do designations of incumbency printed on the ballot. Even the hours and places for polling may have some marginal benefits for one party or the other.

Just how aware the parties and state legislators are of the possible advantages in refining electoral law is not easy to say. It is always difficult to establish the motives of legislators, especially when those motives may not be of the highest type. But occasionally an attempt is just too persistent, too transparent, not to reveal the motives of party or political advantage. Jack L. Walker, for example, comments on Ohio's continuing evolution of the ballot form:

In the state of Ohio the ballot has been changed six times during the twentieth century, and in each case the Republican majority tried to gain an advantage for itself by tampering with the election machinery. In 1940 Governor Bricker tried to avoid the influences of F.D.R.'s "coattails" by calling a special session of the legislature which approved a separation of the ballot carrying national races from the one on which state and local races appeared. Bricker reasoned that if a normally Republican voter who was determined to vote for Roosevelt had to use a second ballot in state races he would be less likely to vote a straight Democratic ticket (the ballots were later consolidated once again to capitalize on Eisen-

---

13 Walker, "Ballot Forms and Voter Fatigue," makes the latter point.

hower's coattails). In 1949 over $85,000 was spent in a campaign to substitute the Office Block ballot for the Party Column ballot in an effort to save Senator Robert Taft from defeat in the bitter 1950 election. . . . The Taft forces thought that by eliminating the party lever they would substantially reduce the number of straight Democratic votes and thus increase the Senator's chances among normally Democratic, working class voters. Key quotes Taft as claiming that the change "was responsible 'for something between 100,000 and 200,000' of his total majority of 430,000." [14]

Finally, in one way above all — the drawing of constituency lines — the American parties have tried repeatedly to steal an advantage in electoral politics. The general tactics have traditionally been two: constituencies of unequal populations and gerrymandered districts. The first and more obvious of the two, the districts of unequal populations, simply involved stretching the popular vote of the majority party by putting fewer people in districts in its strongholds than in the districts located in the other party's areas of strength. In the past the heavily populated districts were usually in urban areas, working to the disadvantage of Republicans in the South and Democrats elsewhere. However, in 1952 the Supreme Court put an end to these inequities. As the courts have applied the "one man, one vote" rule to constituencies of all varieties, they have closed off an indigenously American way of exploiting the rules of the electoral game.[15] The consequences of reapportionment depend on the specific districts being reapportioned. But in the one kind of district that had earlier been the most seriously malapportioned, the state legislative district, reapportionment has on the whole increased Democratic representation.[16]

More subtle and less easy to detect, the gerrymander survives unimpaired. It consists of one party's drawing district lines in such a way as to use its own popular vote most efficiently while forcing the other party to use its vote inefficiently. That goal can be achieved in one of two ways: either by dividing and diluting pockets of the other party's strength to prevent it from winning office, or (if the other party's strength is too great for dilution) by bunching its strength into a few districts and forcing it to win elections by large, wasteful majorities. Frequently but not always, the resulting constituencies, instead of being compact and contiguous, have bizarre and fanciful shapes (see box). (The term "gerrymander" was coined in the early years of the Republic to describe a salamander-shaped congressional district drawn in Massachusetts when Elbridge Gerry was

[14] *Ibid.*, pp. 448–49.
[15] Especially for the political ramifications of apportionment, see Malcolm E. Jewell (ed.), *The Politics of Reapportionment* (New York: Atherton, 1962).
[16] Robert S. Erikson, "The Partisan Impact of State Legislative Reapportionment," *Midwest Journal of Political Science* 15 (1971): 57–71.

## A Gerrymander in New York

Usually the gerrymander is easily identifiable by its bizarre shape. The legislative straining for political effect often violates the traditional criteria of "compact and contiguous" districting. The odd outlines invite the observer to see in them all manner of fantastic creatures. State legislatures have, in fact, beginning with Gerry's salamander, produced a veritable political bestiary. The reader can make what he will of the shape of New York's Twelfth Congressional District in the 1950s, but its explanation is less a matter of fantasy:

"There are very few Republicans in Brooklyn, and distributed in ordinarily shaped districts they would never make a majority anywhere. But the Republican legislature strung G.O.P. areas into a district winding through the borough, and the result was Republican victories until this year."

From Anthony Lewis, *The New York Times,* November 27, 1960.
© 1960 by The New York Times Company. Reprinted by permission.

**Twelfth Congressional District of New York, 1950s**

governor.) Which party reaps the advantage of the gerrymander depends entirely on which party controls the legislature that draws the district lines.[17]

## CAMPAIGN STRATEGY

The folk wisdom about all aspects of American politics is more than ample, but on the subject of campaign tactics it is overwhelming. Much of it has been brought together into little books on campaigning that read like modern how-to-do-it manuals.[18] Since many of the recent books have been written by advertising and public relations specialists, much of the wisdom has a modern tone. Candidates are advised on dress and make-up for TV, and there is a good deal of emphasis on catchy phrases and slogans.

There is much of value in the received wisdom about American campaigning. Generally it represents the distillation of concrete experience. And yet it suffers from two deficiencies that themselves are general warnings about the crafts of political campaigning. The conventional wisdom seems to suggest, first of all, that most political campaigns are run on a master battle plan adhered to with almost military discipline and precision. In reality most American political campaigns lurch along from one improvisation to another, from one immediate crisis to another. They are frequently underorganized, underplanned, and understaffed — and consequently, often played by ear on a surprising lack of information.

The folk wisdom also suggests that there are principles of good campaigning that have an almost universal applicability. In truth, however, optimum campaign strategy depends on a great number of variables, and the only general rule is that there is no general rule. Strategy will vary with:

— *The skills of the candidate:* Does he or she project well on television? At a press conference or an informal coffee hour?
— *The nature of the constituency:* Is it several square miles of urban slum or 30,000 square miles of prairie?
— *The office being sought:* Is it a city councillorship or perhaps a judgeship, which will call for a far more restrained campaign?
— *The nature of the electoral system:* Is the ballot partisan or nonpartisan? Is the general election two or six months after the primary?

[17] For an objective measure of gerrymandering, see Ernest C. Reock, Jr., "Measuring Compactness as a Requirement of Legislative Apportionment," *Midwest Journal of Political Science* 5 (1961): 70–74.
[18] For some recent examples of the how-to-do-it genre, see Edward Schwartzman, *Campaign Craftsmanship: A Professional's Guide to Campaigning for Elective Office* (New York: Universe, 1973); Joe Napolitan, *The Election Game and How To Win It* (Garden City: Doubleday, 1972); and Dick W. Simpson, *Winning Elections: A Handbook in Participatory Politics* (Chicago: Swallow, 1972). A more scholarly approach is represented by Robert Agranoff, *The Management of Election Campaigns* (Boston: Holbrook, 1976).

— *The party organizations in the constituency:* To what extent can their organized resources be counted on? What can they do?

— *The availability of political resources:* What manpower, skills, and money will be available and when?

— *The nature of the electorate:* What are the voters' political norms, party loyalties, perception of issues and candidates? What political styles and tactics do they approve? What turnout and voting record do they have?

There are, of course, other factors. The chief early task of campaign strategists is the sober evaluation of all of the factors and of the consequent demands and limits they place on the nature of the campaign.

It is not only campaign situations that differ. So also do candidates and the way they "see" the voters as well as the structure of the campaign and election. Candidates generally seem to believe that campaigns do affect election outcomes, and most of them are tireless campaigners who — not entirely sure of what will "work" in the campaign — spend every available hour and resource trying every conceivable ploy. One study suggests, however, that candidates do differ in their perceptions of what kinds of appeals voters respond to. Winning candidates saw voters as more influenced by issues and candidates, whereas losers saw them more responsive to party appeals. Candidates may differ even in their understanding of the problem of putting together a majority. The same study found that Democratic candidates tended more than Republicans to see coalitions built of interest groups and organizations rather than individuals.[19] If campaign strategy is essentially a matter of problem solving, then candidates differ in their understanding of the problem.

The nub of the strategic problem in a campaign is selectivity in the expenditures of scarce time, energy, and resources in order to achieve the maximum effect on the electorate For a candidate to spread his resources evenly over a constituency is, in effect, no strategy at all. He and his managers must decide how to spend each unit of campaign resources so that it will return the maximum number of votes. Will they work on areas normally loyal to the other party in hopes of cutting losses there, or will they hammer at the party strongholds? They must also decide how to tailor their appeals to different parts of the electorate. For some of the voters there must be stimuli to party loyalty; for others, appeals of issue or personality. The problem is to know the variety and diversity of the voters, the likely bases of their decisions, and the ways of reaching and stimulating them differentially.[20]

---

[19] John W. Kingdon, *Candidates for Office* (New York: Random House, 1968). It is very possible that the different perceptions of group politics reflect real differences in party traditions.

[20] A number of writers have suggested that the problem of campaign strategy can be approached through "maximization" models such as those of game theory. For example, see John H. Kessel, "A Game Theory Analysis of Campaign Strategy," in M. Kent

The candidate must make these strategic allocations in the face of all kinds of uncertainties and problems.

— Money and the other resources for the campaign will very likely be in short supply. (Problems of money in elective politics will be considered in Chapter 13.)
— Information on the efficacy of various campaign techniques will be sharply limited. Because of the present state of the art, it is virtually impossible to tell whether a day of coffee parties or a day of hand-shaking on the street will be more effective — or when it is better to spend $500 on billboards than on a newspaper ad.
— The campaign will surely confront intractable "givens." The local press, for example, may be committed to the other candidate and freeze other candidates out of the publicity they need.
— The candidate also will need allies in the campaign, and they will have interests and strategies of their own. Interest groups or other political groups or individuals, for instance, may want assurances on specific issues or programs.

There is, in other words, uncertainty about the electorate, about the usefulness of the campaign techniques, about the availability of resources, and about the strategies of both the candidate's allies and opponents. Small wonder that "rational," orderly planning is rare in political campaigns.

Actually, the political characteristics of the election race probably do more to set the limits of campaign strategy than any other factors. The presence or absence of an incumbent in the race and the competitiveness of the constituency exceed in significance all other considerations. Those two factors, perhaps, determine whether there is a possibility of victory. They affect the ability of the candidate to recruit workers and resources, to line up the support of groups (which usually have a taste for joining winners), and to attract the attention of voters.[21] In other words, the fact that a candidate is an incumbent running for reelection in a competitive district or a nonincumbent of the losing party in a noncompetitive district, for example, sets some major limits on campaign strategy before the imaginations of the candidate and his or her advisors even begin to work.

## THE NEW CAMPAIGNING

Within less than a generation, changes amounting to a revolution have altered much of American political campaigning. The skills of the mass

Jennings and L. Harmon Zeigler (eds.), *The Electoral Process* (Englewood Cliffs: Prentice-Hall, 1966), pp. 290–304. For a more general approach to campaign strategy, see Lewis A. Froman's essay, "A Realistic Approach to Campaign Strategies and Tactics," in the same volume, pp. 1–20.

[21] See David A. Leuthold, *Electioneering in a Democracy* (New York: Wiley, 1968).

media specialists have brought new persuasive techniques to bear on the American electorate — with attendant fears that presidents and lesser officials are now sold to the electorate much as Madison Avenue sells a new mouthwash or toothpaste. And with the new techniques have come the new technicians: the campaign management specialists, a new breed of sophisticated, hard-headed advisors, who as political mercenaries deploy their troops and artillery for a suitable fee.

The archetype of this variety of professional campaign organization in recent years has been Spencer-Roberts, Inc. which came to fame in a number of recent California contests, especially Ronald Reagan's primary and general election campaigns for the governorship in 1966 and 1970. (The fee was reported to be in excess of $100,000.) The assets of an organization like Spencer-Roberts are many and impressive. They include a detached professionalism and experience and a familiarity with the arts of advertising, public relations, and the mass media. Furthermore, Spencer-Roberts has extensive mailing lists of Republican activists and loyalists in California and good ties to local Republican workers and luminaries. The scope of the firm's operations can best be seen by describing their exertions on behalf of Nelson Rockefeller in the 1964 presidential primary in California. In that election the Goldwater forces had almost completely tied up the regular Republican organization.

> With absolutely zero troops of their own to start with, Spencer-Roberts had to use money to recruit troops; by opening 40 to 50 Rockefeller headquarters across the state (6 in Los Angeles alone) to show the flag and banner where moderate volunteers might rally; by publishing a newsletter whose circulation rose from 4,500 to 25,000 in a few months; by direct-mail techniques; by billboards, advertisements, television and the drenching of radio, which in automobile-happy California has a dimension of its own.[22]

In addition, Spencer-Roberts organized local committees for Rockefeller, made all the arrangements for local rallies and handshaking receptions, and set up phone campaigns to reach registered Republicans shortly before the primary date. On major matters of strategy it apparently dealt directly with Rockefeller's New York advisors.

Spencer-Roberts demonstrated its sheer size in 1968 by its involvement in thirty or more campaigns. A good share of those were races for Congress, an involvement that represented the confidence of the Republican Congressional Campaign Committee. After a falling out with Reagan forces, Stuart Spencer resurfaced in national politics in 1975 as the manager of Gerald Ford's campaign for the Republican presidential nomination. He helped secure it, of course, in the face of a stubborn challenge by Ronald Reagan.

[22] Theodore H. White, *The Making of the President 1964* (New York: Atheneum, 1965), p. 127.

The entire profession of campaign management is by now a crowded one. Its professional association, the American Association of Political Consultants, counted more than 200 members by the late 1970s. Firms and specialists come in all sizes and shapes. Some are all-purpose organizations such as Spencer-Roberts, which can plan the campaign from the decision to enter through the election-night victory (or condolence) party. Others limit themselves to particular specialties, such as opinion polling or producing tapes for television.[23] But to some extent there is little really new in politics. Much of the new art is a streamlining and sophistication of old campaigning practices. It is generally a more efficient attack on the old demands of any campaign: the assembling of information and the persuading of voters (see box).

## New Sources of Information

The development of modern social science has opened up new sources of information and knowledge to the candidate. Computers and data-processing systems permit a party to keep records about constituencies and to process that information rapidly. Carefully kept records usually yield a faster and more accurate answer to "how the twenty-first ward went four years ago" than do even the most conscientious party workers. Then, too, wily parties and candidates have similarly used the scholarly data and findings on the demographic bases of Republican and Democratic strength. The managers of John F. Kennedy's presidential campaign commissioned a simulation of the 1960 electorate as an aid to campaign planning. The simulation attempted, with the aid of computers, to coordinate and correlate knowledge about the American electorate and to project the effects that various events of the campaign might have on it.[24] Other candidates have computerized records of canvassing so that they can quickly compile lists of voters to contact on election day.

No new avenue to political knowledge, however, has been more fully exploited than the public opinion poll. It may be employed at the beginning of a campaign to assess the political issues uppermost in the minds of voters. Early polls can also develop candidate profiles, information about the way the voting public views the two opponents. If it is found that voters think a candidate too bookish or intellectual, he may be sent to plowing contests, athletic events, or a weekend fishing trip. Polls can also

[23] For a comprehensive survey of the new technicians, see the *Congressional Quarterly* for April 5, 1968. Among the many recent books on the subject see Robert Agranoff (ed.), *The New Style in Election Campaigns* (Boston: Holbrook, 1972): the introductory essay by Agranoff is especially useful.

[24] Described in Ithiel de Sola Pool, Robert P. Abelson, and Samuel Popkin, *Candidates, Issues, and Strategies* (Cambridge: MIT Press, 1964). A fictionalized version can be found in Eugene Burdick, *The 480* (New York: McGraw-Hill, 1964).

---

### The Political Consultants Speak

Interviews with the successful political consultants reveal them to be professionals of candor and insight. Their remarks are worth noting, both for what they reveal of American politics and of themselves and their profession. The following observations were all reported by William J. Lanoutte, "The Selling of the Candidates, 1978," *National Journal* (November 4, 1978), pp. 1772–77.

On the profession's image, Robert Squier: "There's a tendency to exaggerate what we can do. Somehow clients want to believe you're a wizard who can work magic. They don't believe me when I tell them it's mostly luck and a good plan that wins elections."

On issues in campaigns, Robert Goodman: "Voting is emotional rather than intellectual, so we use issues in a campaign as tools or devices with which to express a candidate's personality, integrity."

On success, Matt Reese: "There are three things in this business that are important. Winning, or the reputation of winning — you need a pretty good record; working for people whose names are known; and winning when you're not supposed to."

On the innovations of the consultants, John Deardourff: "Things we pioneered in the mid-sixties, such as long-term planning, voter-trend analysis, targeting of our message, rational resource allocation, were not new ideas then — just new in their application to political campaigns. The whole notion of producing a full-blown written campaign plan was novel then. It's standard practice today."

On coming full circle (or reinventing the wheel), Stuart Spencer: "With the media becoming so expensive, though, I predict you'll see a rebirth of organizational work soon. They'll call it by some new name, but it'll be the same as the old days: five people to a precinct handing out literature, by hand, door to door."

From William J. Lanoutte, "The Selling of the Candidates, 1978,"
*The National Journal*, November 4, 1978. Reprinted by permission.

---

indicate whether the campaign ought to capitalize on party loyalties or whether the candidate would be better advised to divorce himself from an unpopular party or candidate at the top of the ticket. During the campaign a poll or two can chart its progress and indicate where time and resources ought to be concentrated in its waning days.

Parties and candidates have not been uniformly willing to avail themselves of such new techniques. Much of the knowledge thus far accumulated, especially of voting behavior, derives chiefly from presidential campaigns and elections and has only limited applicability. Many of the techniques are also beyond the resources of local campaigns. But the difficulty runs deeper. American political campaigns, despite popular impressions to the contrary, have rarely been run on a solid base of information. Thousands of party organizations around the country never have kept even basic voting data by precincts, wards, townships, cities, and counties. So, such a shift to the "new knowledge" involves a basic commitment to knowledge itself, as well as a willingness to bear the costs of the new knowledge.

## New Techniques of Persuasion

Campaigns are basically exercises in mass persuasion, and increasingly the commercial arts of persuasion have been applied to them. There was a time when strong party organizations were the great persuaders in American campaigns. Changes in them and in American politics, however, have diminished that role. Party organizations, however, do not "control" votes and turn them out as they once did. And yet they have not been quick to pick up new campaign and communication skills. Into the vacuum have come skilled candidates, their advisors and personal staffs, and the firms specializing in the management of political campaigns.

Predominant among the new persuasive techniques is the use of the mass communications media. Frequently now a candidate takes the time and effort to address a rally or meeting largely in the hope that it will produce a news report or a brief film clip on the local TV news. (Of course, the question of whether it produces a news report is not left to chance; the staff prepares news releases and copies of the speech for the local media.) But often candidates have to buy their time and space in the media. Early in the campaign, candidates may vie to commit choice TV time and billboard space for the concluding weeks of the campaign. And as the campaign progresses, the candidates' faces, names, and slogans blossom on billboards, newspaper ads, radio and TV spot announcements — even on lawn signs, automobile bumpers, and construction fences. Full TV or radio coverage of a speech is usually an extravagant waste of money, but candidates may take longer media time for talkathons or "open mike" shows, in which they answer the questions and challenges of all comers.

But to some extent the new techniques are simply new applications of old techniques. Direct mailings, for example, have become increasingly sophisticated means for raising money and reaching voters. In the 1972 presidential campaign of Richard Nixon:

Computers sliced up the nation's census tracts into patterns; the storefront operators in the counties that Malek [Fred Malek of the Committee for the Re-Election of the President] had "prioritized" had identified independents, wavering Democrats and "don't knows"; the 250 telephone batteries in ten key states had poured other names into the computer. And by the end of October the computer was taking over — there would be in the last week eight million "mailgrams" to the nine largest states, cut and coded by county, by age, by income, by Spanish-speaking, by black, by ethnic origin, plus 9,000,000 letters to Republicans. A computer software firm in Texas cut the tapes; mail-list houses around the country sorted names; the Donnelley plant in Chicago printed and mailed — 17,000,-000 pieces in all, in the largest single roundhouse swing by mail in American politics.[25]

Indeed, the new techniques may be no more revolutionary than a new hair style or wardrobe, or perhaps a Dale Carnegie course, for the candidate. Or they may be only a new emphasis on a theme or slogan for the campaign. Often, that is, the new campaigning may be little more than a new application of old advertising wisdom about reaching audiences and consumers.

Nelson Rockefeller's campaigns for public office perhaps represent the acme of the new campaigning. His 1966 campaign for the governorship of New York — then called the most expensive nonpresidential campaign in American political history — cost at least $6 million. The campaign, run by a staff of at least 300, put between 3000 and 4000 television commercials on the stations of the state.[26] In 1968 his expenditures totaled $8 million — a good deal of it in polling and media charges — in the preconvention search for the Republican nomination. His race for another term in the governorship in 1970 topped his own 1966 record with an outgo modestly estimated at $10 million, making *it* the most expensive campaign. The campaign employed almost continuous polling, a budget of a million and a half for television, and enough brochures, buttons, and broadsides to furnish about three pieces for every voter in the state.

All of this is not to argue that the traditional campaign techniques are obsolete. Handshaking on the streets and in the stores, speeches before anyone who will listen, endorsements by local groups and party organizations — all of the old ways are very much alive. The new campaigning is too expensive for many candidates; a minute of prime TV time for a political spot announcement can easily cost $500, and a large billboard in a good city location may well cost the same figure per month. Also, these techniques are inefficient for many local candidates; the radio, television, billboard, and newspaper space they purchase is wasted in great part on readers, viewers, and listeners who cannot vote for them.

Consequently, the new style of American political campaigning has been unevenly used. It is probably employed most often in the campaigns of better financed candidates for state and national office and less often by the candidates for local offices, especially in the less concentrated electorates of the rural areas. At the same time, there is also some reason to think that both party committees and candidate organizations have

[25] Theodore H. White, *The Making of the President 1972* (New York: Bantam, 1973), p. 437.
[26] See also James Perry, *The New Politics* (New York: Potter, 1968).

become more proficient themselves in the new skills and less reliant, therefore, on the professional practitioners. To that extent we may simply be
observing the more general process of the diffusion of knowledge.[27]

## TO WHAT EFFECT THE CAMPAIGN?

More than one candidate, whether his campaign is old or new style, has
wondered about the impact of the campaign's sound and fury. The bar-
rage of words and pictures is staggering, but is anyone listening or watching? Do the spot commercials, the literature, even the canvassing make
any difference in the ultimate voting decision? No one really knows for
sure.

Logical deduction leads to some plausible and probably reliable answers. We know that American voters expose themselves to the campaign
with great selectivity. First of all, they tend to surround themselves with
friends, literature, mass media reports, and even personal experience (such
as rallies and meetings) that support their perceptions and loyalties. They
tend, furthermore, to perceive what they are exposed to in terms of stable,
long-term loyalties, the most stable of which is their loyalty to a political
party. Therefore, what we think of as a campaign may to some extent be
two campaigns — one party and its candidates shouting at their supporters,
and the other party and its candidates doing the same. So, a good deal of
American campaigning has the effect of stimulating, activating, and reinforcing given political predispositions. Far less of it achieves any political conversions. Much of it, too, is directed more to getting people out
to vote than to influencing their voting decision.

We can also make some deductions about the impact of campaigns
just from the data we have about the exposure of the voter to them. Only
a minority of the American adult public reports being contacted by a
party worker in presidential election campaigns. For example, only 29
percent reported being approached by one of the parties in the 1976
campaign. Only 6 percent went to a political meeting, rally, or dinner during the 1976 campaign. Media exposure, on the other hand, reaches the
great majority of the electorate. Significantly, 89 percent of the respondents watched at least one program about the 1976 campaign on TV.[28]

Therefore, most American electoral campaigns are carried on by limited
means within limited ranges of attention and perception. And even if it

[27] At the least, the media now take the professionals more for granted. The flood of articles about them has abated, and *Congressional Quarterly* also appears to have abandoned its reporting of them. For a general study of them, see David L. Rosenbloom,
*The Election Men* (New York: Quadrangle, 1973).
[28] The data of this paragraph come from the Survey Research Center of the University
of Michigan; they were made available through the services of the Inter-University
Consortium for Political Research. Since the postelection interviews were secured with
a reduced subset of the original sample, it is probable that these percentages overstate
the experience of the total electorate.

does "reach" voters, the campaign may not dent their fixed and stable loyalties to a candidate, party, or attitude. Moreover, events outside the campaign — wars, depressions, inflation — may have a far greater impact than the campaign on voting decisions. Therefore, one cannot expect even the most dazzling campaign to achieve a full measure of persuasiveness, for it is directed to a political universe and not a college debating society.

Beyond these generalizations, documenting the impact of a campaign is extremely difficult. For one thing, there are all manner of methodological difficulties. The "campaign" is a whole congeries of events and activities; some of them are the activities of the parties and candidates, and some are not. Consequently, it is difficult to say just what part of the total impact can be attributed to any part of the "campaign" or its context. It is also difficult to determine what part of the campaign the individual voter has been aware of and how he or she has perceived it.

Have we, then, no empirical knowledge of the effects of the campaign? Two studies have indicated that personal contacts activate political apathetics more often than mailed propaganda does and that door-to-door canvassing is more successful in affecting voting decisions than telephone calls.[29] The settings of both studies, however, were local elections in which voter turnout and information were low. Other research has shown in varying degrees of conclusiveness that traditional precinct work by party committeepersons does have an impact on voting, producing from a 5 to 10 percent change in the expected or usual party vote. The research suggests further that the effect of precinct work may well be greater in local elections than in media-centered presidential ones. In local elections there are apt to be fewer alternative cues and sources of information.[30] Those conclusions are buttressed by another set of findings that precinct canvassing in a presidential campaign increases turnout but has little effect on voter choice.[31] Finally, recent scholarship finds that active local party organization (before, during, and after the campaign) is associated with a vote increase over the expected norm,[32] and that specific strategic decisions in campaigns (in this case the decision of some Republican congres-

---

[29] Samuel J. Eldersveld, "Experimental Propaganda Techniques and Voting Behavior," *American Political Science Review* 50 (1956): 154–65; and John C. Blydenburgh, "A Controlled Experiment to Measure the Effects of Personal Contact Campaigning," *Midwest Journal of Political Science* 15 (1971): 365–81.

[30] Phillips Cutright and Peter H. Rossi, "Grass Roots Politicians and the Vote," *American Sociological Review* 23 (1958): 171–79; Daniel Katz and Samuel J. Eldersveld, "The Impact of Local Party Activity upon the Electorate," *Public Opinion Quarterly* 25 (1961): 1–24; Raymond E. Wolfinger, "The Influence of Precinct Work on Voting Behavior," *Public Opinion Quarterly* 27 (1963): 387–98.

[31] Gerald H. Kramer, "The.Effects of Precinct-Level Canvassing on Voter Behavior," *Public Opinion Quarterly* 34 (1970): 560–72.

[32] William J. Crotty, "Party Effort and Its Impact on the Vote," *American Political Science Review* 65 (1971): 439–50.

sional candidates not to associate themselves with Barry Goldwater in 1964) also have an effect on the vote.[33]

To summarize briefly, there are indications that the campaign is more successful in stimulating turnout than in affecting votes. (If that is the case, the implications favor campaigning only among one's probable supporters.) Furthermore, the efficacy of only one kind of campaigning — face-to-face personal contact — seems established, and that appears to be successful under limited circumstances. We know very little about the effectiveness of other techniques, much less about their comparative value. We also have some evidence that campaign strategies do matter. And we have considerable evidence that scholars have a very difficult time measuring the events and techniques of the campaign, and an even harder time accounting for their impact on the electorate. And that is it. For all its vaunted efficiency the new campaign management fraternity has not yet been able to add any answers.

## CAMPAIGN ORGANIZATION

Some American political campaigns are run from under the hat of the candidate. He or she may raise funds (often on a local credit rating), write the speeches and press releases, drive alone from speech to speech. These one-person campaigns are found chiefly in small constituencies, in rural areas, and for less noted offices — for example, the campaign of a rural candidate for state legislator or unimportant county office. A more common and perhaps the modal campaign organization in American politics includes the candidate, the campaign manager, perhaps an office manager, and a small number of faithful political friends, who devote part of their time to major campaign tasks. Together they constitute something of a general council for the campaign. Candidates adopt these modest, practical campaign organizations for very practical reasons. It may be all they can afford, and for many offices, it may be all they need.

The other extreme is the complex campaign organization with full bureaucratic panoply. In its "ideal," textbook form it is headed by a full-time campaign manager, who presides over the functional units that make up the rest of the campaign organization. A research staff examines the political characteristics of the constituency, researches the stands and speeches of the opponent, prepares material for the candidate's speeches, and oversees the gathering of information during the campaign. Canvassers, often a veritable army of them recruited by the party organization, visit or

---

[33] Robert A. Schoenberger, "Campaign Strategy and Party Loyalty: The Electoral Relevance of Candidate Decision-Making in the 1964 Congressional Elections," *American Political Science Review* 63 (1969): 515–20.

telephone voters. A speakers' bureau may provide speakers in addition to the candidate. Public relations and mass media specialists prepare press

---

## Political Humor: Campaigns

A significant percentage of the best political cartooning these days deals with our campaigns for public office. It is interesting, perhaps even revealing, to speculate why that should be so. Maybe cartoonists focus on the campaign because it is the most visible side of our parties and politics. Perhaps, though, it is because they think there is an intrinsically humorous, even absurd, aspect to contemporary campaigning. Whatever the explanation, these two examples have appeared recently in the pages of *The New Yorker.*

*"All in favor of waffling say 'Aye.'"*

Drawing by Stevenson; © 1976 The New Yorker Magazine, Inc.; June 28, 1976 issue.

*"Issue-oriented didn't work for beans."*

releases, ads for the media, and printed literature, and handle the relationships with representatives of the media. A finance committee, possibly supplemented by a treasurer, centralizes the raising of funds, the budgeting of expenditures, the paying of bills, and the keeping of records. Finally, a bureaucracy of a few secretaries and staff people maintains the candidate's headquarters, answers the phone and mail, and organizes large mailings.

These full-scale, maximum campaign organizations are certainly not the norm in American politics. For some campaigns, indeed, they would be organizational overkill. But even when desirable, a shortage of resources may prevent their creation. Also, in some instances, they have been replaced by the organizations of campaign management firms. The candidate with sufficient resources may find it easier to rent a campaign organization. Regardless of the form the campaign organization takes, the key person in most campaigns remains the campaign manager. Most candidates find it necessary to shift the burden of directing the campaign so that their time, energy, and concentration can be spent on the campaign itself.

The larger and more complex the campaign apparatus, ironically, the greater the danger of the endemic "disorganization" that marks American campaign organizations. The candidate, his or her own political following, the activists of the party organization, the financial contributors, the fund raisers, and the campaign staff all may have different incentives for participating and different views of what the campaign should be. What we call "the campaign" may in fact be a number of campaigns only loosely bound together in a common effort. Many of the components of the campaign may indeed be pursuing their own interests, whether they be of ideology, influence, or visibility. A good deal of time and effort must be paid — often by the candidate — to integrate and satisfy all segments of the campaign. The candidate may have to tailor statements to satisfy them. And many campaign speeches are beamed more at the campaign organization, or parts of it, than at the broader electorate. Taken as a whole, the campaign organization itself constitutes one of the major demands on the campaign, its themes, its tone, and its style.

## THE PARTY ORGANIZATION'S ROLE

The campaign for the House of Commons in Great Britain is in the hands of 630 Labour party and 630 Conservative party election "agents." The parties employ the agents, train them in the direction of campaigns, and place them in the individual constituencies as managers of the local campaigns for Parliament. English law buttresses their authority by making them legally responsible for the observance of all election laws and for the management of all moneys spent in the campaigns. The parties, therefore, are guaranteed a guiding role in the parliamentary campaigns.

Not so the American party organizations. Nothing, either of law or tradition, assures them of even a prominent place in the campaign. They must compete constantly for a role in it, just as they fought to control the nominations. Their adversaries in this struggle are would-be independent candidates, the personal campaign organizations they create, and the new professional managers of campaigns. Although the realities of American politics force candidates to run under party symbols that will help them attract the votes of a party electorate, nothing forces them to let the party organization control or even participate in their campaigns.

In some parts of the country, however, the party organization still retains assets that make it indispensable for the campaign. If it can command the armies of local workers, it can provide the candidate with a campaign vehicle (or medium) that ensures success but costs very little. These organizational campaigns occur chiefly in one-party urban areas in which parties control primaries and voters habitually vote the party ticket in the general election. Canvassing and turning out the vote are still relevant there. Furthermore, the urban candidate is much more apt to have been nominated by the party organization through its control of the primary and thus to be its creature in the general election campaign.

Yet, when they can, candidates find it strategically useful to rely on a separate campaign organization composed of friends, followers, and non-party groups. A personal organization may draw on the time and money of people who are chary of party ties or who consider themselves of the "other" party. It enables the candidate to draw support on the basis of his or her own personality and charisma. It permits a campaign that surmounts party lines both in its organization and in its impact. Finally, by running the campaign (and paying for it), the candidate remains free of debt to and hence dependence on the party organization.

Moreover, the candidate has built-in advantages in competing for control of campaigns. The sheer number of campaigns, coupled with the feebleness of many party organizations, has forced those organizations to surrender control by default. Electoral institutions, from the direct primary to the office-block ballot, have been on the side of the candidates, and so have the political norms of many sections of the American electorate. Furthermore, the candidate now has in his favor a whole new set of campaigning skills for which he does not have to depend on the party organization. Some fifty or sixty years ago the party organizations came close to monopolizing the knowledge, skills, and manpower necessary for a successful campaign. They do so no longer; new sources of knowledge, skills, and manpower are for hire.

It is probably a mistake to conclude, as have some of its victims, that a new-style campaign is indispensable. Campaigns in the Shapp and Rockefeller manner are still very much the exceptions — at least in the magnitude of their reliance on the new knowledge and techniques. It is still possible for the careful candidate to win elections without important help from either the party organization or the media specialists. Some candidates, indeed, are as suspicious of the new practitioners as they are of the party organization. Listen to the campaign manager of a successful congressional candidate:

During our first campaign, some fellows from big P.R. outfits who live out here came around and volunteered their time and their talents. We talked with them and looked at the campaign material they'd put together, and we were scared witless. As far as they were concerned, facts and statistics were simply things to be changed. . . . Basically, the P.R. approach is different. Politics has a deeply negative quality. We're convinced that most people vote against somebody. . . . And that's what we concentrate on — making them vote against our opponent. The P.R. crowd feel they have to sell something positively. . . . We believe in being amateurish. Our brochures look as if they were got up in our basement. But the P.R. men want to put out four-color brochures with dazzling artwork and their idea of how the Gettysburg Address should have read.[34]

Because they are exceptions to the rule, however, it would be foolish to deny the rule itself. The new campaigning and the political consultants continue to advance to American politics. Certainly the great majority of Senate, House, and gubernatorial candidates already rely on them in some degree.

The interests of the candidate and of the party organization in the campaign never completely converge. That is the basic truth behind their struggle for its control. The candidate, unless he has been dragooned to fill a ticket in a lost cause, takes himself and his candidacy seriously. Even the longest shot among candidates tends to think he will win; the degree of his ego involvement in the campaign almost demands it. The party, on the other hand, wants to be selective in its use of campaign resources. It may see some races as lost and be glad to turn these candidates loose for their own independent campaigns. Party organizations want to set overall priorities and allocations of scarce resources; they want to eliminate the inefficient and uneconomical parts of the campaign. Furthermore, the party organization wants to activate party loyalty, and candidates may not care to. It may also want to protect a platform and a program, help a presidential or gubernatorial candidate, or win control of a legislature. But these need not be the goals and interests of individual candidates.

To be sure, there are potent advantages to a party-led series of campaigns on behalf of an entire ticket. Such planning can eliminate the embarrassment and futility of two candidates' competing for audiences in the same small town. It can distribute campaign literature for a number of candidates at the same time. And it alone can mount the major election-day activities: setting up operation headquarters, providing cars and baby-sitters, checking voter lists to alert the nonvoters late in the day, and providing poll watchers to oversee the balloting and counting. Efficiency and integration of the campaign, however, often threaten the interests of specific candidates. Although the party organization may prefer to raise money and prevent unseemly competition for the political dollar, an individual candidate may well believe he can raise more on his own. And although the party may prefer billboard posters that celebrate the full party ticket of candidates, some among them may prefer to go it alone.

[34] Richard Harris, "How's It Look?" *New Yorker,* April 8, 1967, p. 63. The article presents an excellent case study of a congressional campaign that relied neither on party organization nor on the new techniques and specialists.

This distance, even estrangement, between candidate and party organization is apparent also in the expectations of candidates and party officials. In many parts of the country neither group expects the party organizations to run the campaigns. Kingdon finds that only a minority of Wisconsin candidates see the party organization as the most important member of their campaign coalition. A slightly higher percentage, in fact, see interest groups as the most important.[35] And there is at least some evidence that state party chairmen do not think of themselves as campaign managers.[36]

Out of this pulling and tugging for control of the campaign emerges a great overlapping of campaign organization. In many instances the struggle and tension for control is really a four-cornered one involving the candidate, nonparty groups and specialists, the local party organization, and state or national party organs. Which one dominates depends largely on which one controls the resources — the money, manpower, skills, and information — that the campaign requires. When party organizations can provide candidates the new expertise and skills that the professionals can, and at a lower cost, they will reassert their control over the business of campaigning. But it will require more money than they now have, and it will demand a greater centralization of party organizational authority. It may well be, therefore, that party organizations will be able neither to beat 'em nor to join 'em.

The new campaigning works against the party and the party organization in another way. It reinforces the development of personalism in politics. It is the candidate, not the party, who is "sold." The image transmitted by TV and the other media is of a person, not of the abstraction known as a political party. The campaign techniques, therefore, foster a tie between candidate and voter — a new personalism in politics — in which the role of party loyalty is less important. The new campaign techniques, therefore, threaten to displace the party "within" the voter as well as the party organization in the campaign.

So the battle between the party organizations and the parties in government intensifies over the control of nominations and election campaigns.

---

[35] Kingdon, *Candidates for Office*, Chap. 3.
[36] On this point two studies report virtually opposite conclusions. In 1970 Charles W. Wiggins and William L. Turk reported that state party chairmen gave last place in importance in a list of five roles to the one described as "helping manage campaigns of state candidates." "State Party Chairmen: A Profile," *Western Political Quarterly* 23 (1970): 329. But Robert Huckshorn in *Party Leadership in the States* (Amherst: University of Massachusetts Press, 1976), finds that chairmen of both parties rate "campaign strategist" and "campaigner" responsibilities in the top third of a list of thirteen responsibilities. It may be that the respondents saw an important difference between managing campaigns and participating and strategizing in them.

If the American parties are indeed electoral parties, then whoever controls the picking of candidates and the staging of campaigns controls the parties. At stake here is not only pride, but the fruits of victory. In the old days the activists of the party organizations were satisfied with electoral victory by itself, for their goals were largely satisfied by power itself and the patronage and preferments that flowed from it. But the new activists seek much more than mere victory; they seek candidates and officials who will pursue specific issues and policy options after victory. And so to achieve their goals the workers of the party organizations need to assert greater control over the party's candidates and officeholders at the very time when it becomes harder and harder to do so.

By controlling their own nominations and elections, candidates are free of party organizational dominance and free to pursue their own relations with their constituencies and their alliances with nonparty organizations. The failures of the party organizations enhance the competitive positions of other groups that want to play electoral politics and influence public policy. At stake in the battle, therefore, is both the control and health of the political parties and the very nature of representative government in the United States.

# 11

# Presidential Politics: The Preliminaries

It has often been said that the American presidency is the biggest, most demanding job in the world. Its size and responsibilities in part reflect the power and concerns of the government of the United States. They also reflect the unique institution of the presidency itself, for the United States is the only major power of the world that chooses a chief executive from a national constituency in free, competitive elections. And as if to match the prodigious demands and responsibilities of the presidency, the American people have evolved a process of nomination and election to that office that for sheer length, expense, attention, and gaudy extravaganza is without peer in the world. It commands front-page coverage in most of the world's newspapers, and in the United States alone media coverage reaches enormous proportions. Approximately 120 million Americans watched at least a few minutes of the televised returns on election night in 1976.

Furthermore, the quadrennial American presidential campaign has become the focal point of all American politics. Its results radiate out to affect other elections — strong presidential winners, for example, carry other candidates into office on their coattails. Its candidates and rhetoric tend to shape party loyalties and identifications, and its regular four-year calendar is the basic pulse of American politics. The presidential election is also the great centralizing moment in American politics, the centripetal force against all of the decentralizing, centrifugal tendencies. It is the brief but influential hour of the parties as national parties. And, for many American citizens who are often apathetic to local elections, its salience and prominence make it virtually the whole of American politics.

Appropriately, this singular campaign and election pivots around two singular American political institutions: the nominating conventions of the summer before the presidential election and that constitutional anachronism, the electoral college. They combine to create a presidential politics of baroque complexity and an electoral process that remains an insoluble puzzle to many of the world's observers. It is a politics that is, to say the least, peculiarly American.

## THE RULES OF THE PRESIDENTIAL GAME

If the American president and vice-president were elected directly by a simple plurality of the American electorate, presidential politics would be vastly different — and vastly simpler. But the presidential constituency, the one national constituency in American politics, is not composed simply of all American adults. It is a complicated constituency from which is chosen an eighteenth-century deliberative body that no longer deliberates. Like any formal electoral system, this one gives a special form to the political competition that goes on within it.

The electoral college as it is set down in the Constitution rests heavily on the structure of American federalism.[1] Each state receives a number of electors equal to its total representation in the two houses of Congress. In other words, to the fixed quota of two senators one adds the number of the state's representatives in the House. The votes of the states in the electoral college, therefore, extend from a fixed minimum of three (two senators and one representative) to an open-ended maximum, currently the forty-five of California. In addition, since the ratification of the Twenty-third Amendment, the District of Columbia has had three electoral votes. Thus the total membership of the college presently is 538, the sum of the membership of the Senate (100), the House (435), and the three votes of the District of Columbia.

The Constitution further provides that the president and the vice-president must be elected by an absolute majority of the votes of the college. At present that would be 270 votes. Should the electoral college not be able to elect a president by this absolute majority, the Constitution has provided for what is in effect a superelectoral college. Under this plan the election of the president would be settled by the House of Representatives, which would choose among the three candidates with the greatest number of votes in the electoral college. However, while each state delegation in the House is to decide whom its state will support (and is not bound by the popular vote of the state), each state has only a single vote in the balloting. The emergency procedure was twice employed in the early 1800s but not since then. Today the procedure's drastic redistribution of political power to the less populous states threatens seriously the assumption that presidents ought to be elected by majorities (or, at least, pluralities) of voters.

The framers of the Constitution intended the electoral college to be a genuinely deliberative body. The choice of a president, argued Alexander Hamilton,

should be made by men most capable of analyzing the qualities adapted to the station, and acting under circumstances favorable to deliberation, and to a judicious combination of all the reasons and inducements which were proper to gov-

---

[1] Article II, Section 1, as amended by the Twelfth and Twenty-third Amendments.

ern their choice. A small number of persons, selected by their fellow-citizens from the general mass, will be most likely to possess the information and discernment requisite to such complicated investigation.[2]

Not all the Founding Fathers were as fearful of direct popular election as was Hamilton, but the majority seems to have accepted the wisdom of selection by a body of respected notables. The transformation of the electoral college began, however, with the rise of political parties. In the states, slates of electors began to run pledged to support a party's presidential and vice-presidential candidates. In other words, the ties of party loyalty assured voters that a vote for a specific set of electors was in effect a vote for party candidates. As soon as that practice of pledged slates became widespread, the electoral college ceased to function as an independent body. And so the electoral college today is perhaps the world's most important governmental body that has neither meetings nor options. In most states the electors meet briefly over lunch or dinner in the state capitol to register their vote formally. Some official of the state then transmits it to the president of the Senate in Washington, and the collective preferences of the electoral college are recorded without the inconvenience of a single meeting of the college as a whole.

Party electoral slates and the party loyalty of those on them have had another transforming effect. The desire of parties to maximize support for a full slate of electors has undoubtedly influenced the states to make the popular election of the electors an all-or-nothing race. A plurality edge for a party, whether of a few votes or many thousand votes, carries all the state's electoral votes. This winner-take-all principle in turn has had two consequences. First, it has forced the parties and the candidates to appeal to the voters of the large, competitive states with the big, indivisible blocs of electoral votes. To fail to carry Nevada or Delaware, with their three electoral votes, is not a major loss. But to fail to win in New York (forty-one electoral votes) or in California (forty-five) is a major setback. The parties tend, therefore, to pick presidential candidates from the large, pivotal states and to beam a great portion of the campaign at them. Second, the winner-take-all arithmetic increases the possibility of the loser in the national popular vote being elected the new president. That result can occur if a candidate wins state blocs of votes by narrow margins and loses others by landslides.[3] Since the Civil War two men have been presidential

[2] *The Federalist,* number 68 (New York: Modern Library, 1937), pp. 441–42.
[3] For example, to reduce the problem to three states of equal voting population and equal electoral vote:

State *A*    Population of 2,000,000 and ten electoral votes
             Democratic vote:    900,000
             Republican vote:  1,100,000
State *B*    Same population and electoral vote
             Democratic vote:    950,000
             Republican vote:  1,050,000

losers even though they led in the popular vote: Samuel J. Tilden in 1876 and Grover Cleveland in 1888.[4]

Although party ties have robbed the electoral college of its deliberative quality, they have not made it completely automatic and predictable. Electors in most states are not legally or constitutionally bound to vote for the presidential candidate under whose name they have run. Five times since World War II individual electors at the "moment of truth" have abandoned the candidate to whom they were pledged. A Virginia Republican bolted the Nixon slate in 1972 to vote for the candidate of the Libertarian party; and in 1976 a Ford elector in Washington voted for Reagan.[5] Furthermore, rebellious state parties may exploit this lack of binding tie for their own purposes. They may deny the voters of their state the chance to vote for their party's national candidates by running either a different slate of candidates or an unpledged slate under the state party label. In 1948, for example, J. Strom Thurmond, the Dixiecrat candidate for president, rather than Harry S. Truman, appeared on the ballots as the Democratic candidate for the presidency in a number of southern states. Mississippi Democrats in 1960 and Alabama Democrats in 1960 and 1964 ran unpledged slates of electors under the Democratic party label. A combination of party decentralization and state control over the presidential ballot, therefore, limits the development of a national, popular election of the American president.

Each of these characteristics and consequences of the electoral college has produced a body of criticism and reform proposals.[6] One school of thought, concerned about the college's artificiality and the possibility of a "minority" president, has sought to abolish it in favor of a direct, popular election of the president. Others, alarmed by the system's emphasis on the indivisible, big-state votes, have proposed various systems of dividing the electoral votes of the state; most of them involve either dividing the electoral vote proportionally according to the candidates' percentages of the

---

State C  Same population and electoral vote
Democratic vote:    1,300,000
Republican vote:      700,000

Here the Republican candidate leads in the electoral vote, twenty to ten, while the Democratic candidate leads in the popular vote by 300,000.

[4] Depending on how one counts the Alabama popular vote in 1960 for both pledged and unpledged electors, a case can be made that Richard Nixon won the popular vote in 1960 while losing the vote in the electoral college. See Longley and Braun, cited in footnote 6.

[5] The Virginia elector, *mirabile dictu*, was chosen the Libertarian candidate for the presidency in 1976!

[6] On the electoral college generally, see Neal R. Peirce, *The People's President* (New York: Simon and Schuster, 1968); Wallace S. Sayre and Judith H. Parris, *Voting for President* (Washington: Brookings, 1970); and Lawrence D. Longley and Alan G. Braun, *The Politics of Electoral College Reform*, 2nd ed. (New Haven: Yale University Press, 1975).

popular vote, or electing some or most of the electors in the congressional districts of the state. (Maine, in fact, decided in 1972 to choose two of its four electors in the state's two congressional districts; the party that carries the state will get two at-large electors, but the loser could conceivably carry one of the districts.) Still others have sought to check the uncertainty of its operation — the possibility of unpledged slates, of state ballots without a national candidate, and of local slates intended solely to deadlock the electoral college. Yet, despite a torrent of polemics and tomes of argumentation, operation of the college remains untouched. It changes today only as it has in the past — by custom, tradition, and state law.

Behind all the attempts to reform or abolish the electoral college lie broader questions of political power and ideology. In defining the national constituency of the president and the vice-president, the electoral college enhances the political power of the large, urban, industrial states with the large blocs of electoral votes. To state the matter another way, the college creates a presidential constituency that is markedly different from the sum of all the congressional constituencies. Because of the equal state representation in the Senate, regardless of population, the political power of the rural and small-city electorates is magnified in the Congress. In the last generation, the presidents, as a result of the nature of the national constituency, have usually espoused the "liberal" social and economic programs favored by the people of the urban areas. The desire of political conservatives to reduce the power of the large urban, industrial states lies behind some of the attempts to alter the college, especially those proposals which would divide the electoral votes of the individual states.[7] And the desire to preserve that power lies behind a great deal of the opposition to change.

The second issue behind reform of the electoral college is no less than direct, popular democracy itself. In the last 130 or 140 years the electoral college has evolved into something very close to a de facto popular election of the presidency. That same period has also seen the spread of democratic norms and a constant broadening of the suffrage. Some of the proposed reforms try to protect the will of the majority either by institutionalizing the popular election of the president and vice-president or by preventing individual electors or state parties from thwarting popular will. Into this category fall both the attempts to abolish the college entirely and those less drastic proposals to limit state party control over the ballot choices and to force electors to vote for the candidates they ran pledged to support. On this point the opponents of change in effect deny the presence of a problem; in every presidential election since 1888 the leader in the popular vote has indeed won in the electoral college.

[7] On this point and also for a general review of the impact of the electoral college, see Allan Sindler, "Presidential Election Methods and Urban-Ethnic Interests," *Law and Contemporary Problems* 27 (1962): 213–33.

Finally, the debate over reform turns on the future of the two-party system. Much of the impetus for reform in the 1970s came from George Wallace's attempt to deny Hubert Humphrey and Richard Nixon a majority of electoral votes in 1968 and thus to give himself a bargaining role in either the electoral college or the "one state, one vote" ballot in the House. But opponents of abolition claim that direct election of the president would do even more to encourage minor parties and independent candidates. They center on provisions in direct election amendments that provide for a run-off apparatus of some kind — another election or selection by a joint session of Congress — if no candidate got 40 percent of the popular vote in the election. The possibility of that run-off combined with direct, national popular vote, they argue, would be an even greater spur to third parties.

So, fair representation, the will of the majority, and the health of the two-party system are goals beyond serious debate. The argument is over what meaning they should have in practice and over what way of selecting a president will best achieve them.[8]

## FIRST STEPS TOWARD THE NOMINATIONS

The national conventions of the two major parties conclude the complicated process of nomination. It is far more difficult, however, to say just when that nominating process begins. For some especially ambitious and farsighted politicians, it may have begun in their own political career planning some six or eight years before. Within the party defeated at a presidential election, jockeying for the next nomination begins the morning after defeat. In a more traditional sense, the nomination process begins as the advance men for would-be candidates straggle into New Hampshire to enter their candidates and delegates in the earliest of the presidential primaries.

Basically, the preconvention part of the nomination process concerns the selection of delegates to the conventions. The major would-be candidates within each party seek delegates bound to them — or at least committed or inclined to them. Conversely, heads of state delegations often want delegates to remain uncommitted so that their bargaining power will remain unexpended until the convention meets. Typically, however, the

---

[8] There are two paradoxes in all of this debate. The first involves the third-party effect. Generally, the electoral college discourages smaller parties, if only because their support is so difficult to translate into electoral votes. However, a "larger" small party, and especially one whose strength is regionally concentrated, can use the electoral college for its own strategic purposes. The second paradox concerns the effect on the smaller states. The informal political consequences of the electoral college lead to the big-state arithmetic and, conversely, to some slighting of candidates from and campaigns in the smaller states. Formally, however, the electoral college, by including the Senate's equal representation in the formula, does overrepresent the small, usually rural states.

party organizations control only part of the picking of delegates to their own conventions. State legislatures decide the crucial matter of how the convention delegates will be chosen: whether by a presidential primary, by a convention or committee of the party, or by a combination of the two.

## Apportionment and Selection of Delegates

The national parties determine the number of votes and delegates each state will have in the Democratic and Republican national conventions. For the first time in a long while the number of votes and delegates to the two national conventions in 1976 were identical. The Democrats in particular earlier had a long tradition of permitting state parties to send more delegates to the national convention than the number of their assigned votes, with the inevitable result that some delegates cast bizarre fractions of a single vote.

To assign the number of votes to each state the national committee or convention of the parties — whichever makes the decision — employs a more than usually complicated formula. The 1976 Republican convention, for example, was chosen according to this formula:

— Each state received six at-large delegates.
— Each state received three delegates from each of its congressional districts.
— Each state received an additional delegate for having a Republican governor and/or senator.
— Each state whose congressional delegation was at least 50 percent Republican received an additional delegate.
— Each state which gave the 1972 presidential candidate its electoral vote received a number of additional delegates equal to four and one-half plus .6 of the state's electoral vote (rounded to the next whole number).
— The District of Columbia received fourteen at-large votes, Puerto Rico eight, the Virgin Islands four, and Guam four.

Virtually the same formula was adopted by the Republicans for their 1980 convention. The Republicans thus favor heavily the areas of heavy Republican strength, and they continue the tradition of overrepresenting the less populous states. Indeed, the 1976 formula was adopted over the strong opposition of about one-third of the 1972 convention delegates, who wanted to increase the representation of the urban, populous states. But those are the states of liberal Republican strength, and the apportionment of convention delegates in both parties tends to reflect the interests of the dominant ideologies within them.

In recent years the Democrats have moved further than the Republicans from the old norm of equal representation for the states modified by bonus delegates for having won recent elections. They started in 1972 to represent more heavily the different populations of the states as well as the factor of Democratic vote strength. The seven largest states — California, Illinois, Michigan, New York, Ohio, Pennsylvania, and Texas — jumped from 36 percent of the convention votes in 1968 to 44 percent in 1972. The effect thus is to increase further the relative strength of the states the Democrats usually carry.

For years the national parties, in preparing for the conventions, had stipulated only the number of delegates the states would have. It was always left to the states or their parties to decide how they would be chosen. In 1968 the Democrats ended that tradition, too. They began to control a number of the other aspects of delegate selection. Best known of those aspects, undoubtedly, was the requirement for 1972 that women, minorities, and young voters would have to be represented in "reasonable" numbers among the delegates. By 1980 the rules of the convention required each state to file affirmative action "goals" for representing all groups in its delegation to the convention in proportion to their strength in the Democratic electorate in the state. They also stipulated that 50 percent of each state's delegation be women. In addition, the rules for 1980 required that in selecting delegates to the convention the states:

— limit participation in primaries and caucuses to Democratic voters who would declare their party preference (thus ruling out selection in open primaries).

— do so largely within a period between the first Tuesdays of March and June 1980 (thus setting limits to state legislatures that wanted to move their state primaries or caucuses to earlier dates).

— require that all would-be delegates be identified either by their presidential preference or as uncommitted (thus banning primaries such as New York's for selecting delegates).

— allocate delegates proportionally by the strength of the various presidential contenders in the state (prohibiting both winner-take-all elections and the use of single delegate districts to avoid the principle of proportional division).

And so ended local autonomy over the selection of delegates to national conventions. The Democratic rules challenge state election law as well as state party options and local political traditions. Taken as a whole the Democratic reforms have been a stunning and unprecedented assertion of the authority of the national party.[9]

The Democrats also ended another tradition with their reforms in the

[9] For a full account of the early steps in the Democratic reform of delegate-selection procedures, see Austin Ranney, *Curing the Mischiefs of Faction* (Berkeley: University of California Press, 1975). Many of the political implications of the reforms are explored in James I. Lengle and Byron Shafer, "Primary Rules, Political Power, and Social Change," *American Political Science Review* 70 (1976): 25–40.

late sixties and seventies. Both parties had for a long time followed similar policies in apportioning and selecting their convention delegates. There had, to be sure, been differences between them, but the main structures of representation and selection had been similar. Now increasingly, as a result of the Democratic reforms, they differ on fundamentals. In fact, the representativeness of the national conventions themselves has become a political issue.

## The Presidential Primaries

The number of states choosing their convention delegates in presidential primaries continues its steady climb. In 1968, only fifteen states and the District of Columbia elected some or all of their convention delegates in ways that offered voters of the state some opportunity to express a preference for the presidential nominee of the party. Together the delegates from these states and the District of Columbia cast 47 percent of the votes at the Democratic convention and 46 percent at the Republican. Additionally, Alabamans elected unpledged delegates to the Democratic convention. By 1976 the total had jumped to thirty-one states and the District of Columbia. Approximately three out of every four delegates at the conventions came from them.[10] With the addition of Texas in 1976, furthermore, there are primaries in all of the ten most populous states.

To speak blithely of presidential primaries is, however, an oversimplification. No two are identical. The major source of their variety lies in their two-part character: They can be devices for selecting delegates to the national conventions, and they can give voters a choice among contestants for the party's nomination. On the basis of the way they combine or divide these two separate functions, the assorted presidential primaries fall into four categories: primaries in which only delegates are chosen, those in which the voters may only show a presidential preference, those which integrate the two features, and those which provide for separate delegate selection and presidential preference polls. (See Figure 11.1 for some sample ballots.)

1. *Delegate selection only.* In Alabama and New York the primary is solely a vehicle to elect delegates to the national conventions. There is no place on the ballot for the names of the contenders for the party nomination, and the delegates do not run formally pledged to any contender. The ballot is, therefore, innocent of any names except those of men and women who seek election as delegates. In New York, however, delegate

---

[10] The nineteen following states did *not* have a presidential primary in 1976: Alaska, Arizona, Colorado, Connecticut, Delaware, Hawaii, Iowa, Kansas, Louisiana, Maine, Minnesota, Mississippi, Missouri, North Dakota, Oklahoma, South Carolina, Utah, Virginia, and Wyoming.

## FIGURE 11.1  Sample Ballots from New Hampshire and Wisconsin (inset) Presidential Primaries: 1976

candidates have often pledged themselves informally to a presidential contender in the campaign, and the supporters of candidates distribute cards with names of delegates supporting them.

2. *Presidential preference only.* In at least two states, Indiana and North Carolina, the presidential primary is nothing more than a presidential preference poll. The voter is confronted by the names of his party's worthies who have entered the primary, and he merely indicates which he would prefer to represent his party in the November presidential contest. State committees or conventions of the parties then pick the delegates to the respective national conventions. Those delegates, however, are usually required to support the candidacy of the winner of the state's presidential poll.

3. *The two elements combined.* A number of states — California, Ohio,

South Dakota, and Wisconsin among them — combine the presidential poll and the election of delegates by a simple device: The delegates pledge themselves to support specific candidates for the party's nomination. That pledge and the name of the national candidate, of course, are linked with the delegate's name on the ballot. In some states every delegate's name on the ballot is associated with a presidential candidate — for example, a statement under each name reads, "Pledged to support John Smith for president." Other states provide that a full slate of delegate-candidates be listed on the ballot under the name of the presidential candidate to which the slate is pledged. On the California ballot, only the names of the presidential candidates appear; a vote for one of them automatically elects the slate of delegates pledged to him.
4. *The two elements separated.* The remaining states — the largest number of them — and the District of Columbia include the two features of the primary but separate them. In these states the ballot has a presidential preference poll in which the party's hopefuls compete for the favor of partisans within the state. In a separate section of the ballot, voters choose delegates to the conventions. Confusion and diversity of practice, however, surround the relationship between the two parts. In only some of the states (e.g., Tennessee) do the results of the preferential polls bind the delegates selected. In the rest of the states they are only advisory.

In outline these are the presidential primaries. There are, though, still other differences among them. First, in some the convention delegates are elected from the state at large; in others, from the individual congressional districts; and in still others, from both. Such a seemingly minor variation, however, can have major political consequences. For example, the chances of a divided state delegation (and its attendant intraparty squabbles) are much greater when delegates are chosen by congressional district. North Carolina also introduced a new twist in 1972. Candidates receiving more than 15 percent of the vote shared the state's delegates proportionately. A large number of primary states, if they are to comply with Democratic rules for 1980, will have to adopt similar plans.

Second, some states in their primaries elect all the delegates the parties will send to the conventions, and some elect only part of them. In Pennsylvania, for example, a quarter of the delegates are chosen by the parties' state central committees. Such a provision helps meet one of the parties' major objections to the presidential primary by permitting them to make sure (through their own state committees) that the important leaders of the state organizations will go as delegates to the national convention of their parties.

Third, the states vary on the issue of whether a presidential hopeful must consent before his name is involved in the state's primary. Most states, but not all, require his approval (or permit his disapproval) before his name may be entered in a presidential preference poll or before delegates run pledged to him. In Oregon the primary law entrusts to a state official the delicate decision of putting on the preference poll the names of all candidates "generally recognized in the national news media" to be candidates for the presidential nomination. A similar decision in Wisconsin is entrusted to an eleven-person committee made up largely of the leadership of the two major parties. The purpose clearly is to make it less possible for potential candidates to avoid some of the primaries and thus diminish competition and interest in them.

Fourth, the presidential primaries differ in the nature of the commitment of the pledged delegates. In some cases the pledge of a delegate to support a certain candidate for the nomination is buttressed only by his enthusiasm for his candidate, by his own code of honor, or by his sense of the political value of integrity. In other states delegates are required by law to take a pledge of loyalty to the candidate. Wisconsin, for instance, specifies by law the content of the pledge:

I will, unless prevented by the death of the candidate, vote for his candidacy on the first ballot; and vote for his candidacy on any additional ballot, unless released by said candidate, until said candidate fails to receive at least one-third of the vote authorized to be cast; and that, thereafter, I shall have the right to cast my convention vote according to my own judgment.[11]

Finally, whereas all the other states and the District of Columbia have closed primaries, Wisconsin and Michigan hold open primaries. The possibility that voters who would normally support Democratic candidates at the general election will drift into the Republican presidential primary — and vice versa — creates an additional uncertainty and unpredictability for the candidates. It is precisely those conditions that the Democratic rules for 1980 seek to end.

## Delegates Chosen by the Party Organizations

The presidential primaries are dramatic and are reported in the most intricate detail. Nonetheless, the parties of approximately a third of the states — as well as the Democratic party in Guam, and both parties in Puerto Rico — choose delegates by assorted internal party processes. Those processes are usually combinations of local caucuses followed by regional and statewide conventions. Generally, the regional conventions choose a fixed and equal number of delegates, and the state convention selects the re-

11 *Wisconsin Statutes*, Chap. 8.12. For a general study of the presidential primaries, see James W. Davis, *Presidential Primaries: Road to the White House* (New York: Crowell, 1967).

mainder from the state at large. In a few states some or all the delegates are chosen by the state central committee of the party.[12]

For years the selection of delegates in the nonprimary states was relatively invisible. The events of 1976, however, changed all of that. A virtually unknown seeker after the Democratic nomination, Jimmy Carter, vaulted himself into serious candidacy by a strenuous campaign in Iowa that netted him both media attention and about 30 percent of the state's Democratic delegates. Within the Republican party Gerald Ford and Ronald Reagan emerged from the primaries almost deadlocked in the delegate count and consequently turned all of their considerable persuasion on what state conventions and uncommitted delegates remained. As a result, the nonprimary states will probably never be invisible again, and party officials in them will find it harder to keep their delegations uncommitted. And since the Iowa selection process begins with caucuses in January, it can fairly be said that the Great Delegate Hunt now begins there rather than in the New Hampshire primary some weeks later.[13]

## THE POLITICS OF SELECTING DELEGATES

The politics of winning a presidential nomination obviously depends on enlisting the support of a majority of the delegates at the national convention. However, the strategies of the presidential aspirants differ in how and when they make their move for delegate backing. But as front-running candidates increasingly attempt to influence the selection and instruction of delegates — as they try to wrap up the nomination before the convention convenes — the significant part of the politics of nomination shifts to the preconvention phase. The intensive preconvention campaign for delegates begun by John F. Kennedy in 1960, in fact, accounts largely for the fact that every nomination in the 1960s and 1970s was won on the first ballot of the convention.

Even though the intensive preconvention campaign is becoming more common, such a strategy makes sense only for some contenders. Front-runners well known to the political public may feel they have no alternative but to make a show of strength and come to the convention with a majority of delegates firmly in grasp or at least in sight. Other candidates,

---

[12] The mechanics and politics of choosing convention delegates are discussed more fully by Gerald Pomper, *Nominating the President: The Politics of Convention Choice* (Evanston: Northwestern University Press, 1963), Chap. 3. On preconvention strategies, see Nelson W. Polsby and Aaron B. Wildavsky, *Presidential Elections*, 4th ed. (New York: Scribners, 1976). For a study of the politics of electing convention delegates in a state convention, see Richard G. Niemi and M. Kent Jennings, "Intraparty Communications and the Selection of Delegates to a National Convention," *Western Political Quarterly* 22 (1969): 29–46.

[13] Jules Witcover reports amply on the preconvention campaigns in the nonprimary states in 1976 in *Marathon* (New York: Viking, 1977).

partially in response to the front-runner's activity, may feel they have to contest the selection of some delegates if only to block the front-runner short of a majority of the delegates. The lesson of the dithering inactivity of moderate Republicans in 1964 while Barry Goldwater kept accumulating delegate support is not apt to be forgotten in the near future. Still other candidates may contest the delegate selection in just a few states for assorted reasons: to garner enough convention votes to have a substantial voice in its deliberations or to extract a political quid pro quo (the vice-presidential nomination or a cabinet seat, perhaps). Some few candidates, the true dark horses who lack a publicized name and a political following, may avoid contests in the states in order to remain acceptable to all wings of the party should a deadlocked convention want to turn to them.

The use of these strategies — and thus the pattern of preconvention contesting — will be determined within a party by a number of factors, among them:

— *The presence of a president.* When presidents are eligible for another term, they are often in a commanding position to dictate their own renomination and to eliminate competition. Even presidents who are not candidates for renomination (such as Eisenhower in 1960 and Johnson in 1968) may influence the nomination by their late decisions or support for a successor.

— *The number of candidates and their strength.* Two leading candidates (such as Ford and Reagan in 1976) force a different form of strategy and counterstrategy than do four or five evenly matched candidates.

— *The resources of the candidates.* Unquestionably the last-minute campaign of Nelson Rockefeller in 1968, lacking support among the party leaders and organizations and thus dependent on the media, could have been undertaken only by a man of considerable resources.

— *The commitments of state leaders and parties.* The heavy support of most Democratic state leaders for Hubert Humphrey was perhaps the greatest disadvantage that Eugene McCarthy faced in his attempt to win his party's nomination in 1968. Their commitment also led to charges that the party's convention in Chicago was bossed.

— *Party rules on delegate selection.* For example, the new Democratic rules outlawing the winner-take-all rule (and thus forcing some kind of proportional representation) will encourage more Democratic candidates. Regional or local candidates (favorite sons or daughters) may wish to bring a handful of delegates to the convention for bargaining purposes.

Within these general political configurations, the candidates must also make personal strategic assessments. A candidate may be forced to greater preconvention activity to counter a popular impression that he cannot win or that he does not enjoy party support. Or he may feel compelled to prove to the skeptical that he is durable enough for the presidential race. He may wish, as George Wallace did, to counter the feeling that his popularity is regional. In 1960 John F. Kennedy entered the presidential primary in Protestant West Virginia to prove that his Catholicism would not hamper him in a presidential campaign. Above all, the candidate's decisions may be governed by his estimates of probable success. There may be a chance of avoiding a primary one is certain to lose, and even if not, the candidate may concede defeat and minimize its impact by doing little campaigning in the state.

The candidates are not alone in having interests at stake in the selection of delegates to the conventions. So also do the state party organizations and leaders, and their interests often run counter to those of the aspiring presidential nominees. For the local and state parties, a hotly contested selection of delegates is often an occasion for intraparty conflict. Battles between Eugene McCarthy and Hubert Humphrey for Democratic delegates in 1968 — both in primaries and in state conventions — created rifts in the party that have been slow to heal. George McGovern's fight for Democratic delegates in 1972 reopened many of these splits in the Democratic party. The McGovern candidacy — heavily supported by the young, female, minority, and very liberal segments of the party — won little favor among the staid and traditional leaders of many of the party organizations. His success in their states, coupled with the party's rules on delegate selection, indeed meant that a good many of them were denied positions as delegates to the national convention.

The interests and goals of the parties in selecting delegates to the national conventions go further than the avoidance of conflict, however. The state party organization (or one of its leaders) may want to pursue its own goals at the convention. It may want to preserve its bargaining power to affect the platform, to win a cabinet seat for a notable of the state party, to affect the vice-presidential choice, or just to enhance its value in the presidential nomination. Its interests may also be the parochial ones of a state party; a number of state Democratic parties, for example, were cool to Kennedy in 1960 for fear of losing the votes of Protestants in the state and thus hurting the party's ticket for statewide office.

For these reasons, the leadership and organization of state parties would often prefer to "depoliticize" the process of selecting delegates. If conflict looms, the party chieftains may prefer an uncommitted slate of delegates or one loyal to a favorite-son candidate rather than chance deep and lasting divisions. Their chances of doing so, however, lessen with each successive presidential election. As candidates intensify the preconvention campaign they guarantee that more and more of the delegates will have loyalties to a presidential candidate. Moreover, for an individual or a state delegation to remain uncommitted while one of the contenders for the nomination is locking up a majority of the convention votes is to squander all influence over the nomination.

## PRIMARY VERSUS PARTY SELECTION

Apart from the interests of parties and candidates, however, has it really made any difference whether delegates to the national conventions have been chosen by primary or by party processes? Does the 75 percent of the delegates chosen by primary behave any differently than those chosen through party bodies? Do the presidential primaries have an impact on the nominations commensurate with the time and money spent in them?

Not too long ago in American politics the processes of delegate selection were sharply bifurcated. In the states of the presidential primaries a more open, popular, candidate-centered politics worked to the advantage of well-known personalities and generally helped insurgents in the party. In the other states the party organization controlled delegate selection and could apply, with few exceptions, tests of party acceptability both to delegates and ultimately to the seekers after the party's nomination. Estes Kefauver in 1952 and 1956 and Eugene McCarthy in 1968 used the primaries to challenge the party apparatus for the nominations. They failed, as did all other challengers with little support outside the primary states. They failed if for no other reason than that there were not enough primaries; the delegates selected in them were 40 percent or less of the whole. Probably the last great conflict of the two selection modes was that of the Democrats in 1968 (Table 11.1). Before the 1970s the party nominees invariably fell into two categories: those, such as Hubert Humphrey, who mixed victories in primary and in nonprimary states, and those such as Wendell Willkie in 1940 and Adlai Stevenson in 1952 who entered no primaries and who won the nomination in brokered conventions.

As the differences between the primary and nonprimary processes diminish in the 1970s, however, the situation has changed. On the one hand

### TABLE 11.1   Humphrey and McCarthy in the Primaries: 1968

|  | Number of votes candidate won on first ballot, 1968 convention | Percentage of candidate's votes won in 15 primary states and D.C. | Percentage of total convention votes of primary states and D.C. won by candidate |
|---|---|---|---|
| McCarthy | 601 | 73.0 | 35.3 |
| Humphrey | 1,760 | 37.4 | 52.9 |

it seems more and more likely that a successful candidate will have won at least some primary victories. It may now be possible to win with a strategy centering largely on the primaries. That seems clear if for no other reason than the growth and spread of the primaries. But on the other hand, the whole question of the alternative route to the nomination seems less and less important simply because the politics of the delegate search under primary and nonprimary conditions seem more and more alike. Delegate selection in either mode is increasingly more open and better publicized in all the states.

The changes are greater under the Democratic party's rules, but there are changes, too, among the Republicans. George McGovern had successes in both selection modes, even though he and his followers were anathema to many state party organizations. In short, we have had a convergence of the two delegate selection processes into a more lengthy, more homogeneous, more important, and more expensive preconvention politics. It is all a part of a general shift to a more open, mass politics. At least in the Democratic party at present the chief strategic problems are just as likely to be the limits and opportunities under the new party rules as the old juggling of separate primary and nonprimary strategies.

To be more specific about it, comparisons of the two delegate selection processes reveal fewer differences than one might expect. The primaries do indeed involve four or five times more the number of partisans. About 30 percent of voting age adults vote in the primary states taken together, whereas caucus turnouts in nonprimary states rarely reach more than 8 or 9 percent. But in both cases the participants are drawn heavily from the strong partisans. That seems self-evident in the nonprimary states, but it is also the case in the primaries. In 1976, for example, the data of the Survey Research Center indicate that whereas adults who identify strongly either as Democrats or Republicans voted at a 38 percent rate in the presidential primaries, only 22 percent of other adults did. Furthermore, with the opening of selection processes in the nonprimary states, the participants in those states now have a range of options comparable to those in primary states, and the popular support of would-be candidates is as fairly represented as it is in the primary states.[14]

Still, the primaries maintain their special role and appeal. Their expansion continues to speak about the way we increasingly view presidential nominating politics. Because of their openness to the voters, their results confer great legitimacy on the winners. Victories acquired in them may still be more important for symbolic purposes than for the number of delegates acquired. The primaries also provide an opportunity for candidates to show their appeals and build a following, and to show their stamina and

[14] These arguments are made effectively and at far greater length by Thomas R. Marshall, "Caucuses and Primaries: Measuring Reform in the Presidential Nomination Process," *American Politics Quarterly* 7 (1979): 155–74.

adaptability under various pressures. And for the successful nominees the primaries build an early name and face recognition which gives them a head start in the election campaign.[15] And, cruelly, too, they help weed out the nonviable candidates. George Romney, for example, dropped from the 1968 Republican race in the face of polls predicting a poor showing in the New Hampshire primary. Edmund Muskie's withdrawal in 1972 was in considerable part the result of failures in a number of primaries. And as Lyndon Johnson discovered in 1968, disappointing results in them may even help drive an incumbent president from office.

## A SYSTEM IN NEED OF REFORM?

The briefs against both the presidential primaries and the party selection of delegates are long and weighty. In fact, they seem to so outweigh the briefs in favor that the observer might easily conclude that once again in American politics he must choose between the lesser of two evils.

The broader question of reform of the delegate-selection process inevitably begins with a hard look at the presidential primaries. The case against them is impressive:

— They consume an enormous amount of time, energy, and money before the presidential campaign has ever begun. Leading contenders for the nomination often run through a series of primary campaigns from February through June, arriving at the party convention personally and financially exhausted.

— They put a tremendous premium on the well-known, familiar name — and thus often on the financial and other resources necessary to build that political familiarity. Consequently, their existence makes it difficult for the party to consider less-known or reluctant candidates.

— Their importance may easily be distorted out of all perspective. In the mass of publicity surrounding them, candidates and voters alike fail often to assess them soberly. Wendell Willkie, for example, bowed out of the 1944 Republican contention after a loss to the Dewey slate in Wisconsin; Dewey, however, polled only 33 percent of the Wisconsin Republican vote (conducted in an open primary at that).

— Victory in the primaries is won by plurality vote, and if the competitors are numerous, often by a small plurality. George McGovern won the Democratic primary in Wisconsin in 1972 with only 30 percent of the vote.

— The scheduling of the primaries is erratic and irrational. In 1976 California, Ohio, and New Jersey, all states with substantial blocks of votes

15 That seems to be the suggestion of Leonard Weinberg and Joseph Crowley, "Primary Success as a Measure of Presidential Election Victory: A Research Note," *Midwest Journal of Political Science* 14 (1970): 506–13.

in both conventions, held their primaries on the same day. There was, however, one other overcrowded Tuesday on which six states all held primaries.
— The presidential primaries frequently result in internal divisions in state party organizations, warring delegations to the national conventions, and delegates not representative of the party organization and leadership in the state. Like any other primary that takes an important party process out of the control of the party organization, it weakens them.

The presidential primary is, to be sure, an institution that only the voters love.

The charges against the party convention or party committee selection of a state's delegates rest on the traditional complaints about party processes — that they are too easily controlled and manipulated by a handful of party oligarchs. That, in any event, has been the charge of the reformers in the Democratic party since 1968. Furthermore, in these states the party electorates and even some of the party activists are excluded from an important and often crucial step in the picking of a president. And it is undoubtedly true that in these states the would-be presidential nominees have had to fight for the access and role they enjoy in the presidential primaries.

Debating points aside, however, we seem to be in the middle of a great revival of interest in the primaries. After a period of disenchantment with primaries, the states are returning to them with the enthusiasm they had fifty years ago.[16] Increasing media coverage has spotlighted their role in the nomination process. And their basic rationale — the twin democratic norms of mass popular participation and fear of party oligarchies — seems more powerful than ever. What is most important, the states *think* the primaries are becoming more important. Clearly some of them are venturing into the primaries for the first time to increase their own political leverage. (In the case of some of the new southern primaries, at least some state legislators see them enhancing the power of the South in national presidential politics by forcing all candidates to be tested — and possibly tarnished — in those states.) No reform movement can ignore, therefore, the presently secure place of the primaries.

If we cannot live without the primaries, is it possible that we might learn to live more comfortably with them? The most drastic reform proposal of recent years was to do away with the national nominating conventions altogether and to choose the presidential nominees in a single national primary. A consideration of that proposal will follow an assess-

[16] For the early development of the presidential primaries, see Louise Overacker, *The Presidential Primary* (New York: Macmillan, 1926). In 1916 at least twenty-three states had some sort of presidential primary.

ment of the conventions in the next chapter. If one assumes the survival of the nominating conventions, however, is no change possible in the way we select delegates to them? Probably the most imaginative and yet realistic proposal was associated some years ago with Walter Mondale when he was a member of the Senate. It was a plan for a series of four regional primaries. Any state wanting to hold a presidential primary would have to schedule it on the day assigned to the region; the election day for each region would be set by lot in each presidential year. Although the proposal received some attention, it has gotten no serious consideration in the Congress. For the near future it would seem that the status quo in delegate selection is not apt to be threatened.[17]

Even at these early stages of presidential politics one sees the beginning of the repetition of an old theme in American politics. It is difficult for the party organizations to control the presidential nomination, just as it is difficult for them to control other party nominations. In part, again, the presidential primary weakens organizational control and shifts it to the would-be candidates. In part, too, the organizations are weak because they have no means of uniting or coordinating their own preferences prior to the nominating conventions. So candidates with comparatively rational and unified national strategies increasingly find it easy to take the initiative from individual state party organizations in this phase of presidential politics. To the extent that they are able to win the commitments of enough delegates to capture the nominations, they and the party in government capture the nomination before the party organizations ever gather themselves together to act as a "national party" at the convention.

[17] In general the best accounts of recent preconvention politics (and the later conventions and campaigns as well) are those of Theodore H. White in his four volumes on the 1960, 1964, 1968, and 1972 elections. See *The Making of the President* for those years, all of them published in New York by Atheneum in the year after the election. The events of the 1976 election are recounted in Jules Witcover, *Marathon* (New York: Viking, 1977).

# 12

# Presidential Politics: The Crucial Decisions

That cynical observer of American politics, H. L. Mencken, especially loved the challenge of reporting a national nominating convention. After ruminating on the Democratic convention of 1924 and the 103 ballots it took to nominate John W. Davis, the Sage of Baltimore wrote:

there is something about a national convention that makes it as fascinating as a revival or a hanging. It is vulgar, it is ugly, it is stupid, it is tedious, it is hard upon both the higher cerebral centers and the *gluteus maximus,* and yet it is somehow charming. One sits through long sessions wishing heartily that all the delegates and alternates were dead and in hell — and then suddenly there comes a show so gaudy and hilarious, so melodramatic and obscene, so unimaginably exhilarating and preposterous that one lives a gorgeous year in an hour.[1]

Former President Dwight D. Eisenhower felt the irritation without experiencing the exhilaration. The conventions, he said, were "a picture of confusion, noise, impossible deportment, and indifference to what is being discussed on the platform." The banner-waving demonstrations that so typify the carnival gaiety of the conventions he dismissed as "spurious demonstration[s] of unwarranted enthusiasm." [2]

Scarcely a convention goes by, indeed, without evoking a series of tongue-clucking appraisals. Calls for convention reform come as regularly as the conventions themselves. And yet the national conventions persist, the chief holdout against the domination of American nominations by the direct primary. How is it that so maligned an institution has so successfully resisted the pressures of change? Has it become an indispensable political institution? And even while offending the canons of taste and decorum, has it really managed to function effectively as a recruiter of presidents?

## THE STRUCTURE OF THE CONVENTION

The conventions are the creatures of the parties themselves. They are subject to no congressional or state regulation, and even the federal courts

[1] Malcolm Moos (ed.), *H. L. Mencken on Politics* (New York: Vintage, 1960), p. 83.
[2] *The New York Times,* June 29, 1965.

have been reluctant to intervene in their operation. Responsibility for them falls to the national party committees and their staffs, although an incumbent president inevitably influences the planning for them. Increasingly, too, the previous conventions and, in the case of the Democrats, the midterm conference are involved.

Planning for the quadrennial conventions begins several years before the event. The first harbinger of that work comes with the selection of the host city. That choice reflects a vast number of considerations, from the size of the financial package the bidding cities offer to such usual convention matters as hotel space. Political considerations enter, too. For 1976 the Democrats selected New York as their site in part as an affirmation of the American city, and the Republicans chose Detroit for 1980 at least in part to broaden their support among urban and minority voters.

Months before the convention, too, its major committees emerge. Like all other major American institutions, both political and nonpolitical, the conventions function in part through committees. Generally there have been four of them:

> *Credentials.* The credentials committee accepts the credentials of delegates and alternates and makes up the official delegate list of the convention. Its prickliest duty is deciding contests (between two delegates or slates vying for the same seats) and challenges (of the qualifications of any delegate or alternate or, indeed, of any delegation).
>
> *Permanent organization.* This committee selects the permanent officials of the convention: the permanent chairman, secretary, and sergeant at arms, for example. Generally its work provokes little controversy.
>
> *Rules.* It sets the rules of the convention, most particularly the specific procedures for selecting the presidential nominee. The main procedures have been fixed for some time, but the committee struggles at every convention with rules such as those governing the length and number of nomination speeches, the number of nondelegate demonstrators that will be permitted on the convention floor, and the method of polling delegations should controversy arise within them.
>
> *Platform (or Resolutions).* This committee's chief responsibility is to draft the party's platform for action by the convention. It holds open hearings to receive the ideas of citizens, party activists, and the potential presidential nominees.

Early appointment of these committees is necessary if only because they begin to function before the convention convenes. Platform committees especially have begun to scour the party and the nation for ideas several months before the convention opens. In 1972 and 1976, in fact, the Democrats completed and distributed a proposed platform some weeks before the convention opened.

The first three of these committees — credentials, permanent organization, and rules — make decisions that define the structure and procedures of the convention. These decisions are no less important for being procedural. Often they have enormous impact on the substantive decisions the convention makes on the nominees or the platform. In the 1976 Republican convention the Reagan forces proposed a rule change to force presidential contenders to announce their vice-presidential choices *before* the selection of a presidential nominee. Ronald Reagan had already announced his running mate (Senator Richard Schweiker of Pennsylvania), and the move was clearly designed to embarrass and weaken the candidacy of Gerald Ford. The proposal was narrowly defeated, and the nomination roll call that gave the nomination to Ford was anticlimactic. It is precisely because procedural battles such as this so affect the distribution of power at the conventions that state parties, the candidates, and the ideological camps within the parties work so hard to win representation on the committees.

In recent years the decisions of the credentials committees have had the greatest repercussions. The 1952 contest for the Republican nomination between Senator Robert Taft and General Dwight Eisenhower hinged in great part on the battle over delegates from Georgia, Louisiana, and Texas. The credentials committee voted to seat the pro-Taft delegates from the three states, but in scenes of recrimination the convention as a whole seated the pro-Eisenhower claimants. If Senator Taft had had the votes of those contested delegates, he would have led Eisenhower on the convention's first ballot. In 1972 George McGovern's quest for the Democratic nomination was aided by the convention's decisions to seat the California delegates loyal to him and not to seat the Illinois delegation loyal to Mayor Daley and the local party. Similar contests over delegates, reflecting either ideological divisions or different candidate loyalties, have in fact afflicted most conventions. Rarely, however, do they reach the number the Democrats achieved in 1972; in that convention more than a dozen disputes received full floor debate.

A somewhat different problem in credentials has plagued the Democratic conventions since World War II: the unwillingness of some southern state delegations to take the delegate "loyalty oath," the pledge to support the candidates and platform of the convention. In 1948 delegates from Mississippi and Alabama marched out of an evening session of the convention after northern liberals nailed a strong civil rights plank onto the platform. Many of those delegates and their state parties later supported the Dixiecrat party ticket or, worse, put the Dixiecrat slate on their state presidential ballot as the ticket of the Democratic party. The loyalty issue in the Democratic party was supplemented in the 1960s by charges that delegate selection processes in some southern states were not fully open to blacks. In 1968 and 1972 the regular Mississippi delegation (and half of the Georgia regulars in 1968) were replaced by challengers loyal to the national ticket. The two Mississippi parties negotiated a merger in 1975, however, and a single integrated, loyal delegation represented Mississippi in 1976.[3]

Credential fights are the major threat to orderly and seemly conventions. The emotions and the stakes are high, and the recommendations of credentials committees have often been overridden in bitter floor battles. Furthermore, the votes on the floor often fall along ideological lines or lines of support for various candidates. The picture is not one of judicious decision. Under their new party charter the Democrats will apparently now try another approach to disputes over credentials. All such matters will go to a party Judicial Council, a body which will also have to certify earlier that state plans for delegate selection comply with national party rules. But the convention itself, the charter clearly notes, remains the final arbiter of credential disputes.

Finally, to complete the organization of the convention the national committee selects the temporary chairperson, who usually delivers the extravagantly partisan keynote address. His or her qualifications are only two — an aloofness from the major contestants for the nomination and a telegenic oratorical style — but the candidates are many. They may remember that Alben Barkley's oratorical flights in praise of the Democratic party won him the vice-presidential nomination in 1948.[4] But even at lower levels of ambition, the assignment is an ideal showcase, one that does no politician's political future any harm.

The description of the formal structure of the convention, of course, fails to convey anything of its ambience. Born of a rough-and-tumble political tradition and related to the institution of the boisterous convention in other areas of American life, the national party conventions have been part carnival, part "fling at the big city," and part (a large part, actually) serious party conclave. At one and the same time they mix well-rehearsed demonstrations of enthusiasm with serious thought about presidential stature, the military precision of floor managers with the aimless amblings of ordinary delegates, the perfunctory afternoon oratorical fillers with the often eloquent messages of the party worthies. If television has now made them somewhat more sedate, they are still part partisan rally and part presidential nomination.

## THE DELEGATES

The combination of large numbers of delegates and equally large numbers of alternative delegates produces gargantuan conventions. The total

---

[3] On the issue of the loyalty oath, see Abraham Holtzman, "Party Responsibility and Loyalty: New Rules in the Democratic Party," *Journal of Politics* 22 (1960): 485–501.
[4] On the contrary case they may remember that General of the Army Douglas MacArthur disappointed his supporters by failing to light any fires with his keynote speech before the Republicans in 1952.

of delegates and alternates exceeded 6000 in the Democratic conventions of 1968 and 1972, for instance, and it will be 5404 in 1980. The national committees are under tremendous pressure from the state party organizations to increase the number of delegates. Party people in the state cherish the prestige of attending a convention, and the experience of being a delegate also is likely to stimulate them to work in the campaign that follows. Large convention size is also increasingly the price of representing the large, populous states in some reasonable ratio to the representation of the small ones. Finally, big conventions create a mass rally atmosphere for television coverage. Especially when the convention is certain to renominate an incumbent president — as the Democrats did in 1964 and the Republicans did in 1972 — the rally aspects of the convention replace its nominating duties.

The delegates to the Democratic and Republican conventions have never been a cross-section of American citizens. Whites, males, the well-educated, and upper income groups have always been overrepresented to some degree. There have also been differences between the two parties. Democratic delegations have had more Catholics, Jews, and trade unionists, the Republicans more Protestants and businessmen. Recently, however, both parties have attempted to broaden the representativeness of their delegations, with the Democrats in 1972 making by far the greater change. For example, 11 percent of the 1976 Democratic delegates were black, against only 6 percent in 1968, and the proportion of women — 33 percent — was a 250 percent increase over 1968.[5]

Ideologically, the delegates are more committed, more aware of issues and issue positions, than the ordinary voters of their party. They also tend more to the ideological poles than do the electorates of their parties; the Democratic delegates are more apt to be liberal and the Republicans more conservative than even the identifiers of the parties.[6] Furthermore, the

---

[5] It is worth noting that 15 percent of the delegates to the 1972 Democratic convention were black and almost 40 percent were women. In that same year almost 30 percent of the delegates to the Republican convention were women. Jeane Kirkpatrick, *The New Presidential Elite* (New York: Russell Sage and Twentieth Century Fund, 1976), Chap. 12. Kirkpatrick's book is both the most ample and sophisticated study in the scholarly literature of any set of convention delegates, and also one of the best studies of women activists in party politics. For other studies of the 1972 and 1976 delegates, see John W. Soule and Wilma E. McGrath, "A Comparative Study of Presidential Nomination Conventions: The Democrats of 1968 and 1972," *American Journal of Political Science* 19 (1975): 501–17; Joseph H. Boyett, "Background Characteristics of Delegates to the 1972 Conventions: A Summary Report of Findings from a National Sample," *Western Political Quarterly* 27 (1974): 469–78; Thomas H. Roback, "Amateurs and Professionals: Delegates to the 1972 Republican National Convention," *Journal of Politics* 37 (1975): 436–67; and John S. Jackson III, Jesse C. Brown, and Barbara L. Brown, "Recruitment, Representation, and Political Values: The 1976 Democratic National Convention Delegates," *American Politics Quarterly* 6 (1978): 187–212.

[6] Herbert McClosky, Paul J. Hoffman, and Rosemary O'Hara, "Issue Conflict and Consensus among Party Leaders and Followers," *American Political Science Review* 54

ideological commitment of the delegates is increasing. The 1964 Republican and 1972 Democratic conventions clearly broke with the rule of
pragmatic compromise and opted for explicitly ideological candidates
(Goldwater and McGovern) and platforms. The ideological gap between
convention delegates and the party's voters results both from the differences between activist and nonactivist and from the way in which the
apportionment of delegates at the conventions overrepresents the areas of
the party's weakness across the country and thus overrepresents some of
the party's electors. Ironically, as Jeane Kirkpatrick has concluded, reforming the party conventions has not made them more representative of the
views and values of the parties in the electorate. To the contrary, the
"reformed" Democratic delegates of 1972 were less representative than the
"unreformed" Democratic delegates of 1968 or the Republicans of 1972.[7]

Actually, differences among the delegates of a single convention may
be more significant than differences between any two party conventions.
A number of observers noted the much larger number of clergymen
and academics among the McCarthy-Kennedy-McGovern delegates than
among the delegates as a whole in the 1968 Democratic convention. Theodore White, in fact, counted twenty-six men of the cloth.[8] The McCarthy
delegates also tended in their style and approach to politics to be amateurs similar to those taking over some of the urban organizations; the
Humphrey delegates were more likely to be professionals — that is, the
McCarthy delegates were more attracted by programs and issues, more
insistent on intraparty democracy, less willing to compromise, less committed to the prime importance of winning elections. Similar differences
carried over to the Humphrey and McGovern delegates in 1972. So the
two sets of delegates differed not only in their candidate preference but
also in their political styles, their perceptions of their political role, and
their political values and outlooks.[9]

As interesting and important as the individual delegates are, the real

---

(1960): 406–27; John W. Soule and James W. Clarke, "Issue Conflict and Consensus:
A Comparative Study of Democratic and Republican Delegates to the 1968 National
Conventions," *Journal of Politics* 33 (1971): 72–91.
[7] *The New Presidential Elite*, Chap. 10.
[8] *The Making of the President 1968* (New York: Atheneum, 1969), p. 272. The White
volumes, beginning with the 1960 election, are the major chronicles of recent presidential politics. For an earlier period similar data are often available in Paul T. David,
Ralph M. Goldman, and Richard C. Bain, *The Politics of National Party Conventions*
(Washington: Brookings, 1960).
[9] John W. Soule and James W. Clarke, "Amateurs and Professionals: A Study of Delegates to the 1968 Democratic National Convention," *American Political Science Review*
64 (1970); pp. 888–98. For a report on "purists" and "professionals" in 1972, see
Dennis G. Sullivan, Jeffrey L. Pressman, Benjamin I. Page, and John J. Lyons, *The
Politics of Representation: The Democratic Convention 1972* (New York: St. Martin's,
1974). See also Kirkpatrick, *The New Presidential Elite*, and Roback and Soule and
McGrath articles cited in footnote 5.

unit of the conventions has historically been the state delegation. Delegates room together at the same hotel and share their experiences with each other; they also often share the same goals and outlooks. They caucus periodically, and they are often bound together by loyalty to the same candidate or party leaders. The 1972 Democratic convention featured the growth of special interest caucuses for blacks, women, youths, Latins, senior citizens, and Jews. They failed, however, to establish a major role in that year or in 1976.

Perhaps the most critical problem for the group caucuses was that their goals were sometimes in conflict with those of other organizations, notably candidate organizations. Delegates who had a stake in the nomination of a particular candidate were unlikely to drop their commitment to that candidate in favor of loyalty to a group caucus.[10]

The state delegations and the candidate organizations thus remain the basic units of both parties' conventions.

## THE BUSINESS OF THE CONVENTION

The convention begins in low key with stiff formalities and the business of organization. It warms up with the keynote address, tries to maintain momentum and expectation through consideration of the platform, and reaches a dramatic peak in the nomination of the presidential and vice-presidential candidates. This general format remains basically the same convention after convention. TV coverage has necessitated some rearrangement into a more compact convention, with the events of major interest reserved for prime evening transmission time, but the tempo of the convention is still governed by the pace of business and not by any dramatic considerations. Ordinarily dramatic suspense is no problem, but it can be in the party of a president eligible to succeed himself. The likelihood of his renomination may be so great that the spectators know how the play will end. President Lyndon B. Johnson himself solved a good share of the problem in the 1964 Democratic convention by creating suspense and uncertainty over his vice-presidential choice.

Aside from the rites of nomination, the approval of the platform is the convention's chief business. The platform committees begin hearings long before the convention opens so that the platform will be in draft form for convention hearings. Those hearings before and during the early phases of the convention are often spiced by the appearance of leading contenders for the nomination. The finished document then is presented to the convention for its approval. That approval is not always pro forma, for the platform has occasioned some of the most spirited recent convention bat-

[10] Sullivan, Pressman, Page, and Lyons, *The Politics of Representation: The Democratic Convention 1972*, p. 68.

tles. In 1968 the forces supporting Hubert H. Humphrey engaged the McCarthy delegates in a virtually unprecedented three-hour floor debate over what the platform would say about the war in Vietnam. The Democrats' discussion of the 1972 platform touched on subjects new to platform discourse (e.g., abortion and gay rights) and set a record for the longest discussion of a platform in American convention history.

Few aspects of American politics so openly invite skepticism, even cynicism, as do the party platforms. They are long and prolix; the Democratic platform of 1972 ran to 26,000 words, almost twenty times the length of the Declaration of Independence. The platforms are not often read; the congressional party generally ignores them, and even presidential standard-bearers reserve the right to disagree with them. Basically the problem is that platforms are the instruments of ideology, and the two major American parties have not been explicitly ideological. They really have no persistent set of political principles, no total political philosophy that unites their followers. The American party platform, rather than being a statement of the party, is much more apt to be a string of pragmatic stands on quite separate issues, one not necessarily related to another.

Whatever it is, though, the platform must generally be acceptable to the presidential candidate and the majority in control of the convention. An incumbent president seeking renomination may virtually write the platform himself, and strong contenders for the nomination (such as Barry Goldwater in 1964) can often make sure that their forces are in firm control of the platform committee. And if it happens that the person likely to be nominated disapproves of the platform, he may insist on its modification. Richard Nixon in 1960, clearly about to receive his party's nomination, bowed to the criticisms of the draft platform by Governor Nelson Rockefeller of New York, rushed to New York to confer with him, and then hurried back to Chicago to force revisions on a very unhappy committee.

Part of the cynicism about the platforms grows from the impression that they are exercises in semantic virtuosity. The words and phrases used are sometimes intended to obfuscate rather than clarify, for phrases that mean all things to all people achieve compromises of a sort. But vague or artful as the platforms may be, they do take stands on some issues, and they are not identical. In recent years they have differed over social security, labor-management relations, farm price supports, medicare, racial integration, and war and peace in Vietnam. Above all, the platforms are campaign documents in which the parties pick their issues and positions selectively to promote the assembling of a majority coalition. The party platform is important, its leading scholar says,

but not as an inspired gospel to which politicians resort for policy guidance. It is important because it summarizes, crystallizes, and presents to the voters the character of the party coalition. Platform pledges are not simply good ideas, or even original ones. In their programs, Democrats and Republicans are not typically breaking new paths; they are promising to proceed along one or another path which has already become involved in political controversy. The stands taken in the platform clarify the parties' positions on these controversies and reveal the nature of their support and appeals.[11]

Finally, the platforms are what they are largely because they are drafted and approved in conventions mainly concerned with picking a presidential candidate. Every convention vote tends to become a test of the strength of the various candidates.[12]

## FINDING A PRESIDENTIAL CANDIDATE

The pièce de résistance of the convention — the picking of a presidential candidate — begins as the secretary intones the litany of the states: Alabama, Alaska, Arkansas. . . . As each state is called, the head of the state's delegation responds in one of three ways: by placing the name of a candidate before the convention, by yielding the state's position in the roll call to another state to make a nomination, or by passing. So as the secretary progresses through the states, the contenders for the nomination are entered, each one by a formal speech of nomination and shorter seconding speeches.

It is at this point that the conventions traditionally reached back to a nineteenth-century political style. The speeches of nomination rolled out in great Victorian periods, often seeming to be parodies; seconding speeches, carefully chosen to provide a cross section of the party, were frequently vest-pocket versions of the main speech. After each set of nomination speeches the supporters of the nominee, usually augmented by young, tireless nondelegates, snaked their way through the crowded aisles of the hall, singing, chanting, and waving banners and signs for almost an hour.

The first modifications of these hoary traditions began with the advent of television, for the endless hijinks often pushed the most dramatic portions of the convention out of prime evening time. And what seemed colorfully old-fashioned in the hall looked grotesque or vulgar on the TV screen. The Democrats, spurred again by the reform impulses springing from their 1968 convention, made further inroads in 1972. They banned all floor demonstrations, shortened nomination speeches drastically, and

---

[11] Gerald Pomper, *Elections in America* (New York: Dodd, Mead, 1968), p. 201.
[12] All the party platforms are available in one volume: Kirk H. Porter and Donald B. Johnson, *National Party Platforms, 1840–1976*, 6th ed. (Urbana: University of Illinois Press, 1978). For a broad discussion of platform making, see Paul T. David, "Party Platforms as National Plans," *Public Administration Review* 31 (1971): 303–15.

made the nomination of favorite-son candidates — those noncontenders with support in only one delegation — vastly more difficult.

Once all the names have been presented to the convention, the task of settling on a single presidential nominee begins in earnest. The secretary of the convention starts again through the states (and the District of Columbia, the territories, and the dependencies), asking each delegation to report how it votes. If no candidate wins the necessary majority of votes, the convention presses on to a second ballot. A number of nominations have been settled on the first ballot, but in 1924 the Democrats plodded through 103 ballots in sultry New York's Madison Square Garden before nominating John W. Davis. (That record number of ballots resulted at least in part from the Democratic rule, abandoned in 1936, that required that the nominee be supported by two-thirds of the delegates.) Since 1952 no nomination contest in either party has consumed more than one ballot (Table 12.1). Furthermore, since 1948 the conventions have averaged only two candidates who polled more than 10 percent of the convention votes on any ballot (Table 12.1). That trend may be attributable to more intensive preconvention campaigning and pressures on delegates that result from the increased publicizing of the convention.

The casting of the votes takes place in a context of some of the most compressed political activity in all of American politics. Even before the opening of the convention, representatives of the various contenders have stalked uncommitted or wavering delegates across the country by mail,

**TABLE 12.1**  Number of Ballots Required to Nominate and Number of Candidates Polling 10 Percent of Votes in Democratic and Republican Conventions: 1948–76

| | Democratic Conventions | | Republican Conventions | |
|---|---|---|---|---|
| Year | Candidates over 10% | Number of ballots | Candidates over 10% | Number of ballots |
| 1948 | 2 | 1 | 3 | 3 |
| 1952 | 4 | 3 | 2 | 1 |
| 1956 | 2 | 1 | 1 | 1 |
| 1960 | 2 | 1 | 1 | 1 |
| 1964 | 1 | 1 | 2 | 1 |
| 1968 | 2 | 1 | 3 | 1 |
| 1972 | 2 | 1 | 1 | 1 |
| 1976 | 2 | 1 | 2 | 1 |

*Source*  Data from *Congress and the Nation* (Washington, D.C.: Congressional Quarterly, 1965), and from newspaper accounts of 1968, 1972, and 1976 conventions.

phone, and personal visit. Once the convention opens, the process is stepped up. Of the 1960 Kennedy organization, Theodore H. White has written:

In all, some forty delegate-shepherds were assigned each to a particular state delegation that was theirs to cultivate; each was given packets of name cards listing the assigned state delegates by name, profession, hobby, children, wife, peculiarity, religion, and sent out to operate. They were instructed, as they found shifts in any delegation, to report such changes to a private tabulating headquarters in Room 3308 at the Biltmore; and there, every hour on the hour from Friday through balloting day, a new fresh total, accurate to the hour, was to be prepared. For five days, the shepherds were told, they were not to sleep, see their wives, relax, frolic or be out of touch with 8315. Each morning, for the five Convention days from Saturday to the Wednesday balloting, they were to gather in Room 8315 for a staff survey at nine A.M., then disperse to their tasks.[13]

Such organizational thoroughness has rarely been seen at conventions before or since, but front-runners generally know they must win quickly. The only strategy the other candidates can employ is to join in a coalition to prevent the first-ballot victory. That imperative can join — however temporarily — men of such divergent views as Nelson Rockefeller and Ronald Reagan, who tried unsuccessfully in 1968 to prevent the first-ballot nomination of Richard Nixon.

If the convention has passed through an inconclusive ballot, negotiations renew with even greater intensity. The leading candidates must take care to prevent a chipping away of their supporters — a genuine danger if they fail to increase their votes on a second or third ballot. New support comes most easily from minor candidates or uncommitted delegates, since delegates bound to candidates are too loyal to those commitments to be lured away.[14] The favorite-son candidate faces the delicate decision whether to cast his lot with a front-runner or to hold tightly and maintain (either alone or in concert) a defensive action. Much of this strategy has, of course, been absent with the first-ballot choices of the last twenty-five years.[15]

Following the naming of the presidential nominee, the secretary begins the roll call ritual again — usually on the next day — to select a vice-presidential nominee. Conventions uniformly ratify the choice of the presidential candidate. Rebellions flash occasionally but always fail; for instance, in the Democratic meetings of 1944 the supporters of Vice-President Henry Wallace tried futilely to resist the decision of President Roosevelt to replace him with Harry S. Truman. And once in recent years the presi-

[13] White, *The Making of the President 1960* (New York: Atheneum, 1961), p. 157.
[14] David, Goldman, and Bain, *The Politics of National Party Conventions*, p. 379.
[15] On the strategies of presidential politics generally, see Nelson W. Polsby and Aaron B. Wildavsky, *Presidential Elections*, 4th ed. (New York: Scribner, 1976).

dential candidate did not indicate his preference. Adlai Stevenson convulsed the 1956 Democratic convention by opening the vice-presidential choice to it; Senator Estes Kefauver was selected on the second ballot.

The method of selecting vice-presidential candidates has recently elicited a crescendo of criticism. It is not so much that they are hand-picked by the presidential candidate but that the decision is made by a tired candidate and tired advisors in so short a span of time. Nonetheless, of the six different men who were presidential candidates from 1960 through 1972, three had been chosen as vice-presidents in the hurly burly of an earlier convention. Moreover, the withdrawal of the initial Democratic vice-presidential nominee in 1972 (Thomas Eagleton) and the eventual resignation of Vice-President Spiro Agnew in the following year gave the unease about vice-presidential selection a new impetus. But little has changed. Ronald Reagan did pick a vice-presidential running mate before the 1976 Republican convention, but the decision was motivated, most observers agree, by the politics of nomination rather than any desire to reform the picking of vice-presidents.

## THE "AVAILABILITY" OF PRESIDENTIAL NOMINEES

There is a bland and misleading term in American politics which describes the personal, social, and political characteristics the parties seek in their presidential nominees. If an individual possesses them, he is said to be *available*. Contrary to its popular use, the word in this idiomatic sense has nothing to do with the candidate's willingness to be a candidate. The assumption seems to be that in that sense every native-born American adult is available for the presidency.

The concept of availability sums up the qualities the parties believe make a politically appealing and acceptable — and thus a winning — candidate. In part, the canons of availability reflect the distribution of political power in presidential politics. It is said, for instance, that the presidential candidate must come from a large state — that is, from a state with a large electoral vote that he can be presumed to carry. From 1896 to the present, only five of the twenty-five men originally nominated for the presidency by a convention came from the smaller states. Eighteen came from eight large states: seven from New York, four from Ohio, two from California, and one each from Illinois, Michigan, Texas, Massachusetts, and New Jersey. One came from Minnesota and one from Georgia, states that would appear to be "in between." None of the five from the smaller states — Landon of Kansas, Davis of West Virginia, Bryan of Nebraska, Goldwater of Arizona, and McGovern of South Dakota — won the presidency.[16]

[16] If one uses the 1976 electoral vote as a measure, none of the seven "large" states referred to here had an electoral vote smaller than fourteen, and none of the "small" states had one greater than seven. Minnesota had ten, and Georgia twelve.

In part, too, the concept of availability is a codification of widely held expectations in the American electorate of what a president should be. It is an aggregate of the characteristics the parties think the American electorate would vote for in a presidential candidate. Some years ago it was commonly said that for a person to be considered seriously for the office he had to be a personal success in business or public life; happily married and blessed with an attractive family; a reasonably observant Protestant; a white male in his late forties or fifties; of Anglo-Saxon or North-northwestern Europe ethnic background; and the product of small city or rural life.

Although there is considerable validity in such a list as a description of past presidential nominees, to project such requirements into the future would be dangerous. The lore of acceptability shifts with changes in social attitudes. Adlai Stevenson, a divorced man, was nominated in 1952 and 1956; an urban and Catholic candidate, John F. Kennedy, was nominated in 1960. Those nominations probably indicate, at least in part, the declining social stigma attached to divorce, the life of the big city, and Catholicism in contemporary America. In coming decades changing attitudes about women in public life will probably also strike the male qualification from the formula of availability.

Finally, related to the issue of availability but somewhat different, is the question of career pattern. Although not all presidential candidates have had prior governmental or officeholding experience, most have. Thus the question arises of what positions provide the better jumping-off points and training for the presidency. What public positions grace a man with an aura of governmental success and competence and yet give him a good base for building party and public support? From 1900 through 1956, nineteen different men ran for the presidency on the Democratic and Republican tickets; eleven of them had been governors (McKinley, Theodore Roosevelt, Wilson, Hughes, Cox, Coolidge, Smith, Franklin Roosevelt, Landon, Dewey, and Stevenson). Only two, the luckless Harding and Harry Truman, had been senators. It had come to be a commonplace in American politics that the Senate was the graveyard of presidential ambitions. Senators, it was said, were forced to cast too many politically sensitive votes and risk too many political enemies. They also were thought to lack the opportunities for national popularity and image.

In 1960, 1964, 1968, and 1972, however, all eight nominees had been senators and none had been a governor. In the presidential politics of 1972 and after, in fact, even a majority of the unsuccessful seekers for presidential nominations were senators or former senators: Birch Bayh, Henry Jackson, Edward Kennedy, Edmund Muskie, Howard Baker, and Robert Dole. In 1976 Representative Morris Udall mounted the first challenge from the House of Representatives in a long time, and President Gerald Ford had been a leader in the House for years before his appointment to the vice-presidency. And for 1980 Representatives John Anderson and Philip Crane seek the GOP's nomination. So, despite Jimmy Carter's gubernatorial route, candidates now come heavily from the Congress, especially from the Senate. Undoubtedly members of Congress find it easier now to keep themselves in the public view, especially with their ready access to the media. Also, the very nationalization of American politics may have convinced large numbers of Americans that their coping with issues of national importance is a good apprenticeship for the presidency. The governors, on the other hand, have found themselves in serious political difficulties in their states in recent years. Problems of taxation and budgeting, abortion and capital punishment, law and order, and legislative reapportionment — as well as the more conventional political conflict resulting from the spread of two-party competitiveness — have caught many of them in damaging political crossfire.

Finally, convention delegates do consider the personal qualities of the contenders and their abilities to meet the demands of the presidency. They do so, however, in the context of loyalties to specific candidates and often, too, to specific ideologies. That is to say, the standards for presidential "timber" are not universally agreed on. Furthermore, delegates may find dilemmas in the fact that the qualities that ensure effective performance in office are not necessarily those which win it in the first place. Difficult as such evaluations of presidential candidates are, they are far less likely to be made in the speed and confusion with which vice-presidential candidates are found.

## CONVENTIONS: YESTERDAY AND TODAY

It is unlikely that small bands of national kingmakers bargaining in smoke-filled rooms ever did control the national conventions to the extent that popular myth has it. Even the celebrated negotiations at the Republican convention of 1920 — in the course of which Warren G. Harding emerged — took place in a convention deadlocked by other candidates with large popular and delegate followings. But whatever power the kingmakers may have had in the past, it is declining rapidly. In a number of important ways the national nominating conventions are not what they were a generation or two ago.

### New Preconvention Politics

More nominations are decided on the first convention ballot these days, and the chances of a party's picking an unknown candidate diminish. It is all the result of a new style of campaigning for delegates that was perhaps ushered in by the 1960 preconvention campaign of John F. Kennedy. More effective organization, greater resources, jet planes, the polls, and expanded media exposure all permit it. The press services keep count of the number of delegates committed to various candidates, and the pollsters periodically report the state of public enthusiasm for them. Both candidates and delegates have fuller information about the entire nomination politics before they get to the convention than they ever did before. Delegates are more likely to be committed to a contender before the convention opens. Consequently, the crucial bargaining and trading of support, the committing of delegates, and the weeding out of candidates take place increasingly at the preconvention stages.

### New Centers of Power

Political power has to some extent shifted away from the state and local party leaders, who at one time came as ambassadors to the convention for the purpose of negotiating within a fragmented, decentralized party. Power in the parties in the mid-twentieth century is less decentralized as national issues, national candidates, presidents, and congresses dominate the political loyalties and perceptions of voters. National party figures and national concerns — and party identifications shaped by national politics — have cut into the autonomy of state parties and leaders. So, too, has the increased power of potential candidates in the convention, power that is largely a product of their preconvention successes in rounding up delegates. We find, therefore, in many recent nominating conventions a tension among the old and new centers of power. Both Richard Nixon and Hubert Humphrey were in 1968 supported by the leaders of the states and localities; their major challengers, Nelson Rockefeller and Eugene McCarthy, staked their campaigns on national issues and their support in a broader national public. Similarly, the McGovern delegates of 1972 were generally less experienced and influential in their local parties than the Humphrey delegates.

As ideologies and issues become more important in the parties generally, they structure more and more of the choices in the conventions. Ideological factions or tendencies thus become new centers of power. The battle for the Democratic nomination in 1972 clearly was a battle between the liberal and moderate centers of gravity within the party. In the Republican party those ideological clusters were evident in the contest for 1976, and they were as well geographically clustered (Table 12.2). To the extent that such geographical concentrations are stable, we see the emergence of a new kind of sectionalism. The population and economic development of the "sun belt" are clearly reflected in a sectional conservatism.

### The New Media Coverage

The mass media have increasingly turned the conventions into national political spectaculars, intended as much for the national audience as for

TABLE 12-2   Regional-Ideological Divisions in the Republican
Party: The Choice of a Candidate for the Presidency in 1976

| Delegates pledged to: | Delegates from: Northeast and Middle West | South and West |
|---|---|---|
| Gerald Ford | 945   (77%) | 191   (19%) |
| Ronald Reagan | 277   (23%) | 790   (81%) |
| | 1222 (100%) | 981 (100%) |

Note   These data are only for the 48 states of the continental United States
and the District of Columbia. The Northeast and Midwest states (in addition
to the D.C.) are these: Connecticut, Delaware, Illinois, Indiana, Iowa, Kansas,
Kentucky, Maine, Maryland, Massachusetts, Michigan, Minnesota, Missouri,
Nebraska, New Hampshire, New Jersey, New York, North Dakota, Ohio,
Pennsylvania, Rhode Island, South Dakota, Vermont, West Virginia, and
Wisconsin.

the delegates in attendance. Party officials have given key roles to telegenic
partisans, speeded up the pace of business, and virtually eliminated serious
business from daytime hours. The strategic moves of major candidates, the
arrival of powerful figures in the party, and the defection of individual
delegates are reported fully. Even the formerly sacrosanct hagglings of
platform and credentials committees are done in the public eye. For the
party, then, television coverage offers a priceless opportunity to reach
voters and party workers and to launch its presidential campaign with
maximum impact. So the media spotlight shifts the role of the convention — not completely but perceptibly — from the conduct of party business to the stimulation of wider political audiences.

But media coverage is a two-edged sword, and its results may not be
the ones the parties want. A restless television medium searches for excitement and makes news out of the merest incidents and rumors. Often
the excitement needs no search; in 1968 scenes of violence in the streets
and parks of Chicago provided a running counterpoint to the business of
the Democrats within the convention hall. Media exposure is also prob-
lematic in other ways. The "openness" of the 1972 Democratic convention
kept it far behind its media-oriented schedule. As a result, George McGovern began his acceptance speech at 2:48 A.M. before a TV audience one-
fifth what it had been earlier in the evening.[17]

The conventions have therefore lost some of their freedom and deliber-

17 For fuller studies of the impact of television on the conventions, see Herbert Waltzer,
"In the Magic Lantern: Television Coverage of the 1964 National Conventions," *Public
Opinion Quarterly* 30 (1966): 33–53; and David L. Paletz and Martha Elson, "Televi-
sion Coverage of Presidential Conventions: Now You See It, Now You Don't," *Political
Science Quarterly* 91 (1976): 109–32.

ative character. Genuinely "brokered" conventions and last-minute compromise candidates seem now to belong to the past. The unlikelihood of lightning striking the unknown statesman does not, of course, signal the end of the convention. In some years at least, delegates will have to choose from among a small number of candidates who established themselves in the preconvention stages. And when the choice must be made among these well-known hopefuls, it will be made by a freer, more open bargaining that involves the majority of delegates as well as the prominent bosses and kingmakers.

Furthermore, the conventions reflect as never before a heterogeneous mix of roles and expectations. There are the old state and local leaders representing the interests of their party organizations, and now there are also new national party leaders, national officeholders, and powerful candidates with blocks of loyal delegates. Old organizational styles also mix uncomfortably with new styles of media-based politics, professional party leadership rubs elbows with volunteer, amateur party activists. The old electoral pragmatism — the traditional convention emphasis on picking the "winning" candidate — clashes with the new ideologists' unwillingess to compromise. In reflecting all these conflicts the conventions only mirror the broader conflicts and divisions of American party politics. But the stresses and strains that result are debilitating nonetheless.

Taking a broader overview, one may put the matter of change another way. Aided by media-reported campaigning and by the results of periodic polling, the entire process of nominating a president has fallen under the spell and evolving influences of a national, popular democracy. More and more people are becoming aware of the candidates and the choices before the party, and more and more of them are formulating views about those choices. Therefore, to nominate an unknown candidate today is doubly dangerous — first, for the seeming affront to the popularly supported contestants and, second, for the handicap of running an unknown candidate against the well-known candidate of the other party. Even the style, manners, and seriousness of the convention are under a new mass, popular scrutiny. To the extent that secretive or apparently manipulated party conventions are incompatible with the "democratization" of the presidential nominating process, they have to change.[18]

Although change and declining power may beset the conventions, the parties are not about to abandon them. They will gladly make the com-

[18] William G. Carleton offers another reinterpretation of the national conventions in "The Revolution in the Presidential Nominating Convention," *Political Science Quarterly* 72 (1957): pp. 224–40. William Lucy finds that eventual presidential nominees had in most recent instances been leaders in the opinion polls even before the presidential primaries and suggests that the linkages between mass opinions and convention outcomes have been more direct than we suspect. "Polls, Primaries, and Presidential Nominations," *Journal of Politics* 35 (1973): 830–48.

promises that are necessary to shore up the conventions' credibility. Even in its altered condition the national convention of the 1960s and 1970s is too precious an institution to surrender. It is the only real, palpable existence of a national political party. It is the only occasion for rediscovery of common traditions and common interests, the only time for common decision making and a coming together to celebrate old glories and achievements. It stimulates the workers and contributors to party labors, and it encourages party candidates in the states and localities. Its rites may not mean a great deal to the majority of Americans passively peering at the TV screen (and a bit sullen over missing the summer reruns), but they do mean something to the men and women of the party organization. The conventions are, in short, a vital, integrative force in the life of the American national parties.

Not surprisingly, the parties have resisted the varying proposals for a national presidential primary advanced over the past several generations. Such a primary would replace the nominating conventions with a national primary for nominating the presidential and vice-presidential candidates. Its rationale is the general rationale of the direct primary. The objections to the proposals are considerable. First of all, there are the practical problems: a uniform national date, the provision of a run-off primary if candidates are not to be chosen by small pluralities, and the implications of such a primary in open primary states. There is, too, the staggering burden in time and resources that a nomination campaign in fifty states would place on the parties and candidates. (Very possibly, too, a national primary would encourage a lengthy preprimary politics, in which the leading contenders would seek the endorsement of the state organizations.) But, above all, most scholars and political leaders are not convinced that a national presidential primary would result in the selection of more able candidates for the presidency. It might well result in the nomination of candidates best able — in money and personal charisma — to mount an effective mass-media campaign. From the party's point of view, it might also result in the nomination of candidates less likely to unify the party or appeal to its activists.[19]

## THE PRESIDENTIAL CAMPAIGN

Tradition has long dictated that the presidential campaign open in early September. After the July or August conventions, the presidential and vice-presidential candidates rest and map strategy for the approaching campaign. Then it all begins with the Democratic candidate's traditional opening speech on Labor Day, often in an industrial center. (Jimmy Carter, however, chose to open his 1976 campaign in Atlanta.)

[19] For a defense of the convention, see Aaron Wildavsky, "On the Superiority of National Conventions," *Review of Politics* 25 (1962): 307–19.

The campaign for the presidency is in many ways the generic American political campaign "writ large." Its main problems and tasks are different in degree but similar in kind. The candidate and his campaign managers must still print literature and flyers, contract for ads and media time, schedule travel and speeches, put together an integrated campaign organization, and amass the necessary research. The candidate also faces similar strategic choices. On what mixture of appearances or radio-television speeches will he rely? What timing will he adopt — the full-speed-from-the-beginning strategy of Kennedy in 1960 or the pointed, paced buildup favored by Nixon in the same year? Will he play primarily on the appeal of the party, of the candidate ("I like Ike," "All the way with LBJ"), or of issues and ideology (Barry Goldwater: "In your heart you know he's right")? And like candidates all over the country, he faces problems in presenting himself to voters: Nixon's problem with a reputation for deviousness; Kennedy's problems of youthfulness, Catholicism, and wealth; Goldwater's reputation for "shooting from the hip"; Johnson's for the ruthless exercise of power (arm-twisting); Humphrey's for garrulousness; and McGovern's for radicalism.

Yet, many of the usual campaign problems are heightened by the nature of the presidential office and constituency. The candidate's problem of keeping posted on how the campaign is going, on his progress with the electorate, is tremendous. The expanse of the country, the variety of local conditions, and the candidate's isolation from the grass roots make any kind of assessment difficult. In this dilemma the presidential candidates have increasingly relied on professional pollsters to supplement the reports of local politicians. That same expanse of continent plus the length and pace of the campaign put exceptional physical strains on the candidate. The jet airplane adds to the strains by making more and more travel possible within a few months. Virtually every presidential candidate comes to election day on the fine edge of exhaustion. Perhaps these developments in the presidential campaign can best be illustrated by the changes of a century. During the 1860 campaign Abraham Lincoln never left Springfield, Illinois. During the 1960 campaign the two candidates together traveled more than 100,000 miles and gave almost 600 speeches.

There are, however, some important ways in which the presidential campaigns are really quite different from others in American politics. The most significant one concerns their financing. Beginning in 1976, presidential candidates had the option of accepting federal campaign funds if they would raise and spend no other money. Both candidates did so. Aside from money spent on their behalf by separate individuals and by national party committees, they were limited to the $21.8 million grant. In one fell swoop they were released from the heavy burden of fundraising. In return for that advantage, of course, the presidential candidates did have to scale back their campaigns. The $43.6 million they received together was con-

siderably less than the candidates spent in 1972. (The details and implications of public financing of campaigns will be explored at greater length
in the next chapter.)

The electoral college and the nature of the American parties also give
a special shape to the presidential campaigns. Because of the electoral
college, presidential candidates allocate their time and resources in a
special way. In all other American constituencies a candidate can pick up
useful votes in his areas of weakness, even in those areas he will lose. Not
so in the electoral college, where the candidate gains only if he wins a
plurality of the vote in a state. This fact drastically alters the strategy of
a presidential campaign. Presidential candidates generally pick a group
of states they feel they can carry and then devote their time to them. As
a result, presidential campaigns have tended to be concentrated in the
close, two-party states, with the candidates largely avoiding each other's
areas of strength. At the bottom of virtually every presidential campaign
strategy is some reckoning of what states the candidate has the best chance
of winning in order to produce a majority of electoral votes.

The rambling, decentralized character of the American parties places
special problems of its own on the campaign, chiefly on its organizational
aspects. Neither the presidential campaign staff nor the national committee controls the whims and activities of the state parties. Most candidates
work pragmatically (and inefficiently) through the maze of state and local
organizations, finding useful leaders and contacts as best they can. Barry
Goldwater in 1964, however, made the best known and best chronicled
attempt to establish a single national organization with direct lines of
authority and a comprehensive campaign plan (down to vote quotas for
each precinct in the country).[20] By most judgments the loose, untidy
nature of the American parties triumphed over Goldwater's attempt to
impose some order and central planning.

The Nixon administration carried domination of the presidential campaign to new lengths in 1972. Its instrument, innocently entitled Committee for the Reelection of the President, came to be known by the
not-so-innocent acronym, CREEP. It was a long step beyond the usual
presidential campaign organization in two ways. First, its leadership was
limited to personal loyalists of the president; at the outset, at least, it had
very few people of any experience in the Republican party. Second, it was
controlled by the president's closest aides in the White House; in that way
there was virtually no separation of the campaign and the government.
Beyond all of that, CREEP achieved a kind of sordid immortality by
spawning the major case of corruption in presidential politics in American

---

[20] For two good reports on 1964 campaign organization, see Karl A. Lamb and Paul A.
Smith, *Campaign Decision-Making* (Belmont: Wadsworth, 1968); and John H. Kessel,
*The Goldwater Coalition* (Indianapolis: Bobbs-Merrill, 1968).

history. Most of its unwholesome activity actually took place before the nominating conventions and included, *inter alia,* the break-in and attempted bugging of Democratic National Committee offices (in the Watergate complex), the keeping of intelligence files on Democratic candidates, a vast series of "dirty tricks" in the presidential primaries (e.g., a bogus billboard in Florida purporting to be sponsored by Democrat Edmund Muskie and urging "More Busing"), and the collecting and spending of illegal and unreported campaign funds. All in all, the committee's activities helped to bring down a president and to contribute to an already hefty cynicism about the ethics of campaigning in the United States.[21]

## RADIO, TELEVISION, AND THE THIRD ESTATE

For several special reasons, presidential campaigns depend more heavily than most others on campaigning through the mass media — radio, newspaper, and television ads and appearances:

— Media exposure costs dearly (in the record year, for example, the two presidential candidates in 1972 spent $28 million on radio and television alone), and presidential candidates command larger sums of money than other candidates.
— Media exposure is more efficient for presidential candidates. They have none of the usual problems of paying for an audience that lies partly outside their constituency.
— The presidential candidates have a more receptive audience for a media-centered campaign. The voter who wouldn't pass up a TV quiz show for a congressional candidate may do so for a presidential aspirant.
— The size of the presidential constituency dictates that this is the only practical way for the candidate to reach large numbers of voters. The alternative, especially as the states become more competitive, is an exhausting travel schedule.

So the dependence of presidential campaigners on the media grows, and there is no end in sight. To a greater extent than in most other campaigns, the masters of the media — public relations men, pollsters, ad agencies, TV production experts — form a new political elite in the presidential races.

No candidate can escape the exposure the media provide. A good deal of it will come without cost or effort. Every speech or foray, no matter how trivial, will be reported. Some of this kind of exposure can be controlled, however. Barry Goldwater's campaign managers persuaded him to forego press conferences during the 1964 campaign in order not to be goaded into rash and ill-considered retorts. In their commercial uses of the media, the

---

[21] What we have come to call collectively the Watergate affair, of course, also involved abuses of executive and presidential power far beyond the 1972 campaign.

**From a Dictionary: "Campaign Promises"**

There is an amazing amount of American political folklore that we are in danger of losing as the oral tradition dies and as interest in things political wanes. William Safire, newspaper columnist and former presidential speechwriter, has brought together a good deal of it in his *Safire's Political Dictionary* (New York: Random House, 1978). It is a dictionary in providing definitions and in its alphabetical entries, but Safire uses the dictionary form for recording a great deal of additional folk and historical material. Here is his entry under " Campaign Promises":

*Campaign Promises* pledges made by a candidate to gain certain things for his constituents after election.

This is probably the oldest form of politicking since elections began. Said a sign on a first-century Roman wall: "Genialis urges the election of Brutius Balbus as duovoir (commission member). He will protect the treasury." A candidate's promises, like a party platform, are rarely taken as literal commitments. Often they seem part of a game in which candidates out-promise each other, accuse each other of making rash promises and cite the opposition's unfilled promises left over from previous elections.

Occasionally a particular promise takes on major — even historic — importance. One such was Dwight Eisenhower's pledge to go to Korea if elected in 1952. But for the most part, Bernard Baruch's admonition seems valid. "Vote for the man who promises least," said Baruch. "He'll be the least disappointing."

The classic campaign-promise story is recounted by Senator Russell Long (D.-La.) about his uncle, Governor Earl Long. He had promised voters the right to elect their local sheriffs, but once in office, went in the opposite direction. When a delegation came to "Uncle Earl's" office to protest, Senator Long tells the author, "Uncle Earl told his right-hand man, 'I don't want to see 'em — you see 'em.' His aide said, 'What'll I tell 'em?' And Uncle Earl said, right out, 'Tell 'em I lied!' "

candidates have full control. Candidates may choose their form of exposure: Will it be full speeches or spot announcements? The former run the danger of boring voters; the latter have been criticized for merchandising presidents. Richard Nixon in 1968, for instance, developed a novel TV format. He appeared in ten hour-long programs in which he answered questions from panels of six or seven usually friendly questioners. An enthusiastic studio audience of carefully chosen Republicans watched and cheered.[22]

[22] For a generally acerbic account, see Joe McGinniss, *The Selling of the President 1968* (New York: Trident, 1969).

Something of an apogee in the trend to media-centered presidential campaigns was reached in the presidential debates of 1960 and 1976. In 1960 the television networks contributed free time when the Congress waived the "equal time" rule and thus freed them of the necessity of granting time to minor party candidates. In 1976 the League of Women Voters Educational Fund sponsored the debates, and the networks simply covered them as a public event. The format of the debates in 1960 and 1976 were different, but in 1976 there were three debates of ninety minutes each, with most of the time devoted to questions directed first to one candidate and then to the other by a panel of three media reporters. (In 1976 there was also an unrelated vice-presidential debate between Walter Mondale and Robert Dole.)

The impact of such debates is not easy to measure. Most observers and scholars of the 1960 debates thought they did more for John Kennedy than Richard Nixon. At the least they enabled Kennedy to close the publicity gap between himself and the better-known vice-president and to establish his credibility as a possible president. Indeed, the size of the audiences — 85 million and more than 100 million in the two years saw at least one of them — mark the debates as a unique opportunity for a candidate. Moreover, the composition of the audience is as remarkable as its size. Candidates perpetually face the problem of speaking largely to their supporters, but the debates brought each before the partisans of the other party and before the self-defined independent and undecided voters.

Such media confrontations, however, are not without their traps and pitfalls. President Gerald Ford unquestionably hurt himself and his campaign in 1976 by asserting that there was no Soviet domination of East Europe. No amount of explaining and clarifying could repair the damage to his ethnic support and to his reputation for experience in matters of foreign policy. Because both the stakes and the dangers of the debates are so great, some presidential candidates between 1960 and 1976 were not willing to participate in them. Lyndon Johnson was far ahead in the 1964 campaign and disinclined to risk a debate, and Richard Nixon, having once been burned, ruled them out in 1968 and 1972. In fact, there may not be many presidential elections in which both candidates will think it to their advantage to debate.[23]

Presidential campaign politics are thus both typical and atypical of American campaigning generally. On the one hand, the sheer magnitude of the office and its national constituency puts a special stamp on the campaign for the presidency. It is also contested within a special nomination process and the unique constraints of the electoral college. And yet on the

[23] On the debates of 1960 see Sidney Kraus (ed.), *The Great Debates* (Bloomington: Indiana University Press, 1962). For an account of the 1976 debates, Jules Witcover, *Marathon* (New York: Viking, 1977).

other hand, the campaigns for the presidency grow out of the same norms, styles, and traditions that shape other American campaigns. The art of presidential campaigning is also the basic art of American political campaigning — the art of defining the various audiences of the campaign and reaching them as efficiently and effectively as possible.[24]

## THE NATIONAL PARTY

If there is a national party in the United States — despite all the influences that fragment it into fifty state parties and innumerable local ones — it must materialize as the parties contest the one national election in American politics. And it must be able to function as one and to identify some goals and interests beyond those of the state and local parties. Does, then, the quadrennial race for the presidency see the emergence of a national party?

If by the term "national party" one means a national party organization, then clearly there is no national party. The national committees, even during the presidential campaigns, are usually weak, unused auxiliaries of the campaign organizations of the presidential candidates. The candidates have the right to appoint the chairmen of the national committees, and that traditional right in many ways symbolizes the subordination of the national committee to them. In fact, in the entire business of nominating and electing a president, the dominance of the candidates is greater even than in the rest of American politics. So, if there is a national party, it is almost exclusively the party in government, and we have every right and reason to call it the presidential party.

Even during presidential elections the localism of American political organization asserts itself. The incentives of patronage and preferment, of political career and social advantage, depend on the winning of state and local elections and the maintenance of an effective state party organization. The goals and incentives of party activists, however, appear to be shifting from these locally rooted incentives to issue, interest, and ideology. And these tend to be national, since the great public policy concerns with which they are involved are national concerns that will be resolved largely by national political institutions. The party worker, therefore, must look to national politics — to the election of a president and a Congress — for the achievement of these goals. That trend is probably matched by an increasingly national focus within the loyal party electorate. The political information and goals of the American voter, as well as his party identification, are increasingly dominated by the personalities and issues of national politics.

Thus there are forces making for a national party and forces resisting

[24] For a thoughtful essay on the presidential campaigns generally, see Stephen Hess, *The Presidential Campaign*, rev. ed. (Washington: Brookings, 1978).

one. The conventions themselves illustrate that ambivalence. In some states the state organizations may be strong enough to send to the convention delegates who will protect the interests of the state party. In other cases the delegates may be loyal primarily to a would-be candidate and committed to support him, regardless of the competing interests of the state party. The result is an unstable amalgam of state-oriented and national-oriented presidential politics in the conventions.

With the state party organizations and delegates thus divided between local and national outlook, and with the national committees unable to function effectively, the national party is easily dominated by the presidential candidate and his followers. His is the only organization with purely national goals and incentives. Frequently the party activists whose incentive to action is a national personality or a national ideology find their best avenue to national political involvement in the voluntary organizations (e.g., Citizens for Eisenhower), the campaign organizations, or the personal followings (e.g., the Robert Kennedy personal organization) of the present or potential presidential candidates. So, what is loosely called the national party is really the party of the presidential candidate. His main problem in presidential politics, in fact, is to override and unite all the local, separatist interests and loyalties within the party. He must nationalize the attention of voters and the activities of party activists for at least the brief time of the presidential campaign.

The politics of nominating and electing a president also create for each party a national image. What the party does in nominating a candidate and what he does in the campaign put a stamp on the party, give it profile and salience for millions of Americans. For them the business of presidential politics defines what the party is, what it stands for, and who its supporters are. The creation of that image of the national party is, then, one of the major stakes of the presidential nomination and campaign. In this sense the conservatism of the Goldwater candidacy in 1964 rubbed off on the Republicans, and the painful events of the 1968 Chicago convention had an impact for the Democrats far beyond issues of control within the party. Similarly, the Watergate sins of CREEP in 1972 attached to the Republicans, even though the major sinners had few ties to and little experience in the Republican party organization.

Thus the American party is something of a hierarchical hybrid. It combines a steadfastly decentralized organization with a politics in which the focuses — party identifications, personalities, and issues — are increasingly national and centralized. Taken as a national entity, the American party is an illogical, even contradictory mixture of a decentralized party organization and an increasingly centralized party in government. One wonders how long the party organizations will be able to remain so determinedly decentralized at a time when all other influences in American government and politics are thrown on the side of centralization.

# 13

# Financing
# the Campaigns

At some time in the future it may be possible to draw up a great balance sheet for the parties in which all the resources they recruit — the manpower, skills, and money — are balanced against all the resources they spend. We would then know the sources and the value of all party resources and the costs and activities on which they were spent. However, that kind of total input-output accounting is beyond us at the moment and so, therefore, is the kind of analysis of party effort that it would sustain.

The resources needed by the parties fall into two main categories: those of the party organization and those of the party in government (Table 13.1). The discussion in Chapter 4 on the recruitment of manpower and skills into the party organizations approached the question of resources for the organizations. But it dealt almost exclusively with their principal resource: the efforts of active individuals. The party's candidates and public officials — the party in government — recruit and spend another substantial sum of political resources. The party in government needs resources for its political expenses while in public office; congressmen, for example, may collect funds for trips back home for political fence mending. But the vast bulk of what the party in government needs are the cash resources for its collective campaigns for election. It is that money with which the chapter is primarily concerned.

Again, in the best possible of all scholarly worlds, we might be able to account for all the contributions to campaigns for nominations and elections — to account, that is, for all the hours of work, all the goods, all the skills and expertise, and all the cash contributed. But difficult as they may be to identify, the cash contributions are easier to total than the others, and this chapter will be largely limited to them. Although that limitation is forced by sheer lack of information, one can build a substantial rationale for it at the risk of seeming to make a virtue of necessity. Whereas the work of the party organizations has largely employed valuables other than cash (e.g., goods and services), the campaign activities of the party in government have been based mainly on cash contributions (Table 13.1).

The increasing importance of money as a political resource can be easily documented. There is abundant evidence scattered through this chapter that the cash inputs into American political campaigning have risen

TABLE 13.1   Total Party Resource Needs

|  | Party organization | Party in government |
|---|---|---|
| Type of resource | More services (especially manpower) than cash | More cash than noncash contributions |
| Purpose | General expense of maintaining the organization | Largely for election campaigns |
| Schedule | Continuous | Periodic; at elections |

steeply. As candidates free themselves from the control of campaigns by the party organization, they need cash to pay for the information, skills, and manpower that party organizations once furnished for no charge (other than a mortgage on their political loyalties). It is doubtful that the noncash inputs are increasing, at least at such a pace.

## HOW BIG IS THE MONEY?

A forbidding secrecy long veiled the budgets of parties and candidates. Contributors were hesitant to be publicly identified, and candidates feared both an unknowing violation of some law regulating campaigns and public disapproval of even the most modest expenditures. The 1970s, however, brought extensive requirements to report contributions and expenditures in federal campaigns and in most states. There is no doubt that we now have more information on American political finance. Where once the problem was secrecy, it now is a flood of data.

Despite these difficulties, Alexander Heard and Herbert Alexander, the two most authoritative experts on the question of money in American politics, have estimated that total campaign expenditures — for all offices at all electoral levels, including both nominations and general elections — in the presidential years almost quadrupled from 1952 to 1976 (see Table 13.2).[1]

Not surprisingly, the most expensive campaign for public office in the United States is that for the presidency. Just to win the party nomination — that is, the right to run — may cost $10 million. Even the underdog cam-

[1] The data from 1952 and 1956 come from Alexander Heard, *The Costs of Democracy* (Chapel Hill: University of North Carolina Press, 1960). Those for 1960 through 1976 are from Herbert E. Alexander's five studies: *Financing the 1960 Election* (Princeton: Citizens' Research Foundation, 1962); *Financing the 1964 Election* (Princeton: Citizens' Research Foundation, 1966); *Financing the 1968 Election* (Boston: Heath, 1971); *Financing the 1972 Election* (Boston: Heath, 1976); and *Financing the 1976 Election* (Washington: Congressional Quarterly, 1979).

**TABLE 13.2    Total Campaign Expenditures for All Offices in Presidential Years: 1952–72**

| Year | Sum expended | Percentage increase over previous election |
|------|--------------|--------------------------------------------|
| 1952 | $140,000,000 | — |
| 1956 | $155,000,000 | 10.7 |
| 1960 | $175,000,000 | 12.9 |
| 1964 | $200,000,000 | 14.3 |
| 1968 | $300,000,000 | 50.0 |
| 1972 | $425,000,000 | 41.7 |
| 1976 | $540,000,000 | 27.1 |

*Source*    The sources of these data are fully explained in footnote one.

paign of Eugene McCarthy for the 1968 Democratic nomination cost over $11 million. With the renomination a certainty for President Richard Nixon in 1972, the preconvention contesting was limited to the Democrats. Even so, Democratic candidates spent $37 million; George McGovern accounted for almost $12 million of it. The Federal Election Campaign Act of 1974 set an effective limit of approximately $13.1 million per candidate in the preconvention campaigning. Candidates Ford, Reagan, and Carter all exceeded $12 million, and the total bill for all candidates in the two parties approached $46 million. And that, to repeat, was before the conventions ever named a candidate.

The presidential campaign raises the ante conspicuously (Table 13.3). Even a third-party candidacy is increasingly expensive; George Wallace spent more than $7 million in 1968. Richard Nixon and his supporters spent about $25 million in 1968 and then went on to set a new presidential campaign record of $68 million in 1972. That latter figure reflects both a prodigious ability to raise political money and the good fortune of not having to spend any of it on a campaign for nomination. The McGovern campaign in 1972 spent approximately $35 million, after having spent $12 million in the preconvention drive. The 1972 total of $103.7 million and the Nixon portion of it are apt to stand as records in American presidential politics for the foreseeable future. The 1974 Election Campaign Act imposed sharp limits on presidential spending as a condition for accepting public funds for the campaign. Thus, the drop of $15 million between 1972 and 1976. The combination of the cut itself and the inroads of inflation meant a drop of almost 50 percent in purchasing power for the 1976 campaign.

It is difficult to generalize about the cost of a race for the Senate, but it is not unheard of to spend several million dollars in one. John Tower of Texas spent over $2.5 million seeking reelection in 1972, and John Heinz

TABLE 13.3   National Level of Spending by Presidential
and Party Committees: General Elections, 1960–76

| Year | Amount | Republican percentage of two-party expenditures |
|------|--------|-------------------------------------------------|
| 1960 | $ 19.9 million | 49 |
| 1964 | 24.8 million | 63 |
| 1968 | 44.2 million | 65 |
| 1972 | 103.7 million | 67 |
| 1976 | 88.7 million | 56 |

*Source*   Herbert Alexander, *Financing the 1976 Election* (Washington:
Congressional Quarterly, 1979).

spent $3 million for his Senate election in 1976. More typically, Senate
races in fairly competitive states may cost well over a million; the *average*
Senate winner spent $617,000 in 1976 and $920,000 in 1978. Of course, it
is possible for a firmly entrenched senator from a small state to spend
considerably less. It is no easier to generalize about the cost of House
campaigns. Two candidates together spent over $1 million contesting a con-
gressional district on Manhattan's east side in 1978, but the average winning campaign for the House in that year cost $108,000. Costs also fluctuate
erratically in successive congressional campaigns. It is not unusual for a
successful candidate for the House to spend twice as much beating the
incumbent than he will in his first defense of the office two years later.

Beyond these quests for national office are the thousands of campaigns
for state and local office. Hard information is rare, the generalizations
questionable. Many of these campaigns involve almost unbelievably small
sums. Each year hundreds of candidates win office in the United States in
campaigns that involve cash outlays of a few hundred dollars; on the other
hand, the mayoralty campaign in a large American city may cost a candidate and his supporters several hundred thousand dollars. Campaigns for
governor of the larger states often exceed $500,000. And Nelson Rocke-
feller spent more than $10 million winning renomination and reelection in
1970; it was probably the most expensive nonpresidential campaign in the
history of American politics. Campaigns for referenda in California, the
home of the most elaborate noncandidate campaigns, have been known to
exceed a million dollars. The various groups on both sides of the 1978 referendum on property tax reduction (Proposition 13) spent well over $2
million.

The levels of campaign spending, therefore, are related to a number of
factors. Clearly the importance of the office and the size of the constituency
are two. Important also is the degree to which the party organization con-

trols campaigning and uses its own apparatus as the chief campaign vehicle. The competitiveness of the race also affects levels of spending. A pair of major-party candidates will generally spend more when and where the election outcome is uncertain.[2]

To repeat, all of these figures reflect only cash outlays. Therefore, they do not reflect the true economic costs of the campaign. They do not usually include the gift or loan of goods or services. Volunteer workers contribute time for canvassing, typing envelopes, phoning voters, writing press releases, and dozens of other campaign jobs. Partisans may also donate goods: free paper for literature, the use of a plane or auto, or their home and their refreshments for fundraising parties. Nor do these totals include the costs of campaigning borne indirectly by the public treasuries. In cities and states with old-style patronage systems, the city halls and county courthouses and all of their employees may be a vortex of campaign activity for the weeks before elections. Senators and congressmen customarily use their offices, their staffs, and even their franking privileges for some campaign help. Heard suggests that these additional contributions, exclusive of part-time volunteer labor, would add another 5 percent to the bill; the value of contributed labor seems greater but it is virtually impossible to estimate.[3] One might venture the opinion, however, that these noncash expenditures form a larger chunk of local campaign costs and that with a shift from party organization campaigning (noncash) to media campaigning (cash), the percentage of noncash costs is, on the aggregate, declining.

The most important question about the "big money," however, is whether it is getting bigger. Heard, writing in 1959, plotted the rises in costs from 1940 through 1956 and concluded that the increases of 54 percent in that period were no greater than increases in the price level — that is, no greater than increases in the general cost of living.[4] After that, however, the increases have far exceeded the rise in the price level. Between 1956 and 1972 the aggregate sums increased by 174 percent, while the price level rose about 54 percent. Most observers attributed the rise to greater dependence on the technology of campaigning: jet travel, opinion polling, computer management of data, and reliance on the media. Then, from 1972 to 1976 the total increase of 27 percent was less than the approximately one-third increase in the cost of living over the four years. Had there not been the statutory limits on the 1976 presidential campaign, of course, the increase would very likely have exceeded the inflation rate by a substantial amount.

[2] For a fuller development of these points, especially the one on competitiveness, see David Adamany, *Financing Politics* (Madison: University of Wisconsin Press, 1969). Adamany's study is the best one on party finance in a single state (Wisconsin). Most of its findings parallel those of Alexander at the national level; that is, the patterns and relationships that prevail nationally also prevail in the main within Wisconsin.
[3] Heard, *The Costs of Democracy*, p. 372.
[4] *Ibid.*, p. 376.

These then are preliminary answers to the question of how big the political money is. Unanswered is the more difficult question of how big it *really* is — how big it is when measured by relative values and utilities rather than the fixed measure of the dollar sign. Even in the American economy of 1976 the $540 million figure represented only about .032 of 1 percent of the gross national product. If one is looking for comparative benchmarks, it becomes clear that many smaller countries spend far more on political campaigns (measured by money per voter) than does the United States. A country such as Italy may spend four times what American parties and candidates do per voter, and the two candidates in the Philippine presidential elections of 1965 spent just a bit more than the two American contestants of 1964.[5] And that $540 million total for 1976 is not much more than the $468 million the manufacturers of toiletries and toilet goods spent on television ads alone in 1976.

## PATTERNS OF EXPENDITURES

The modern arts of mass communication — and especially the television tube — have revolutionized American political campaigning. In so doing they have, of course, upset and restructured the patterns of expenditures in campaigns. In 1948's presidential election there were no expenditures for television, but twenty years later in 1968 the campaigns of Richard Nixon and Hubert Humphrey together spent $13.5 million for network and local television time. Additions of those magnitudes not only help to explain the absolute rise in campaign costs in recent years, they also reflect shifts and dislocations in the proportions of campaign budgets going for various purposes.

The reports of the Federal Communications Commission to Congress (through 1972) permitted an unusually precise definition of radio and television campaign costs. The total Democratic and Republican election costs for radio and television increased more than four times between 1956 and 1968, from $9.8 million to $40.0 million. The figure for 1968 could be boosted to $58.9 million if one included the nomination expenditures. Part of the increase reflects the spread of television sets and stations; part, however, reflects a growing reliance on TV. The limits placed on media expenditures in 1971, however, altered sharply the pattern of reliance on radio and television in 1972 (Table 13.4). Totals jumped again in 1976, reflecting both the repeal of the 1971 limits and the increased reliance on the media in a campaign in which overall spending was reduced.

Television and radio expenditures, however, do not fall evenly on all

[5] The entire edition of the *Journal of Politics* for November 1963 (vol. 25, no. 4), was devoted to studies in comparative political finance; see especially the article by Arnold Heidenheimer, "Comparative Party Finance: Notes on Practices and Toward a Theory," pp. 790–811.

**TABLE 13.4   Comparisons in Expenditures for Radio and Television in the 1968, 1972, and 1976 Elections**

|                                                    | 1968          | 1972          | 1976          |
| -------------------------------------------------- | ------------- | ------------- | ------------- |
| All presidential candidates, nomination and election | $28.5 million | $14.3 million | —             |
| Republican presidential ticket                     | 12.6 million  | 4.3 million   | $7.9 million  |
| Democratic presidential ticket                     | 6.1 million   | 6.2 million   | 8.7 million   |
| All candidates in all elections                    | 58.9 million  | 59.6 million  | —             |

*Source   Congressional Quarterly Weekly Report,* May 12, 1973; and Alexander, *Financing the 1976 Election,* Chap. 7.

candidates and party levels. Presidential campaigns rely far more heavily on them than do the others. Although the 1968 presidential campaign accounted for only 19.8 percent of total campaign costs in that year ($59.4 million out of $300 million), the bills of the presidential campaign ($11 million) explain 33.4 percent of the total radio and TV bill for the 1968 campaign. Some other campaigns do match this concentration of funds on radio and TV. Robert Kennedy in his 1964 race for the Senate allocated over half of his expenditures for radio spots and television presentations, some $900,000 on TV alone. But campaigns for the Senate and House, not to mention state and local office, rarely rely to such an extent on radio and TV. For many, such as the congressional candidate whose district is a small patch of a great urban center, TV time is a costly, inefficient, buckshot method, striking perhaps one in eight or ten listeners who can vote for him.

Other costs related to the shift to media campaigning are greater in the presidential campaigns. The arts of opinion polling do not come cheaply; in 1968 Nixon and Humphrey together spent $650,000 on polls and surveys. Advertisements on the printed page can also cost thousands of dollars; an eight-page insert in the *Reader's Digest* cost the Goldwater forces about $300,000 in 1964. Given the nature of the presidential office, the campaign for it involves far greater costs for travel and communication; major items are jet fares, postage, long-distance phone bills, and telegrams. The costs of moving presidential entourages — advance men, press contacts, speech writers, diction coaches, friends, advisors, and family — increase not only because of the greater amount of traveling but also because of the higher costs of jet travel itself.

On the other hand, state and local campaigns rely more on newspaper advertisements and campaign literature. Other sources of communication — the lapel button, the bumper sticker, the signs on the lawn or in the window, for example — can also account for a sizable part of the candidate's expenditures. State and local campaigns also bear heavy costs in staff salaries and expenses, and in maintaining headquarters or offices. In almost every campaign, in fact, the major expenses are two: communication costs and overhead and staff costs.

Finally, what difference is there in the expenditure patterns of the two parties? The evidence of recent presidential years suggests that there is not much. Both parties, for example, spend approximately the same percentage of their budget on radio and television. But although general patterns are the same, the level of Republican expenditures has stayed above that of the Democrats. Even if one includes the transfers that Democratic national committees make to state and local committees and the spending of labor on behalf of Democratic candidates, it appears that the Republicans at the national level have been spending between 10 and 20 percent more than the Democrats. It may well be, however, that greater noncash expenditures by the Democrats — volunteer labor and work by party activists and patronage holders — would narrow the margin if they could be calculated.

## SOURCES AND WELLSPRINGS

Political expenditures are comparatively obvious; the voter sees them in the nature and events of the campaign. Not so with the political input. Although the mechanics of fund raising, the ways in which the parties and candidates get their money, may be no great secret, the contributors have been. They are thought to be the secret movers of American politics, and their motives are the objects of the greatest suspicion.

The techniques by which the parties and candidates raise their funds are limited only by their ingenuity and by the prevailing political norms. The chief methods include:

*Personal solicitation.* Personal visits, phone calls, letters, door-to-door solicitation, and all other personal approaches by the candidate or his solicitors raise substantial sums for the party. This is the method most generally used to reach the big contributors, the so-called "fat cats" of American politics. The success of these solicitations depends, of course, on the skill of the solicitor and on his access to those willing and able to contribute. Given the well-known propensity of many "fat cats" to give and give again, it may be largely a matter of contacting the right list of prospects.

*Mail solicitation.* Appeals by mail, now recognized as the most effective way of raising money in small sums, have enjoyed increasing success. The Goldwater campaign of 1964 established their importance; almost a third of the Goldwater revenue came by way of mail solicitation. George Wallace followed suit in 1968, and George McGovern topped even those successes in 1972. Close to 700,000 contributors gave him about $15 million, close to 60 percent of all the money the McGovern campaign received. The secrets of mail solicitation are the same, whatever the object. The specialists polish carefully the printed message of the candidate, and they are always in search of the profitable list of prospects. (Goldwater's solicitation scored with a list of Americans who had bought an automobile polishing cloth by mail.) The importance of the mail appeal, great already, is likely to increase as new laws prohibit the very large campaign contribution.

*Dinners.* As unlikely as it may seem, a considerable amount of the fiscal stability of American politics has been built on a foundation of banquet chicken, mashed potatoes, and half-warm peas. For a "ticket" price, usually between $10 and $100, one has dinner in a large ballroom, listens to endless political exhortations, rubs elbows with the other party faithful, and perhaps observes a senator, a cabinet member, or a president. It is an occasion, it offers something in return for the contribution, and it may also permit some expense account sleight-of-hand. The sums raised are significant; senators or a state party may net between $50,000 and $250,000 with the right "name" guest as a drawing card. Party committees traditionally also use the dinner for fund raising. The Lincoln Day dinners of the Republicans and the Jefferson-Jackson dinners of the Democrats are traditional annual events all around the country.

*Other diversions.* Taking their cue from the success of the political dinner, money raisers have begun to rely on related occasions: the cocktail party, the theater party, the reception, the wine-tasting party, rock concerts, the beach party, and the trip to the races. They are adaptable to all levels of giving and are especially apt for local candidates who cannot risk the pretentiousness of a "dinner."

*Telethons.* An increasingly popular way of raising money for all manner of causes, the telethon features a nonstop media show mixing entertainment, messages for the cause, and pleas for phoned-in pledges. (A variant for radio also exists.) Because the Democratic party in recent decades has had the lion's share of support from the entertainment industry and because the format aims to tap new small contributors, telethons have been more common in Democratic fund raising. The Democratic National Committee has used them, and Jimmy Carter raised a valuable $328,000 in one for his campaign for the party nomination. Beamed throughout Georgia, it was called "Spend Valentine's Day with Jimmy Carter (and some of his famous friends)."

*Patronage.* Although patronage has virtually passed from national politics, it does yield contributions in many states and localities in which the holder of a public job is expected to contribute a fixed percentage of his salary at campaign time. In Indiana, the state patronage holders are referred to as the "Two Percent Club." Crude as it may seem, the patronage system comes close to governmentally financed campaigns in a few American states. In addition, of course, the patronage workers make an even more substantial noncash contribution in their labors for the party.

*Miscellaneous.* One can only suggest the richness of the ingenuity with which other sums are raised. Syracuse Democrats in 1960 offered trading stamps (at a rate higher than that of supermarkets) for contributions. In 1964 the Goldwater enthusiasts opened retail shops in some cities to sell the usual campaign buttons and stickers, Goldwater sweatshirts, tumblers, and pens. At George Wallace rallies in 1968 a Miss JaNeen Welch offered her kisses for $20 contributions; the Wallace forces, however, raised greater sums by passing an old-fashioned yellow "suds-bucket."

Finally, the budget of any single candidate or party committee may show two other sources of campaign funds. One is a transfer from another political committee. Large numbers of candidates for the Senate and House, for example, receive sums from their party's campaign committees in the Congress. Some, too, may rely in the short run on debt. But both these sums must ultimately be raised in the ways suggested above. Some years after the events of 1968 the Democratic National Committee was still trying to settle debts from that campaign, often on the basis of a few cents for the dollar.

Whatever may be the nature of the solicitation some individual or group of individuals for some political goal or reason has added to the political assets of a candidate or party. But who are these individuals and how many of them are there? Why do they make their contributions?

Despite all the innovative techniques of fund raising, candidates and parties have always relied heavily on the very big contributor. In 1964 about $2.2 million was raised by the two parties in gifts of more than $10,000 apiece; by 1972 similar gifts totalled $50.7 million. In that same year there were also some 71,800 contributions of $500 or more, a threefold increase over 1968. Even at the lower political levels (where a large contribution often is defined as a minimum of $100 rather than $500), many state and congressional candidates have relied on large contributors for more than 50 percent of their political campaign funds.[6]

The 1974 Election Campaign Act undercut the reliance on big contributors — at least in federal elections. It set a limit of $1000 for contributions to any primary or general election campaign. The United States Supreme Court upheld the constitutionality of these limits on contributions — *except* as they applied to candidates spending their own money on their campaign. That is, the Court upheld limits on contributions but struck down those on spending, and the use of one's own personal wealth it

[6] Data of this paragraph are from the Alexander studies cited in footnote 1.

viewed as an expenditure rather than a contribution.[7] Ironically, therefore, wealthy candidates were left as the only class of large "contributors" for the 1976 campaigns. John Heinz spent $2.5 million of his own fortune (out of total campaign expenditures of about $3 million) in his 1976 Senate race, and Carter Burden used close to $700,000 of his own in an unsuccessful campaign for the House in New York City in 1978.

Although the importance of the big contributor diminished in 1976 and 1978, the importance of the "political action committee" (PAC) increased sharply. Organizations are limited to $5000 in contributions to any one campaign, but the law imposes no overall limit. In 1976 political action committees — largely organizations formed specifically for the purpose of making monetary contributions — gave $22 million to congressional campaigns, twice their 1974 total. But by 1978 their total contribution had risen to $35 million — a more than threefold increase in just four years. By 1979 approximately 2000 PACs had registered with the Federal Election Commission — organizations representing business, labor, agriculture, professional, and specific issue interests. Some, indeed, encompassed only the employees of a single corporation (e.g., the Texaco Employees' Political Involvement Committee). Organized labor, with the oldest tradition of working through political action committees, kept its number of committees fairly stable, but the number with business and corporate ties has increased dramatically. Since both presidential candidates in 1976 accepted public funds and thus the fund-raising limits that accompanied them, group giving was diverted largely to races for the House and the Senate. And among congressional candidates by far the largest amounts went to committee chairmen running for reelection. PAC contributions to House chairmen averaged $45,000 in 1978, and their total sum accounted for 56 percent of all the funds those chairmen raised.

Yet, the attempts of the parties and candidates to broaden the base of party finance go on. Early attempts in the 1950s to stimulate small contributions by door-to-door solicitation and by mass advertising campaigns had little success. But in the 1960s the new computer technology for organizing and printing mailing lists and the new knowledge gained from direct mail merchandising provided a breakthrough. The Republicans netted large sums of small amounts by mail in 1964 and 1968, and then in 1972 George McGovern raised unimagined sums in small contributions — $15 million from some 700,000 Americans. Attention to small contributions then received a new stimulus in the 1974 Election Campaign Act. Contenders for the presidential nominations qualify for federal subsidies in the preconvention period only if they raise at least $5000 in each of

----

[7] *Buckley* v *Valeo,* 424 U.S. 1 (1976).

twenty states, with federal funds matching only the first $250 of individual contributions.

In short, the parties and candidates have never ignored small contributors, and now the incentives to reach them are greater than ever. Nonetheless, the task is not an easy one. Many Americans will not contribute to their party even if asked. Less than 8 percent of the sample of American adults in the SRCs 1976 survey reported having given money in the campaign. And in no year so far has even 30 percent of tax-paying Americans been willing to channel a dollar of their tax liability to the federal election fund on the checkoff provision of the income tax return — a decision that takes the dollar not from them but from the United States Treasury. And despite some successes with mail solicitations, there are also stories of failures with them. Local candidates often find that their attempts yield little more than enough to cover the costs of printing and postage. And even at the national level mail soliciting seems to yield large returns only in causes or candidates identifiably of the right or the left.

## COMPETING FOR THE DOLLAR

The solicitation of political money is as decentralized and dispersed as American campaigning is. Chaotic organization, inefficient overlap, and even an unseemly scramble for cash are the rule. In this competition the parties find themselves hard pressed to raise money as parties; the individual and personal appeal of a candidate or officeholder is far more effective. In part the party organizations' problems are merely a reflection (and a cause) of the basic difficulty the parties have in controlling and coordinating campaigns for office. But the problems also spring from the fact that it is much easier to raise political money for campaigns (the power and goal-oriented activity of the parties) than it is to raise it for the continuing, monthly costs of party organization. Consequently, most American party organizations limp along on small budgets. For example, it is not uncommon for a state party's organizational costs for a year to be just about the cost of a single senatorial campaign (i.e., less than a million dollars). Periodically, parties try to establish a list of regular monthly contributors to a sustaining fund or to make levies on candidates, but in the long run they often fall back on the funds from a few dinners and a handful of loyal contributors.

The competition for the political dollar has another dimension: the uneasy relationships among national, state, and local levels of the party. The interests of the national party organization are two. First, it wants to bring some order out of the chaos of competing party bodies and committees. And second, in the close competition for political gifts, it wants to ensure an adequate source of funds for itself. Behind all of these at-

**Campaign Finance from the Other Side of the Checkbook**

An unusually reflective and usually candid Hubert Humphrey confided to two interviewers, late in 1974, his great distaste for the fund raising a candidate has to do. His thoughts may indicate some of the reasons the two candidates in 1976 chose to accept public subsidies that forbade them from raising additional money:

"Campaign financing is a curse. It's the most disgusting, demeaning, disenchanting, debilitating experience of a politician's life. It's stinky, it's lousy. I just can't tell you how much I hate it. I've had to break off in the middle of trying to make a decent, honorable campaign and go up to somebody's parlor or to a room and say, 'Gentlemen and ladies, I'm desperate. You've got to help me. My campaign chairman is here and I'm going to step out of the room.' You even have to go through all that kind of fakery. You ask 'em and you just have to feel like a louse. When you are desperate, these are the things you just have to do.

"... And you see people there — a lot of them you don't want to see. And they look at you, and you sit there and you talk to them and tell them what you're for and you need help and, out of the twenty-five who have gathered, four will contribute. And most likely one of them is in trouble and is somebody you shouldn't have had a contribution from...."

From Flora Rheta Schreiber and Stuart Long, "A Candidate's Eye View of Campaign Finance," *The New York Times*, October 13, 1974. © 1974 by The New York Times Company. Reprinted by permission.

A quite similar view came less than two years later from a retiring fund raiser, Harold Willens, who had secured major contributions for the McCarthy and McGovern campaigns in 1968 and 1972. Of that latter year he wrote in *The New York Times:*

"My decision to do it again four years later reflected the fact that the McGovern campaign became another chapter in the antiwar crusade. As in 1968 I cringed for the candidate when we would drag him through the dung heap of fundraising antics and charades, awaken him from desperately needed sleep for a bleary-eyed breakfast with a few fat cats, march others in late at night to "chat" with a candidate close to collapse, or put him through a photographic musical chairs routine at a fat-cat function so that pictures with warm personal notes could be sent to dozens, or hundreds, of potential contributors."

From Harold Willens, "Dogging Fat Cats No More," *The New York Times*, March 23, 1976. © 1976 by The New York Times Company. Reprinted by permission.

tempts by national organizations to exercise some control over the competition for the political dollar there is another, scarcely hidden issue. If the national parties can control more of the business of political finance, they will have strengthened themselves immeasurably against the decentralizing forces of state and local parties.

Historically the Republicans have coped more effectively than the Democrats with these intraparty competings. Until the 1960s the Republicans had a reasonably effective system of coordination centering in a Republican National Finance Committee, which negotiated a budget for all the national organs of the party (including the congressional campaign committees) and assessed fund-raising quotas for the state parties. The system, never fully effective, broke down in the conservative domination by Barry Goldwater in 1964 and in the Nixon-centered fund raising of 1968. The Democrats managed a brief and very ineffective attempt at a similar plan in 1960. What little coordination they have enjoyed has come through the personal force and persuasiveness of the treasurer of the national committee.[8] (The party chairman from 1972 to 1977, Robert Strauss, held that position before assuming the chairmanship.)

The national committees seek funds that will sustain their own year-round activities and that they can disperse to candidates for their campaigns. The former are essential to their existence, but the latter have the potential for drastically altering the basic distribution of power within the party. The implications are tremendous when an incumbent president such as Lyndon Johnson through a vehicle such as his President's Club reverses the direction of monetary flow by collecting funds that might otherwise have gone to local fund raising and then dispersing them back to state and local campaigns. The implications are similar when a Congressional Campaign Committee (the so-called Hill committees), a national committee, or an ad hoc national organization does the same thing. Despite the occasional successes of Democratic presidents at it, the successes continue to be largely Republican. The assorted national organizations of the Republican party spent $40.1 million in the presidential and Congressional campaigns in 1976, while the Democratic committees spent only $19.3 million. The major disparity was in the transactions of the Hill committees. The Republican House and Senate campaign committees spent $11.3 million versus $2 million for their Democratic counterparts.

The main obstacle to centralized party finance remains the voluntary campaign committees of the candidates. Party organizations may systematize their own solicitation of funds, but they do not easily control the solicitations of candidates and their committees. It is the problem of the party organization against the party in government all over again. And

---

[8] See Adamany, *Financing Politics,* for the organization of solicitation within the two Wisconsin parties.

once again the advantage is with the candidates and officeholders. Contributors prefer to give to specific candidates and causes rather than to
the umbrella-like concerns of the party organization. They would rather
be selective themselves than give the party organizations the power to be
selective and, thus, more influential.

## REFORM IN CAMPAIGN FINANCE

The regulation of campaign finance in the United States was for a long
time a jerry-built structure of assorted and not very well integrated federal
and state statutes. Periodically reformers attempted to bring order out of
that legislation and at the same time to strengthen legal controls over the
getting and spending of campaign money. A new episode of reform was
under way in the early 1970s when the Watergate scandals broke over the
country. The result in 1974 was the most extensive federal legislation on
the subject in the history of the Republic.

The 1974 law was, as as usual, set down on an already-existing web of
legislation, superseding some of it and supplementing some of it. Some
of it, in turn, was invalidated by the United States Supreme Court in late
January of 1976. It was then supplemented by amendments passed in
1976. The resulting structure of federal legislation in the late 1970s falls
into two main categories: the limitations on campaign contributions and
spending, and the provisions setting up a system of public funding of national politics.

### Limitations on Contributions and Expenditures

The chief provisions of existing federal law are these:

1. *Restrictions on sources of money:*
   Each individual is limited to a contribution of $1000 per candidate in
     primary elections, $1000 per candidate in the ensuing general elec-
     tion, $5000 to a political action committee, and $20,000 to a national
     party committee. The contributor is also limited to a total of $25,000
     in all such contributions in any one calendar year. (In addition, the
     contributor is also permitted extra expenditures for fund raising and
     for an advertisement supporting a candidate or candidates.)
   Organizations are limited to contributions of $5000 to any candidate
     in any election.
   Corporations and labor unions themselves may not contribute. (They
     may, however, set up "independent" political action committees.)
   Federal employees may not solicit funds from other federal employees
     on the job. The same limitation also applies to state or local employees
     whose activities are financed by federal loans or grants.

The new limits on size of contribution in the 1974 legislation have already curbed the role of the very large contributor. Even with the loopholes (and the possibility that all adults in a family can contribute within the ceiling), there is no possibility that we will again see gifts of the magnitude of Clement Stone's $2 million-plus to Richard Nixon in 1972 or Stewart Mott's in excess of a million to both McCarthy and McGovern. The Motts and Stones will be unlimited only in their personal, independent efforts on behalf of candidates (e.g., newspaper ads). Organizational gifts (such as those of political action committees) have already become more important, as have small contributions and the personal funds of wealthy candidates.

2. *Restrictions on expenditures:*
   If presidential candidates accept federal subsidies for the prenomination and general election campaigns (see below for details), they must agree to spend no more than the sum of the subsidies. They are therefore limited to $12 million before the convention and to $20 million after it (in 1974 dollars). Thus, with the correction for rises in the consumer price index, the limits were $13.1 million and $21.8 million in the 1976 elections. (In addition, national party committees may collectively spend up to two dollars a voter in the presidential election campaign; that allowance totalled $3.2 million in 1976.)
   If presidential and vice-presidential candidates accept the public subsidies, they are also limited to expenditures of no more than $50,000 of their own, or their family's money, on the campaigns.

The 1974 law's limits on spending in House and Senate campaigns were the chief casualties of the Supreme Court's decision of 1976 (*Buckley* v *Valeo*). The challengers to the statutes — an unlikely coalition extending from Senator James Buckley and *Human Events* to Eugene McCarthy and the New York Civil Liberties Union — had argued that restrictions on campaign expenditures infringed the rights of free speech and political activity. The Supreme Court agreed. Expenditure limits, therefore, are permissible only when they are a condition of the voluntary acceptance of public subsidies. Congress could reinstate the expenditure limits on its own campaigns apparently only as a part of a plan for subsidizing them. Candidates, of course, would have to be free to reject the subsidies, as are the presidential candidates. (The restriction of contributions to $1000 makes rejecting subsidies a hazardous option for the presidential contestants.)

3. *Requirements for accounting and reporting:*
   All contributions to a candidate must go through and be accounted for by a single campaign committee.

Each candidate must file quarterly reports on his finances and then
supplement them with reports ten days before the election and thirty
days after it.
All contributors of $100 or more must be reported and identified.

The publicity provisions of earlier legislation have not been notably effective. Reports have always been sketchy at best and missing at worst. But
the new legislation has improved the quality of reporting by centralizing
candidate responsibility in a single committee. In any event, whether it
is because of the new legislation of 1971 and 1974 or the post-Watergate
sensitivity, experts agree that the election of 1976 was the most fully reported in recent history.

### Public Funding of Presidential Campaigns

Although the Congress has not yet been willing to fund its own challengers
from the public treasury, it has embarked on a program of public support
for presidential candidates. The 1976 elections marked its inauguration.
Candidates seeking their party nominations were aided only if they first
passed a private funding "test." They had to raise at least $5000 in con-
tributions of $250 or less in each of at least twenty states. If they so estab-
lished their eligibility, public funds matched every contribution up to
$250 to a total of $5 million. In addition, each of the major parties received
up to $2 million to offset the costs of its national nominating convention.
Provisions for funding the election campaign are somewhat simpler.
Candidates may draw on a public fund for some or all of their expenses
up to the $20 million ceiling. (That provision, of course, presumes suffi-
cient money in the fund created by voluntary check-offs on each year's
individual income tax return.) Minor parties fare less well. They receive
only a fraction of the $20 million maximum and then only *after* the elec-
tion and after they have received at least 5 percent of the vote. (If they
drew at least 5 percent of the vote in the previous election, they can receive
their payment before the election.) It is, in fact, this section dealing with
minor parties that has received a major part of the criticism directed at
the 1974 statute. Critics charge that it will enfeeble minor parties, certainly
making it hard for them to reach major-party status and, in view of the
need to pay cash for many campaign expenses, hard even for them to
finance a modest campaign.[9]

### First Results: 1976 and 1978

The largely new structure of federal regulation and subsidy worked a
number of changes in its first applications in 1976 and 1978. Although any

[9] For an evaluation of this and other public funding plans, see David W. Adamany and
George E. Agree, *Political Money* (Baltimore: Johns Hopkins University Press, 1975).

conclusion based on so short an experience must be tentative, the main results of the new legislation appear to be these:

— Obviously the 1974 law achieved its stated and explicit purpose of lowering the scale of presidential campaign expenditures and of ending the role of the giant contributors to them and to congressional campaigns. At the same time, alternative sources of money — PACs, wealthy candidates, and small contributors — became more valuable and important.

— As expenditure ceilings were lowered for the 1976 presidential campaign, the patterns of spending changed. Candidates cut down less on media advertising and travel costs, more on other advertisements (e.g., billboards), organizers and professional staff, and the traditional paraphernalia of campaigns: buttons, leaflets, and bumper stickers, for example.

— Tighter planning and setting of priorities became the order of the day in presidential camps. Candidates had to select audiences and media "targets" more rigorously (see box). They also had to restrict their organizing and travel; there was by general agreement less activity in the smaller states, for instance.

— Most observers thought the new subsidies and expenditure limits helped Jimmy Carter to the White House. The preconvention grants obviously help the less well known candidate, especially the one with a limited

---

**Scarce Money and Hard Choices**

Public financing of the presidential campaigns in 1976 unquestionably forced the candidates to set priorities in a way not altogether common in American politics. When campaign funds are plentiful and their use relatively unrestricted, candidates are free to "try everything." When they are not, candidates and their campaign managers face hard choices. Stuart Spencer, campaign manager for Gerald Ford in 1976, addressed himself to the problem:

"People accuse us of having written off the black vote. That's a crude way of saying that when you have only $21.8 million to spend in the general election, you have to prioritize. You have to decide where your votes are and go after them.

"We prioritized all sorts of groups. . . . Most were ahead of blacks because our research showed that — based on Carter's demonstrated strength with blacks during the primaries — that we'd be wasting our dollars trying to penetrate the black voter market."

From Finlay Lewis, *Minneapolis Tribune*, January 2, 1977.
Reprinted with permission from the Minneapolis Tribune.

financial base. (They may also have helped Ronald Reagan mount his almost successful challenge to the renomination of an incumbent president.) The grants and limits in the presidential campaign in 1976 erased the usual GOP advantage in spending and prevented the Ford campaign from developing a late media blitz that could conceivably have carried a close election.

In one important way, however, the 1976 experience did not have the result many expected. It has not yet led to public subsidies for elections to Congress. Despite support from the president and some of the leadership in Congress, proposals for extending the subsidies never made it to serious consideration. The main issues were two. There was, first of all, a good deal of concern about voter reaction — that voters would view subsidies as an improper use of tax monies or as a congressional "raid" on the treasury for its own advantage. (In truth, the lack of public support was evident.) The second issue concerned the possible goring of oxen. A few congressmen grumbled that they would be encouraging their own opponents, but the Republicans and many observers thought the plan would further entrench the incumbent Democrats. What scholarly evidence there is on the point suggests that there is indeed a significant relationship between a challenger's level of expenditures and his ability to give an incumbent a close race.[10]

### State Regulation and Financing

To the maze of federal legislation one must add the even more complicated fabric of state regulation. The states have long set at least some limits to campaign activity. Most, for example, have some law prohibiting certain election-day expenditures; all prohibit bribery and vote buying, and some prohibit such practices as buying a voter a drink on election day. Most states also require the making of reports on campaign contributions and expenditures. In general, however, state regulations never even achieved the modest effectiveness of the old federal legislation.

Watergate spurred a new round of state legislation after 1972. The new state legislation on campaign finance was often set in a broader frame that included legislation requiring registration by lobbyists, open meetings by government bodies, and the disclosure of the personal finances of public officeholders. By the 1976 campaigns, consequently, virtually every state had a disclosure statute that forced reports on campaign giving and spending. Many of the states that had long had such requirements tightened them up after Watergate. By the same time about thirty of the states had set limits on expenditures candidates could make, and twenty-two

[10] Stanton A. Glantz, Alan I. Abramowitz, and Michael P. Burkhart, "Election Outcomes: Whose Money Matters?" *Journal of Politics* 34 (1976): 1033–38.

limited contributions. Most of the state limits on expenditures are now constitutionally suspect since the decision in *Buckley* v *Valeo*.

Half of the states have undertaken some form of direct or indirect aid to political campaigns. The majority — fourteen — have taken the indirect route of encouraging private contributions through either tax credits (two) or tax reductions (ten) or both (two). Another eleven directly disperse public funds gotten either from an income tax check-off (like the national government's) or voluntary tax surcharge. Not surprisingly, the former method yields larger sums. Most of the eleven states give the funds to the candidates (as does federal law), but four channel the subsidies to party organizations. For that reason the funding programs in those four states are unquestionably the ones with the most profound implications in this entire body of legislation.[11]

The record of state and federal regulation before 1972 was not one of success. Too many loopholes and too little administration led to a conspicuous ineffectiveness. Moreover, the mass of regulatory legislation had unfortunate side effects. It stimulated the proliferation of candidate committees and the decentralization of candidate finance in order to sidestep the limitation on both individual contributions and candidate expenditures. Furthermore, it encouraged — as does any failure in regulation — a cynicism about the motives of everyone involved. But the post-Watergate legislation begins a new era in campaign regulation. More and more of the legislation reaches the nomination process in addition to the general election campaign. And both state and federal laws increasingly centralize campaign finance in a single committee and thus include more of the total campaign in their scope. It may well be that the reform successes of the 1970s will break out of the old cycle of hopeful reform followed by disappointing results that has so long characterized attempts to end the excesses of American campaign finance.[12]

## RESOURCES AND THE FUTURE OF THE PARTIES

We have failed to cope with campaign money in the past at least in part because large numbers of Americans view the question with a mixture of unrealism and self-righteousness. They accuse the wealthy candidate who finances his own campaign of buying public office; the Kennedy campaign for the presidency, for example, was dogged by references to "Jack's jack." If the candidate relies on large contributions from a business or labor

[11] For a fuller explanation of state policies, see Herbert E. Alexander, *Financing Politics* (Washington: Congressional Quarterly, 1976), Chap. 7. To be exact, the District of Columbia is here considered a "state," and thus the universe is 51 "states."
[12] For a survey of these and other issues, as well as for a review of recent literature on them, see David Adamany, "Money, Politics, and Democracy: A Review Essay," *American Political Science Review* 71 (1977): 289–304.

group, he may be accused of selling out to special interests. And yet the average voter is generally unwilling to make a political contribution; many indeed will not even allocate a dollar of their income tax payment (at no cost to themselves) to the fund that will support presidential campaigns. One can only suppose that many Americans think a political stork brings campaign funds.

Beyond the general problem of voter attitudes, there are three more pervasive problems in campaign finance. The first is the basic one of influence in the parties and electoral processes. Political contributors have political goals and incentives, just as do activists who contribute their skills and labor to the party organization or to a candidate's campaign. Large numbers of Americans wonder what kinds of demands or expectations accompany their financial contributions. Money is obviously a major resource of American politics, and its contributors clearly acquire some form of political influence. What we have not been able to decide is the nature of the influence and the differences, both quantitative and qualitative, between it and the influence that results from nonmoney contributions to the parties and candidates.

It is not easy to specify with certainty the goals or incentives that motivate the financial contributor. Very likely they come from the same range of incentives that stir the activist to contribute his or her time to the party organization: patronage, preferment, a political career; personal, social, or psychological satisfactions; an interest, issue, and ideology. Unquestionably the chief incentive is the combination of interest, issue and ideology — the desire, that is, to influence the making or administration of some kind of public policy. The concentration of PAC contributions on Congressional committee chairmen is a case in point. Their desire may be for direct access or for the ear of the powerful. More commonly, it is only a desire to elect public officials with values and preferences that promise a sympathy for the goals of the contributor. Thus the demands of the contributor are largely indirect; certainly very few contributors seek a direct quid pro quo.

Two brief footnotes to the subject of financial contributors and their goals ought to be added: (1) These contributors are not a group completely separate from nonmoney contributors; many of the smaller contributors especially are also activists who give time, skills, and labor to the party. In 1976 more than half of the workers in campaigns also made financial campaigns, according to the SRC survey. But less than 7 percent of the nonworkers did. (2) The general concern for the goals of contributors is accentuated in American politics because of the failure of the American parties to develop either nonpolitical or widely distributed sources of money. The British Labour party, for example, distributes the burden of finance more widely by means of individual and group payment of membership dues. Some local Labour parties also raise substantial sums by running soccer pools; the advantage of such methods is that contributors to the parties do so indirectly and thus do not make any political demands on them.

Second, in addition to the issue of influence on policy there is the question of power within the party. The status quo in American political finance supports parties in government and helps them maintain their independence from the party organizations. As long as candidates and officeholders continue to finance their own primary and general election campaigns, they block the organizations' control of access to public office. Unquestionably the reluctance of Congress and state legislatures to disturb the present patterns of political finance grows in large part from their satisfaction with the political independence it ensures them. Despite the spate of reforms of recent years, candidate spending — as opposed to party organization spending — remains entrenched. The candidate, rather than the party, gets and spends large sums of money. Even in the sorties into public financing of campaigns, the funds go to candidates (and not to party organizations) in all but a few states. To be sure, there has been some indirect supporting of a party role — the federal legislation permitting party committees to spend beyond candidate expenditure ceilings, for example — but it is far less than would be necessary to establish strong and disciplined parties with sanctions over their candidates and officeholders.

Third, party reform, especially reform in campaign finance, never affects all individuals and parties alike. It works to some people's advantage and others' disadvantage. The cumulative effect of the reforms of the 1970s will surely be to diminish the influence of wealthy contributors and to make the "little" contributor more valuable than ever. (In that respect one ought to note, however, that it is hardly certain that one contributor of $10,000 actually made more effective demands on the recipient than 100 contributors of $100 will.) New advantages may well also accrue to the technicians who can raise small gifts as well as to group contributors and incumbents. New limits on contributions may, indeed, put a new premium on the noncash contribution in politics. The ability of labor to turn out a disciplined vote without a major expenditure of cash may assume a greatly enhanced value.

The American way of campaign finance reflects the American way of politics. Its costs reflect the vastness of the country, the many elective offices on many levels of government, the localism of American politics, and the unbridled length of our campaigns for office. The domination of spending by candidates reflects our candidate-dominated campaigns, and more generally, the dominance within American parties of the party in government. The importance of the mass media in major American campaigns speaks volumes about the media themselves while it also reflects the sheer size of our constituencies. By contrast, campaign finance in Great Britain involves far smaller sums more firmly in the control of the party organizations. But in Britain there is free time on the government-run BBC and a long-standing tradition of the "soft sell" in all forms of public persuasion. Moreover, the election campaign runs for only about three weeks, and the average constituency in the House of Commons has less than one-fifth as many people as the average American congressional district. And, most significantly, there is no larger constituency, no office with a constituency as vast as most American states, not to mention the American presidency's national constituency.

Aided by institutions such as the direct primary and the office-block ballot and supported by their ability to recruit the resources they need, the American parties in government thus largely escape the control of party organizations. In many states and localities, indeed, they dominate them. But at what price? Certainly at the price of a loss of cohesion as a party in government — for example, in the loss of a unified presence as party representatives in American legislatures. Certainly, too, at the price of a weakening of party organization, not only vis-à-vis the party in government, but also internally in terms of its ability to achieve the goals of its activists. And nowhere in the life of the parties is the competition between party in government and party organization any clearer than in the competition for campaign funds and campaign control. As the costs of campaigning rise and as all participants are forced to shift to a cash economy of enormous magnitude, the future is with the sector of the party with access to those cash resources. So far the advantage is clearly with the candidates and officeholders.

# V

# THE
# PARTY IN
# GOVERNMENT

The charge that the American parties cannot govern is an old one, and few scholars of American politics have made it as pungently as E. E. Schattschneider:

Yet, when all is said, it remains true that the roll calls demonstrate that the parties are unable to hold their lines on a controversial public issue when the pressure is on.

The condition . . . constitutes the most important single fact concerning the American parties. He who knows this fact, and knows nothing else, knows more about American parties than he who knows everything except this fact. What kind of party is it that, having won control of government, is unable to govern? [1]

In campaigns political parties in effect try to convince the American electorate that it does matter that they, rather than the opposition party, win office. But can it matter that much when the parties in Congress are so easily fragmented in votes on important issues? For instance, in the roll call votes in 1978 in which a majority of one party disagreed with a majority of the other party, the average Democrat in Congress voted with his party only 64 percent of the time and the average Republican only 67 percent. [2]

Yet, in the face of this and other evidence that the American parties do not and cannot govern, it still remains true that party lines, however loosely drawn, are the chief lines in American legislative voting behavior. In the roll calls of Congress and the states, there is a degree of party cohesion that cannot be lightly dismissed. Furthermore, recent scholarship suggests that the party winning the presidency even succeeds in carrying out a goodly portion of its party platform. [3]

The evidence on party government in the United States thus points in a number of directions. It suggests that the parties do not fail entirely

[1] E. E. Schattschneider, *Party Government* (New York: Rinehart, 1942), pp. 131–32. Italics in the original have been eliminated.
[2] *Congressional Quarterly Almanac* 34 (1978): 30-C.
[3] Gerald M. Pomper, *Elections in America* (New York: Dodd, Mead, 1968), Chap. 8.

in enacting their programs into public policy. And yet it betrays the frequency with which officeholders of the same party disagree on matters of public policy. More surely, it suggests that an individual's assessment of the parties' ability to govern depends on how and to what extent he expects the parties to govern.

Some distinctions are important here. We are talking of *party* government, not merely the governing and policy making of office holders elected on party tickets. Certainly men and women who seek legislative or executive office do intend to govern, to take their responsibilities seriously, but that is not the issue. We are talking about the ability of public officials of the same party to enact the program of their party. If it is *party* government about which we inquire, which parts of the party do we expect to set policy and which will govern by it? All three sectors, or just the party in government? By the entire party in government? Or is it possible that the executive party has propensities and abilities to govern different from those of the legislative party?

It is well to remember, too, that although the three sectors of the party are brought together in the search for power at elections, each has its own goals and motives. The activists of the party organization may seek to translate a program or ideology into policy, but they may also seek patronage jobs, other forms of reward or preference, the sensations of victory, or the defeat of a hated opposition. The party's voters may be stimulated by an issue, a program, or an ideology, but they also respond to personalities, to incumbency ("time for a change"), to abstract and traditional loyalties to a candidate or party, or to the urging of friends and family. The candidates and officeholders seek the office, its tangible rewards, its intangible satisfactions, its opportunities to make public decisions. The important point is that none of the three sectors is committed wholly — or possibly even predominantly — to the capture of public office for the purpose of working out party policies or enacting them into law.

The classic American statement on party government (or "party responsibility") was made in the late 1940s by a committee of the American Political Science Association in a report entitled *Toward a More Responsible Two-Party System.*[4] It argued that the American parties ought to articulate more specific and comprehensive policy programs, nominate candidates pledged to those programs, and then see to it that their successful candidates enact the programs while they are in office. In other words, the major parties ought to serve as the mechanisms through which American voters could choose between competing programs, and through which the winning majority of voters could be assured of the enactment of its choice.

---

[4] The report was published by Rinehart in 1950. It also appears as a supplement to the September, 1950, issue of the *American Political Science Review.*

In such terms the question of party government (or responsibility) concerns not just the nature of the parties but also the nature of the American democracy itself. If the parties were to become policy initiators, they would assume a central representative role in the American democracy. They would bring great, amorphous majorities in the American electorate into alliance with groups of officeholders by means of some kind of party program or platform. They would forge a new representative link between the mass democratic electorate and the powerful few in government. Or, to put the issue another way, responsible parties would bring electorates closer to the choices of government by giving them a way of registering a choice on policy alternatives. In part those choices might be "before the fact" (in the mobilization of grassroots support behind proposed programs), and in part they might be post facto judgments on the stewardship of two different, distinguishable parties in government. Behind the proposal is thus an attempt to restore initiative and significant choice to the great number of voters.

The critics of such proposals for party government have concentrated on one insistent theme: the nonideological, heterogeneous, and pragmatic nature of the American parties. They argue that agreement on and enforcement of a coherent policy program is therefore very difficult, if not impossible. Yet the party organizations are increasingly oriented toward programs and ideology — and thus toward the uses of governmental authority for specific policy goals. There was a time when the activists of the party organization contested elections for the spoils at stake: jobs, contracts, honors, access, and other forms of special consideration. It made little difference to them what uses public officeholders made of the governmental power in their hands. That time is passing. As more and more citizens are attracted to the party organizations and electorates for reasons of policy, important intraparty pressure builds for some degree of party responsibility.

In other words, the general question of the role of parties within the institutions of government is really two questions. First, it is a question of the party's contribution to the decision making of public officials, of the party's role in a democratic political system. These concerns one may call the issue of the party's impact on the broader political system. But the relationship of party to government is also a question of the government's impact on the party. The achievement of party goals (the goals of all three sectors) is closely related to the holding of governmental power. But in what way? What, to put it bluntly, does governmental power do for the parties? What kind of rewards does it generate for the men and women who have invested so much in politics and the party? How does it contribute to the health and vitality of the party and its various sectors?

Talk of more programmatic and disciplined political parties leads always to the European parties, especially those of England. Parliamentary institutions foster the kind of legislative cohesion and discipline — the sharply drawn party lines — that the advocates of responsible parties have in mind. Party leaders in Britain and on the continent, especially those of the parties of the left, also seek to enforce the party's program on its legislators. In some cases they have succeeded — in many of the socialist and communist parties, among others. In others they have not, but even in these cases the national party leaders speak powerfully for the party's program. One often sees a concerted effort on the part of the party in government (all of which sits in Parliament) and the party organization to carry out a program that was adopted with the help of the party members at an earlier party conference. Indeed, so strong is party discipline in the legislative process in some European countries that scholars complain about the decline of parliaments, and journalists write darkly of "partyocracy." Ironically, in these circles it is not uncommon to hear envious talk of the flexible, nondogmatic American parties and uncontrolled American legislatures.

The European experience is important for perspective and for the comparison of American party practice with parties in parliamentary regimes. It is additionally important because the European variety of party government, with its focus on parliamentary discipline, has dominated the thinking of many Americans about party government. Any change in the American parties toward greater responsibility, however, will probably follow no conventional route, European or otherwise. The role the parties now have in American politics and the roles to which they move will be as uniquely American as the institutional complex of American federalism, separation of powers, and electoral processes. Especially in view of the power of the executive in American government, it is necessary to look beyond the legislature to the executive party for the ability to convert party goals or platforms into public policy.

The first two chapters of this part examine the present role of the political party in the organization and operation of the three branches of government. They are basically concerned with the degrees of party direction or party cohesion in legislative and executive policy decisions. (Needless to say, most Americans would consider party direction in judicial decision making grossly improper.) The chapters deal also with the relationship between party organization and the party in government, especially with the ability of the latter to achieve the goals of the former. In short, they deal with the impact of internalized party loyalties and external party influences on public officials. The third chapter of this part faces the general question of party government, its desirability and its possibility. It is especially concerned with the question of whether the new programmatic orientations within the parties create conditions hospitable to the development of party government.

# 14

## Party
## and Partisans in
## the Legislature

The political party assumes an obvious, very public form — yet a very shadowy role — in American legislatures. In the legislatures of forty-nine states and in the United States Congress, the political parties organize majority and minority power, and the legislative leaders and committee chairmen are party oligarchs.[1] Yet, despite the appearance and panoply of party power, the voting on crucial issues often crosses party lines, not to mention party pledges and platforms. The party in many forms stalks the American legislatures; yet the effect of party effort and loyalty is often negligible. On this paradox turns much of the scholarly concern and reformist zeal expended on American legislatures.

The character of the American legislative party has been deeply affected by the American separation of powers. In a parliamentary regime, such as that of Great Britain, a majority party or a multiparty coalition in the Parliament must cohere in support of the cabinet (and its government), thus creating a constitutional presumption and pressure on behalf of unity within the legislative party. When the parliamentary majority no longer supports the cabinet, the cabinet falls. Either reorganization of the cabinet or a reshuffling of the legislative coalition supporting it ensues, or else the Parliament is sent home to face a new election.

No such institutional and constitutional pressures weigh on American legislators. They may divide on, dispute with, or reject executive programs, even if that executive is of their own party, without similar consequences. In these American legislatures, the party role is not institutionalized as it is in parliaments. The American legislature may not run as smoothly without party cohesion and discipline, but it can run, and executives survive its faithlessness.

---

[1] The Nebraska legislature is chosen in nonpartisan elections. On the subjects of this chapter, see the bibliography of Charles O. Jones and Randall B. Ripley, *The Role of Political Parties in Congress* (Tucson: University of Arizona Press, 1966), and the relevant parts of the bibliography in Malcolm E. Jewell and Samuel C. Patterson, *The Legislative Process in the United States*, 3rd ed. (New York: Random House, 1977).

## PARTY ORGANIZATIONS IN LEGISLATURES

In forty-nine of the state legislatures and the Congress, the members come to their legislative tasks as elected candidates of a political party. The ways in which they form and behave as a legislative party, however, differ enormously. In some states the legislative party scarcely can be said to exist; in others it dominates the legislative process through an almost daily regimen of party caucuses. Parties in the great number of state legislatures and in the Congress fall comfortably in the territory between these two poles.

### Parties in the Congress

Party organization in the United States Congress stands as something of a benchmark for observations of the American legislatures because it is the best known of them. Both parties in both houses of Congress caucus at the beginning of each congressional session to select the party leadership: a party leader, an assistant leader, a whip and assistant whips, and a party policy committee. In addition, the party caucus presents its candidates for the position of Speaker of the House and president pro tempore of the Senate, and it sets up procedures for the appointment of party members to the regular committees of the chamber. In effect, then, the basic unit of party organization, the caucus (or the conference, as some prefer to call it), begins the business of organizing the chamber. From its decisions rises the machinery of the party as a party (the leaders, whips, policy committees) and the organization of the chamber itself (the presiding officer and the committees).

And yet, for all the machinery they create the parties in Congress do not easily organize themselves for action as parties. When the party caucuses or conferences do meet on important issues during the session, they only rarely undertake to bind the individual members. Indeed, they do not even meet regularly during the session. Moreover, the policy committees set up in the Reorganization Act of 1946 have not succeeded as broadly based instruments of party policy making or strategy setting, even though they were created for the "formulation of overall legislative policy of the respective parties," as the act puts it. One study found that they lacked any internal agreement on party policy and that instead of being a collective party leadership, they had lapsed into the practice of representing the assorted blocs and wings of the party.[2] Despite the original hopes, the policy committees have operated primarily as advisory boards and channels of communication between the party leaders and influentials and the full party membership.

[2] David B. Truman, *The Congressional Party* (New York: Wiley, 1959), pp. 126–30.

Dissatisfaction with leadership control of the policy committees breaks out periodically, especially among the liberal Democrats. In 1963 in an attack on the "Senate Establishment" Senator Joseph Clark (Pennsylvania) included strictures about conservative and leadership domination of the Democratic Policy Committee.[3] In the same year the overthrow of Representative Charles Halleck, the Republican leader, by Representative Gerald Ford was accompanied by an increase in the number of younger Republicans on that party's policy committee in the House. But despite the agitation, the policy committees remain at best a means for increasing consultation and communication within the legislative party; they are a very long way from becoming the authors of party policy. In the reform of party machinery in the 1970s the House Democrats, however, formed a new Steering and Policy Committee with elected representatives from the caucus. Since 1975 it has at least begun to function as the party's Committee on Committees. However, the Democratic liberals of the House, in the absence of an effective House Democratic policy committee, some years ago formed a policy committee of their own: the Democratic Study Group. The DSG does some staff research, takes policy stands, and represents the liberal views of its members. It has even developed its own whip system.[4]

To the extent that there is "party policy" in the houses of Congress, it is largely set by the party leadership. The floor leaders and the powerful figures of the party consult widely throughout the party, but the final codification of party policy, the sensing of a will or consensus, rests primarily on their judgment. If they are of the president's party, their actions and decisions are limited by his legislative program and his influence within the Congress. Within the nonpresidential party, the leadership in the House and Senate may act not only without a continuing check by the legislative party but also without a continuing check by any party organ or spokesman. Senate party leaders such as Lyndon Johnson in the 1950s and Everett Dirksen in the 1960s, in fact, established themselves as spokesmen for both the legislative and the national parties.[5]

What emerge as the decisions and priorities of the party leadership, however, are not really "party policy" — except in the sense that they are voiced by leaders of the legislative party. They are rather an amalgam of or a negotiated compromise among the goals of the senior party members (who hold committee power), the party leaders themselves, the rank and

[3] Joseph S. Clark, *The Senate Establishment* (New York: Hill and Wang, 1963).
[4] See Arthur G. Stevens, Arthur H. Miller, and Thomas E. Mann, "Mobilization of Liberal Strength in the House, 1955–1970: The Democratic Study Group," *American Political Science Review* 68 (1974): 667–81.
[5] More generally on party leadership in the Congress, see Ralph K. Huitt, "Democratic Party Leadership in the Senate," *American Political Science Review* 55 (1961): 333–44; and Randall B. Ripley, "The Party Whip Organizations in the United States House of Representatives," *American Political Science Review* 58 (1964): 561–76.

file of the legislative party, and (in one party) the president. They rarely flow from any national party program or platform. They speak instead of the powers and perquisites of the legislature, the need to support or oppose a president, and the demands of the legislative constituencies. The party leaders, in other words, do not enforce a prior party policy; they "make" policy for and with their fellow legislators in an ad hoc way. Their party policy is purely that of the legislative party. In view of the party leadership's brokerage role in making it, therefore, it is mandatory that party leaders come from the "mainstream," the dominant wing of the party.[6]

### Parties in State Legislatures

Among the state legislatures are those in which daily caucuses, binding party discipline, and autocratic party leadership make for a party far more potent than exists in the two houses of Congress (see box). But there are also legislatures — especially those of the traditional one-party states — in which party organization is perceptibly weaker than in the Congress. Even in states having a complete apparatus of party organization, the parties fail more frequently than the congressional parties to make it operate effectively. The party caucuses in Congress at least maintain cohesion in their initial organizational tasks; they always agree on candidates for the presiding officers. State legislative parties have on occasion found themselves too riven by factionalism even to organize the legislature. In January of 1965, for example, the Democrats of the New York legislature, the majority party in both houses, split so badly that they could not agree on a single set of leadership candidates. After a hiatus of a month during which the unorganized legislature could conduct no business, the Republicans threw their votes to one of the Democratic factions and thus elected leaders for both chambers.

In a one-party state, the party caucus has little excuse for being. Disagreement over organization, leadership positions, and policy issues in these states usually falls along factional lines within the party or along the lines of followings of powerful personages. In the heyday of the Long dynasty in Louisiana, one Democratic faction adhered to the Longs and others supported their opponents. In this particular case and in others as well, factional lines built on personal and family followings coincide with differing regional loyalties. Alternatively, the legislative caucuses in one-party states may reflect ideological lines; from 1910 to the 1930s in Wisconsin, the La Follette Progressive Republicans organized one legislative caucus, the conservative Republicans another, and the very feeble Democrats a third.

Party leadership in the state legislatures assumes a number of forms.

[6] Robert L. Peabody, *Leadership in Congress* (Boston: Little, Brown, 1976), Chap. 16.

## The Party Caucus in Pennsylvania

The party caucuses of the United States legislatures are generally secret, and that secrecy encourages speculation about the grossest forms of party coercion in them. One observer of Pennsylvania politics writes about the legislative caucuses of that state in a way that is closer to the political reality of the caucuses than the dark suspicions of press and public.

"A politically significant part of the caucuses' work is, of course, on policy bills that affect the fortunes of the governor and the parties themselves. Between 10 and 15 per cent of the bills voted on in recent legislative sessions have found the two parties opposed to each other as parties on the floor. Here the caucuses, again principally the majority's caucus, may devote weeks and even months to working out a party position on an issue acceptable to most party members. Negotiation rather than pressure would be the best noun to describe this process. The very slender margin of control each party has had when it has been in control in recent sessions has made it necessary to secure nearly total agreement of the members on a bill. Sometimes the caucus may re-write an unpopular bill that the governor needs to have passed. The House Republican caucus in 1963, for example, scrapped Gov. Scranton's dual proposal for a one-half per cent rise in the state sales tax, and extension of that tax to cover clothing. Instead, it worked up a bill — successfully as it turned out — raising the tax by a full one per cent, but limiting the tax to items previously covered. All but one of the House Republicans supported this measure on the floor. All but two House Democrats voted against it."

Kenneth T. Palmer, "The Pennsylvania General Assembly:
Politics and Prospects," a paper on the state legislatures
prepared for the Pennsylvania Assembly, 1968.

---

The traditional floor leaders and whips exist in most. In others the Speaker of the House or a spokesman for the governor may mobilize the party's legislators. State party officials, unlike the relatively powerless national party officials vis-à-vis Congress, may have a powerful voice in the legislative party. As Lockard reported of the heyday of party control in the Connecticut lower house

the "outside" party leaders are in daily attendance at the capitol and can be seen in corridor conferences with the great and small alike. Each party chairman sits in on his respective party policy conferences and not infrequently he is the real leader of the conference. With few exceptions the men who reach the party pinnacle of the state chairmanship can expect (and they certainly receive) proper deference from their fellows in the legislature.[7]

[7] W. Duane Lockard, "Legislative Politics in Connecticut," *American Political Science Review* 48 (1954): 167.

But whatever may be their relationship with state party leaders, the legislative leaders enjoy enormous power in the day-to-day workings of the legislature. Their influence on party caucuses is great, and they do not often have to contend with steering or policy committees in state legislatures.

One is probably warranted in saying that the range of extremes in party influence in state legislatures is in recent years narrowing. Jewell and Patterson write about one state:

> For many years the classic example of a powerful caucus was found in New Jersey, where the majority party caucus in each house met daily and decided which bills would be passed and which would die. . . . The power of the caucus was so great that the standing committees had no significant functions and seldom met. In recent years, however, the caucuses in both houses have reduced the scope of their activities, and now take action only on a limited number of bills designated by the leaders as party policy measures. As a consequence, the committee system in the New Jersey legislature has begun to develop some independent authority.[8]

As the strong party discipline of a few states dissipates and as two-party competition brings legislative parties to states that had not known them, practice in the states becomes more similar, more homogeneous.

## THE EFFECTS AND INFLUENCE OF PARTY

The shape of party power is clearly evident in American legislatures. But power for what? For organizing party support for a set of party programs or merely for parceling out the perquisites of legislative office? Or does the legislative party seek both policy and perquisites?

### In the Congress

The parties in the United States Congress have amply illustrated over the last century that they can impose party sanctions on only one issue: the failure of a member of the legislative party to support its presidential candidate. A congressman or senator can freely vote against the party's platform, majority, or leadership — or against the program of his party's president. But he risks punishment if he undercuts his party's presidential candidate. In 1925 the Republican caucus in the Senate expelled Senators La Follette, Ladd, Frazier, and Brookhart after they had supported La Follette and the Progressive ticket in the 1924 elections. That decision also robbed the four senators of their Republican committee assignments and seniority.

In 1965 the Democratic caucus in the House invoked a lesser sanction

---

[8] Jewell and Patterson, *The Legislative Process in the United States*, 3rd ed., pp. 159–60; the authors also cite an unpublished paper by Alan Rosenthal and the Eagleton Institute of Politics, *Studies of the New Jersey Legislature* (New Brunswick, 1970).

on two Democrats from the South who had supported the Republican presidential candidate, Barry Goldwater, in the 1964 elections. Although they were not expelled from the party, they were stripped of their legislative seniority and placed below even the new congressmen of the 1964 class in committee seniority. In 1968 the same fate befell Representative John Rarick, a Democrat of Louisiana, for supporting George Wallace. Disloyalty in presidential elections is not always punished, however. A number of conservative Democratic congressmen rejected the presidential candidacy of George McGovern in 1972 — and a few even supported President Richard Nixon — without suffering any consequences. In dissent, too, there is safety in numbers.

Beyond these rare disciplinary actions, the party organizations in Congress can exert informal pressure. The president's wishes and influence are often funneled through his party's leaders. They confer with him and carry his proposals to the Congress, and, in fact, they are often called "his" leaders in the Congress. In other instances the legislative leaders may report and transmit the feelings of party leaders outside of the Congress. But as they try to organize consensus within the Congress, they organize it chiefly around the image and interests of the legislative party — around the congressional view of the nation's problems and around its concern for its perquisites and reputation. Their role is classically that of the broker trying to mediate between the local pressures of congressional constituencies and the imperatives of national policy making, and trying also to form majorities out of disparate views and loyalties within the party. The chief limit to their success is always the need of the individual congressman to satisfy a constituency in order to win reelection. Responsiveness to the constituency often outweighs the calls for party unity in Congress.[9]

Attempts to build party discipline in Congress have been undercut in the past by the power of the committees and by a tradition of seniority that awards committee chairmanships to legislators of longest service. The independence of the committees places them, as a system of influence, squarely in opposition to any influence that the parties might exert. Seniority as a key to power in the committees puts a premium on getting reelected rather than on party loyalty or regularity within Congress. So attempts of the parties to reform seniority and the committee system — such as those of the House Democrats in the 1970s — are nothing less than struggles for control of the business of Congress. The Democrats of the House succeeded by modifying the power of committee chairmen and establishing the principle that the party caucuses would vote every two years to approve the continuance in power of every committee chairman. Indeed, as a result of the reforms three Democratic chairmen who had held

[9] David R. Mayhew, *Congress: The Electoral Connection* (New Haven: Yale University Press, 1974).

their positions by reason of seniority were deposed in 1975. As committee power was diminished one more barrier to the influence of party organization was removed.

## In the State Legislatures

In some state legislatures, party leadership and organization operate far more effectively than they do in the Congress. Positions of party leadership and committee power much more frequently go to legislators loyal to the party and to its program. Furthermore, either the party leaders, the party speaking through a periodic caucus decision, or the party's governor or state committee may expect the legislator to support the party program or stand on a particular issue. For excessive lapses of party loyalty state legislators may suffer sanctions inconceivable in the United States Congress. Their influence may wane in the legislature, and they may ultimately lose positions of power. In a patronage state they may find that the applicants they sponsor fare less well than formerly. They may also find in the next election campaign that they no longer receive campaign funds from the state or local party, or worse yet, that the party is supporting competitors in the primaries.

Clearly the parties in some of the competitive, two-party state legislatures have advanced the art of discipline far beyond its state in the Congress. Their contrast with Congress and the less assertive legislative parties of other states affords an opportunity to examine the determinants of such control. Disciplinary success in some state legislatures can be attributed to the following reasons among others.

*Absence of Competing Centers of Power.*   In the Congress the committees have traditionally been the centers of legislative power. A vast amount of the real business of the Congress goes on in them. They are a set of screens that sift through the great mass of legislative proposals for those relatively few nuggets of legislative metal. The result is the creation of important centers of power in the Congress that owe nothing to the parties and do not necessarily reflect the party organization or aims. (In fact, one can argue that since seniority and its power accrue to congressmen from non-competitive one-party areas, they are definitely unrepresentative of the party in the country at large.)

In the states, on the other hand, legislators accumulate less seniority (turnover is greater), and deference to seniority in allocating positions of power is far less common. A 1950s survey of the state legislatures concluded that seniority "figured prominently" in the selection of committee chairmen in only fourteen senates and twelve lower houses in the states.[10]

---

[10] Belle Zeller (ed.), *American State Legislatures* (New York: Crowell, 1954), p. 197.

The parties are freer to appoint their loyalists to positions of legislative power; the committees and other legislative agencies of the states generally operate as instruments of party power in a way they cannot in the Congress.[11]

*Patronage and Preferences.* Patronage and other forms of governmental preference still exist in some states to a far greater extent than they do in the national government. Especially in the hands of a vigorous and determined governor these rewards may be potent inducements to party discipline in state legislatures. The legislator who ignores his party, if it is the party of the governor, may not be able to secure the political appointments that his constituents and local party workers have been waiting for. Conversely, the loyal and faithful party legislator is amply rewarded. In the Congress little such patronage remains with which to induce party discipline. Its last, gaudy twilight came in the early 1930s as Franklin Roosevelt mustered what remained of the federal patronage and told his patronage chief, Postmaster General James A. Farley, not to dole out the jobs until the voting records were in from the first congressional session.

*Influence of the State Party Organization.* The state legislator is subject to far more sanction and control from his state party organization than is the member of Congress from the feeble national committee of the party. In the states the party organization and the legislative party are far more apt to be allies. State party leaders may inhibit the political ambitions of party mavericks or deny them advancement within the party, especially in states in which they can control the nomination processes. They may even prevail on local parties to deny renomination to the disloyal. Indeed, state party leaders may occupy positions of legislative leadership; powerful figures such as the former Democratic Speaker of the California Assembly, Jesse ("Big Daddy") Unruh, combined state party influence with legislative leadership. Lockard reported that Republican legislators in Rhode Island had "a policy committee comprised of important senators, a few representatives, the state party chairman, and a few members of the state central committee." [12] By contrast, the national political party is relatively powerless in dealing with its congressional parties. Even so powerful a party figure as Franklin Roosevelt was unable to purge a group of conservative Democrats for failing to support his program. Congressmen are protected by decentralized party power. State legislators are not.

*Electoral Dependence of State Legislators.* State legislators are far more dependent on the local and state party for nomination and election than

---

[11] On seniority in state legislatures generally see Jewell and Patterson, *The Legislative Process in the United States,* 3rd ed., Chap. 8.

[12] W. Duane Lockard, *New England State Politics* (Princeton: Princeton University Press, 1959), p. 218.

are the members of Congress. And what the local party has given, it may take away. Congressmen and senators build their own political organizations, their coteries of local supporters, and their own sources of campaign financing. But state legislators are less well known and therefore more dependent. In some states the parties control the election of state legislators to such an extent that these positions approach an "elective patronage," which the party awards to loyal toilers in its organizational ranks. (About 70 percent of the candidates for the Pennsylvania House of Representatives in the election of 1958 had held some party office.)[13] Even where control of elections is less certain, a lack of party support creates unwelcome campaign problems.

*Greater Political Homogeneity.* Greater party cohesion in some state legislatures reflects also the greater homogeneity of state parties. Although a legislative party in Congress reflects the full range of differences within the nation, that same party in any given state embraces a narrower spectrum of interests and ideologies. This greater political homogeneity of the states produces legislative parties in which the ranges of differences and disagreements are smaller and in which there are fewer sources of internal conflict. The political culture of the state also is more homogeneous, and in some cases more tolerant of party discipline over legislators than is the national constituency. Legislative party strength, for example, has traditionally flourished in the northeastern part of the country (Rhode Island, Connecticut, Pennsylvania, New Jersey, for example), the states of party organizational strength, patronage, weak primaries, and, one infers, a political culture tolerant of the exercise of political muscle.

## PARTY COHESION IN LEGISLATIVE VOTING

Party organization in Congress and the state legislatures — with caucuses, leaders, whips, and policy committees — is only the most apparent, overt manifestation of the party in the legislature. Its efforts on behalf of party unity and discipline among its legislators are tangible, even if difficult to document. But party influence in legislatures is broader, more pervasive, than the enforcing activities of the organized legislative party. "Party" in a broader, more figurative sense also may operate "within" the legislator as a series of internalized loyalties and frameworks for organizing his legislative decisions. To speak of party only in the organizational sense of leaders and caucuses, therefore, is to miss the richness and complexity of "party" influence on the legislative process. It is also to risk an overestimation of its importance.

---

[13] Frank J. Sorauf, *Party and Representation* (New York: Atherton, 1963), p. 86.

The legislator often faces sharply conflicting expectations for his vote. The cues, even the articulate demands, he or she gets from the constituency electorate may differ from the demands of the more ideological and militant souls who make up the party organization in the constituency. And one or both may be at odds with the presidential or gubernatorial party interests. Then, too, party pressures often conflict with nonparty pressures, such as those of nonparty organizations, the interests of the constituency itself, and the values of the legislator's own belief system. The dilemmas arising from these conflicts are the staple of legislative conflict.

Although no single legislative decision is in any sense typical of the work of even one legislature, an illustration of the cross-cutting influences may be useful. The continuing financial crisis of New York City came back to the Congress in 1978. In order to enable New York to sell its bonds — and thus to avert bankruptcy — the Congress agreed to guarantee up to $1.5 billion of the city's bonds. The vote for passage in the Senate was 53–27, with Democrats voting 35–12 and Republicans 18–15. Both parties were, therefore, in the majority with the Democrats providing more support for a bill that had the support of a Democratic administration. At the same time the vote also illustrated how easily the parties in the Senate fragment under constituency and regional-ideological considerations. Only three senators from the urban, industrial states of the Northeast and the Midwest voted against the bill. But in the southern, southwestern, mountain, and western states the vote totalled sixteen for the bill and twenty-four against.

Gauging the various party influences on legislative behavior is no easy matter. But the collective consequences of party influence ought logically to be apparent in the actions of legislatures. The proof of the pudding comes as the roll calls begin. If the legislative party is to govern, it must be able somehow to muster cohesive support for party positions on policy issues.

## Incidence of Party Cohesion

Answers always depend on the form of the question, and so it is with the question of just how much cohesion or discipline the American parties generate in legislatures. The answer depends to a considerable extent on the operational definition of the term "cohesion."

One more or less classic measure of party cohesion in legislatures has been the "party vote," any legislative roll call in which 90 percent or more of the members of one party vote yes and 90 percent or more of the other party vote no. By such a stringent test, party discipline appears frequently in the British House of Commons but far less often in American legislatures. Julius Turner found that from 1921 through 1948 only 17 percent of the roll calls in the House of Representatives met such a criterion of party discipline. In the 1950s and 1960s it dropped steadily to about 2 or 3 per-

**TABLE 14.1   Party Cohesion in Nonunanimous Roll Calls in Selected State Legislatures**

| State and Year(s) | Percentage of Roll Calls with Majority vs. Majority | | Average Index of Cohesion (Median Session)[a] | | | |
|---|---|---|---|---|---|---|
| | Senate | House | Senate D | R | House D | R |
| Pennsylvania (1959) | 82 | 29 | 82 | 90 | — | — |
| Massachusetts (1959, 1965) | 74 | 72 | 78 | 77 | 53 | 73 |
| Ohio (1959–69) | 74 | 51 | 84 | 83 | 61 | 66 |
| Iowa (1965–74) | 49 | 55 | 79 | 70 | 72 | 70 |
| Illinois (1959) | 27 | — | 75 | 63 | — | — |
| Utah (1965) | 8 | 20 | 60 | 52 | 70 | 65 |
| New Mexico (1951–59, 1963) | 24 | 20 | 42 | 53 | 42 | 57 |

[a] The Index of Cohesion is a simple measure in which one subtracts the percentage in the minority from the percentage in the majority; hence, if 75 percent of a party are together in a vote, the index is 50.

Source   Data from Jewell and Patterson, *The Legislative Process in the United States*, 3rd ed., 384–85. In some of the years the data are for only one house of a state legislature.

cent. Recently in the British House of Commons the percentage of "party votes" averaged very close to 100.[14]

Although the "90 percent versus 90 percent" standard discriminates between British and American party cohesion — indeed, between parliamentary and other systems — it is too stringent a standard for comparisons within the American experience. Scholars of the American legislatures have opted for less demanding criteria. Whatever the criterion one accepts, it may be used to describe both the overall incidence of cohesion in the legislatures and the party loyalty of individual legislators. In other words, one may make statements about the percentage of instances in which the majority (or 80 percent) of one party opposed a majority (or 80 percent) of the other; and one can also figure the percentage of times that an individual legislator votes with his party when party opposes party. In their study of American legislatures, Jewell and Patterson have collected data from various other studies and sources on party cohesion in state legislatures, drawing on a number of these measures of party cohesion. Table 14.1 indicates the enormous variation in party cohesion in the decisions of a number of state legislatures. It illustrates also the high degree of cohesion

[14] Julius Turner, *Party and Constituency: Pressures on Congress*, rev. ed. by Edward V. Schneier (Baltimore: Johns Hopkins University Press, 1970), pp. 16–17.

TABLE 14.2  Party Cohesion in Congress for 1963–78:
Percentage of Roll Calls with Majority vs.
Majority

| Year | Both houses | Senate | House |
|------|-------------|--------|-------|
| 1963 | 48% | 47% | 49% |
| 1964 | 41 | 36 | 55 |
| 1965 | 46 | 42 | 52 |
| 1966 | 46 | 50 | 41 |
| 1967 | 35 | 35 | 36 |
| 1968 | 33 | 32 | 35 |
| 1969 | 34 | 36 | 31 |
| 1970 | 32 | 35 | 27 |
| 1971 | 40 | 42 | 38 |
| 1972 | 33 | 36 | 27 |
| 1973 | 41 | 40 | 42 |
| 1974 | 37 | 44 | 29 |
| 1975 | 48 | 48 | 48 |
| 1976 | 37 | 37 | 36 |
| 1977 | 42 | 42 | 42 |
| 1978 | 38 | 45 | 33 |

*Source*  Data from *Congressional Quarterly Almanacs* for each year.

in the urban, two-party states of the northeastern section of the country.[15]

By similar measures the degree of party cohesion in the United States Congress falls somewhere between the extremes of party cohesion among the states. In recent years the two houses of Congress have been pitting majorities of Democrats against majorities of Republicans in 30 to 50 percent of the roll calls (Table 14.2). And within those votes in which party majority opposed party majority in the 1970s the average Index of Cohesion was in the range of 30 to 35, below the score of most state legislatures.[16]

## Occasions for Cohesion

The incidence of cohesive voting among members of the same legislative party varies significantly with the types of issues and questions the legislatures face. Studies in the Congress and the state legislatures find that three kinds of legislative concerns are most likely to stimulate high levels of

[15] See also Table 1 of the study by Hugh L. LeBlanc, "Voting in State Senates: Party and Constituency Influences," *Midwest Journal of Political Science* 13 (1969): 36.
[16] See the note under Table 14.1 for an explanation of the Index of Cohesion.

party discipline: those touching the interests of the legislative party as a group, those involving support of or opposition to an executive program, and those concerning the socioeconomic issues and interests that tend to divide the party electorates.

The interests of the legislative parties as parties — as interest groups, one might even say — often spur the greatest party unity in legislatures. The range of this type of issue is broad. It includes, especially in two-party legislatures, the basic votes to organize the legislative chamber. In the Congress, for example, one can safely predict 100 percent party cohesion on the early session votes to elect a Speaker of the House and a president pro tem of the Senate. Discipline runs high in the state legislatures over issues such as patronage (and merit system reform), the laws regulating parties and campaigning, the seating of challenged members of the legislative chamber, election and registration laws, or the creation or alteration of legislative districts. Whatever form these issues take, they all touch the basic interests of the party as a political organization. They threaten some aspect of the party status quo: the party's activists, its internal organizational structure, its system of rewards, its electorate, its electoral competitiveness.

Second, legislators of a party rally around the party's executive, or they unite against the executive of the other party. Perhaps the reaction to an executive program is not so predictable as it is in a parliamentary system, for American presidents freely court the support of the other party. Nonetheless, it is a significant partisan issue even in the American context. The *Congressional Quarterly* periodically measures the support that each legislative party gives to the president on those issues he has clearly designated a part of his program (Table 14.3). This executive-oriented cohesion in the Congress and in the state legislatures reflects a number of realities of American politics. It may result from the executive's control of political sanctions — patronage in some states, his personal support in fund raising and campaigning, his support of programs for the legislator's constituency. It also results from the fact that the executive increasingly symbolizes the party and its performance. Legislators of the president's party or the governor's party know that they threaten their party and their own political future if they make the party's executive look ineffective.

Finally, legislative cohesion remains firm on some policy issues, especially those bearing directly on the socioeconomic interests of the electorate. Certainly in those states in which the SES foundations of party loyalties produce an issue-oriented politics, this fact is not surprising. Such issues include labor-management relations, aids to agriculture or other sectors of the economy, programs of social security and insurance, wages and hours legislation, unemployment compensation, and relief and welfare programs. These issues involve, in the oversimplifications of American politics, the welfare state, the whole complex debate over government re-

TABLE 14.3   Percentages of Times That Congressmen Supported Bills from President's Program: 1963–78

| Party of President | Year | Senate Democrats | Senate Republicans | House Democrats | House Republicans |
|---|---|---|---|---|---|
| Democrat | 1963 | 63% | 44% | 72% | 32% |
| Democrat | 1964 | 61 | 45 | 74 | 38 |
| Democrat | 1965 | 64 | 48 | 74 | 41 |
| Democrat | 1966 | 57 | 43 | 63 | 37 |
| Democrat | 1967 | 61 | 53 | 69 | 46 |
| Democrat | 1968 | 48 | 47 | 64 | 51 |
| Republican | 1969 | 47 | 66 | 48 | 57 |
| Republican | 1970 | 45 | 60 | 53 | 66 |
| Republican | 1971 | 40 | 64 | 47 | 72 |
| Republican | 1972 | 44 | 66 | 47 | 64 |
| Republican | 1973 | 37 | 61 | 35 | 62 |
| Republican | 1974 | 39 | 56 | 44 | 58 |
| Republican | 1975 | 47 | 68 | 38 | 63 |
| Republican | 1976 | 39 | 62 | 32 | 63 |
| Democrat | 1977 | 70 | 52 | 63 | 42 |
| Democrat | 1978 | 66 | 41 | 60 | 36 |

*Source*   Data from *Congressional Quarterly Almanacs* for each year.

sponsibilities that we sum up in the liberal-conservative dualism. For example, on issues that the AFL-CIO's Committee on Political Education (COPE) considered a test of labor-liberal positions between 1947 and 1966, the Senate Democrats supported the COPE position 72 percent of the time, the Senate Republicans 28 percent of the time.[17] Such substantial cohesion, however, does not obscure the fact that senators differ in the degree of their personal support. In 1978 Republicans varied from a high of 95 percent (Javits of New York) to a low of 5 percent (Garn of Utah).[18]

To single out these three groups of issues is not to imply that they are the only instances of party cohesion. The structure of the choice itself may encourage or discourage cohesion. In the Congress (and probably in the states, too) party discipline seems to be easier to maintain on the complex, almost invisible procedural issues before the chamber. Apparently the simple, substantive questions attract publicity and thus attract the attention

[17] William J. Keefe and Morris S. Ogul, *The American Legislative Process: Congress and the States,* 3rd ed. (Englewood Cliffs, N.J.: Prentice-Hall, 1973), p. 276. Unquestionably there is considerable overlap between this issue category and the previous one of support for or opposition to the executive; cohesion in reaction to the executive may well be in part an artifact of issue consensus.
[18] *Congressional Quarterly Weekly Report,* June 2, 1979.

and activities of nonparty pressures. In the House of Representatives, at least, party leadership finds its task easier when it is working on an obscure issue.[19] Also, in the Congress issues of federalism and states' rights produce partisan voting.[20]

### The Constituency Basis of Cohesion

Party cohesion in legislative voting is greatest in those states of competitive, two-party politics. One-partyism in a state legislature invites the disintegrating squabbles of factions and regional or personal cliques within the dominant party. The South has in recent years been the region of the least cohesive legislative parties. But this is perhaps to labor the obvious; the very concept of cohesive parties and party government presumes two healthy, competitive parties locked in the struggle to make public policy.

Party cohesion, furthermore, is at its maximum in the legislatures of urban, industrialized states (see Table 14.1). The key here — and perhaps the key to the entire riddle of legislative party cohesion — is in the types of constituencies the parties represent. In these urban, industrial states the parties tend to divide the constituencies along urban-rural and SES lines, and they develop an issue-oriented politics that reflects those lines. Party cohesion in the legislature, therefore, reflects the relative homogeneity of the interests and constituencies the party represents. It also reflects, of course, the fact that the other party represents a different configuration of interests in different constituencies. Moreover, the legislators of one party may themselves have different background characteristics and life styles from the legislators of the other party — that is to say, differences in their own values and experience reinforce the party differences in constituencies. So, in such state legislatures an attempt to revise an unemployment compensation program will put two cohesive parties in sharp opposition, with the prolabor and promanagement sides each reinforced by their roots in their home districts and by their own lives and values.

There do exist urban, industrial states with relatively little legislative party cohesion. California has become the most famous example. California's two parties represent districts that by the usual SES measures are fairly mixed. The Democratic party, for instance, has an important rural wing, a possible result of the long-time overrepresentation of rural areas in the state legislature. To put the matter another way, in California each party represents a relatively heterogeneous set of constituencies. In such states — and more commonly in the less urban states — there probably exists no single, sharp dualism of interests on which to develop clearly marked, grassroots differences between the parties.

[19] See Lewis A. Froman and Randall B. Ripley, "Conditions for Party Leadership: The Case of the House Democrats," *American Political Science Review* 59 (1965): 52–63.
[20] Turner, *Party and Constituency*, rev. ed., Chap. 3.

Within the legislature of a particular state, the degree of any individual legislator's party loyalty also appears to be related to constituency characteristics. Party cohesion is greater among those legislators who represent the typical or modal constituency when typicality or modality is measured by some index of SES or urbanness. In the example of MacRae's study of the Massachusetts legislature, Republicans tended to represent districts with a high rate of owner-occupied housing; Democrats tended to come from areas in which fewer people owned the homes they lived in. Republicans from low owner-occupancy areas and Democrats from high owner-occupancy districts — that is, legislators from districts not typical of those their party generally represented — tended to be the party mavericks on roll calls.[21] This kind of analysis pointing to the influence and limitations of constituency loyalties is based on the assumption that each party has differing typical districts and that differences are chiefly in SES interests. In short, we appear to be examining here the same constituency effect on the individual legislator that we saw working on entire legislative parties several paragraphs ago.[22]

### The Other Bases of Cohesion

Clear and unmistakable though the constituency bases of party regularity may be, they do not explain all party cohesion in the state legislatures. The parties as operating political organizations do account for some. Daily caucuses, state party representatives roaming the legislative corridors, and the party pressures of a vigorous governor do count for something. Even though it is difficult to measure their influence, few observers of the state legislatures deny it. What actual organizational pressure the legislator feels, however, probably comes from the state party, the party in the executive, or the legislative party itself. It rarely comes from the local party, which, if it makes any demands on him at all, generally makes them on purely local, service issues. The varying strength and capacities of constituency political parties may affect legislators' relationships with their constituencies, but they seem not to affect their votes at the state capitol or in Washington. The local party is much more concerned with matters of

[21] Duncan MacRae, "The Relation Between Roll Call Votes and Constituencies in the Massachusetts House of Representatives," *American Political Science Review* 46 (1952): 1046–55. See also Thomas A. Flinn, "Party Responsibility in the States: Some Causal Factors," *American Political Science Review* 58 (1964): 60–71.

[22] For a useful exploration of the relationship between party cohesion and constituency variables, see LeBlanc, "Voting in State Senates," pp. 44–53. There is also considerable evidence to suggest that constituency differences lay beneath the high degree of party cohesion in the United States Congress at the turn of the century. See David W. Brady and Phillip Althoff, "Party Voting in the U.S. House of Representatives, 1890–1910: Elements of a Responsible Party System," *Journal of Politics* 36 (1974): 752–75.

local interest and its own perquisites than it is with questions of state or national policy.[23]

Party regularity may also be related to the political competitiveness of the legislator's constituency. Legislators from the unsafe, marginal districts with finely balanced parties are more likely to defect from their fellow partisans in the legislature than are those from the safer districts. To be sure, it is likely that many of these marginal districts are the districts of SES characteristics atypical of the parties' usual constituencies. But marginality may also be a product of the organizational strength of the opposing party or the appeal of its candidates, and it may therefore force the legislator to be more than usually sensitive to the constituency.[24]

Finally, as obvious and even banal as it may seem, parties must cohere in order to get the business of the legislature done. If bills are to be passed and the public's business done, majorities must be put together. The putting together of those majorities is the prime task of the party leadership of the majority party. That leadership is in truth far more likely to be concerned with the smooth operation of the legislative body than with the enactment of some stated party policy. It is also persuasive and influential at least in part because it dominates the group life of the legislative party and controls access to its esteem and camaraderie.[25]

In summary, the northeastern states provide the prototype of the state legislature with greatest party cohesion. They are largely competitive, two-party states. Drawing on urban-rural lines and the SES differences of a diverse population, their major parties represent fairly homogeneous and markedly differing clusters of constituencies. Those differences give rise to a politics of issue and even of ideology, which is in turn reinforced by the similar axes of national politics. These are also the states of old-line, vigorous party organizations and party control of nominations. Here, too, one finds that the hardship politics of favors and patronage has armed the parties with impressive arsenals of sanctions and rewards. Organizational strength carries over, too, into the legislative chambers, where regular caucuses and the apparatus of party discipline are often in evidence. Here also party differences and party conflict have a greater salience for the in-

[23] David M. Olson, "U.S. Congressmen and Their Diverse Congressional District Parties," *Legislative Studies Quarterly* 3 (1978): 239–64.
[24] The scholarly evidence on this point is very mixed. A recent article by Barbara S. Deckard makes a strong case for the argument that there is no relationship between electoral marginality and party disloyalty in roll calls; the article also summarizes a good deal of the recent literature on the point. "Electoral Marginality and Party Loyalty in House Roll Call Voting," *American Journal of Political Science* 20 (1976): 469–81.
[25] Some observations of state legislatures and the logic of coalition theory would suggest that the size of the legislative party itself would have some effect on party cohesion, that the smaller the margin of the majority the greater the pressure on it to cohere. Eric M. Uslaner finds no such relationship in the Congress in "Partisanship and Coalition Formation in Congress," *Political Methodology* 2 (1975): 381–414.

dividual legislator (and the individual voter, too). In a now-classic study of four state legislatures, the legislators were asked to indicate the kinds of conflict that were important in their legislature; 96 percent of the members of the New Jersey lower house designated party conflict as "important"; comparable percentages for Ohio, California, and Tennessee were 49, 26, and 23 respectively.[26]

It is not easy to bring the United States Congress into this discussion of the conditions leading to cohesion in legislative voting. There is nothing among the state legislatures to which Congress can be compared. Perhaps it is because of the unique scope of its politics and its powers as a legislature that it does not lend itself to the relatively simple generalizations we have made about the state legislatures. The members of Congress come from fifty different political systems, not one, and the diversity of the constituencies and constituency politics they represent may be too great for a continuous, simple set of party battle lines to encompass. The parties in Congress have a more complex pattern of party cohesion than do the state legislative parties. Because of the special case of the South, the Democratic party achieves varying degrees of cohesion on various issues. The Republicans often manage a greater cohesion on foreign policy issues than on the conventional welfare-state issues of domestic politics. And not until one narrows the members of Congress to the non-Southerners do the constituency bases of party cohesion appear.[27]

## LEGISLATIVE PARTIES AND PARTY GOVERNMENT

Even though party cohesion in American legislatures falls far short of the standards of some parliamentary parties, it remains the most powerful determinant of roll call voting in American legislatures. Party affiliation goes further to explain the legislative behavior of American legislators than any other single factor. Their normal disposition seems to be to support the leadership of their party unless some particularly pressing commitment intervenes. All other things being equal (i.e., being quiescent and not demanding), party loyalty usually gets their votes.

Yet, despite the relative importance of party cohesion, the fact remains that most American legislative parties achieve only modest levels of it. Party lines are often obliterated in the coalitions that enact important legislation. Interest groups, powerful governors, local political leaders, the mass media, influential legislative leaders — all contend with the legislative party for the ability to organize legislative majorities. In this system of fragmented legislative power the legislative party governs only occasion-

[26] John C. Wahlke et al., *The Legislative System* (New York: Wiley, 1962), p. 425.
[27] Lewis A. Froman, *Congressmen and Their Constituencies* (Chicago: Rand McNally, 1963). See also David R. Mayhew, *Party Loyalty Among Congressmen* (Cambridge: Harvard University Press, 1966).

ally. It often finds itself in conflict with other party voices in the struggle
to mobilize majorities in the legislatures. The governor or president as a
party leader and expounder of the party platform may find himself repeatedly at odds with legislators of his party whose roots are deeply im-
planted in local, virtually autonomous electorates.

So, the fragmenting institutions of American government once again
have their impact. With the separation of powers there is no institutionalized need for party cohesion, as there is in the parliamentary systems.
Two recent studies of Canadian parties suggest, indeed, that the presence
of a parliamentary form primarily accounts for the greater cohesion of
legislative parties in Canada.[28] It is possible for government in the United
States to act, even to govern, without disciplined party support in the
legislature. In fact, at those times when one party controls both houses of
Congress and the other the presidency — or one controls both houses of
the state legislature and the other the governorship — it would be difficult to govern if high levels of cohesion behind an a priori program did
prevail in each party.

Even where one finds party cohesion or discipline in an American legislature, however, party government or party responsibility need not result.
Cohesion is a necessary but not sufficient condition of responsibility, and
that's the rub. The American legislative party tends to have only the most
tenuous ties to the various units of the party organization. The legislative
parties of Congress do not recognize the equality — much less the superiority — of the party's national committee. Most state legislative parties
similarly escape any effective control, or even any persistent influence, by
their state party committees. Nor do the legislative parties have a great
deal of contact with local party organizations. Many legislators depend
on personal organizations for reelection help, and even those who rely on
the party at election time receive no continuing advice from the party
back home. The local party organizations are usually preoccupied with
local issues and local services, and, furthermore, they do not often sustain
enough activity between elections to keep even the most fleeting supervisory watch over their legislators.

The American legislative party, therefore, has often found it easy to
remain aloof from and independent of the party organization and its platforms and program commitments. It creates the major part of its own
cohesion, employing its own persuasions, sanctions, and rewards. What
discipline it commands generally serves a program or a set of proposals
that originate in the executive or within the legislative party itself. Only
rarely is the legislative party in any sense redeeming earlier programmatic commitments or accepting the overriding discipline of the party

[28] Leon D. Epstein, "A Comparative Study of Canadian Parties," *American Political
Science Review* 58 (1964): 46–59; Allan Kornberg, "Caucus and Cohesion in Canadian
Parliamentary Parties," *American Political Science Review* 60 (1966): 83–92.

organization. As a legislative party it is politically self-sufficient; it controls its own rewards to a considerable extent. In some cases it attempts also to control its own political future; the party campaign committees of both houses of Congress are good examples. So long as its members can protect their own renomination and reelection, it is able to keep the rest of the party at arm's length.

This freedom — or irresponsibility, if one prefers — of the legislative party grows in large part from its unity and homogeneity of interests in a total party structure where disorder and disunity prevail. The legislative party and executive party are wary and suspicious allies in the party in government, and the decentralized party organization (decentralized even within the states) can define no common goals or programs for them. Even if local party organizations were to establish supervisory relationships with their legislators, no party responsibility would result unless those relationships were unified and integrated within the state as a whole. In other words, there exists no unified political party that could establish some control over and responsibility for the actions of its legislative party. There is only a party divided geographically along the lines of American federalism, functionally along the dimensions of the separation of powers, and politically by the differing goals and commitments its various participants bring to it.

At the most, therefore, the American legislative parties are tied to the rest of their parties by some agreement on an inarticulate ideology of common interests, attitudes, and loyalties. In many state legislatures and in the United States Congress, the mute "ideology" of one party and its majority districts differs enough (even though roughly) from that of the other party to promote the tensions of interparty disagreement and intraparty cohesion. These modal sets of interests and attitudes may or may not find expression in platforms, and they may or may not be articulated or supported by the party organizations. Legislative parties may in the short run even ignore them. Nonetheless, they are there, and they are the chief centripetal force in a political party that has difficulty articulating a central set of goals for all its activists and adherents. Whether this inarticulate ideology can produce a measure of party responsibility, however, is another question, and it will wait until the considerations of Chapter 16.

# 15

# The Party
# in the Executive
# and Judiciary

The American involvement of the executive and the courts in party politics
stems in considerable part from the traditions of nineteenth-century popular democracy. The belief that democratic control and responsibility can
best be guaranteed through the ballot box led to the long ballot, on which
judges and all manner of administrative officials (from local coroners to
state auditors) were elected. Popular election led easily to party influences
in those elections. At the same time, the tenets of Jacksonian democracy
supported the spoils system and the value of turnover in office, justifying
the use of party influence in appointments to office. Thus in the name of
popular democracy 'the access of parties to the executive and judicial
branches was established to an extent quite unknown in the other Western
democracies.

It is one thing for the political party to influence — or even control —
the recruitment or selection of officeholders. It is, however, quite another
for it to mobilize them in the exercise of their powers of office. The parties
have had only limited success in mobilizing American legislatures. The
pertinent question here is whether they have had equal success with the
executive and judicial branches. To put the matter another way: In the
decisions that affect us all, has it made any difference that the men and
women making them have been selected by a party? Do they carry out
party programs or values? Does the pursuit of public office by the political
parties serve only their internal organizational needs for rewards and incentives, or does it also promote the enactment of party programs and
platforms?

## THE EXECUTIVE AS A PARTY LEADER

The twentieth century has often been proclaimed as the century of mass
political leadership, in both the democracies and the dictatorships of the
world. In the democracies, electorates have expanded to include virtually
all adults. At the same time the revolutions in mass media and communications have brought political leaders closer than ever to them. In the

United States these changes have culminated in the personal leadership of the presidency in the twentieth century — a trend summed up merely in listing names such as Wilson, Roosevelt, Eisenhower, and Kennedy, names that signify both executive power and a personal tie to millions of American citizens. Not even the post-Watergate reaction against the "imperial presidency" is apt to reverse the trend. Even the parliamentary systems and their prime ministers have been energized by the growth of personal leadership. It is no longer true that the British prime minister is merely "first among equals" in the cabinet, and British elections increasingly are contests for national leadership.

Unquestionably one important ingredient of executive leadership in the United States has been the leadership of a mass political party. When Andrew Jackson combined the contest for executive office with leadership of a new popular political party, he began a revolution in both the American presidency (and governorship) and the American political party. The presidency ceased to be the repository of elitist good sense and conservatism that Hamilton saw in it and became, slowly and fitfully, an agency of mass political leadership and representation. It was ultimately the president rather than the Congress who became the tribune of the people in the American political system. Popular democracy found its two chief agents — a popularly elected leader and a mass political party — merged in the American chief executive, the power of the office reinforced by the power of the party.

It is easy to speak glibly of the American chief executive as the leader of a party. The chief executive — whether president or governor — wears many hats at once, and one of them surely is the hat of party leadership. Although leadership of a party demands his time and concern, it supports him in his dealings with the legislature and with his administrative underlings. But the specifics of executive leadership of a party are more elusive, for the president and governors are rarely formal party leaders. National and state party chairmen hold that responsibility. The chief executive's role as party leader is really a subtle, complex combination of a number of overlapping partisan roles. Among them certainly are these:

## Party Leader as Representative of the Whole Constituency

James MacGregor Burns has written of an American four-party system composed of the two "presidential parties" and the two "congressional parties." [1] But even if one does not see the basic divisions of the American party system in executive-legislative differences, it is evident that the two branches represent different constituencies. The national constituency the

[1] James M. Burns, *The Deadlock of Democracy* (Englewood Cliffs, N.J.: Prentice-Hall, 1963).

president represents differs from the sum total of the congressional constituencies. Whereas the congressional constituencies are local and particularistic ones that collectively overrepresent the rural areas of the country, the president's overrepresents the large, urban, industrial states on which the electoral college places such a premium. His constituency is more concerned with the problems of the big cities, their industrial workers, and the racial and ethnic minorities that live in them. It is a constituency that makes its incumbent more "liberal," more committed to government responsibility for solutions to social problems than his congressional party. Furthermore, since his is the only truly national constituency — especially in contrast with the localism of the congressional party — the president or the presidential candidate *is* the national party. Apart from the party's national convention, he is its only manifestation.

Many of the same observations may be made of the American governors. They, too, represent the entire state in contrast to the local ties of the state legislators. Other public officials may also have statewide constituencies (the constitution-writers of the states have seen fit to elect treasurers, attorneys general, and state insurance commissioners), but unlike these less known and less public fellow executives, the governor embodies the party on the statewide level. He or she is the political executive and is so recognized by the voters of the states. Like the president, most governors must make political and policy records appealing to the voters of the entire state, and like him they symbolize concern for the problems of the whole constituency.

## Party Leader as Organizational Leader

At the same time the American executive may choose to be concerned with the organizational affairs of his political party. Some, like President Eisenhower in the 1950s, may choose not to be. But though Eisenhower "preferred to leave the operation of the political machinery to the professionals," [2] not many other recent presidents have.

The opportunities for organizational leadership, however, are generally greater for governors than for the president. Their constituency and political power coincide with a viable level of party organization. In the state party organization there is an organization worth leading and capable of being led. The president, confronted with an often divided and usually futile national committee, is less fortunate. Not all governors assert themselves in positions of party leadership, of course. They may have no taste for party organizational leadership, or they may even represent a dissident faction within the party. But many governors do lead. Their control of the state patronage establishes them as party leaders, since they control

---

[2] Sherman Adams, *First-Hand Report* (New York: Harper, 1961), p. 25.

a major element of the party's reward system. Powerful county chairmen must pay them periodic homage.

The president traditionally asserts his organizational control over his national committee. Its chairman, if not his personal choice, must be acceptable to him. Even more important, he determines the role of the committee and its officers. In his relationships with the state and local organizations of his party, he may be less secure. Is it wise for a president to take sides, however covertly, in a deep-seated split within one of the party's state organizations? That unpleasant question confronted Presidents Kennedy and Johnson in the 1960s as they stepped carefully through the debris of battle between the New York Democratic organizations and the reformers. How is he to apportion his political resources — the dwindling patronage, his own presence, the prestige of the vice-president and the cabinet — among the parties within his party? For what goals or purposes should they be used?

To find a way through all of these political thickets, presidents do not usually rely on the national committee or its officers. Earlier in this century presidents used the cabinet position of the postmaster general as the post for an advisor knowledgeable in the intricacies of the party's many organizations. Franklin Roosevelt relied on James Farley, and Dwight Eisenhower chose Arthur Summerfield; each had extensive party organizational experience, and each served simultaneously as the national party chairman. It was the tradition that Lyndon Johnson honored in 1965 by appointing Lawrence O'Brien, his predecessor's shrewdest political counselor, as his postmaster general. Now that the postal service is reorganized and the postmaster general no longer sits in the cabinet, political advisors hold positions on the White House staff. In the case of Jimmy Carter they are largely his trusted, early supporters from Georgia.

### Party Leader as Electoral Leader

The chief executive is often a party leader in the additional sense that his electoral successes or failures affect the electoral fortunes of other office seekers within his party. Presidential coattails are widely thought to carry into office a certain number of congressional and state candidates. Although specific candidates may be able to isolate themselves from the effect of presidential or gubernatorial success or failure by building their own personal organizations or by cultivating nonparty support, many do not.[3] The basic nature and mechanism of the effect are obscure — is there, for example, a downward coattail effect as well as an upward one? — but the relationship is often present. In the 1964 Democratic landslide, North

---

[3] Malcolm Moos, *Politics, Presidents, and Coattails* (Baltimore: Johns Hopkins Press, 1952).

Dakota Democrats won a house of the state legislature and half of the state's congressional delegation for the first time in history. In Iowa the Johnson sweep turned the state's congressional delegation from six Republicans and one Democrat to six Democrats and one Republican. (Although the president garnered 62 percent of the vote and the popular Democratic governor, Harold E. Hughes, won 68 percent, all of the Democratic congressmen won with less than 54 percent.) In fact, the Republicans controlled twenty lower houses in state legislatures before the 1964 elections, but only nine after it. Thus the glitter of executives or candidates for executives — the candidates at the head of the tickets — can rub off on other party candidates (Table 15.1). In other words, the short-term judgment that grows out of executive performance or potential can overcome to some extent the patterns of voting that stem from long-term party identifications.[4]

It is, however, easy to exaggerate the ability of presidents and governors to influence the elections of other candidates for office. First, there are genuine limits to the coattail effect. They are not always strong when they are the coattails of an executive of a "minority" party. The landslide elections of Dwight Eisenhower in 1956 and Richard Nixon in 1972 did help some Republican candidates for the House of Representatives, but they were not enough to prevent Democratic control of the House in both years. Moreover, attempts to spread their coattails in elections in which they are not themselves candidates have not been successful for most executives. For example, despite his personal popularity President Eisenhower's appeal in 1958 for a Republican Congress with which he could work more effectively met total defeat. The Democrats, in fact, increased the margin of their control.

Presidents have failed, furthermore, in most of the few instances in which they have intervened openly in a primary of their own party to try to defeat a disloyal or unacceptable candidate. Governors who control a strong party organization and its resources have succeeded in the task at times, but such victories are not common. The impact of the executive on specific primaries and elections is in fact close to negligible unless it is exercised through a party organization. Executive appeals made directly to the voters seem not to have a great deal of effect, no matter how great the popularity and personal strength of the executive. All the traditions and pulls of localism in American politics are against them.

---

[4] On the general subject of the coattail effect, see *ibid.;* also Warren E. Miller, "Presidential Coattails: A Study of Political Myth and Methodology," *Public Opinion Quarterly* 19 (1955): 353–68; Charles Press, "Presidential Coattails and Party Cohesion," *Midwest Journal of Political Science* 7 (1963): 320–35; Milton C. Cummings, *Congressmen and the Electorate* (New York: Free Press, 1966); George C. Edwards III, "Impact of Presidential Coattails on Outcomes in Congressional Elections," *American Politics Quarterly* 7 (1979): 94–108.

TABLE 15.1   Johnson Landslide of 1964: The Impact in
the House

Elections to the House of Representatives

| Year | Percentage of vote cast for Democratic candidates | Percentage of Democrats in House | Percentage of vote cast for Democratic presidential candidate |
|------|------|------|------|
| 1962 | 52.5 | 59.3 | |
| 1964 | 57.2 | 67.8 | 61.1 |
| 1966 | 50.9 | 56.8 | |
| 1968 | 50.0 | 55.9 | 42.7 |

*Source*   Data from *Statistical Abstract* ( 1968 ).

## Party Leader as Symbol of the Party

Closely related to the role of electoral leader is the executive's role as party
symbol, for the president or the governor is its most salient representative.
In the public's mind, executive programs are party programs. The successes and failures of executives are party successes and failures; their
imaginativeness and vigor are the party's. For a public that views politics
chiefly in personal terms, a president or a governor is the personification
of the party. It is in this sense that chief executives are party leaders by
virtue of being chief executives. They can choose not to lead their party
organizations, not to lead their party in the legislature, not to intervene
in local or congressional elections, or not to cater to their special constituency — but they cannot avoid their symbolic impact on their parties. That
impact springs not from their intentions but from the voters' perceptions
of their performances.

Again, however, it is easy to overestimate the impact of the executive
on the party. During the Eisenhower years, for example, the president's
personal popularity rode high. Yet, the survey data on party identifications
for that period indicate only a slight Republican increase — certainly in
dimensions far below the president's personal popularity. In the long run,
popular chief executives such as President Eisenhower do not convert
their personal popularity to their political party *unless* they succeed in
altering the voter coalition supporting the party or its organizational structure and leadership.

However, if one looks for presidential impact not on long-run party
identifications but on short-run voter choices, the effect is clearer. Table
15.2 suggests graphically that a sag in one president's popularity was al-

TABLE 15.2  Relationship between Popularity of President Nixon and
Vote Intentions of Voters: 1973–74

|  | Percentage approving Nixon's conduct of presidency | Percentage intending to vote for Republican congressional candidates |
|---|---|---|
| January 1973 | 68 | |
| April 1973 | 48 | |
| May 1973 | | 35 |
| September 1973 | 33 | |
| October 1973 | | 30 |
| December 1973 | 29 | |
| January 1974 | | 29 |
| April 1974 | 25 | |
| May 1974 | | 30 |
| August 1974 | Nixon resigns | |
| October 1974 | | 35 |

*Source*  Gallup polls for months indicated.
Used by permission of the Gallup Organization, Inc.

most directly reflected in his party's electoral fortunes. More systematic
evidence makes it clear that mid-term elections — those in the states as
well as the congressional elections — are influenced by voters' evaluations
of the president in the two years since his election. All other considerations
held equal, voters disapproving of the president's performance vote for
the candidates of the other party to a greater extent than those approving
of it. Independents seem especially affected by their views of the president,
and there is also evidence that negative reactions have a greater impact
than do positive ones.[5] Small wonder, then, that the leaders and potential
candidates worry when the president of their party dips in popularity in
the Gallup poll.

These facets of the executive's role as party leader are in fact too closely
linked to separate them in practice. They buttress and reinforce each other,
and the skillful party leader draws on one to be effective in another. They
should more properly be thought of as interdependent aspects of the
single phenomenon of executive leadership in the party.

Imposing as these ties between the chief executive and the party may

[5] James E. Piereson, "Presidential Popularity and Midterm Voting at Different Electoral
Levels," *American Journal of Political Science* 19 (1975): 683–94; Samuel Kernell,
"Presidential Popularity and Negative Voting: An Alternative Explanation of the Mid-
term Congressional Decline of the President's Party," *American Political Science Review* 71 (1977): 44–66.

be, they are not without real and tangible limits. First of all, the executive may be limited by his own political experience and taste for political leadership. Some presidents and governors do not want to lead a party, or they do not think it proper for an executive to do so. And even those who do want to be party leaders may find that the representational demands of the office — the pressures to be a president or governor of "all of the people" — limit their partisan work and identification.

Presidents and governors may also lead only part of a party. For example, governors from one-party states often lead only a party faction. Executives also may share leadership of the party with other partisans. Presidents who are not especially secure in national party affairs may find the more experienced leaders of the congressional party asserting major leadership in the national party. Governors also may find senators and congressmen of their party pressing parallel leadership claims over the state party. These legislators and state party leaders may fear that the governor will use party control for his own political ambitions.

Nonetheless, the president heads, and occasionally even unifies, the national party. He dominates the national committee and the rest of the national organization, and through a combination of his powers of office and his party leverage he often exerts enough mastery of the legislative party to speak for the party in government. Most important, perhaps, for millions of American voters he is the symbol of the party, its programs, and its performance. The national constituency is his, and his nomination and campaign are the chief activities of the national party. They are the *only* activities with any visibility. Within the state parties, the governors have the same unifying, symbolizing role, and they too have their leverage on legislative parties and state organizations.

Therefore, it is no exaggeration to speak of the American parties as "executive-centered coalitions."

The party primacy of the chief executive lies not only in his advantage in establishing himself as the party leader in the state or nation, but also in the difficulties facing any alternative leader in attempting to do more than limit the impact of his titular status. The loose structure of the party is a coalition which necessarily centers on the chief executive, even though his influence within this coalition may vary widely depending on his skills and opportunities. No other source of party leadership has the legitimacy or the range of sources of influence.[6]

Even in the parties out of power the executive office and its opportunities dominate. Opposition to the other party's executive and his coalition, as well as planning for the next election's assault on the office, provide the chief unifying focus. It is, moreover, the headless quality of the party out of power that most typifies its melancholy condition.

---

[6] Judson L. James, *American Political Parties* (New York: Pegasus, 1969), pp. 163, 169–70.

The executive-centered party to some extent is a coalition of the executive-dominated party in government with the party in the electorate. That leaves the party organization increasingly as the odd man out. The identifications and loyalties of voters are not to the party organization but to the party symbols, meaning for which comes largely from executives and their programs. The men and women of the party in government often build their own supporting organizations and thus bypass the party organizations in their quest for office. One need only mention once again the fatal strategy of Richard Nixon in 1972. Even in the use of patronage, executives often try to maximize support for their programs and their own political futures rather than maintain or rebuild the strength of the party organization.

Once in office executives generally put the leverage they derive from their position as party leaders into the business of governing rather than into any concern for the party per se as an organization. The president, for example, often finds himself without sufficient constitutional powers to hold his own in the struggles of the American separation of powers. Indeed, if the proverbial man from Mars should obtain a copy of the United States Constitution, he could not imagine from its niggardly grants of power to the president what the office has come to be. American presidents, faced with that shortage of formal powers, have had to rely heavily on their extraconstitutional powers, such as those they derive from party leadership.

## PARTY LEADERSHIP AND LEGISLATIVE RELATIONS

The American chief executive does not possess a large area of policy-making autonomy. Aside from the president, who enjoys a primacy in the fields of defense and international relations, little major policy is reserved for the American executive to set. What impact the executive is to have on the making of policy or on the enacting of a party program must come about through the formal actions of the legislature. In this pursuit of policy by influencing a legislature, the president and the governors turn repeatedly to their identification with, and embodiment of, their political party.

The coordination of legislative and executive decision making under the aegis of a unifying political party is not easily accomplished, however. Between 1961 and 1969 only thirteen states (Idaho and South Dakota were the only two states of the thirteen outside the South or its border) did not experience at least some period in which one house of the legislature was of a party different from that of the governor. The reasons for those divided regimes are several: overlapping terms of office, differing constituencies, the impact of a politics of personality and localism, and legislative malapportionment. At such times the executive has no choice but to minimize partisan appeals. In view of the closeness of the party split in many legislatures and the unreliability of some legislators of his own party, he must also curry the favor of some legislators of the opposing party. Thus the president and governors follow a mixed strategy: partisan appeals and sanctions for their own party and nonpartisan or bipartisan politics for those of the opposition.

The role of the president vis-à-vis the Congress is too well known to bear a great deal of repetition here. Presidents rely on their nonparty sources of leadership, of course — on their lingering patronage, their prestige and persuasiveness, their command of the communications media, their own attention and favors. Overtly or not, they also use their identification with the party and their ability to influence coming elections. Members of the president's party know that if they make him look bad, to some extent they also make themselves and their party look bad. That awareness surely accounts for their rallying around a presidential veto of their own legislative preferences (Table 15.3). Nor can they escape the fact that the president heads the party ticket when he runs and that his performance becomes the party's record when he does not. In fact, even congressmen who benefitted in the past from presidential coattails are more apt to support the president's program than those who did not. Legislators thus appear both to anticipate and to react to presidential leadership at the polls.[7]

There are, however, signs that the president's party leverage on the Congress is diminishing. For example, the effect of presidential coattails on congressional elections appears to be dropping off.[8] To look at the matter from another direction, incumbent congressmen are increasingly secure in their constituencies. The quantity and the closeness of the competition they face are not as great as they were a decade ago. A congressional politics of cultivating the constituency with greater attention to its interests and increased services to individual constituents secures these congressmen's political futures and isolates them from the electoral influences of the presidency.[9] As they lose party leverage, then, presidents are forced back on the nonparty components of their influence.

Governors, on the other hand, are frequently in a position to exercise far greater and more direct party organizational power over the legislators of their own parties. In many states their legislatures are unbound by the traditions of seniority, and governors may take an active part in selecting

[7] J. Vincent Buck, "Presidential Coattails and Congressional Loyalty," *American Journal of Political Science* 16 (1972): 460–72; and Jeanne Martin, "Presidential Elections and Administration Support among Congressmen," *American Journal of Political Science* 20 (1976): 483–90.
[8] George C. Edwards III, "Impact of Presidential Coattails on Outcomes in Congressional Elections," *American Politics Quarterly* 7 (1979): 94–108.
[9] See, for example, Morris P. Fiorina, "The Case of the Vanishing Marginals: The Bureaucracy Did It," *American Political Science Review* 71 (1977): 177–81.

TABLE 15.3   Republican Voting on Vetoed Bills in Congress: 1973 and 1976

| Bill and Chamber (year) | Vote on original passage | | Vote on veto | |
| --- | --- | --- | --- | --- |
| | Republican voting | Percentage supporting Nixon or Ford position | Republican voting | Percentage supporting Nixon or Ford position |
| Vocational Rehabilitation Act — Senate (1973) | 35–2 | 5 | 10–31 | 76 |
| Water-Sewer Program — House (1973) | 105–48 | 31 | 24–161 | 87 |
| OMB Confirmation — Senate (1973) | 16–17 | 52 | 14–22 | 61 |
| OMB Confirmation — House (1973) | 20–164 | 89 | 18–167 | 90 |
| Cambodia Bombing Halt — House (1973) | 63–120 | 66 | 53–133 | 72 |
| Public Works Employment — House (1976) | 62–71 | 53 | 56–82 | 59 |
| Public Works Employment — Senate (1976) | 20–16 | 44 | 12–25 | 68 |
| Aid to Day Care Centers — Senate (1976) | 18–16 | 47 | 11–26 | 70 |
| Hatch Act Revisions — House (1976) | 49–93 | 65 | 22–113 | 84 |

*Source*   Randall B. Ripley, *Congress: Process and Policy,* 2d ed. (New York: Norton, 1978), p. 202. Reprinted by permission.

committee chairmen and influential party floor leaders at the beginning of the session. They often view the party's legislative leaders as "their" leaders, chosen to steer their programs through legislative waters. Governors may attend party caucuses and even direct the strategy of the party's legislative leaders. They may also lead powerful, ongoing state party organizations. To cross them may be to run the risk of falling from party favor; a legislator's career in the legislature, not to mention his future ambition, may be at the mercy of a determined, politically skillful governor. In short, the average governor has far greater control over party rewards and incentives than a president. But, on the other hand, in the symbolic aspects of party leadership he usually exerts far less influence than a president. Though the party sanctions and organizational power many governors command are impressive, these governors suffer from undersized political coattails.

## PARTY POWER AND ADMINISTRATIVE POLICY

Administrative agencies now regulate vast areas of the economy — the airlines, atomic and nuclear energy, radio and TV, for example — under only the vaguest legislative mandates. Even the question of tariff barriers, long the occasion for protracted congressional politicking, Congress has largely delegated to the president, the State Department, and the Tariff Commission. Obviously, then, any concept of party responsibility or party government cannot be restricted to legislatures. The administration clearly shapes policy in its application, and party programs require sympathetic administrative leadership to be effective.

There are however, substantial limits on the executive's ability to unify his administration and hold it responsible to a party program:

— The legislature may place administrative positions outside of executive control by stipulating terms of appointment that last beyond a president's or governor's term, by limiting the executive's power of removal, or by placing policy makers under merit system and tenure. It may extend a special legislative protection to others. So potent were the legislative supporters of the late director of the Federal Bureau of Investigation, J. Edgar Hoover, that he was independent of presidential authority.

— Special precautions may also be taken to thwart partisan control of an administrative agency. Federal agencies such as the Securities and Exchange Commission, the Federal Trade Commission, and the Civil Aeronautics Board are headed by five-person commissions or boards, but not more than three of the members of each may be of the same political party. (Republican presidents often meet that formal bipartisan requirement by appointing conservative Democrats, and Democrats seek out liberal Republicans.)

— In a number of states the top administrative positions, like the gubernatorial office, are filled by election. At worst that places members of both parties — a Republican governor and a Democratic state treasurer, for example — in an uncomfortable alliance. Even if the offices are filled by candidates of the same party, they are often politically and constitutionally independent. In Minnesota, for example, eleven different men held the governorship between 1930 and 1969. In that same period there were only two auditors, four secretaries of state, and six treasurers. Thus the governor may confront a number of entrenched "executive parties" as he enters office; they may even be there as he leaves.

— Furthermore, American executives suffer some diminution of political
power as their terms approach a predetermined end. The Twenty-sec-
ond Amendment to the United States Constitution limits the presidential term to between eight and ten years, and a majority of the states
limit the gubernatorial time in office.
— Finally, political realities may force executives to share the instruments
of party leadership with others. Senatorial courtesy and other political
considerations guarantee that the Senate's confirmation of presidential
appointments will be more than pro forma. And in forming a cabinet
the president cannot ignore the feelings and aspirations of groups
within the party that contributed to his victory.

Establishing control of the executive branch is, however, far more complex than simply putting fellow partisans into positions of power. Control
over their operations and decisions comes with the greatest difficulty. The
chief executive faces essentially the same problem in enforcing party discipline on his administrative subordinates that a party leader in the legislature faces. In both cases the problem is loyalty to and the power of a
constituency. Just as the legislators identify with the problems and outlooks of the citizens they know and represent, so administrators often
identify with the problems and outlooks of the groups and individuals with
which their agencies deal. And just as legislators must depend on the folks
back home to protect their political careers, top-level administrators know
that the support of client groups is their best personal political protection
and the only protection for an agency, its mission, and its budget. In this
way the Veterans Administration enjoys the protection of the American
Legion and the Veterans of Foreign Wars, and the Environmental Protection Agency depends on the support of organized naturalists and en-
vironmentalists. Only with the greatest difficulty does the pressure of party
loyalties and party sanctions overcome the power of these administrative
constituencies. For in the executive as well as the legislative branch, the
party has less to give and less to take away than does the constituency.

Only in that part of the administrative establishment closest to the chief
executive is there the possibility of party responsibility. At these top administrative levels, the appointee has often been politically active and has
associated actively with a political party. He or she has very likely come
to recognize the claims of the party organization and developed a commitment to party goals and programs. The cabinet of a president such as
Richard Nixon (see box) illustrates the classic combination of party and
governmental experience that mark the cabinets of the more partisan presidents of both parties. The 1977 cabinet of President Jimmy Carter was,
however, less experienced in party politics and less closely associated with
the political career of Carter. It was, to be sure, the cabinet of a man
who had billed himself as an outsider to Washington and Democratic

## The Nixon Cabinet and the Republican Party

The original appointees to the 1969 cabinet of Richard Nixon typify the interplay of both the personal connections to the president and the broader activity within the president's party that one finds in many cabinets. Their political histories indicate party-based recruitment and also a potential on their part for reinforcing the party leadership of the president.

1. William P. Rogers (secretary of state): old friend and advisor of Richard Nixon and fellow campaigner in 1952; attorney general in the Eisenhower administration
2. David M. Kennedy (secretary of treasury): no apparent history of Republican activity
3. Melvin R. Laird (secretary of defense): member of House of Representatives and chairman of House Republican Conference; at least fifteen years on Republican convention platform committees (including 1968)
4. John N. Mitchell (attorney general): campaign manager for the 1968 Nixon-Agnew national campaign
5. Winton M. Blount (postmaster general): active for many years in Republican politics in the South; active in the Nixon campaign in 1960 in the South
6. Walter J. Hickel (secretary of interior): early supporter of Nixon in 1968 as governor of Alaska; cochairman of 1968 Nixon campaign in western states; had earlier been member of Republican National Committee
7. Clifford M. Hardin (secretary of agriculture): no apparent history of Republican activity
8. Maurice H. Stans (secretary of commerce): director of Budget Bureau in Eisenhower administration; chief fund-raiser in the 1968 Nixon campaign
9. George P. Schultz (secretary of labor): no apparent history of Republican activity
10. Robert H. Finch (secretary of health, education, welfare): national campaign manager for Nixon in 1960; active in Nixon's 1962 bid for California governorship; lieutenant governor of California; advisor to Nixon in 1968 campaign
11. George Romney (secretary of housing, urban development): governor of Michigan; early contestant for Republican presidential nomination in 1968
12. John A. Volpe (secretary of transportation): governor of Massachusetts; active in 1968 Nixon campaign as a speaker and as the head of the Nixon-Agnew Nationalities Committee

politics. Of the traditional cabinet seats, only one went to an old political associate: Griffin Bell, a fellow Georgian and the attorney general. As a group, the cabinet appointees had far more administrative than party experience; five had indeed held high-level appointments in the administration of Lyndon Johnson.[10]

But when one looks a step below in the administrative structure to the assistant secretary level, party and governmental experience dwindles. These are individuals most often chosen for their skills and experience in administration and only secondarily for their political credentials. In the selection of many of them, the role of the party organization may not have extended beyond determining whether they were politically acceptable (i.e., inoffensive) in their home states. Often the partisans who seek these positions through the party organizations lack the basic job qualifications. The party role in appointment suffers, therefore, because executive and managerial considerations weigh more heavily than political ones with most presidents.[11]

For what purposes, then, do executives use the executive party and their leadership role in it? Their power and influence go chiefly for the tasks of governing, of meeting their executive decision-making responsibilities. Only secondarily can they attend to the goals and interests of the party organization. Many governors use some chunk of their patronage purely for party goals, and presidents often use cabinet appointments to assuage and satisfy the need for recognition of various groups or factions within the party and the need to govern. A concession such as a cabinet seat that satisfies the political demands of the party may build party cohesion, but it may also thwart the executive or administrative goals of the president. Ultimately, chief executives use what party loyalty and cohesion they can build for their own programs and, if they are in their first term, their own reelection. It is the goals of the office and not of the party that they pursue.

## THE MYSTERIOUS CASE OF THE JUDICIAL PARTY

Nothing illustrates quite so clearly the difficulties of evaluating the party in office as the examples of cohesive party voting in American appellate courts. Several recent studies point to the presence of party-rooted blocs in state appellate courts in cases such as those involving workmen's compensation. Another broader study cutting across a number of states finds

[10] By giving cabinet status to his appointees Andrew Young (U.S. ambassador to the United Nations) and Bert Lance (director of the Office of Budget and Management), President Carter did expand the number of personal associates in the cabinet. The five who held appointments in the Johnson administration were Cyrus Vance, Michael Blumenthal, Harold Brown, Joseph Califano, and Patricia Harris.
[11] Dean E. Mann, *The Assistant Secretaries* (Washington: Brookings, 1965).

that Democratic and Republican judges differ significantly in the ways they decide certain types of cases. For example, Democrats on the bench tend to decide more frequently for the defendant in criminal cases, for the government in taxation cases, for the regulatory agency in cases involving the regulation of business, and for the claimants in workmen's compensation, unemployment compensation, and auto accident cases.[12] To be sure, no one suggests that the incidence of party cohesion in judicial decision making approaches that in legislatures. It appears only in certain types of cases; and the amount of disagreement within an appellate court that can be explained by party division falls far below the amount of legislative division that can be explained by party. But, in any event, there does appear to be party cohesion in the American judiciary.

It may infrequently happen that an American judge is swayed by some subtle persuasion of his political party. If it does happen, though, it doesn't happen frequently enough to explain party cohesion in the courts. The explanation rests in the different sets of values, even the different ideological stances, that the major parties represent. Quite simply, judges of the same party vote together on cases for the same reasons of ideology and outlook that led them to the same political party. In other words, two judges vote together on an issue of the administrative regulation of utilities because of deepseated values they share about the relationship of government and the economy. Those same values or perceptions led them some years earlier to join the same political party, or they were developed out of experience in the same political party.

The impact of the party on the decision-making processes of the judiciary, therefore, is indirect. It stems largely from the role of the party as guarantor of its members' commitments. That this should be so ought not to surprise anyone, for the appointment of judges in the United States has classically taken the values and attitudes of judges into account. Although we have only recently accepted in any overt way the notions of judicial law making — the notion that in some instances judges have options and that in these choices they may in part reflect their own prior experiences, perceptions, and values — we have acknowledged it implicitly for some time. President Theodore Roosevelt, considering a replacement for Justice Horace Gray on the Supreme Court, wrote Senator Henry

[12] On the general subject of party blocs or voting affinities among justices of the same party, see Sidney Ulmer, "The Political Party Variable on the Michigan Supreme Court," *Journal of Public Law* 11 (1962): pp. 352–62; Stuart Nagel, "Political Party Affiliation and Judges' Decisions," *American Political Science Review* 55 (1961): 843–50; Glendon A. Schubert, *Quantitative Analysis of Judicial Behavior* (Glencoe, Ill.: Free Press, 1959), pp. 129–42; and David W. Adamany, "The Party Variable in Judges' Voting: Conceptual Notes and a Case Study," *American Political Science Review* 63 (1969): 57–73. Similar differences in decision making in the federal judiciary are reported in Sheldon Goldman, "Voting Behavior on the United States Courts of Appeals, 1961–1964," *American Political Science Review* 60 (1966): 374–83.

Lodge inquiring about a certain Judge Oliver Wendell Holmes of the Massachusetts Supreme Court:

In the ordinary and low sense which we attach to the words "partisan" and "politician," a judge of the Supreme Court should be neither. But in the higher sense, in the proper sense, he is not in my judgment fitted for the position unless he is a party man, a constructive statesman, constantly keeping in mind his adherence to the principles and policies under which this nation has been built up and in accordance with which it must go on.

Now I should like to know that Judge Holmes was in entire sympathy with our views, that is, with your views and mine and Judge Gray's, just as we know that ex-Attorney General Knowlton is, before I would feel justified in appointing him. Judge Gray has been one of the most valuable members of the Court. I should hold myself as guilty of an irreparable wrong to the nation if I should put in his place any man who was not absolutely sane and sound on the great national policies for which we stand in public life.[13]

Congress, too, has often implicitly examined such issues in approving appointments to the federal judiciary. The Senate in 1969 and 1970 rejected two appointees to the Supreme Court (Clement Haynsworth and G. Harrold Carswell) at least partly because of the general conservatism of their views on race and labor.

Whether or not it should be within the province of a president or a governor to consider such matters in proposing judicial appointments, the appointee's political party loyalties serve as some indication of his or her values and attitudes. Indeed, it is one of the reasons that in the last century American presidents have appointed judges largely from their own parties. They have generally chosen more than 90 percent of their appointments from their own partisans, and in every case from Cleveland through Johnson the percentage has been above 80 (Table 15.4).

Since the inauguration of Jimmy Carter in 1977, the appointment of federal court judges has apparently been transformed. Judicial selection committees in the states, usually appointed by the senators of the state, have been charged with screening candidates and making recommendations to the justice department and the president. It is difficult to pinpoint the results of the new process, both because it is too early and because its impact differs widely from state to state. It does seem likely, however, that federal judgeships will be less available as rewards for party service than they have been. Indeed, even the chances that an appointee will be of the president's party will probably decline. Certainly it is clear that President Carter's intention is to diminish party control of judicial appointments in favor of wider access and considerations of professional merit.

In the majority of the states, the judiciary is not appointive; it is filled

---

[13] The Roosevelt letter is quoted more fully in Walter F. Murphy and C. Herman Pritchett, *Courts, Judges, and Politics* (New York: Random House, 1961), pp. 82–83.

TABLE 15.4   Percentages of Judicial Appointments from the Party of the President: Grover Cleveland through Lyndon Johnson

| | | | |
|---|---|---|---|
| Cleveland | 97.3 | Coolidge | 94.1 |
| Harrison | 87.9 | Hoover | 85.7 |
| McKinley | 95.7 | F. Roosevelt | 96.4 |
| T. Roosevelt | 95.8 | Truman | 90.1 |
| Taft | 82.2 | Eisenhower | 94.1 |
| Wilson | 98.6 | Kennedy | 90.1 |
| Harding | 97.7 | Johnson | 94.6 |

*Note*   No data are available on the appointments of Richard Nixon to the federal bench.

*Source*   Data from Evan A. Evans, "Political Influence in the Selection of Federal Judges," *Wisconsin Law Review* (May 1948), pp. 300–51, and Harold W. Chase, *Federal Judges: The Appointing Process* (Minneapolis: University of Minnesota Press, 1972).

by either partisan or nonpartisan elections. In the partisan elections of seventeen states, of course, the judge is elected as a member or candidate of a party, and one can reasonably suspect that his party tie represents certain generalized value positions. But the state parties vary greatly in the active way they contest these elections. In a few states, such as New York, the party organizations make primary endorsements and actively support energetic partisans for the judgeships. In other words, they would make the position a form of elective patronage. Other state parties pay far less attention to judicial elections; in some cases the same candidate — often with the endorsement of the state bar association — will run on both party tickets.

Party pressures and activities are far less obvious and important in nonpartisan elections. But regardless of the election process and politics, the judge still may come to the bench with the values that a party represents, and party lines may even be apparent in the divisions of a nonpartisan judiciary.[14] Judicial terms tend to be so long that many elective judgeships become appointive. Death often takes a nonpartisan judge from the bench in mid-term, and the vacancy is filled before the next election by a gubernatorial appointment. The political considerations attending such appointments may then prevail, and with the advantage of even a brief period of

[14] Even in a state in which judges are chosen on a nonpartisan ballot, partisan blocs may be apparent in some kinds of issues. In Minnesota, for example, the state supreme court has in recent years shown a high degree of party cohesion in two celebrated, "political" issues: an important question of procedure in the early stages of the recount of the state's 1962 gubernatorial election and the question of the authority of the governor to veto a legislative reapportionment.

incumbency the appointee usually wins a full, regular term at the next election.

The point, then, comes down to this. There is no way to eliminate the values and preferences, the important frames of reference, that judges bring to their work. Judges have been men and women of the world; they know the issues of their times and the ways the parties relate to them. Furthermore, given the tradition of political activity of the American lawyer, there is a good chance that the judge has had some active, political party experience. Beyond this, the political party has an opportunity for active and overt influence in the selection process through the initiatives of governors or the president of the party or through the usual processes of a partisan election. In these selection processes, the party has the opportunity to achieve two goals: the selection of judges who are sensitive to the values for which the party stands, and the appointment of deserving (and qualified) lawyers for service to it.

The use of the federal or state bench as a desirable bit of political patronage obviously politicizes the American courts to a degree unthinkable in many other nations. But the relationship between judge and party may even extend beyond the politics of appointment. In some parts of the country the local district or county judge sometimes still retains hidden ties to local politics. In some American counties he is the *éminence grise* of the party, slating candidates behind the scenes, directing party strategy, arbitrating among the conflicting ambitions of the party's candidates. Moreover, the local administration of justice occasionally opens new reservoirs of patronage for the party. The judge who is a loyal member of a political party may parcel out guardianships, receiverships in bankruptcy, and clerkships to loyal lawyers of the party. In a 1966 battle in New York for the Democratic nomination for a judgeship in Manhattan's Surrogate Court, it developed that the surrogates had in the preceding year issued 428 guardianships, with lawyers' fees running into many millions, in that one borough of the city alone. Many commentators and journalists, and many party officials, believe that such appointments go chiefly to attorneys active in the party ranks.[15]

How is it that the tie between the judiciary and the parties is so substantial in the United States? The factors are complex and mixed. The phenomenon of the elective judiciary, compounded by the political appointment process, is one. Then, too, we have no career vocation, no special training process or examination for the judiciary; any lawyer can be a judge. By contrast, in many continental European countries the career of judging requires special preparation, study, and apprenticeship,

---

[15] On judicial patronage see Charles E. Merriam and Harold F. Gosnell, *The American Party System*, 4th ed. (New York: Macmillan, 1949); and Herbert Jacob, *Justice in America* (Boston: Little, Brown, 1965), pp. 87–89.

and one enters it by special civil service examination. In the American context, then, the additional factor of the dominance of our politics by the legal profession is free to operate. Lawyers are everywhere in American political and public life, and many of them hope for ultimate reward in appointment to the bench.

## CONCLUSION

Surprisingly, the influence of the political party on the executives and judiciaries of the American political system differs in degree but not in kind. The main avenue of party influence is indirect, and in both cases it stems from the kinds of commitments and values that membership in a party — or loyalty to one — represents. It depends, in other words, on the ideological impact or presence of the party *within* the men and women who hold administrative or judicial office.

Furthermore, in both the executive and the judiciary one observes the conflict between the policy purpose — even when pursued within the limits of judicial propriety — and the demands of the party. The administrative position and the judgeship are two of the few available positions with which to reward party leaders, and the party is not anxious to have them pass to party "nobodies." In the filling of positions in both branches, however, one sees again the struggle between the party's own important need for organizational incentives and the need to recruit people who can best meet the responsibilities of governing. It is a dilemma without end or resolution.

# 16

## The Quest for Party Government

Political parties are everywhere in American legislatures and executives, and even in American judiciaries. All American executives, all American legislatures but one, and about half the American judiciaries are selected in processes that weigh heavily the party affiliation of the office seeker. Moreover, the appearances of party power are plentiful in the party leaders and whips of the legislatures and in the clearly partisan cast of many executive appointments. Even the elemental struggle between government and opposition, between ins and outs, largely follows political party lines in the American system, just as if the parties controlled cohesive parties of the government and the opposition. Yet, despite the trappings and portents of power, the American major parties do not govern easily. They find it hard to mobilize cohesive groups of officeholders behind programs and ideologies to which they and especially their organizations and activists have committed themselves.

The discontent with this inability of the American parties to "govern" is an old one within academic political science.[1] But the dissatisfactions are with more than the American parties. They extend to the entire American political system and its fragmented centers of authority, its tendency to blur political alternatives and differences, and its built-in barriers to strong and vigorous governmental initiatives. The critics, many of them admirers of the cohesive parties in the British Parliament, have long hoped that by joining electoral majorities and officeholders to party programs they could surmount the diffusion of power in the American polity. The 1950 report, *Toward a More Responsible Two-Party System*,[2] gave the controversy its major recent stimulus. The ensuing academic controversy has slowly simmered down, but it is by no means quiet today.

While the controversy over party responsibility and party government has embroiled academic political science for the past generation, a parallel

[1] Austin Ranney, *The Doctrine of Responsible Party Government* (Urbana: University of Illinois Press, 1962).
[2] Committee on Political Parties of the American Political Science Association, *Toward a More Responsible Two-Party System* (New York: Rinehart, 1950).

concern has agitated the world of American politics. From the ideologically oriented activists in both parties have come wails of dissatisfaction with the issuelessness of American politics and the tendency of the major parties to take similar centrist positions. They complain, much as did Lord Bryce some seventy years ago, that the American parties are as similar as Tweedledum and Tweedledee (see box). In 1964 the Republican conservatives inveighed against the "me-too-ism" of the party's liberals and moderates; in working for the nomination of Barry Goldwater they pleaded for "a choice, not an echo." Eight years later the major ideological pressures were from the left: The New Left and a coalition of the young, the disadvantaged, and the disaffected spearheaded a movement that won the 1972 Democratic presidential nomination for George McGovern. It, too, rejected the American status quo and the centrist politics of the established leadership of the Democratic party.

At first blush it may seem that the ivory tower controversy over party responsibility has not a great deal to do with the development of distinct programs for the parties. In any event, one would not ordinarily expect such a conjunction of academic debate and popular political controversy. But the two questions are to a great extent the same. The groups of scholars favoring party government or responsibility and the ideologues of the left and right in American politics both want the major American parties to present more specific and differentiated programs. Both groups also want the parties to govern by carrying their programs into public policy. To the extent that such goals require some degree of consensus on basic values and long-term philosophies within the parties, they both also want greater ideological clarification and commitment within the parties.

## THE LOGIC OF THE RESPONSIBLE PARTY

Despite the nomenclature, the doctrines of party government (or party responsibility) are only secondarily concerned with political parties.[3] They are fundamentally doctrines of democratic government — or, more precisely, doctrines advocating one particular variety of American democracy. Much of the debate over them has been over the kind of democracy

---

[3] A word of semantic elaboration may be helpful here. Even though the two terms, party government and party responsibility, are used synonymously here, there are authors who make distinctions between them. Party government denotes leadership by a major political party in the important decision-making processes of government. For some observers the concept of party responsibility is more than party government in that it suggests party government in which there is, additionally, responsibility to a priori party programs and to the voters who have chosen officeholders loyal to them. For others, however, party responsibility is "less" than party government; it identifies a degree of party program and discipline greater than the present but perhaps not great enough to provide cohesive majorities with which to enact party programs.

## Tweedledee and Tweedledum

It has become a commonplace to compare the similarity of the Democratic and Republican parties on issues to those two identical little fat men in Lewis Carroll's *Through the Looking Glass,* Tweedledee and Tweedledum. Carroll borrowed their names from an earlier English poet, John Byrom, but it was his adoption of them in 1872 that secured their modern fame. James Bryce, later Lord Bryce, was apparently the first to use them to describe the American parties; he did so in his *American Commonwealth* (1888). Some years after Carroll's masterpiece, Tweedledee and Tweedledum also developed a stereotyped appearance, complete with schoolboy caps — doubtless the creation of some influential illustrator. After all these years, the twins are alive and well in American politics, as witness the cartoon below. It carried no caption, except perhaps the words on the briefcase that identify the visitor as a "pollster." Ironically, the artist is Charles Addams, best known for his ghoulish and gothic imagination.

Drawing by Chas. Addams; © 1975 The New Yorker Magazine, Inc.

we are to have. The whole movement for party government has sprung from discontent over what some scholars and citizens have seen as the ills of American democracy.

The proponents of party government begin with a belief in strong, positive government as a necessary force for the solution of problems in the American society and economy. And like so many of the advocates of positive government in the context of the American separation of powers, many of them see a need for strong executive leadership if the whole complex governmental apparatus is to move forward with vigor and a semblance of unity. Yet, they know all too well that the institutions and traditions of American government diffuse and divide governmental power in ways that prevent the generation of aggressive and responsive governmental programs. Theirs is the old complaint that American political institutions, suited perhaps for the minimal, gingerly governing of the eighteenth and nineteenth centuries, are far less adapted to the present century's need for positive government action. And, clearly, decentralized political parties, each of them divided by a vast diversity of interests and points of view, only accentuate the problem of diffusion. In a sense, therefore, doctrines of party responsibility are American attempts to find a viable alternative to parliamentary government.

A second thread of argument runs through the political diagnoses of the proponents of party government: concern for the miniscule influence of individuals in a mass, popular democracy. Contemporary government becomes complex and remote, and individuals find it hard to have the time, attention, and political knowledge for an active role in it. They find it especially difficult to assess what their elected representatives have been doing in public office. Into the political void resulting from their ineffectiveness and ignorance rush well-organized and well-financed minorities — local elites, interest groups, party bosses, or ad hoc alliances. Consequently, so the argument goes, important decisions are frequently made by public officials and organized minorities without the participation or even the post hoc judgment of the great majority of individual citizens. Individuals drift from one meaningless decision to another; they do not know what the candidates stand for when they first elect them, and they have no standards or information for judging their performance in office when they come up for reelection.[4]

This sense of alarm about the American democracy, to be sure, is by no means limited to the proponents of party government. It is a more or less standard critique from those quarters of American life committed to the "liberal" confidence in the usefulness of a broad governmental role and to the "liberal" belief in the rationality and desirability of citizen in-

---

[4] See Ranney, *The Doctrine of Responsible Party Government*, Chaps. 1 and 2, for an analysis of what party government presumes about democracy.

volvement in a popular democracy.[5] What sets the school of party government apart is its reliance on the organizing and consolidating powers of the competitive political party. A reconstructed (and responsible) pair of political parties, it is hoped, would bring together masses of voters behind meaningful party programs and candidates loyal to them and then hold their elected candidates to the obligation of carrying those programs into public policy. The responsible political party thus would bridge the gulf between the politically disoriented individual and the distant, complex institutions of government.

In essence, these are proposals for the reinvigorating and animating of popular democratic institutions through the prime organizing role of the political party. Why the political party for so crucial a role?

As mobilizers of majorities the parties have claims on the loyalties of the American people superior to the claims of any other forms of political organization. They have extended the area of popular participation in public affairs enormously and have given elections a meaning and importance never before thought possible. ... Moreover, party government is good democratic doctrine because the parties are the special form of political organization adapted to the mobilization of majorities. How else can the majority get organized? If democracy means anything at all it means that the majority has the right to organize for the purpose of taking over the government.[6]

Only the parties, their supporters believe, are stable and visible enough to carry this representational burden. As the only completely political of the political organizations and the only one with a public or semipublic character, the political party alone has the capacity for developing the essential qualities of responsibility.

The call for responsible political parties, therefore, is a call for political parties with new capacities and new goals. Specifically, the responsible political party must:

— Evolve and enunciate a reasonably explicit statement of party programs and principles.
— Nominate candidates loyal to the party program and willing to enact it into public policy if elected.
— Conduct its electoral campaigns in such a way that voters will grasp the programmatic differences between it and its opposing party and make their voting decisions substantially on that basis.
— Guarantee that public officeholders elected under the party label will carry the party program into public policy and thus enable the party to take responsibility for their actions in office.

[5] I am using "liberal" in the sense it is used in contemporary American politics. The liberal position favors popular, participatory democracy and positive government. Conservatism, on the other hand, generally connotes a preference for limited government and for the wisdom of political leaders and elites.
[6] E. E. Schattschneider, *Party Government* (New York: Rinehart, 1942), p. 208.

The entire argument, therefore, rests on replacing individual or group responsibility for governing with the responsibility of the political party.

Concern for developing and enacting programs must infuse all relationships within the party and all steps in the contesting of elections. As the report of the committee of the American Political Science Association argues in its very first paragraph:

While in an election the party alternative necessarily takes the form of a choice between candidates, putting a particular candidate into office is not an end in itself. The concern of the parties with candidates, elections and appointments is misunderstood if it is assumed that parties can afford to bring forth aspirants for office without regard to the views of those so selected. Actually, the party struggle is concerned with the direction of public affairs. Party nominations are no more than a means to this end. In short, party politics inevitably involves public policy in one way or another.[7]

The whole idea of party government is policy- and issue-oriented. It is concerned with capturing and using public office for predetermined goals and not merely for the thrill of winning, the division of patronage and spoils, or the reward of the office itself. The winning of public office becomes no more than a means to policy ends.

There still remains, however, a sizable platoon of American political scientists and political leaders who, despite the persuasiveness of the advocates of party government, are definitely unconvinced.[8] The journals of American political science were, in fact, dotted with rejoinders for several years after the publication of the report of the Committee on Political Parties in 1950. Their collective case against party government and responsibility divides into two related but independent arguments: the *undesirability* of party government and its *impossibility* (or at least its improbability). Although the two points are related, both logically and polemically, one does not have to make both points to venture one.

On the grounds of undesirability, the skeptics argue across a number of fundamental issues of political philosophy. They fear that an embrace of party government would stimulate a more intense politics of dogmatic commitment — one in which the softenings and majority building of compromise would be more difficult. They fear, too, that by making the political party the prime avenue of political representation, the advocates of party government would destroy the present richness and multiplicity of representational mechanisms in the American democracy. Interest groups

[7] Committee on Political Parties, *Toward a More Responsible Two-Party System*, p. 15.
[8] The bibliography critical of the concept of party responsibility is a long one. Pendleton Herring's *The Politics of Democracy* (New York: Rinehart, 1940) early presented a view contra the reformers. A recent article by Evron Kirkpatrick refers to a great portion of the writing on the subject; see his "Toward a More Responsible Two-Party System: Political Science, Policy Science, or Pseudo-Science?", *American Political Science Review* 65 (1971): 965–90.

and other nonparty political organizations, they feel, are necessary means
of political representation in a large and heterogeneous polity. To channel
the representation of such a diversity of interests into the party system
would overload two parties and risk the development of multipartyism.
Furthermore, the skeptics are concerned lest party government destroy
the deliberative quality of American legislatures, for legislators would
cease to be free, independent men and women and would become the
mandated, committed representatives of a fixed party position. In short,
they fear what European critics often call "partyocracy" — the domination of politics and legislatures by a number of doctrinaire, unyielding
political parties, none of them strong enough to govern and none willing
to let others govern.

On the related grounds of realism (i.e., the question of possibility and
probability) the critics of responsible parties have argued that:

— The American voter remains insufficiently involved in issues to be
  coaxed easily into viewing politics and electoral choices in programmatic terms.
— The complexity of American society and the diversity of interests it
  generates are too great to be expressed in the simple set of alternatives
  a two-party system can frame.
— The parties themselves are too diffuse and decentralized — too lacking
  in central disciplinary authority — ever to take a single national position and then enforce it on their assorted partisans and holders of public
  office.
— The institutions of American government stand in the way at a number
  of crucial points. For example, the direct primary makes it difficult for
  the parties to choose nominees loyal to their programs, and the separation of powers (and bicameralism) often prevents the control of all
  executive and legislative authority by a single party.

In other words, the model of the responsible, governing political party
appears to the critics to demand too much of the American voters, the
major parties, and the institutions of American government.

If the major American parties are to meet the demands and roles of
party government, they must find some way to overcome their egregious
disunity. The problem is really one of uniting the party organization, the
party in the electorate, and the party in office in active and responsible
support of a party program — despite their different political goals, different political traditions and interests, and different levels of attention, information, and activity. Three sources of the cohesion or unity necessary
for party government seem at least to be logically possible:

— Cohesion may be promoted by *constitutional imperatives*. The parliamentary system demands that the majority party maintain cohesion in

the legislature — and to a lesser extent in the electorate and party organization — if it is to stay in office. In the case of the United States the constitution works against cohesion; federalism and the separation of powers are, in fact, roots of the problem at hand.[9]
— Cohesion may also be promoted by *organizational discipline*. A strong party organization may impose its discipline and cohesion on balky partisans in office if it can control renomination to office.[10] The American direct primary, however, makes that a hard task. Alternatively, powerful party leaders or executives may enforce it through the manipulation of the rewards they control (patronage, preference, access to authority, etc.). But the value of these rewards is shrinking, and political ethics in the United States no longer easily accept an enforced line-toeing. Although the available rewards and a tolerant political culture permit this kind of discipline in some American states and localities, it is impossible in many others.
— Finally, the cohesion may be produced "naturally" by an all-pervasive, intraparty *agreement on ideology or program*. All three components of the party may reach some consensus on a basic party ideology or program — or at least on a "silent ideology" of commonly held interest. The activists and identifiers of the party would then achieve a cohesion arising from common philosophy and goals, and their cohesion to a considerable extent would be a result of internalized and self-enforced commitment to those goals. Distasteful external constraints and restraints would thus be less necessary.

Because it seems that only the third avenue to party government is a likely one for contemporary American parties, the issue of party government becomes one of ideological — or more nearly ideological — politics and parties. A pervasive ideological commitment appears to be the necessary condition for cohesion, which in turn is a necessary condition for responsible governing parties. Organizational discipline may supplement and buttress the ideology, but it does not appear to be an alternative to it.

## IDEOLOGICAL PARTIES IN THE UNITED STATES

The complaint of the American ideologist with the major American parties is an old and familiar one:

[9] See Leon D. Epstein, "A Comparative Study of Canadian Parties," *American Political Science Review* 58 (1964): 46–59.
[10] A highly centralized party such as the Indian Congress party can maintain control over nomination and renomination of candidates to the national Parliament and thus exercise a potent sanction upon those parliamentarians of the party who break party discipline. In 1957, for example, the national Parliamentary Board of the party, the agency that selects and approves the candidates for local constituencies, declined to renominate almost one-third of the party's incumbent members of Parliament.

The elections this November will prove totally irrelevant because the American electorate will have no substantive choice among the candidates. Naturally, there will be the traditional rhetoric about the "great liberal policies of the Democratic party" and the "great Republican tradition of fiscal responsibility," but if one pierces the rhetoric of each party, one sees that while each may say varying things, each pursues a common policy, i.e., the preservation of the status quo.[11]

If the complaint is clear, its author and occasion are not. The admonition could be from the political left or the political right, and it might well have been spoken at virtually any national election since World War II. As it happens, it opened an article by a prominent spokesman of the New Left shortly before the 1966 congressional elections. From the conservative right in 1971 came similar sentiments:

I favor the two-party system. But the two parties should represent distinct positions; the reason for the demise of the modern system has been too much sameness and liberal-financed convergence. . . . A "broad-based" party is possible and desirable. To be a "party," an interest, it must have discernible principles, not just a roost for "personalities," engaging or otherwise.[12]

The Democrats and Republicans are guilty, so the charges go, either of suppressing positions subscribed to by significant numbers of Americans or of failing to promote a wide-ranging debate on public issues. In other words, they smother existing ideological differences, and they close off an important opportunity for others to develop.

Some academic and nonacademic reformers seek full-blown, total commitment to ideologies in the parties. But some seek only a crisper, bolder set of programs or issue positions from the parties. The differences between issue and program on the one hand and ideology on the other — and the relationship between them — lie at the heart of the problem. Some distinctions between them are probably overdue.

Terms such as "issues" and "programs" denote the stands that parties and politicians take on specific policy questions — on defense, foreign policy, medical care, labor-management relations, and protection of the environment. Traditionally the parties have, however hesitantly, taken programmatic stands in their platforms. Presidents and presidential candidates take theirs in speeches, messages, position papers, and press con-

[11] Edward M. Keating, "The New Left: What Does It Mean?" *Saturday Review,* September 24, 1966, p. 25. The second paragraph of the essay is also illustrative:

"Republicans and Democrats in 1966 are snarling and snapping at each other, vainly attempting to deceive the voter into thinking that there are choices, not echoes, on the political horizon. This is to dissemble. Both parties know that neither will attempt to alter basic American policy, which, on the national level, is to obfuscate the social sickness that is consuming us all, and, on the international level, is intended to extend Americanism to the rest of the world by military blackmail."

[12] From Anthony Spinelli, "Hooray for the Two-Party System," *The New York Times,* July 17, 1971. © 1971 by The New York Times Company. Reprinted by permission.

ferences. "Ideology," by contrast, denotes the broader values or philosophies that give rise to coherent sets of stands on issues. Liberalism or conservatism, to illustrate, provides an underlying structure of values that
leads an individual to a logical, even predictable, position on a number
of issues.

In a descriptive sense it is unquestionably true that there are parties
of issue (or program) and parties of more explicit ideology.[13] Certainly
not many of the reformers can hope to develop in the American political
context the kind of total *weltanschauung*, the all-embracing concern, of
an East European Communist party or an Asian Moslem party. Theirs is
an ideology encompassing virtually all social relationships, and it spawns
a politics of limitless scope and total involvement. Because of the general
American agreement on basic institutions, ideological differences between
the American parties are not apt to involve dispute over the Constitution,
the general outlines of the American economy, or the basic fabric of American society. Nor will American parties commit themselves dogmatically
to irrevocable political ideologies in the manner of some doctrinaire European parties. And so, ideological parties as one finds them elsewhere —
and especially in the bitter class politics of the European democracies
— do not exist in the United States.

However, it would be a mistake to draw the distinction too broadly
between issue stands and ideology. Both are really points on the same
continuous dimension; one blends into the other. Individuals take stands
on specific policy issues, but those stands are often related to some more
basic value or goal. Their disapproval of income taxation (or any taxation)
may be related to their desire to toughen eligibility requirements for welfare programs. In other words, although few Americans develop total, all-
encompassing ideologies, many do develop rudimentary, restricted ideologies, which at their minimum are little more than expansions of a single
value or interest. The result is an ideology — or quasi ideology — in the
sense that it guides the individual to a reasonably logical, interrelated set
of positions on a group of issues.

The modest form of ideology one finds in American politics perhaps
can be explored and explained in another way. The American parties have
often differed on the major political issues of the moment. In recent years
their national platforms have differed over American foreign policy in the
Far East, government medical insurance and aid for the aged, fiscal policy
and the balanced budget, and government regulation of labor-management
relations. Beneath these differences on the policy issues were the different
constellations of attitudes, interests, and goals each party had embraced.

---

[13] Leon D. Epstein, *Political Parties in Western Democracies* (New York: Praeger,
1967), Chap. 10, distinguishes between parties of program and ideology.

Each party, in other words, had developed a "silent ideology" based on the common interests and views (and in a few cases on the full-blown ideologies) of its activists and its party electorate. Its leaders are a group of like-minded men and women whose views on public issues separate them from the like-minded leaders of the other party.[14] Such a silent ideology stops short in only one main way from being an ideology in the more conventional sense; it is not usually codified or explicated — either by the party or the individual voter — into a systematic, coherent, and consistent pattern of political values. The classic American political style focuses the party's attention not on fixed, abstract principles of ideology but on immediate, concrete issues of public policy.

All these distinctions and definitions are not merely an arid exercise in precision. Some kind or degree of ideology is implicit in every demand for party government. In a heterogeneous society of many conflicting interests, parties cannot take stands on ten or fifteen separate issues if there is no similarity among the coalitions on each issue. That is to say, there must be some clustering of one group of voters on one set of issue positions and another group on the opposing sides (see Table 16.1). That alignment of voters along a single axis in turn presumes some kind of ideology, some basic commitments or values that connect separate issues into logical structures and govern stands on a number of them. So, call it what one will (the APSA report refers at several points to general party principles), greater programmatic commitment in the American parties depends on underlying values or philosophies to reduce the vast number of policy issues to a few dimensions. In the absence of constitutional pressures and sheer organizational discipline, there appears to be no other possible cohesive force for programmatic parties.

By these modest standards the American major parties have never been indistinguishable, but there are ample signs that attention to issues and even ideological concerns within the parties is on the rise. For example:

— Men and women are increasingly being drawn to party work out of their involvement with issues and ideologies. The triumph of political ideas and values thus becomes a major incentive to party activity. To some extent it replaces the older incentives of patronage and preference.[15]

— Ideologically motivated partisans have increasingly formed ideological organizations both within and parallel to the party structure. The club-style organizations of some urban Democrats are a case in point. Recently, also, the Republicans have been proliferating extra-party organizations (e.g., the Free Society Association and the Ripon Society),

[14] Thomas A. Flinn and Frederick M. Wirt, "Local Party Leaders: Groups of Like Minded Men," *Midwest Journal of Political Science* 9 (1965): 77–98.
[15] See Chap. 4.

TABLE 16.1   The Alignment of Voter Preference on Separate Issues in
Ideological and Non-Ideological Parties

If one assumes two political parties (parties 1 and 2) with positions on each of
four issues (issues A, B, C, and D), the first party assumes positions A1, B1, C1,
and D1, while the second takes positions A2, B2, C2, and D2. Then if one furthermore assumes five voters (V, W, X, Y, and Z) taking stands on some or all of
issues A, B, C, and D, one can construct schema for both the ideological and the
nonideological parties:

| Voters | Ideological Parties | | Nonideological Parties | |
| | Party 1 | Party 2 | Party 1 | Party 2 |
| --- | --- | --- | --- | --- |
| V | A1, C1 | | A1 | C2 |
| W | | A2, B2, C2, D2 | A1, B1 | C2, D2 |
| X | B1, C1, D1 | | C1, D1 | B2 |
| Y | | A2, C2, D2 | A1 | C2, D2 |
| Z | | B2, C2 | B1 | C2 |

and groups such as the New Democratic Coalition have grown up on
the fringes of the Democratic party.
— The labels of liberal and conservative are freely accepted by increasing
  numbers of political activists, in contrast to the widely expressed belief
  of less than a generation ago that to accept the labels, especially the
  conservative label, was gross imprudence.
— In 1964, one of the major political parties chose an avowedly ideological
  candidate and wrote an unabashedly ideological platform. One observer termed it the end of the "reign of pragmatism" within the GOP.[16]
  A similar unwillingness to make the usual pragmatic compromises
  marked the unsuccessful campaign of Eugene McCarthy for the 1968
  Democratic nomination and the successful pursuit of the same nomination by George McGovern in 1972.

There are other symptoms of the ideological renaissance. George Wallace
ran programmatic campaigns for the presidency in 1968 and 1972. As a
number of observers noted, he appealed to a cluster of goals and interests
(an ideology?) we often describe as populism, as well as to rather specific
racial attitudes. In 1970, a Conservative party candidate for the United
States Senate from New York, James Buckley, defeated both the incumbent Republican and a well-heeled Democratic candidate.[17]

[16] James Reichley, quoted by Theodore White, *The Making of the President 1964*
(New York: Atheneum, 1965), p. 217.
[17] It is important to keep in mind that there were no other third-party winners in congressional elections in the 1970s. There were several successful "independent" candidacies, however.

Most of these signs of increased ideological concern are visible chiefly among the activists of the party organization. But what of the American voters, especially the less partisan electorate? The existence of ideological political parties does not guarantee an ideological politics. It may very well be that only the small core of party activists is moving to greater ideological sophistication and concerns and that the broad American public is accepting them only selectively and cautiously. There is always the possibility, in other words, that more ideological party cadres will bring their new involvement to a deaf or hostile public, that their "ideologizing" will only bore or alienate the majority of the electorate.

The issue of the differences in ideological concern between activists of the party organization and the electorate is, moreover, not merely a scholarly one. The ideologists of American politics have long claimed that a horde of ideological voters is increasingly alienated by parties unwilling or unable to give them clearly defined ideological alternatives. Much of the 1964 rationale of the Goldwater Republicans, for example, hinged on the argument that a frankly conservative Republican candidate would mobilize the disenchanted, stay-at-home conservative vote.[18] Are, then, the American parties reflecting a nonideological electorate or suppressing an ideological one?

## IDEOLOGY IN THE AMERICAN ELECTORATE

In the late 1950s the authors of *The American Voter* found that by the most generous criteria only about 15 percent of the American electorate employed an ideological framework or ideological terminology as either a primary or marginal means of evaluating parties and candidates.[19] That is to say, less than one in six American voters applied to the presidential politics of the time some ideological abstractions greater than a single issue or group of isolated interests. Beneath this thin stratum of ideologists and near ideologists, some 45 percent of the electorate operated on an interest-oriented level — a level that we have earlier called the level of the silent ideology. Their subideological identifications and valuations were nonsystematic projections of the interests of a group or the fervor of an issue position. For example, they characterized the Democratic party as the party of the worker, the Republican as the party of business or fiscal responsibility.

The 1950s were, however, years of consensus in American politics, a period in which increased affluence seemed to have produced a new politics to replace the SES politics of the New Deal and the 1940s. The consensus was, however, either illusory or short-lived. From 1960 on it became clear

---

[18] It should be noted, of course, that none materialized in the 1964 elections and that no scholarly study of the American electorate, either before or since those elections, has confirmed the presence of such a body of voters.

[19] See Angus Campbell et al., *The American Voter* (New York: Wiley, 1960), Chap. 10.

TABLE 16.2    Percentages of Voters Perceiving Different Party Stands on Two Issues: 1956–72

| | Government responsibility for Guaranteeing Jobs | | | | |
|---|---|---|---|---|---|
| | 1956 | 1960 | 1964 | 1968 | 1972 |
| Strong Democrat | 73.0 | 74.5 | 80.3 | 78.1 | 86.9 |
| Weak Democrat | 54.2 | 66.3 | 69.3 | 65.4 | 82.0 |
| Independent | 36.4 | 57.6 | 55.2 | 54.2 | 60.2 |
| Weak Republican | 50.3 | 50.5 | 61.3 | 64.1 | 76.8 |
| Strong Republican | 63.7 | 42.5 | 76.7 | 79.1 | 89.5 |
| | School Integration and Busing | | | | |
| | 1956 | 1960 | 1964 | 1968 | 1972 |
| Strong Democrat | 55.6 | 50.6 | 70.0 | 75.9 | 72.7 |
| Weak Democrat | 55.6 | 34.9 | 63.7 | 62.5 | 64.1 |
| Independent | 42.3 | 30.8 | 59.0 | 51.1 | 61.3 |
| Weak Republican | 50.0 | 36.4 | 52.1 | 53.1 | 72.0 |
| Strong Republican | 57.5 | 39.2 | 66.2 | 60.5 | 74.0 |

Source   Data from Table 8.2 in *Voters' Choice* by Gerald Pomper. Copyright © 1975 by Harper & Row, Publishers, Inc. Reprinted by permission of the publisher.

that the scholarship of the 1950s had reflected a period of complacency in American politics. It had also probably underestimated the extent of emerging policy disagreements.[20] By the 1970s it seemed clear that the differences between Democrats and Republicans on major issues of public policy were increasing. The alternatives they represented were becoming clearer and clearer. Indeed, there was also some reason to think they had also been clearer before the 1950s and that the soundings taken in those years merely represented a dip in the level of issue concern and awareness in the American electorate.[21]

As things have turned out, the late 1960s and the early 1970s were the high point of recent issue and ideological content in American politics.[22] Voters were more alert to and informed about issues than they had been. More important, they saw the two parties increasingly as presenting alternatives in the major areas of public policy (Table 16.2). Issue voting also reached new highs in the period. In the 1972 presidential election, issues

[20] John C. Pierce, "Party Identification and the Changing Roles of Ideology in American Politics," *Midwest Journal of Political Science* 14 (1970): pp. 25–42.
[21] Everett C. Ladd and Charles D. Hadley, "Political Parties and Political Issues: Patterns in Differentiation Since the New Deal," vol. 1 of Sage Professional Papers in American Politics (Beverly Hills: Sage, 1973).
[22] See, for example, Gerald Pomper, *Voters' Choice* (New York: Dodd, Mead, 1975), and Norman H. Nie, Sidney Verba, and John R. Petrocik, *The Changing American Voter* (Cambridge: Harvard University Press, 1976).

assumed an importance equal to party loyalty in shaping voter choices. Democrats abandoned McGovern to vote for Richard Nixon because of his stands on the important issues.[23] Finally, there is some evidence, although disputed, that American voters also became more consistent in their issue stands, more able to relate a stand on one issue to their stand on another — in short, more ideological in their responses.[24] All in all, it appeared to most observers that the American electorate had moved to a new stage of politicization in which issues would count for more and party loyalties for less in American politics.

The developments of the 1964–72 period were, however, to be remarkably short-lived. It may have been that scholarship overestimated them, at least in part.[25] But it is also clear that the American electorate made one of its unexpected shifts following the events of the 1972 election. Voters no longer saw the differences between the parties as sharply, and their consistency in finding similar "sides" to related issues also declined.[26] An extensive New York Times-CBS poll also found a blurring of differences between self-proclaimed liberals and conservatives. They no longer differed as sharply as they once did on issues such as social welfare programs.[27] And, as if to clinch the retreat from issue and ideology, Americans made their vote decisions in the 1976 presidential elections as if it were 1956! That is to say, there was a marked decline in issue voting, and party loyalties were more influential in voter decisions than in any election since 1960.

At the risk of more premature generalizing, it is beginning to look as though the American electorate periodically raises and lowers its concerns for issues. The salience of issues and ideologies reflects the events of the time and the extent to which campaigns and candidates play on concerns for them. It is surely not a coincidence that the period of 1964 through 1972 featured the principled, issue-centered rhetoric first of Barry Goldwater in 1964 and then of Eugene McCarthy in 1968 and George McGovern four years later. By contrast, the Ford-Carter campaign of 1976 featured low key appeals to trust and confidence and, indeed, a conscious avoidance of well-defined policy initiatives. It may even be the case that after the intense politics of the late 1960s and early 1970s American voters found by 1976 that politics itself was less compelling and important. The

[23] Arthur H. Miller, Warren E. Miller, Thad A. Brown, and Alden Raine, "A Majority Party in Disarray: Policy Polarization in the 1972 Election," *American Political Science Review* 70 (1976): 753–78.
[24] John L. Sullivan, James E. Piereson, and George E. Marcus, "Ideological Constraint in the Mass Public: A Methodological Critique and Some New Findings," *American Journal of Political Science* 23 (1978): 233–49.
[25] Michael Margolis, "From Confusion to Confusion: Issues and the American Voter (1956–1972)," *American Political Science Review* 71 (1977): 31–43.
[26] John R. Petrocik, "The Changeable American Voter: Some Revisions of the Revision," paper presented at the annual meetings of the American Political Science Association (September 1978).
[27] *The New York Times,* January 22, 1978.

middle 1970s were, in short, a time of alienation and cynicism about politics, of conspicuous nonvoting, and of a muting of rhetoric in presidential campaigns. In retrospect it seems not to have been a time for a national debate on issues or ideologies.

Issue commitments, therefore, apparently come and go in American parties. Two other discontinuities in the issue content of American politics are also worth mentioning. First, not only does issue salience come and go — so also do specific issues. A whole set of social issues — abortion, racial integration, legalization of marijuana, for example — rose to prominence before and after 1970. By 1976, though, Americans had returned their primary attention to the economic issues they had thought most important in the 1950s. Second, issue concerns are also very unevenly spread across the American adult population at any one time. They are clearly more marked among college-educated Americans and among political activists.[28] To a considerable extent, of course, these are the same people; the active elite in American politics comes heavily from college graduates. But in addition to being better informed about issues and more prone to ideological voting, this active, educated elite tends to locate itself on the outer ideological reaches. Ideological Republicans tend to be to the right of other Republicans, and ideological Democrats tend, if less certainly, to be to the left of their fellow partisans.[29]

Not even the importance that issues and ideology assumed in 1968 or 1972, however, met all of the assumptions of responsible party government. The Pierce study, for example, found that the increase in numbers of "conceptual" ideologues (those perceiving parties and issues in ideological terms) was not matched by increases in the numbers of "informational" ideologues (those with specific knowledge about ideologies in the parties).[30] Voters may think in ideological terms, in other words, but they may lack information about candidates and campaigns on the basis of which to make specific ideological choices. For instance, despite all of Eugene McCarthy's explicit campaigning against American participation in the war in Vietnam in 1968, 60 percent of the people who voted for him in the New Hampshire primary of that year favored a tougher, more hawkish policy on the war![31] Furthermore, James Piereson has reminded the advocates of party responsibility that ideological awareness must be accompanied by "ideological alignment" (of exactly the sort depicted in

[28] On the college-educated, see Ladd and Hadley, "Political Parties and Political Issues."
[29] Ibid.; Herbert McClosky, Paul J. Hoffman, Rosemary O'Hara, "Issue Conflict and Consensus Among Party Leaders and Followers," American Political Science Review 54 (1960): 406–27; and David Nexon, "Asymmetry in the Political System: Occasional Activists in the Republican and Democratic Parties: 1956–1964," American Political Science Review 65 (1971): 716–30.
[30] Pierce, "Party Identification and the Changing Role of Ideology."
[31] Philip E. Converse et al., "Continuity and Change in American Politics: Parties and Issues in the 1968 Election," American Political Science Review 63 (1969): 1092.

Table 16.1). Voters in large numbers must agree substantially with the issue stands of one party or the other. But he finds that there has been no increase in the incidence of such alignment from 1960 to 1976. The extent of alignment in 1976 was, in fact, less than in 1956! [32]

In summary, we have evidence both of the expansion and the contraction of issue concerns in the American electorate. Certainly the experience of the last twenty years suggests that many of the conditions are present — or can be present — for an ideological politics. Increased education and literacy among American adults, combined with new means of communication, make widespread political ideology possible, for ideology is by its nature abstract and intensely verbal. The nationalization of American politics, too, promotes political ideology by focusing political attention on a single, dramatic set of issues or a single ideological dimension. Finally, presidential politics between 1960 and 1974 doubtless sensitized millions of Americans to issues and ideologies. With candidacies such as those of Goldwater, McCarthy, Wallace, and McGovern, ideology begets more ideology.

But the politics of ideology is abstract and remote, and it thrives with difficulty in the folksy, face-to-face politics of personal followings, family political traditions, and patronage and preference. In the increasing reliance on campaigning in the mass media, furthermore, all advantages are with the campaigns that stress personal appeal and punchy sloganeering. Most voters cannot sustain the interest or provide the intellectual sophistication that ideas demand; theirs is not the ideologist's view of American society. Once the short term ideological stimulus has disappeared, the concern with issues abates. Thus, although an ideological minority within the parties and the electorate will see American politics largely in ideological terms, the American majority will apparently do so only under special circumstances. What is an easy and natural way to understand American politics for some is an unusual, even unnatural way for many others.

## THE ANGUISH OF IDEOLOGY

In general, the uneven and uncertain rise of ideology risks a discontinuity between the ideological minority within the parties and the essentially nonideological majority in the electorate. At best, the full electorate is only sporadically given to ideologies. It responds selectively to issues, to be sure, but it also responds to a personality, a deeply felt personal in-

[32] James E. Piereson, "Issue Alignment and the American Party System, 1956–1976," *American Politics Quarterly* 6 (1978): 275–308. It is interesting to speculate why, in view of greater issue salience, there should be no increase in alignment. The multidimensionality of issues during 1964–72 may be at fault. It may also be that the strength of party identification in the 1950s promoted the acceptance of a partisan issue alignment as a consequence or derivation of loyalty to a party.

terest, a campaign, a group loyalty, an ancient tradition. To that gulf between the ideological minority and the nonideological majority, the parties and their candidates may respond with appeals on a number of levels — ideological arguments for some parts of the audience, non-ideological ones for others. But always there is danger of alienating a majority irritated and ultimately repelled by a discourse that is to them obscure, irrelevant, and even fatuous.

Moreover the increasingly ideological activists and organizations run the risk of alienating even the ideologists in the party in the electorate. The ideological positions of the activists need not be those of the party's electorate. McClosky's study, for example, documents the fact that Republican leaders and activists are far more conservative, less willing to accept the social welfare reforms of the last generation, than are the rank-and-file loyalists of the party.[33] Caught in the middle of these differences are the party's candidates and officeholders. The only alternatives open to them — conflict with the party's activists, lack of candor with the electorate, or defeat at the polls — are not very attractive. Similarly, the 1972 elections ultimately proved that the Democratic activists who nominated George McGovern and wrote the party platform stood to the left of the party's electorate.

So, a major American party, faced with the development of ideological activists, may develop an internal, private ideology or issue consensus at odds with the stance necessary to win elections. That divergence aggravates, in one more way, the tensions and strains among the party organization, the party in government, and the party in the electorate. There are periodic eruptions of dissatisfaction among the conservatives of the Republican organization with the moderation of the party in office. Even so conservative a "moderate" as President Gerald Ford found himself rejected by many of the organization Republicans in favor of the more conservative Ronald Reagan.

Beyond the external threats to the party as an organization, however, there are the internal threats from ideology. It may presage the factionalism of "true believers" — perhaps the most virulent form of factionalism. It produces scenes of bitterness and irreconcilability such as those of the southern delegations storming from the 1948 Democratic convention after the adoption of a strong civil rights resolution, the closing hours of the conservative triumph in the 1964 Republican convention, and the three-day-long shambles of the 1968 Democratic convention in Chicago. Furthermore, it threatens divisions between the ideologists and the pragmatists. Their disagreements within the organization escalate as one side charges sellout and vote buying while the other alleges dogmatism and extremism.

The American party organizations, for all these reasons and many more,

[33] See McClosky, Hoffman, and O'Hara, "Issue Conflict."

find it hard to contain an expanding ideological ferment. They are decentralized and fragmented by American federalism and the separation of powers. Lacking unifying structures, they speak in a babel of ideological voices. They have no annual conference and no other instrument for arbitrating the conflicts and fashioning a doctrine. They have no apparatus for political education or socialization; they have no way of propagandizing a doctrine or even an issue position. Their quadrennial platforms are instruments of the presidential campaign for votes rather than lucid declarations of party principles. And the institution of the direct primary makes it impossible for them to ensure the ideological loyalty of their candidates. In short, the major American parties are structurally incapable of articulating — much less monopolizing — the ideological content of American politics.

Discouragement with the party organization and its electoral pragmatism drives some ideologists out of the party and party activity. They work instead for groups involved in the issue or issues most salient for them. In other cases it presses them into the quasi-party activity of the Democratic club reformers in New York and California. They affiliate with the party while expressing a distaste and reforming zeal for the regular party organization and its bosses and other pragmatists. Still others find specialized, issue-oriented groups within the parties. For some it may be a group such as the liberal Ripon Society within the Republican party or the New Democratic Coalition, a remnant of the "new politics" of the 1960s. Others now find a home in the various issue caucuses in the parties, the best known of which are the women's groups.

Along with the increase in the sheer quantity of issue involvement, we have recently seen a slow spread of the scope and breadth of ideology. The debate spurred by the Goldwater candidacy of 1964 seems (perhaps in nostalgic retrospect) almost classic in its simplicity. Most of it turned on a single ideological dimension: the traditional liberal and conservative differences over the proper and useful role of government. It was strong, positive government and the welfare state versus very limited government and individual responsibility. By 1968 and after, however, the ideological dimensions were no longer simple. Differences along an axis of war-peace-defense-military establishment had been added. So, too, had differences touching racial equality and the aspirations of minorities. The politics of 1972 added concern for unrest and violence in American society and for the "new morality" and its proposals, for example, of the legalization of abortion and marijuana. What was largely a unidimensional ideological politics in 1964 became a multilevel ideological universe in less than ten years.

Thus ideology comes with many difficulties and complexities to the American parties. What is more, it comes increasingly in forms that attack the status quo and the consensus of the political center. For the parties themselves, the question surely must be whether they can contain an increasing dose of ideological conflict. The threat to the parties is in part one of factionalism, conflict, and splintering — the usual forms of intraparty bickering. Beyond that threat is another: greater numbers of ideologues threaten the party organizations with an inflexibility of goals that rejects the parties' traditional electoral pragmatism. Many delegates to the Republican convention of 1964 and the Democratic conventions of 1968 and 1972 were prepared to nominate candidates without considering greatly their electability. Some, indeed, preferred defeat with principle to victory with compromise. If the importance of the ideological goal of the party ever crowds out the electioneering role, then the parties themselves will be greatly altered. So, too, will most of American electoral politics.

## PARTY RESPONSIBILITY AMERICAN-STYLE

The model of the responsible political party is an ideal. One does not look for it in reality, for no political system yet has developed the cohesion, discipline, and unity that its pure form demands. Even in Great Britain, home of the hopes of the American reformers, practice falls considerably short of the model. Party cohesion in the British Parliament, though significantly greater than in the American Congress, is by no means perfect. British cabinets and parliamentary parties, in fact, have long insisted that constitutional traditions forbid them to be bound by party decision or commitment. Even within the Labour party, historically committed to the binding discipline of party decisions, Labour prime ministers have made it clear that although a Labour government will consult with the party's national executive, it cannot be bound by it.

American practice is even further from the model. To be sure, one finds in some state legislatures a high order of party discipline behind or in opposition to the program of the majority or the governor. The programs or principles, however, spring not so much from a party organization or the decision of the electorate as from the initiative of the governor or the party's legislative leadership. What responsibility there is to the voters for their program is established at later elections as the voters reward or punish their programmatic stewardship.[34] Under the best circumstances a sophisticated voter may be able to identify a past policy or decision with a party, but such a quasi responsibility diverges from the model in one major way: There is little role in it for the party organization, since the legislative party or the executive originates the program and enforces discipline be-

---

[34] This is largely the point V. O. Key makes in *The Responsible Electorate* (Cambridge: Harvard University Press, 1966). On the American voter's lack of the perceptions and decisions the goals of party responsibility would demand, see Donald E. Stokes and Warren E. Miller, "Party Government and the Saliency of Congress," in Angus Campbell et al., *Elections and the Political Order* (New York: Wiley, 1966), pp. 194–211.

hind it. The responsibility rests not on the overt program of party activists and organizations but on the homogeneous interests of the voters, party leaders, and constituencies supporting the legislative and executive parties. It is a cohesion and responsibility that springs essentially from the coalescing of common interests in electoral politics.

Occasionally under the stress of crisis or catastrophe, American politics approaches even more closely the model of party responsibility. A strong case can certainly be made that at the presidential election of 1936, the Democrats and Republicans were identified with sharply differing solutions to the nation's economic woes. If their positions were not truly ideological, they were at least determinedly programmatic. The burdens of the depression may have focused voter attention on the hopes and remedies of policy to an unusual degree. Much of the campaign oratory centered around the Roosevelt program for social and economic change and his opponent's charges that he proposed radical changes in the American polity and economy. The programmatic rhetoric and identification, combined with high voter attention, may well have produced something close to a mandate election and a mandated congressional contingent of Democrats. If the supposition about the presidential election of 1936 is correct, it indicates that the kind of ideology or programmatic concern necessary for "pure" party responsibility is a product of crisis conditions which have prevailed only for short periods of time in recent American experience. The necessary ideological focus and attention are not expressions of ordinary American politics; rather they are the product of occasional heightened, extrapolitical crisis.[35]

More common than the case of crisis-stimulated responsibility is the type of responsibility resulting from presidential government. Strong presidential leadership, especially when aided by majorities of the same party in the Congress, produces a somewhat cohesive program that becomes the program of the president's party. Indeed, some presidents have been able to organize the enactment of large parts of the party platforms on which they ran for office.[36] Presidential government, of course, produces only the kind of post hoc responsibility that we noted above. And it need not produce the kind of clear programmatic alternative the reformers want. (Platform differences between the two parties, although they can be observed, are not generally great enough to satisfy the same critics.) But presidential government does stamp some differences on the parties, and it does fashion points of reference for the approval or disapproval of voters.

Can one expect more than this of the American parties? It is true that

---

35 Barbara Sinclair relates these conditions to the immediate aftermath of the 1928–1932 party realignment in "From Party Voting to Regional Fragmentation: The House of Representatives, 1933–1956," *American Politics Quarterly* 6 (1978): 125–46.
36 Gerald M. Pomper, *Elections in America* (New York: Dodd, Mead, 1968), Chap. 8.

the new ideological activists, a more sophisticated electorate, a slowly centralizing pair of party organizations, and the development of nationally recognized issue differences between the parties create some of the conditions for greater party responsibility. But several notes of caution ought to be mentioned:

1. The American institution of the direct primary (and its undermining of party control of nominations), combined with the decentralizing effect of federalism and the separation of powers, continues to work against party responsibility even in the presence of ideology. It opens the way to the nonideological candidate. It also permits a candidate or an officeholder to defend to the political death a program or ideology at odds with that of his party or his president or governor. To be ideological is not necessarily to be "responsible."

2. Much of the increasing ideological or programmatic commitment has not followed the single, unidimensional pattern necessary if ideology (or issue) is to provide the unity essential for party government. If the issue divisions along SES lines do not coincide with those on minority rights or civil liberties, or with those on foreign policy, the resulting crosscutting (multidimensional) ideologies divide much more than they unify. Only if multiple patterns of issue or ideological differences coincide do they offer the basis for two unified, cohesive programmatic parties.[37]

3. Ideology thus far has not been translated into party organizational strength. There are only a few signs of an important growth of authority within the parties; the national committees remain hostages to the traditional decentralization of the parties. Nor has the cohesion of legislative parties increased. We have not yet, therefore, developed the mandate elections or the party discipline with which to convert issue unity into public policy.

Thus while the spread of ideology and issue salience may be a necessary condition for government by responsible parties, it is not a sufficient one in and of itself. Especially in the context of fragmenting political institutions — particularly the institutions of federalism and the separation of powers — the growth of ideology can even work to defeat the goal of party responsibility.

If the advent of ideology will not automatically (or willy-nilly) bring the party to a greater governing role, will the more conscious and overt proposals of the reformers? The breadth of the problem of converting the American major parties into prototypic responsible parties can be gauged by examining the scope of the reformers' proposals. The Committee on

[37] Donald E. Stokes, "Spatial Models of Party Competition," Campbell et al. *Elections and the Political Order*, pp. 161–79, develops this and related points. See also the Piereson article in footnote 32.

Political Parties of the American Political Science Association, for example, proposed:[38]

A *massive shoring up of the national parties and their organizations.* The committee recommended that the national conventions meet at least biennially and exercise greater control over the national committees. Above all, it suggested a national party council of some fifty members that would draft a platform for the national convention, interpret and apply it to issues between conventions, make "recommendations . . . in respect to congressional candidates" and about "conspicuous departures from general party decisions by state or local party organizations," provide a forum for "the discussion of presidential candidacies," and coordinate relations among national, state, and local party organizations.

A *perfecting of the instruments of ideology.* The committee in essence proposed that the platform mean something and that it bind the party officeholders and organizations. The platform ought to deal at least partially with the party's "permanent or long-range philosophy," and it ought also to be carefully prepared and systematically interpreted. "The party programs should be considered generally binding" on both officeholders and state and local parties.

An *asserting of party control over the congressional party.* To tackle so protean a task, the committee recommended both a consolidation of the present congressional party organizations into a single party leadership group and the elimination of practices (such as the seniority system and the traditional power of the House Rules Committee) that undermine party discipline.

A *remodeling of the American parties into membership, participatory parties.* The committee's hope was perhaps best expressed in these words:

> With increased unity within the party it is likely that party membership will be given a more explicit basis. Those who claim the right to participate in framing the party's program and selecting its candidates may be very willing to support its national program by the payment of regular dues. Once machinery is established which gives the party member and his representatives a share in framing the party's objectives, once there are safeguards against internal dictation

---

[38] The direct quotations in the following list are from the report of the committee, *Toward a More Responsible Two-Party System* (New York: Rinehart, 1950). The italics in the original have been eliminated. One of the members of the committee has also recently published some reflections on its work; see Evron M. Kirkpatrick, "Toward a More Responsible Two-Party System: Political Science, Policy Science, or Pseudo-Science?" *American Political Science Review* 65 (1971): 965–90.

by a few in positions of influence, members and representatives will feel readier to assume an obligation to support the program.[39]

The committee's report ranged beyond these general points. It dealt with other barriers to party responsibility: the direct primary ("the closed primary deserves preference"), the electoral college (it "fosters the blight of one-party monopoly"), political finance, and barriers to full and meaningful adult suffrage (e.g., the long ballot). In short, it becomes clear that to achieve the goal of government by responsible parties, the committee would undertake — and probably would *have* to undertake — a wholesale reconstruction not only of the American parties but of the American electorate and political environment as well.

However, some other proponents of party responsibility have been more modest in their goals. One of the most persistent, James MacGregor Burns,[40] touches many of the same themes as the ASPA Committee. There is the same emphasis on the building of grassroots, membership parties, the buttressing of the national party (the presidential party), and the reconstructing of a vigorous congressional party. There is the same recognition of the need for change in the parties' political environment (e.g., the restrictions on adult suffrage and the status quo in political finance). Yet the reforms Burns suggests are less drastic and more realistic, even though their direction and their pinpointing of the causes of the present lack of responsibility are not greatly different. Perhaps Burns' relative moderatism springs in part from his recognition of an essentially Madisonian political culture that has not tolerated any instrument — party or other — of national majoritarian political power.

For the immediate future, barring the special conditions of crisis, it seems likely that the American parties will continue their modest governing roles — a post hoc responsibility for carrying out programs that generally promote the interests of the party's activists and loyal electorate. Neither the American parties nor the voters can meet the demands that the classic model of party responsibility would impose on them. It is true, to be sure, that the various sectors of the party are increasingly bound together by a commitment to a set of issue positions that separates the activists, candidates, and voters of one party from those of the other. In a loose, often distressingly imprecise sense, each of the two parties is a distinct group of like-minded men and women. That tentative and limited agreement on issues, reinforced by executive leadership of the party in

---

[39] Committee on Political Parties, *Toward a More Responsible Two-Party System*, p. 70.
[40] See James MacGregor Burns, *The Deadlock of Democracy* (Englewood Cliffs, N.J.: Prentice-Hall, 1963), especially Chap. 14. Note also that Burns is dealing with the parties in terms of his own, somewhat different frame of reference, especially the distinction between the presidential and the congressional parties. See also Stephen K. Bailey, *The Condition of Our National Political Parties* (New York: Fund for the Republic, 1959).

government, may produce enough cohesion for a modest, variable degree of responsibility. Such a degree of party responsibility will, ironically, be achieved without the central role — drawing up a program and enforcing it on candidates and officeholders — that the reformers planned for party organizations. It will be a party responsibility of the party in government, and that is a very significant difference.

Of the relation between party responsibility and the new ideological and issue concerns in American politics, two things must be kept in mind. First, such concerns will in their purest form very likely be limited to a minority of Americans. The ideological view is one pattern of perception that the party develops with one segment of the electorate. To the non-ideological segment the party continues to make appeals on other than ideological grounds — on a mixture of issues, traditions, interests, and personalities. Second, the salience of issues or even of ideologies is a consequence of events in the broader political context. American politics apparently reached one peak of issue salience in the 1930s, and the years from 1964 through 1972 may well have been another. By 1976, in contrast, the electorate was returning — but who knows for how long? — to an electoral politics dominated more by partisan loyalties and less by commitments on issues.

To conclude, parties in government govern for a great many goals and reasons. They want to satisfy the multiple and complex demands of the electorate. They want to meet the goals — also complex and contradictory — of the activists of the party organization. Furthermore, they have their own goals to meet, goals that range all the way from individual desires for power and the perquisites of office to their obligations to public office and service. In the aggregate, those various goals are extraordinarily complex. Although program or ideology is an important goal for many people in each of the three party sectors, it does not necessarily dominate all others. Nor does it dominate the perceptions of the American electorate. The present extent of party government — that is, of the parties' ability to enact cohesive programs into public policy — probably reflects the present place of program and ideology in the total structure of the goals and incentives of American government and politics.

# VI

# THE POLITICAL PARTIES: ROLE AND THEORY

Textbooks change with the subjects they treat. Some years ago the concluding chapters in books of this sort invariably discussed the place of the parties in the broader political system and in the smooth operation of American democratic processes and institutions. Those questions are still important and almost obligatory. But political science has changed in the last generation. Since World War II, political scientists have been caught up in explanations of the empirical behavior, institutions, and processes they study. That new commitment of the profession of political science thus creates a new expectation here: the final theoretical essay.

The theoretical aspirations of political scientists vary greatly. The more confident and optimistic of them aspire to propositions that not only will explain past behavior but also will meet the higher test of predicting future behavior. Less hopeful ones are content with specifying major variables and relationships, with the understanding that the arrangement of them into a final, integrated theoretical pattern of explanations will have to await the collection of more observations and more explanatory fragments. The pages of these last two chapters will make it clear that the choice here is for the second, more modest route. The development of theoretical statements about most political institutions and processes is in an early, rudimentary stage, and modesty becomes such a state.

One begins the theoretical task by attempting to explain why the American parties are what they are and why they do what they do. One of the best strategies for this purpose is to observe changes in them over time. As the parties develop new activities, depend on new incentives, take new organizational forms, for example, one is naturally led to wonder how and why the changes came about. What changes in the parties' environment accompanied those changes in the parties? Is there a causal relationship between the changes in the parties and those outside of them? If the decline of patronage accompanies the decline of the old-style urban machine, does it cause the change in the party organization? Or has the decline of the machine reduced the need for patronage and thus caused *its* demise? We learn much about the parties if we put the changes together into a pattern and adduce explanations for them.

Chapter 17 undertakes the analytical task by examining the changes presently under way in the American parties. It brings together the trends and changes that have been mentioned throughout the book and concludes with an explanation of those changes and a series of projections of what's ahead for the American parties. The central theme — already more than hinted at in earlier chapters — is that the major American parties have lost their powerful, predominant role in American electoral politics. Of necessity, we also face the questions of what produced that change and what electoral politics will look like in their release from party domination.

The last chapter carries the analysis beyond the specific changes presently abroad in the American parties to the level of parties in general and the American parties in other periods of time. In that last chapter, too, the theoretical problems and issues suggested by the contemporary changes will be brought together into some more general categories. The chapter will be concerned with changes in the parties' roles and activities within the larger political system. It concludes, in fact, with the proposal of a developmental approach to the parties, an approach suggesting that parties usually enjoy their heyday when electorates are less educated, less secure, and politically unsophisticated, and that as populations develop political knowledge and sophistication, the parties become less important to the mass electorate.

"Theory" may well be too pretentious a word for the tentative suggestions that follow. At least their goal is a modest one: to raise the understanding of the American political parties beyond the level of analysis of specific events to a more general knowledge that provides insights into continuing trends and into groups of events or phenomena. After a journey through a book such as this, one ought at least to be able to explain why the American parties differ at any one time and from one time to another.

# 17

# The Future
# of the American
# Parties

A great deal has turned sour for the American parties in the last few years. The late 1960s saw the decline of their prestige; and along with other institutions of American government and politics, they have borne a good deal of the blame for the general malaise and the decline in public confidence that beset American society. From all sides critics blame the parties and the other institutions of the "system" for the ills which afflict American society.

Whether or not the parties deserve such disfavor depends in great part on one's estimate of the problems and progress of American society. But whatever may be the current reputation the parties enjoy, their most fundamental problems predate the dip in public esteem. Their time of troubles had started by the 1950s and early 1960s. Furthermore, their troubles resulted more from long-run changes in American society and politics than from any recent events.

## CHANGES IN THE THREE SECTORS

The American parties have long been characterized by the loose set of relationships that have bound the three party sectors together. That looseness, or lack of integration, is indeed one of their most fundamental signs. The party organization has not been able either to bring a substantial part of the party electorate into membership or to assert its leadership or discipline over the campaigns and policy making of the party in government. Not surprisingly, therefore, the recent widespread changes in the parties have hit the three sectors separately and differently.

### The Party in the Electorate

The American electorate seems to be losing its long-run attachment and loyalty to the American parties. More and more American adults consider themselves independents rather than members of or identifiers with a major party. And even among those who profess a loyalty or attachment

**397**

to a party, the attachment to a political party no longer dominates the decision on how to cast the vote as it once did. So we have a decline both in the quantity and the power of party identification in the American public. Since those changes are now more apparent in the eighteen- to thirty-year-old group, they will likely accelerate. The result, obviously, is a shrinking of the size of party electorates and an eroding of the quality of their loyalty. More serious than the loosening of identifications, of course, is the increasing rejection of party altogether, evident perhaps in the declining confidence in the parties and the increased nonvoting of the 1970s.

It has been the stability of party identification, of course, that has undergirded the stability of the two-party system. The unchanging adherence to the party as a reference symbol and an object of loyalties — and operationally as the key to the voter's decisions — has left no opportunities for a new party to gain a foothold in the electorate. Not surprisingly, therefore, the decline of party identification in the American electorate has been reflected in the victories of independents and third parties in increasing numbers since 1960. Independents and third-party candidates won seats in the Senate, an independent was elected governor of Maine, and George Wallace ran with amazing strength as a third-party candidate in 1968. Even the little-advertised independent candidacy of Eugene McCarthy for the presidency in 1976 drew more than 750,000 votes. Furthermore, ticket-splitting and nonparty voting are on the increase. In 1972, for example, the voters in 45 percent of the congressional districts selected presidential and congressional candidates of different parties.[1] And after a long string of presidential elections in which party loyalty governed the outcome, the voters' issue preferences actually accounted for as much of their vote decisions in 1972 as did party loyalty.

If the American electorate is not responding as eagerly to its party loyalties, to what does it now respond? Some segments of it are attuned to the new appeals of program and ideology. The Goldwater campaign of 1964, the McCarthy and Wallace appeals of 1968, and the McGovern candidacy of 1972 — along with those of many state and local issue-oriented candidacies — drew on and activated higher levels of issue awareness. For less sophisticated voters, the appeals that now register most effectively are those of candidate personality and image. The handsome faces, ready smiles, and graceful life styles that the television screens convey so fully attract some of the support that party symbols once commanded. And since candidates and issues change far more frequently than parties, the consequence is an increasingly unstable, less predictable pattern of voting.

---

[1] Gerald M. Pomper, *Voters' Choice* (New York: Dodd, Mead, 1975), p. 215. Even in an election in which a president and the congressional majorities came from the same party (1976), 29 percent of the congressional districts voted across party lines. Michael Barone et al., *Almanac of American Politics 1978* (New York: Dutton, 1977).

## The Party Organizations

In the party organizations, the machines have been passing from the scene, and with them their activists and incentives. Even the Daley organization in Chicago has stumbled. Many organizations no longer can depend on the patronage and preferments or the guaranteed election to public office that once recruited their full-time, vocational activists. Instead, they draw the better-educated, part-time leadership, whose incentives more often incline to issues or ideology and who bring with them new demands for intraparty participation. The new party activists tend to seek their payoffs in the triumph of principle or program. Indeed, some among them increasingly reject the politics of compromise, accommodation, and pragmatism that resulted from the assumption that the capture of public office is the alpha and the omega of American politics. And if their ideological goals are not satisfied — or even recognized within the party — they may leave it for particular candidates or issue organizations.

Increasingly, too, the internal, intraorganizational processes cease to be under the organization's control. Under the force of growing participatory expectations, these processes are becoming progressively more public; the private sphere of the party organization shrinks accordingly. The direct primary began the process of taking decisions from the party organization, and some seventy-five years later it continues apace. Also, one can now see the "publicizing" of the national convention processes. The convention is no longer a device for the organization's deliberation and choice making. Its processes are public, and, more important, its options have been sharply restricted in recent years by the activities of the would-be candidates in the preconvention politicking. Even the preconvention scramble for votes increasingly moves from the hands of party organizations as three-fourths of convention delegates are chosen in states with presidential primaries.

At the same time that they are undergoing internal changes, the party organizations are losing their capacity for controlling American electoral politics. No longer do they consistently control either nominations (thanks to the direct primary) or the politics of election campaigning. Candidates increasingly find themselves able to build their own campaign organizations, raise their own campaign funds, and go their own merry ways in the campaign. All the campaign assets they once received from the party organizations and their workers — skills, information, pulse-readings, manpower, exposure — they now can get from pollsters, the media, public relations people, volunteer workers, or even by "renting a party" in the form of a campaign management firm. Especially because the party organizations have been unwilling or unable to provide the new arts for the candidates, they have waned in influence in the contesting of elections. Their fairly primitive campaign skills have been superseded by a new campaign technology, and more and more they are finding themselves among the technologically unemployed.

Furthermore, the party organizations remain decentralized in the face of the increasing centralization of life and politics in the United States. The electorate looks more and more to national political symbols and figures, but the party organizations remain collections of state and local fiefdoms. The futility of national party organization results partly from the suppressing power of the American presidency and partly from the unwillingness of state and local organizations to share incentives and resources with national party organs. The national committees and the national conventions are loose confederations of powerful local organizations and seem destined to remain so. But even those assertive local organizations no longer prosper. They do not easily recruit full-time, concerned leadership with the new incentives, and they do not have (and never did) a competent or ample party bureaucracy to fall back on.

## The Party in Government

The men and women of the party in government, freed from reliance on the party organizations by the direct primary, by access to the media, by independent sources of funds, and by supportive personal followings, increasingly establish a direct appeal to the voters. No longer able to rely as heavily on abstract party loyalties, they develop more personal appeals and rely on personal style, physical appearance, even what personal magnetism they can generate. They find in many ways that it is quite a different matter to be sold by media than by party canvassers.

The successful candidates are the parties' contingents in American legislative bodies. And there, in direct relationship to the decline of party loyalties among voters and the decline of party organizations' power over their legislators, they vote as legislative parties with decreasing party cohesion. The instances in the Congress in which a majority of one party opposes a majority of the other in recorded roll call votes have, over the last decade, been at an all-time low. Freed from the party demands of both voters and the party organizations, they are more vulnerable to the nonparty pressures — the local interests of the constituency, primarily. More important, perhaps, with the decline of competition (especially for incumbents) in congressional elections, they are not very vulnerable to anyone.

As the legislative party loses its cohesion and strength, the executive party rushes into the vacuum. Presidents and governors enjoy governmental power and leadership of the executive branch at the very time at which they increasingly represent the party and its programs to so many voters. They personify the party and give tangible content to its labels and symbols. In a period when many partisans seek programmatic goals, they alone formulate programs and control policy initiatives. Therefore, it is no exaggeration to speak of the parties as executive-centered coalitions. And nowhere is the phenomenon clearer than in the ability of presidents to dominate the national party organization of their parties, to give life and meaning to the symbol of their parties, and, with the help of federal subsidies, to mount campaigns free of obligation to the party organization.

This much is merely summary of what has been said in greater detail in earlier chapters.[2] The changes cumulatively amount to a vast shift of power within the American political party from the party organization to the executive-led party in government.

The crucial fact, perhaps, is the progressive isolation of the party organization in the American political parties. The organizations had their days of glory in some of the larger cities, but they never succeeded in integrating any significant measure of the party electorate into the organization on a membership basis. Isolated from the electorate and without any broad-based support or participation, they have always been vulnerable to suspicions that they were run by irresponsible oligarchies. The smoke-filled room myths have never died, the cries of bossism are as alive at today's party conventions as they were at the turn of the century.

What assets the party organizations once had they are losing rapidly. They no longer control the chief incentives for political activity as they did when it was patronage and preference that made the activists active. They no longer control the resources and technology of campaigning and of electoral politics. And they no longer invoke the feelings of party loyalty in their electorate. But what kind of a party is it in which the party organization loses a preeminent or even equal position? Is not the party organization the only sector of the party that has more at stake than the winning of elections, that offers some possibility of life and principle beyond specific elections and even beyond electoral defeat?

In the case of the American parties, in any event, a coalition of an executive-led party in government and a somewhat restive and fickle party electorate has resulted. The executive rather than the party organization controls and manipulates the party symbols. The alliance of the executive with the party electorate rides on the message of the mass media and political personalism; the organization as a channel of communication no longer matters as much. That coalition is all the easier because party organization has been unable to centralize while the other two party sectors have done so. Especially in national politics, that centralization or nationalization of party messages, cues, and personalities unites the president-led party in government and the large numbers of voters who react primarily to national issues and faces.

[2] The "decline of party" literature is extensive. Its major recent contributors include: Walter Dean Burnham, "Revitalization and Decay: Looking Toward the Third Century of American Electoral Politics," *Journal of Politics* 38 (1976): 146–72; Jeane J. Kirkpatrick, *Dismantling the Parties: Reflections on Party Reform and Party Decomposition* (Washington: American Enterprise Institute, 1978); and Gerald Pomper, "The Decline of the Party in American Elections," *Political Science Quarterly* 92 (1977): 21–42.

## THE NEW CONTEXT: THE NEW POLITICS

These changes in the contemporary American parties are taking place in
the context of broader ferments and upheavals in American politics and
even in American society. Most of them matured in the middle and late
1960s. In an American society that believes change is inevitably good and
innovation always newsworthy, it was perhaps inevitable that the new
politics would be called "the new politics." The term is, however, one of
considerable variety and looseness, and one commentator's description of
the new doesn't always match that of another. There is some consensus,
however, that it includes these elements:

— *Concern for issues and principles.* In substance the new politics connotes a heightened concern for issues and ideology, often even new
   issues such as those of the environment, the war in Vietnam, and abortion. At a more abstract level it also marks a commitment to values and
   principles in public policy and a concomitant reluctance to compromise
   them.
— *Increased citizen participation.* The new politics exalts the mass participatory ethic to broaden the base of American politics. (It is, of course,
   opposed to elites, bosses, establishments, and all other forms of limited
   decision makers.) It demands a voice in government down to the local
   neighborhood, and it is committed to more representative participation
   that includes women, minorities, and the disadvantaged. At a less active
   level it pays new attention to mass opinion (e.g., the polls) and devices
   for citizen "consultation." With some reason, therefore, it has been said
   that there is a new populism in the new politics.
— *Personalism and the New Individualism.* In a rejection of institutions
   and "structures" the new politics has put new value on the individual,
   whether as citizen, candidate, or officeholder. Candidates run for office
   on personal magnetism and govern on the basis of personal trust. It is,
   of course, a political style perfectly adapted to the messages of the mass
   media, except perhaps that the media easily trivialize them. The individual too easily becomes merely an image, a smile, a well-clothed
   appearance, or a celebrity. (On the subject of celebrity, one need only
   refer to professional athletes and astronauts as United States senators.)
   At the level of the individual voter the new individualism translates into
   a new independence of parties and into a hesitation to make any form
   of collective action possible by moderating one's views or interests.
— *Reformism and political skepticism.* The new politics has certainly been
   marked by a skepticism, even a cynicism, about traditional social and
   political institutions. It has questioned traditional processes (the "system") and traditional leadership (the "establishment"), and it has
   fueled a vigorous program of reform for the parties, presidential nominations, and campaign finance, among others.

The "new" has not, to be sure, completely replaced the old. It joins the older political styles and modes in the mainstream of American politics. It is only a part of a new amalgam, but an important part nonetheless. One need only look at the 1976 elections and the candidacies of Ronald Reagan and Jimmy Carter for illustration. Both ran as critics of and outsiders to "Washington," and both traded heavily on personal appeal and trust. Reagan furthermore ran frankly as an ideologue, and Carter's campaign was in substantial part an exercise in the new populism.

Thus, for the parties the advent of the new politics seems to mean a sharp division — in all three sectors — between old and new style politics, and, so, between old and new style activists. On the one hand, there are the upper-middle-class ideologues, the so-called amateurs, who demand a politics of differentiation, attention to issues and ideology, and a major participatory role in the party. On the other hand, there are the older, more traditional partisans whose politics are centrist and consensual, whose incentives for activity are varied, and who are willing to accept the old modes of authority in the party organization. It was that difference that lay in good measure behind the battle in the Democratic party in 1972 between the McGovernites and their opponents and in the Republican party in 1976 between the Reagan and Ford forces. But it is a difference beneath an increasing number of factional divisions in the parties, and it promises to remain with them for the foreseeable future.

The impact of the new politics on the political parties is readily apparent if one looks at one of its chief by-products: single-issue politics. The parties have traditionally been committed to the building of consensus and the fashioning of majorities — with all the compromise and pragmatism that implies in a complex society. They build those majorities to win elections, to organize cohesive legislative parties and, in their fashion, to govern. Single-issue politics threatens all of that. It is by definition a commitment to an issue position that is so deep and principled that compromise is often ruled out. The single issues spawn political organizations, activity in which is for many of the new activists more satisfying than activity in a political party. Loyalty to a single-issue position — and the rewarding or punishing of a candidate or officeholder on its basis alone — is quite different from the pragmatic acceptance of a number of candidates and issue positions that loyalty to a political party assumes. And perhaps most troubling of all for the parties, the organization of political activity single issue by single issue bespeaks in the aggregate a degree of politicization, a sheer quantum and intensity of political feeling, that the major American party cannot integrate or contain.[3]

---

[3] It should be noted that single-issue politics has to some extent begun to develop within the parties. Feminist, prolife, ethnic, rural, minority, and labor caucuses can now be found within the national conventions, some legislative parties, and some state organizations.

Two caveats about the new politics and the changes in the parties must be entered. The first is merely that predictions about American politics are very perishable. Only a few years ago there were many predictions of sweeping and fundamental changes in American politics, and the turmoil on the campuses and in the streets did indeed seem to promise major changes in other parts of American society. It also seemed that a new dawn of ideology had arrived for all time. But the issues, causes, and enthusiasms that stir Americans also shift with unexpected speed. Thus the new politics and the contemporary phase in which the American parties find themselves may turn out to be, contrary to expectations, an interlude of no lasting force in American politics. For the moment, though, one can only note its importance.

Second, it is terribly important to realize that these developments in American politics are not of a single piece. They constitute no one movement or logical, coherent program. (Nor should we expect logic or consistency in a politics marked by a history of diversity and accommodation.) To some extent they pull and tug against each other as well as against the traditions of the past. The commitments to issue and ideology flower simultaneously with an increase in personalism, life-style appeals, and media images. Not only is most of the personalism distinctly *not* issue or policy oriented, but in its most attenuated form — the concern for the profile, the smile, the hair, the clothes of the candidate — it is supremely nonpolitical. At its worst, ironically, it is less political than the reliance on party loyalties and identifications that it replaces. The choice made on the basis of party label certainly weighs more political factors than the choice made on the basis of the candidate's self-confidence in front of a TV camera.

## THE DECLINE OF THE PARTIES

It is one of the comforting beliefs of the conventional wisdom that social systems contain their own self-adjusting mechanisms. The free-market, competitive economic system, which freely adjusts prices and production to changes in supply and demand, offers a ready example. So, too, does the self-correcting system of checks and balances that generations have trusted to keep the American separation of powers in a well-tuned equilibrium. We have long had similar hopes for the party system. For the ills of unresponsiveness and dissatisfaction in the electorate, the cure is said to be a readjustment of party appeals (spurred by competition) and a consequent realignment of party loyalties in the electorate.

Is it possible that realignment may yet come as a response to the disaffection with the parties? Indeed, it is possible. The external symptoms that ordinarily precede a realignment are evident: a third-party surge named Wallace and the instability of the vote from one election to another, for instance. It may be that the increasing disposition of voters to identify as independents and to split tickets will be reversed by a party realignment restoring the aggregate confidence in and identification with the parties.

The realignment, however, appears to be overdue. Perhaps the most striking aspect of the 1968 and 1972 elections was the fact that in the end there was no realignment, that despite all the ticket splitting the old party identifications held and that, indeed, American voters returned to them in 1976. Furthermore, an issue or ideological axis on which realignment might take place has not appeared. Alternatively, it may be that realignment cannot take place once the voters' confidence in the party system has slipped below a certain point. A considerable number of Americans may simply decide to rely on cues and political organizations outside the parties. Thus they will have no incentive to change party loyalties; new nonparty symbols and loyalties will be added to the old party ties. Perhaps, too, our politics — at least for the moment — are too complex to produce the simple dualism, any dualism, around which voters can cohere in a new alignment. Most of the party realignments of the past formed along the classic lines of "ins" and "outs" at a time of national crisis.[4]

Even if the parties should find an issue and a catalytic event for realignment, however, it is by no means certain that realigning will restore the parties to their political preeminence. Realignment is no solution to the erosion of party organizational capacity to nominate and elect candidates. Nor is it any guarantee that large numbers of Americans will return to an unswerving partisanship or that they will again mark the straight party ticket. The truth is that a party realignment is only a readjustment of the parties to new cleavages in the society. Moreover, it may even depend on the very kinds of confidence in party and need for party symbols that the American parties appear to be losing.

For the moment, therefore, a good many signs point beyond the cure of realignment to a decline of the parties generally and of party organizations in particular. Both the parties' dominance of our electoral politics and the stability of the two-party system have rested on the acceptance of the party label as a cue for action. Large numbers of voters now have cues and sources of information outside the parties. Many of them also are less and less inclined to accept the omnibus commitments that party loyalty implies. They want to pick and choose among issues and candidates. Party loyalty demands that they buy a whole collection of commitments; in effect, it asks them to divide the political world into two simple categories, ours and theirs. The simple, dichotomized choice that party loyalty within a two-party system demands no longer appeals to an educated, issue-

---

[4] On realignments, see James L. Sundquist, *Dynamics of the Party System* (Washington: Brookings, 1973), and Walter Dean Burnham, *Critical Elections and the Mainsprings of American Politics* (New York: Norton, 1970).

oriented electorate. Knowing, confident, even assertive adults are less and less willing to surrender their selective judgment in favor of an unquestioning loyalty to party.

To look at it another way, the Republican-Democratic loyalties of the American two-party system actually require a politics of low-intensity and moderate involvement in issues. The willingness of millions of voters to buy the diverse bag of candidates and issues assumes that they can compromise their feelings about any one of them. Loyalty to the party as a least common denominator can bind diverse populations into one party electorate only when the other lines that divide them are weaker. But what happens when large numbers of voters repeatedly feel more strongly about a candidate or an issue than they do about a party? What happens when large numbers of voters decide that they no longer need the ready-made, all-purpose, prepackaged judgment of a political party? Above all, what happens when that voter disenchantment takes place at the same time that candidates find ways of communicating with voters outside the usual channels of the party organization?

It must be clear, however, that all of this is not to predict the imminent decline and fall of the political parties, American or otherwise. There is considerable danger of exaggeration when one draws a series of indicators into one concentrated argument. A good many of the necessary qualifications and counter-indicators get lost. There are, indeed, ample signs that the parties have and will continue to have a creative role in American politics, even if they no longer dominate the channels and resources of our electoral politics. There are hundreds of thriving party organizations, aggregate trends to the contrary notwithstanding. There are still thousands of ardent party loyalists, and millions of voters still cast straight party tickets every four years. When we talk of decline, we do not mean death.

Furthermore, we ought not to assume that the decline will lead irreversibly and inevitably to death. On the contrary, there are signs that the decline of the parties is beginning to level off. The growth of the independents in the American electorate slowed down greatly between 1972 and 1976. Voters resorted to their party identifications in 1976 with an old-time confidence. And legislative party cohesion (in those legislatures for which we have time series data) seems not to be declining further. There are, after all, a good many traditional and institutional forces ensuring some role for the parties. They act collectively as a brake or a barrier against the infinite decline of the parties. It may well be the case that they are taking hold now and the parties are, consequently, settling into a new and stable, if reduced, role in American politics.

So the parties are alive, if not well, in America. But they will increasingly become a part of a richer, more diverse pattern of American politics. We may well see the repeated emergence of third parties as expressions of deeper discontent with the parties and American society. Eugene Mc-

Carthy talked freely of a third-party attempt for the presidency in 1976 before settling on an independent candidacy. And some scholars of American politics have also begun to reexamine the long-accepted case against multipartyism.[5] Other political organizations — interest groups, candidate organizations, ideological movements, ad hoc issue organizations — will assume a greater importance in the electoral politics once dominated by the parties. In 1968, in fact, organized labor's efforts registered close to 5 million voters, distributed 115 million pamphlets and leaflets, and recruited almost 100,000 election-day workers. The total bill ran around $10 million.[6] The flourishing and financing of the PACs in the 1976 and 1978 elections speak to the same point. And all these nonparty organizations will reflect and embrace the new ideological politics in a way the parties never could.

What seems likely, in other words, is a politics of greater fluidity and instability, carried on by a wider range of political organizations. The parties will exert their influence over nominations, elections, and policy making, but so will other political organizations. In many instances the personable candidate — aided by the media — will attract the voter loyalties and activist labors that the party organizations once did. The erosion of the one, stable, long-run loyalty in American politics will contribute to a politics more often dominated by the short-term influences of the charismatic candidate or the very salient issue. In its volatility, its lack of continuity, and its lack of predictability, the new electoral politics may increasingly resemble that of the one-party factional and personal politics Key described in the American South in the 1930s and 1940s.[7] Or perhaps it will most closely approximate the nonpartisan politics of school board elections in many American cities.

Diversity and specialization thus characterize the changes in American politics. The diversity of goals and needs, multiplied by the intensity of feelings about them, cannot easily be met by two traditionally pragmatic, compromising political parties. Voters, too, appear to want more specialized cues for political choice and action, and the activists among them want to discriminate among the causes and people for whom they will work. All of that leads to an increased specialization and division of labor among the political organizations. Just what specialized role we may anticipate for the parties is not altogether clear. Some voters will still find the party a useful cue-giver and an effective vehicle for their political goals. Indeed, there will be locales in which the party organizations maintain control of nominations and elections and in which the party loyalty of the electorate remains firm — that is, in which the old party roles persist.

[5] See, for example, Lawrence C. Dodd, *Congress and Public Policy* (Morristown: General Learning, 1975).
[6] Theodore H. White, *The Making of the President 1968* (New York: Atheneum, 1969), p. 365.
[7] V. O. Key, *Southern Politics* (New York: Knopf, 1950).

Where the parties do lose some of those traditional roles, they may well turn into more ideological, issue-oriented parties. The changes will be less marked in areas in which the electorates are less educated and less politicized. Where voters are politically more sophisticated and less dependent on party symbols, ideological activists will more often control the party organization.

## AFTER THE REIGN OF THE PARTIES

Political life in the United States without the guiding dominance of two assertive political parties is not unthinkable. Much of our local politics has been nonpartisan in reality as well as in name for some time. But a diminished role for the parties throughout much more of electoral politics suggests impacts of a greater magnitude. The consequences not only for the political processes but for the quality of American democracy trouble many observers.

Burnham has put the concern directly and simply:

Political parties, with all their well-known human and structural shortcomings, are the only devices thus far invented by the wit of Western man that can, with some effectiveness, generate countervailing collective power on behalf of the many individually powerless against the relatively few who are individually or organizationally powerful. Their disappearance as active intermediaries, if not as preliminary screening devices, would only entail the unchallenged ascendancy of the already powerful, unless new structures of collective power were somehow developed to replace them, and unless conditions in America's social structure and political culture came to be such that they could be effectively used.[8]

The American parties — and all others for that matter — mobilize sheer numbers against organized minorities with other political resources, and they do so in the one avenue of political action in which sheer numbers of individuals count most heavily — elections. Thus the parties have classically been the mechanisms by which newly enfranchised and powerless electorates rose to power. The old-style urban machine in the United States, for example, was the tool by which the powerless, often recently arrived, urban masses won control of their cities from older, largely "Wasp" elites. In a more fluid politics of bargaining among a larger number of political organizations and millions more uncommitted voters, the fear is that the advantage will be on the side of the well-organized minorities with other political resources.

The further decline of the parties, therefore, could have ironic elitist consequences. The educated, sophisticated, and involved political minority may help impose a new kind of political tyranny on the less involved,

[8] Walter Dean Burnham, "The End of American Party Politics," *Trans-action*, December 1969, p. 20.

lower SES segments of the electorate. It increasingly tries to impose an ideological politics that lacks salience and may indeed be incomprehensible to the less sophisticated. At the same time it contributes to the decline of the most useful cue-giver, the major political party. The removal of the political party as an organizer and a symbol in our present nonpartisan elections helps upper SES elites, both of the right and the left, to dominate those politics.[9] The political party, in other words, is the political organization of the masses who lack the cues and information — as well as the political resources of status, skills, and money — to make a major impact on public decisions via other means. The diminished power of the parties makes the game of politics more difficult for them to play and win.

A continued decline of the parties would threaten to rob the political system of an important builder of majorities. Although imperfectly, the major American parties have pieced together majority coalitions. American presidents have enjoyed the legitimacy of majority coalitions most of the time, and the party majority in legislatures has at least permitted them to organize for action. With weakened parties, how are we to find majorities in a fragmented politics? Are we to rely on the personal appeals and promises of national candidates? Or do we face the kind of political immobilism that has resulted elsewhere from the splintering of intransigent groups and deeply felt loyalties and sentiments? To be sure, it is easy to overestimate what the parties have traditionally contributed to our politics, but the contributions, if more modest than many believe, are real and important. Certainly, a mature political system can and will work out its adaptations. There are indeed alternatives to stable, two-party systems which dominate electoral choice. The issue is whether they can pull together the separate pieces of American politics and political institutions as effectively as the parties have.

It may be that the parties will come out of their present decline and enjoy a resurgence in ways we cannot foresee. Were the party organizations to acquire the resources for distributing the new campaigning skills to candidates, they might redress their recent losses to the new campaign technicians and to other political organizations. The key to the future of the parties is clearly in a recaptured ability to control the major resources of American politics: money, organization, people, and know-how. Perhaps, too, the parties would fare better if the current mood of national self-doubt and political cynicism were to lift. But for the short run, at least, important trends are afoot in the parties and in American politics. Regardless of whether they last, they will have their short-run effects, and the long run is often nothing more than a series of short-run trends.

[9] Willis D. Hawley, *Nonpartisan Elections and the Case for Party Politics* (New York: Wiley, 1973).

# 18

# Toward
a Theory
of the Political
Party

The political parties have never been able to contain the splendid diversity of American politics. We have always pursued many routes to influence — by dealing directly with public officials, by working through interest groups and other nonparty groups, by engaging in various forms of direct representation and demonstration, and by making choices through a political party. It has never been the case, in other words, that all of our politics has gone on through the political parties. Indeed, the parties have not even monopolized our electoral politics.

It is important to keep the parties in a realistic perspective because a good deal of scholarship on them attributes to them a role far more central and impressive than they have played in reality. It is as if the sheer pervasiveness of the party label in American elections and public office guaranteed a position of primacy for them. But in reality the American parties do not easily control nominations or elections, nor do they readily govern on behalf of party programs. Their place today in American politics is not easy to square with the view that considers them the "indispensable instruments of government,"[1] or even the originators of the American democracy.

Behind the attributions of a prime, central role for the parties is a false theoretical assumption, and that is what concerns us here. It is that the parties are causes rather than effects, that they are perpetually independent rather than dependent variables. They are said to cause, to shape, to produce. The fact that they themselves are caused, shaped, and produced is overlooked. Simply because the rise of the American parties accompanies the rise of democratic institutions and the expansion of the adult suffrage, we cannot assume that they somehow "caused" the rise of democracy. Both political parties and American democracy arose more or less simultaneously because of the interplay of the same general social forces and conditions. Parties do indeed have their impact on political processes

[1] Committee on Political Parties of the American Political Science Association, *Toward a More Responsible Two-Party System* (New York: Rinehart, 1950), p. 15.

and institutions, but other political and nonpolitical forces in turn have their effects on them. The parties are "in" and "of" the political system, and one cannot expect that they alone among political organizations and institutions can escape the influences that shape everything around them.[2]

The mission of this chapter, therefore, is to identify the reasons why political parties — especially the American parties — are what they are and why they have developed as they have. What shapes the particular structure of the parties, the relationships among their three sectors, and their various activities and roles in the political system? What accounts for change in them over time, and for variation in them from place to place? And why do they differ from the parties of the other Western democracies?

What follows is *not* a full-blown, systematic explanation or a comprehensive and tidy wrapping up. This chapter is in truth built around four analytical ways of looking at the parties. It can perhaps be said to be four fragments in search of a theory. For when we search for explanations about parties and party systems, we tend to segment the problem, to break it into manageable parts. These four fragments reflect, in other words, four very common ways of looking at political parties. They are different perspectives, views of the parties from different sides or analytical points of view.

## I — THE IMPACT OF THE EXTERNAL ENVIRONMENT

In the first chapter we discussed briefly the major environmental influences that impinge on the parties (Table 18.1). Subsequent chapters have elaborated on them, and especially on the ways in which they shape and mold the parties. For instance, the effect of the direct primary on the parties' ability (inability, really) to control nominations was set out in great detail. So, too, was the effect of the separation of powers — and the absence, therefore, of parliamentary government — on the legislative party and the national committees.

The political parties are, in other words, surrounded by a context, an environment, of the most varied sort. One can visualize it only imperfectly in two-dimensional images (Figure 18.1). But such an illustration helps to convey the comprehensiveness, even the oppressiveness, of the political world external to the parties. One point about Figure 18.1 does need to be elaborated a bit. The argument this far might suggest that there is an

---

[2] One very extensive attempt to treat the political parties as a dependent variable — an effect rather than a cause — has of course been the persistent urge to reform them. Austin Ranney in *Curing the Mischiefs of Faction* (Berkeley: University of California Press, 1975) describes the attempts with enormous insight. On the recent reform attempts within the Democratic party see William Crotty, *Decision for the Democrats: Reforming the Party Structure* (Baltimore: Johns Hopkins University Press, 1978).

TABLE 18.1  Major Categories of Influences in the
Environment of the Political Parties

| Influences | Examples |
|---|---|
| 1. Political institutions | Federalism, separation of powers, development of presidency |
| 2. Statutory regulation | Legislation on campaign finance, structure of party organization |
| 3. Electoral processes | Definition of franchise, the direct primary |
| 4. Political culture | Attitudes about politics and the two-party system |
| 5. Nonpolitical forces | State of economy, age distribution of population, use of TV |

assumption that the direction of cause to effect runs exclusively from the environment to the parties, that the parties are always the dependent object of external, independent forces. That would be an overstatement of the relationship. Although the direction of the relationship is indeed primarily from environment to party, the parties do have some direct and indirect control over their environment. They do, for example, participate in the making of public policy on who votes, the kind of ballot they mark their choices on, and the kind of primary election at which candidates will be nominated. They also shape, by education and by their own performance, public attitudes toward them and more generally toward politics. There are, of course, many more examples one could cite.

The diagram of the political party in Figure 18.1 should not go unnoticed either. It suggests a way of thinking about the parties: as an input-output mechanism. Parties both get and spend. They "get" in the sense that they recruit the inputs or resources that they need to function: money, skills, manpower, and loyalty. They "spend" in that they convert these resources into outputs or party activities: the contesting of elections, organizing of public officeholders, and propagandizing on behalf of issues or ideologies. All three sectors of the party in their various ways must mobilize resources, and all three generate results, outputs, in their special ways.

Thus the political party in such a conception is first of all a conversion mechanism for changing resources and demands into goal-seeking activities. It must mobilize resources to maintain itself and undertake its activities. Obviously a change in the statutes regulating campaign finance or a further contraction of patronage impinges there. The vitality of the party organization, an essential element of the conversion mechanism, depends

## FIGURE 18.1   The Political Party: Structure and Environment

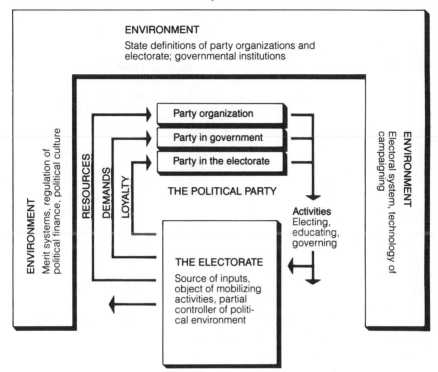

as well on the network of state legislation setting its outlines and powers. The outputs — the activities or functions — of the parties are similarly sensitive to changes in the environment. Any change in electoral law — whether it is the closing of a primary in one state or the abolition of the electoral college — clearly impacts on their electoral activities. The electorate itself is shaped by birth rates, patterns of education, and the spread of democratic and participatory expectations. And the demands the party activists and electorate bring may reflect issues of war or depression, or alienation and trust in government.

There is a sense in which all the elements of their environment generate "needs" or "demands" on the parties. Those concepts offer a way of viewing that environment. More precisely, they refer to the conversion or impacting of the environment on the party. They are an elaboration of the connection between them. Thus:

— a parliamentary system operates in a specific way, and that operation "requires" or "needs" or "demands" certain kinds of parties and certain kinds of party capabilities and activities.

— as the new campaign experts broke the party's monopoly of the skills
and information for contesting elections, candidates no longer "needed"
the party organizations as they once did.

The use of demands and needs in this explanatory sense, in this way of
relating one phenomenon to another, is simply another way of stating the
cause-effect relationship. Some observers are more comfortable intellectually with it than with bald statements of cause.[3] But — and it is a big
"but" — we use the concept of demand in another, more direct way. We
refer, for example, to the demand of citizens for government action of one
kind or another or the demands of party activists for patronage or for a
voice in party affairs. These are demands as *goals* of voters and party
workers. Those individuals may seek those goals, those demands, through
the political party. They, too, are shaped by the broader political and social
environment, just as the party is.

Obviously the environment of the parties embraces an enormous range
of components — from laws regulating the registration of voters in one
state to the social-medical-technical forces affecting the national birth rate.
Is it not possible to group the components into a manageable set of categories? Or to establish some hierarchy of importance that will enable us
to say that this element of the environment is more important than that
one? It is possible to do so to some extent, but that attempt should be
postponed until we look at the other three theoretical fragments.

## II — TWO TYPES OF PARTY STRUCTURES

Nothing typifies the parties as political organizations quite as much as
their three-part structure. Much of what they are, what they do, and how
they do it is suggested merely by calling to mind that political parties
include a party organization, a party in government, and a party in the
electorate. Differences among them, not surprisingly, often get down to
questions of the activities of the three parts or sectors and the various
relationships among them. For the relationships of the three sectors describe both a division of labor and a hierarchy of authority within the
parties.

When measured by the roles and influence of their sectors, political
parties in democratic regimes tend to fall into two main groups: those
dominated by the party organization and those dominated by the party in
government. The American parties, of course, are moving increasingly to
the type headed by the party in government — that is, by the party's can-

---

[3] There is an old tradition in political science of avoiding direct statements of cause and
effect. Political scientists have in fact developed an extensive vocabulary that avoids the
word "cause" while suggesting causation. I have in mind nouns such as force, factor,
influence, condition, determinant, and variable.

didates and officeholders. In their glory days at the turn of the century one might have argued that they were organization dominated, but no longer. The American party in government increasingly contests elections, controls the party image and reputation, and governs in office without important constraints or even contributions from the party organizations.

The party dominated by its organization differs in a number of very fundamental ways from the party led by its party in government (Table 18.2). They differ obviously in their activities and in the control of them. The party controlled by the party in government is almost by definition a heavily electoral party. The concerns of the party's officeholders are in winning elections, and they establish both the priority of the electoral mission and their control over the resources and choices for it. Once elected they govern in political response to the need for securing reelection and for making a record of accomplishment in governance. The alternative — the party dominated by its organizational sector — is best typified by the parties of the European parliamentary democracies. The issue commitments or ideologies of the organization's activists assume a greater importance in the life of the party. And they have an impact within the party precisely because the organization speaks for the party, picks its candidates, and maintains some degree of leverage over its parliamentarians.

One can summarize many of the differences between the party models in terms of their ability to integrate their three sectors. In the organization-centered model the three sectors are bound closely by ties of loyalty and

---

TABLE 18.2   Characteristics of Two Types of Political Party Structures

| Party Organization Dominates | Party in Government Dominates |
|---|---|
| 1. Party in electorate assumes (in part) a membership role in the organization | 1. Little or no membership component in party organization. |
| 2. Party organization controls nomination of candidates and much of election campaign. | 2. Party in government largely freed of organizational control of nomination and election. |
| 3. Relatively high degree of cohesion in legislative party. | 3. Relatively low degree of cohesion in legislative party. |
| 4. High degree of integration of three sectors. | 4. Low degree of integration of three sectors. |
| 5. Unified by goals of party organization's activists. | 5. Unified by goals and programs of executive party. |
| 6. Activities substantially electoral, but programmatic as well. | 6. Activities almost exclusively electoral. |

discipline. A substantial part of the party electorate, in fact, joins the organization as members, and the debts of candidates for nomination and election assistance bind them to the party organization. The key to the organization-centered party, in fact, lies in the ability of the organization to unite the party in government to it and to the goals of its activists. In the classic urban machine of patronage and preference, both sectors were united in the overarching goal of electoral victory and the electoral pragmatism it demanded. Alternatively, the two sectors might be united, as the "party responsibilitarians" argue, by loyalty to the same principles or issue positions. In the party controlled by the party in government, however, everything depends on the pragmatic alliances of convenience at election time. The dominant party in government, indeed, is free to form alliances with nonparty organizations, such as interest groups, rather than work with its own party organization. The substantial distance between the congressional parties and the national committees illustrates the point. The party in government establishes contact with the party electorates without relying greatly on the party organization.

Obviously the differences between these two varieties of political party run to deeper, more basic issues. Ought a political party to be something more than the sum total of the candidates choosing to run on its label? At the very least it seems unlikely that the party led by its party in government can provide the continuity and breadth that sets the party aside from other political organizations. The parties that are strong for their ability to dominate or monopolize certain forms of activity have been those led by the organizational sector. Only the party organization has the range of skills and resources, as well as the commitment to all party goals and even to the party itself, to fill this leadership role within the party. Only such a party can approach the model of the responsible party. Only strong parties exerting policy leadership as well as leadership in the recruitment of public officials — and in providing a stable cue to millions of voters — can augment or support the officeholder's electoral responsibility to the people who elected him. The crucial question is whether a party controlled by officeholders does that — or whether the executive-centered coalition is not an alternative to, or a mutation of, the more traditional political party.

These two kinds of party do not occur without reason or explanation. What differences are there in the different environments from which they come that will explain their differences? One can also put the question in more parochial terms. Since the American parties are the archtypical parties controlled by the party in government, what accounts for the differences between them and parties dominated by their organizations?

— Scholar after scholar has noted that the American party is not associated with parliamentary institutions and that the organization-dominated party is. The very nature of a parliamentary system demands discipline and integration of the parties; the American separation of powers does not.

— American electoral law (primaries, the regulation of finance, for example) is all on the side of the party in government, giving it easy access to nomination and renomination and a great freedom from the party organization in waging the campaign.

— State regulation of and legislation on parties has placed a set of heavy constraints on the party organization; the reformist urge has indeed been heavily antiorganization in its goals. The states have imposed cumbersome forms and a weakening openness and permeability on the organizations while making it difficult for them to develop a large membership.

To be sure, there are additional secondary and reinforcing explanations. The availability of the new campaign arts and technologies is clearly one. It has provided the party in government with an alternative to party organizations by destroying their monopoly over election campaigning. But the new campaigning is available to parties everywhere, and one must ask why it has freed the parties in government in the United States and not elsewhere. The answer, of course, is that elsewhere there are parliamentary institutions and election legislation that buttress the central, dominant role of the party organization.

## III — THE SOCIAL PSYCHOLOGY OF THE VOTER

Among political organizations the parties alone attach their names to candidates for public office. On the surface the point appears to be trivial. On closer look, however, one sees that it involves the willingness or need to respond to that label on the part of large numbers of Americans. So the durability and special character of the parties result in great measure from the needs and perceptions of the American voters. In fact, political parties originated in major part from the need of voters for a guide, a set of symbolic shortcuts, to the confusing and often trackless political terrain. The labels, activities, and personages of the parties ran as a clearly perceptible thread through the jumble of political conflict and the baffling proliferation of American elections. When that cue giving, in addition, produced loyalties and identifications with the parties, when those loyalties were stable and enduring, and when they dominated so many voting decisions, the conclusion was inescapable that this pattern of reliance and loyalty was a primary determinant of the American political parties.

In other words, political parties are historically a reflection of the ability or inability of the electorate to cope with its citizenly responsibilities. Their symbolic importance, the value of their labels in elections, reflect directly the informational needs and problems of a new, mass electorate. But those needs change over time. Note, for example, the reduced incidence of and reliance on party loyalties in the American electorate. Voters simply are better educated and better informed than they were sixty or eighty years ago. They are more involved and active in the things of politics — more "political" than they once were. They are also more often bombarded by nonparty political messages — especially those of the personalities and personal images that the mass media carry so effectively.

This is not to say that American voters no longer need cues or labels. Rather, they increasingly seek the mixed and different cues that the party organization will not provide. The integrated party dominated by an organization suited an earlier American electorate seeking a single, consistent cue to a great many political decisions and judgments. But as voters become more political they are prepared to handle a wider range of political perceptions and loyalties and to sift through a greater variety of political messages. They may form an attachment on an issue or two — or to an entire ideology — and they are not prepared to surrender that loyalty or those loyalties to an overriding loyalty to a political party. And although they may find many of the candidates of "their" party perfectly acceptable, they accept no overriding party loyalty as a reason to favor all of its candidates. In short, voters increasingly want to pick and choose in their political decisions. The American parties in the electorate thus find the candidate-centered party better tailored to their preferences than the party dominated, integrated, and unified by a party organization.

In another, more general sense, too, parties reflect the political-psychological needs of voters. The rise of personalism in political campaigning is a case in point. It is easy — too easy — to attribute this personalism to the new campaign technology and reliance on the mass media. Behind the personalism is the need of many citizens for personal leadership, for flesh-and-blood embodiment of distant government, even for the vicarious ego strength of a confident public figure. Perhaps, too, the new personalism reflects a dissatisfaction with the parties (and other political organizations) as lifeless and impersonal abstractions.

## IV — DEMOCRACY AND THE DEVELOPMENT OF PARTIES

That the origin and rise of the political parties is intimately bound up with the sweep and spread of democracy is abundantly evident. The parties grew as the first mobilizers of electoral power while the electorates expanded. The relationship of the parties to democracy, however, extends beyond their origins and initial growth. Democracy presupposes a degree of citizen participation and choice. By definition it involves a broad distribution of political power and requires organizational intermediaries to mobilize the political power of individuals in order to make it effective.

The entire development of the parties reflects these imperatives of democracy, and changes in the parties have mirrored changes in the very nature of democracy and its electorates.

The democracy of the mass political parties, however, is not necessarily democracy's pure or final realization. Democratic expectations, institutions, and processes change, and with them so do the parties. The political parties may have been essential, as many have suggested, during the initial politicization of the uneducated, economically disadvantaged masses. But when education and affluence open new channels of political information and activity, then competitors arise with new organizational forms, new appeals, and new political resources. We see the growth of a politics that is more issue-oriented, more committed to goals and values, and less pragmatic and compromising. The argument that only the parties can aggregate or mobilize political influence no longer is as convincing as it once was.

The relationship of the changes in the parties to those in the democratic processes is closer than one might infer from mere assertions that everything changes. In the United States and many of the other Western democracies, the changes in the parties occur in phases related to the development of democratic politics and modern political institutions. In all of those changes three phases are evident.[4]

1. Initially the parties began in most of the Western democracies as parties of limited access and narrow appeal. Originated at a time of a restricted, aristocratic suffrage, they were limited in personnel, confined largely to electioneering, and closed to mass participation. This formative, premodern period in the American experience came before 1830 or so.

2. As the electorates expanded, the parties also expanded their organizational forms to include more activists and members. (Although the American parties resisted more than most the development of mass membership parties, they were no longer largely legislative caucuses.) The parties dominated the political loyalties and even the political socialization of the new electorates. As the dominant political organization of a citizenry marked by relatively low levels of political information and sophistication, they became the chief givers of political cues. In the American experience, of course, this stage of their development reached its zenith at the beginning of the twentieth century. (In many of the new nations of Asia and Africa, which began with virtually complete adult suffrage, the parties entered the second stage very quickly.)

3. Finally, as electorates mature along with democratic processes, as polit-

---

[4] For another developmental approach to political parties, see Samuel P. Huntington, *Political Order in Changing Societies* (New Haven: Yale University Press, 1968), especially Chap. 7. His four stages seem to coincide with the first two here.

ical loyalties and interests become more complex, politics becomes more diverse and differentiated. The political party in this phase becomes merely *primus inter pares*. Its sole control of the mobilization of power ends amid growing competition from other political organizations. The party remains both a potent organization and a powerful reference symbol, but its total role in the politics of the nation diminishes. This clearly is where the American parties are today.

These stages in party development reflect no organic growth or inherent life cycle. They are direct responses to changes in democratic electorates and processes, and they certainly do not appear to be limited to the United States. Parties in Western Europe, for example, are losing members and appear to be entering the third phase, too.[5] When an electorate reaches a certain point of politicization, party loyalties and parties themselves are no longer as useful as they once were to large numbers of voters.

Are the American parties becoming relics of an earlier and simpler political age? Will their decline continue indefinitely? Those questions force speculation about the unknown tomorrows of American politics. Possibly other stages will follow the third. But for the moment, at least, it does not look as though the parties will disappear. They are deeply rooted in American law, and the advantages they afford in political organizing — largely the result of their statutory and ballot status — would alone ensure their continued life. They also remain deeply set as important reference symbols in the political worlds within countless citizens. Too many party processes and too many political expectations are too deeply embedded for the parties simply to pass away.

## WHAT SHAPES THE PARTIES?

Two main influences, or sets of influences, from the environments of the American parties meet to shape their outlines and dimensions. They are, first, those which define and mold the electorate, and second, those which set the basic electoral and governmental structures of the political system. They are not special influences that shape only the American parties. All scholarly evidence suggests that they set the outlines of the parties in all the Western democracies.

That these should be the chief influences on the parties reminds us once again that the parties are first and foremost electoral organizations. They and their candidates contest elections, and their party labels furnish the electorate a variety of cues, symbols, and information. It is a small but very

[5] Anthony King discusses this and related points in his excellent essay "Political Parties in Western Democracies," *Polity* 2 (1969): 111–41.

significant point that the party label appears with the candidate's name on the ballot. Thus the parties are what they are primarily because of the ways in which they contest elections and relate to their successful candidates after election. It is true that some parties are more purely electoral in their mission than others, but in the Western democracies the major parties are all electoral parties. It is that fact, indeed, which accounts for most of the differences between them and the minor parties.

## The Definition of the Electorate

That first set of influences, the one defining the electorate, is in fact made up of a number of components. It includes those legal statements, both constitutional and legislative, defining what individuals will be in the electorate. It also includes those social conditions which determine the numbers, the age distribution, the education, the affluence, and the other social characteristics of the electorate. And it includes those influences which shape the levels of political awareness and information, the attitudes and expectations, and the sheer political understanding of the electorate. What causes the cognitions of the adults of a society is a question far beyond the scope of this book. It is enough to take them as a major set of causes acting on the parties.

The nature of the electorate, in all of these facets, clearly changes over time. The changes in the Western democracies appear to be almost invariably in one direction — from lesser to greater politicization, from fewer to more democratic and participatory expectations, and from a limited to a larger or universal adult suffrage. All these changes obviously are interrelated, although they happen at different rates and sequences in different political systems. Taken together they constitute the rise of mass, popular democracy, a process that began in the United States at the beginning of the Republic and that extended virtually to today. Only one trend in the American electorate appears to move in the opposite direction: rates of political participation, especially voter turnout. Their recent downturn may be temporary or may signal a fundamental, long-term change in the electorate.

At this point in this long book, not much needs to be said about the specific ways in which the nature of the electorate impinges on the parties. It shapes the pattern of party loyalties and the reliance on them for political decisions such as the casting of a vote. It affects the nature of campaigns and candidates; it affects, too, the relationship of the officeholders with the parties and with their constituencies once they are elected. It is indeed a truism to say that the shape of electoral politics depends to a great extent on the nature of the electorate. Finally, it is the electorate from which the party activists are drawn, and changes in it change the personnel of the parties.

## The Governmental and Electoral Institutions

This second cluster of influences on the parties is, in effect, the chief governmental institutions and constraints within which they work and to which they relate. Foremost within it is the basic configuration of political institutions — federalism or unitary government, parliamentary forms or a separation of powers, the nature of the executive, and the extent of governmental authority. Second, it includes the myriad laws and constitutional provisions that define the election processes (and those for nominations, too, where that is a matter of public policy). Finally, there are the regulations of the parties per se and of the activities carried out under their label. They run the gamut from laws creating their organizational structure to those regulating the spending of money in campaigns. Often, too, they merge almost imperceptibly into the legislation creating election machinery. Again, the impact of all of this on the parties is an old subject. One need only reiterate, as examples, the effect on the democratic parties and party systems of the separation of powers (or, to put it another way, the absence of a joining of legislature and executive in parliamentary government), the impact on party organizations of the direct primary as a way of choosing party candidates, and the use of single-member districts rather than proportional representation from multimember constituencies.

These segments of the parties' environments change, too. Constitutions and electoral systems are often replaced, although not in the United States. If one compares the United States and Great Britain to the nations of continental Europe on this point, the contrast is striking. Although their constitutions change and adapt, there have not been any abrupt breaks with the past in the last 100 years in either Britain or the United States. In that time, however, France has launched five entirely separate republics, each one intended to be a break with, even a repudiation of, its predecessor. Similarly, large numbers of European countries have tinkered with various election systems; Britain and the United States have stayed with plurality election from single-member constituencies. On the other hand, though, the American parties have been subjected to a range of legislation on themselves and their activities quite unknown anywhere else. The direct primary constrains their selection of candidates, for example, and state laws defining the party organizations have no parallel elsewhere. The effect, and in some cases the intention, of this regulation is to restrict the party organization, and thus to favor the party in government. What is more, the reformist zeal behind much of this legislation lives on and has recently begun to work within the parties themselves. One need only mention the reform of the national party conventions.

These two sets of variables interact in a special way on the American parties to produce their rather different, "special" qualities. First of all, a good many of the important institutional-structural influences on them are rare or uniquely American — the direct primary, the separation of powers, the nationally elected executive, and the network of regulatory legislation on the parties. It is precisely these factors which are instrumental in shaping the American two-party system and in vaulting the parties in government to a dominant place in the American parties (at the expense of the party organizations). Second, although the first set of influences — those shaping the electorate — have changed over time in both the United States and the other democracies, the second set has remained fairly constant in the United States. For that reason, changes in the American parties seem more directly related to changes in the specification and behavior of the American electorate.

There is also a third set of environmental variables that ought now to be mentioned: those of the nonpolitical environment. They are the events and trends beyond the political system that nonetheless so very much shape our politics — the wars, international crises, recessions, economic prosperity, birth and mortality rates, energy shortages, and new moralities, for instance. Their effect on the parties is, however, not really *on* the parties. They define the policy issues of a time, and thus they shape the demands and goals that individuals try to achieve *through* the parties, whether as activists in them or simply as voters. They originate outside of the parties and the political system, and they are to a great extent beyond their influence. Their ultimate impact is beyond the parties. In other words, their effect is not primarily on the parties as conversion mechanisms but on the goals for which the mechanism is employed.

Finally, after an intensive look at the political parties and the influences that make them what they are, one ought to step back a bit and take a broader perspective. Political parties are not caused or shaped, not changed or modified, in a vacuum or in isolation. They contribute to a broader, aggregative politics and, in a sense, they compete with other organizations and avenues for aggregating and representing large numbers of individuals. If there are other more effective ways for individuals to seek their political goals than through political parties, they will take them. If a relationship with a congressman and his attentive staff secures a social security check or access to federal contracts, why work through a party? If an interest group is more forthright and effective in opposing abortions or gay rights, why work through a party? What the parties are at any given time, therefore, is in part determined by the alternatives to them that are available. And if those alternatives should be fostered by public policy — as the PACs have been by the federal campaign finance laws — the parties will in a sense be shaped by the political environments of their competitors.

Indeed, the major problem for the American parties today arises from the increased differentiation in American aggregative politics. As the American electorate continues to develop more complex interests, it acquires more differentiated loyalties and responds to more complex and differentiated cues. It maintains identifications with parties, but it responds also to candidates and to issues, programs, and ideologies. It responds differentially to different elections and even to the choice between electoral and nonelectoral politics. The ultimate consequence is a more diverse, complex politics that no single set of loyalties, and thus no single set of political organizations, can easily contain.

So the American parties find it increasingly difficult to be all things to all citizens. There probably will never again be a dominant, all-purpose political organization in our politics. The parties especially cannot easily meet the expectations of ideological politics and pragmatic electoral politics at the same time. And their symbols cannot continue to work their old magic on all elements of so diverse a political population. The new challenge for them in this fragmented politics is for the first time to fight for a place and a role in American politics — to cope with the fact that they do not have a guaranteed future.

# INDEX